Exploring Nature
with Your Child

Exploring
Nature
with Your Child

AN INTRODUCTION TO THE
ENJOYMENT AND UNDERSTANDING
OF NATURE

BY

Dorothy Edwards Shuttlesworth

Contributing Editor, *Junior Natural History Magazine* of The American Museum of Natural History

GREYSTONE PRESS

11598—5M

ACKNOWLEDGMENTS

The writing of this book would have been quite impossible without the wholehearted interest of my husband, Melvin Shuttlesworth. His excellent advice and suggestions, as well as practical helps, have been invaluable. I am grateful also to Frederick Drimmer, editor of The Greystone Press, for his guidance and enthusiasm all along the way. My deep appreciation goes also to C. M. Goethe of Sacramento, California, who through a lifetime of nature exploring has caused innumerable parents and children to follow his example, and whose interest in my work over many years has been a constant inspiration.

It is impossible to express adequately my debt to the American Museum of Natural History, where my work gives me the privilege of discussing the various aspects of nature with brilliant scientists who are devoting their lives to the study of some particular field of the natural sciences. Particularly am I indebted to the following members of the Scientific Staff who have read and helpfully criticized chapters of this book: Dr. John T. Zimmer, Curator of Birds; T. Donald Carter, Assistant Curator of Mammals; Francesca R. LaMonte, Associate Curator of Fishes; Bessie Matalas Hecht, Scientific Assistant, Amphibians and Reptiles; John Pallister, Research Associate, Insects and Spiders; Farida A. Wiley, Instructor, Department of Education; Dr. Henry K. Svenson, Curator, Forestry and Botany; Robert R. Coles, Chairman, Astronomy and the Hayden Planetarium. Also my thanks to Dr. George H. Childs for reading the section of seashore life, and to Dr. George G. Goodwin, Associate Curator of Mammals for reading the section on whales.

I am grateful for the kind permission of Dr. Arnold Gesell and of Ginn and Company to include (in Chapter One) an excerpt from *The Normal Child and Primary Education,* by Arnold and Beatrice Chandler Gesell.

D. E. S.

To Mel
and to our two young explorers,
Lee Ann and Gregory,
this book is affectionately dedicated

The Illustrators

Mammals, Reptiles, and Insects . . . .

THOMAS VOTER, *Art Director*
American Museum of Natural History

Fish . . . .

LLOYD SANDFORD, *Staff Artist*
New York Zoological Society

Birds . . . .

ROBERT F. SEIBERT, *Formerly Staff Artist*
"Audubon Magazine"

Flowers and Trees . . . .

MATTHEW KALMENOFF, *Staff Artist*
American Museum of Natural History

Contents

snakes move—snake tracks—how snakes breed—snake eggs—how
snakes kill—how poison fangs work—hearty eaters—the ways of a
rattler—the rattle rings—what the rattle is for—kinds of rattlesnakes—the good-natured boa—pythons: the largest snakes—the
cobra's double personality—the garter snake—hognose snakes:
ham actors—the maligned milk snake—king snakes: harmless and
dangerous kinds—how to recognize a poisonous snake—when you
encounter a snake—snakes as pets—proper diet for a pet snake—
turtles—armor plate for defense—how to take care of turtle pets
—turtle ailments and remedies—chameleons and other lizards—
the secret of the chameleon's color changes—how to keep a
chameleon pet—lizards of the Southwest—alligators and crocodiles
—how alligators and crocodiles differ—frogs—the hobby of collecting frogs' eggs—how a tadpole grows—biggest and smallest frogs—
toads—basis for the "wart" myth—how toads drink and breathe—
how toads defend themselves—where to find toads—salamanders
—the red eft—the care of amphibians—how to catch a frog—how
to feed an amphibian pet.

What is an insect?—how insects are able to move—the lowly bug
—millions of kinds of insects—the magic of metamorphosis—eyes
with thousands of facets—the insect's detecting equipment—how
insects eat and breathe—the delicate structure of legs and wings
—butterflies: insects with glamour—the beautiful black swallowtail
—the migrating monarch butterfly—the hibernating mourning
cloak—moths: how they differ from butterflies—silk manufacturers
—the woolly bear caterpillar: weather prophet—caterpillars as a
hobby—the pleasures of cocoon collecting—how to collect butterflies and moths—how to handle the butterfly net—the best hunting
grounds—how to mount butterflies and moths—beetles: 23,000
species in North America—the firefly—the ladybug: pest exterminator—the ground beetle: nighttime hunter—beetles with gas
bombs—beetles near water—how to collect beetles—ants—inside
the ant colony—savage ant warriors—grasshoppers and their music
—katydids: fiddlers, not singers—crickets as weather forecasters—
cricket on the hearth—how to keep cricket pets—bees—the bee's
sting—very few kinds of bees store honey—the underground
bumblebee—playing bee detective—what goes on in a beehive—
wasps: clever papermakers—the wood-eating termites—flies—blood-
thirsty mosquitoes—crane flies—the dragonfly—beautiful, and useful too—the damsel fly—insects that live in the water—the
whirligig: "lucky bug"—the speedy water strider—the upside-down

feed on—fungi that prey on living things—precautions against
poisonous mushrooms—mosses favor moist places—the moss as a
compass—the best-known moss—ferns, fronds, and "fiddle heads"
—ferns for decoration—how to make fern prints.

Tree rings and what they tell us—watching a tree develop—buds:
new life for the tree—how to grow tree buds indoors—trees have
their own birthday candles—how trees are nourished—the most
famous tree food of all—why leaves change color and fall—how
knots and knotholes are formed—trees prune their own branches
—the underground life of trees—keeping a tree biography—how to
recognize the trees—the white oaks—the black oaks—oak buds—
sugar maples—red maples—Norway maples—sycamores: massive
shade trees—"the button-ball tree"—American elms: graceful and
tough—poplars: including the quaking aspen—the popular cottonwood—willows: generally found near water—the pussy willow:
children's favorite—beeches: handsome and practical—ash trees:
pliant but tough—the paper birch—the gray and yellow birches—
the cherry birch — horse-chestnuts: imported from abroad:
ginkgos: admirable for city streets—firs for Christmas—Canada
balsam—how to recognize a black spruce—the Norway spruce—
hemlocks: useful and ornamental—pines: majestic trees—needles:
the key to identification—pine cones—massive sequoias: thousands
of years old—the towering redwood—how to mount evergreen
specimens—some spring beauties—flowering dogwoods—magnolias
—apple blossoms—shrubs—witch hazel and its popgun seed—
lovely mountain laurel—staghorn sumac: brilliant scarlet—poison
sumac—poison ivy and poison oak—relief for poison ivy—making
leaf collections—how to make spatter prints—how to make prints
with printer's ink—growing trees at home.

Things are not what they seem—looking at the sky—galaxies and
more galaxies—what telescopes tell us—telescopes for everyday
use—choosing a telescope—how planets differ from stars—how to
locate the planets—why life is possible on our earth—Mars:
science-fiction favorite—Mars through the telescope—the "canals"
of Mars—life on Mars—Mars without a telescope—Martian invasion—Mercury: submerged by the sun's brilliance—life is impossible on Mercury—when Mercury is visible—Venus: most brilliant
of the planets—the atmosphere of Venus—earth: just another

Exploring Nature
with Your Child

What Nature Exploring Can Do for Your Child

C HILDREN are natural explorers. They have the true explorer's interest in their immediate surroundings as well as in faraway places, and they are eager to know why things are as they are. If you are a wise parent, you will look upon these qualities in your child as a sacred fire—always to be fed, allowed to die out never. An inquiring mind and zest for living are essential for a rich, interesting, and worth-while life. Childhood is the time to nourish and strengthen these fine qualities.

Just as your child is a natural explorer, you are a natural guide. You help him find security and a sense of direction in the broad and bewildering world that men have made; so, too, you can guide him along nature's ways—and give him a happy outlet and satisfaction for his natural curiosity and exuberance.

You can be a fellow explorer, too, enriching your own life as well as your child's. As you look back on your own early years, you may recall the first time you noticed a bud opening into a flower, a bird building its nest, two colonies of ants battling each other. You may remember that such intimate glimpses of nature gave you a real thrill. Now, as a parent, you can find still more pleasure in learning about the ways of animals and the wonders of plants as you share your observing with your child. No need to go on a safari through Central Africa—delightful discoveries await you in your own back yard, in city parks and suburban gardens, along forest trails where you may hike, and by the side of lakes and streams or the ocean where you may vacation.

There is no end to the wealth of experiences nature holds in store for you and your child. In a park you can see squirrels burying nuts, providing for lean times in a season of plenty. You may observe a flock of wild ducks landing on a park lake for a stopover in their long flight from summer to winter homes. Bees, butterflies, and ants have strange and wonderful ways that you and your child can watch with fascination for hours.

The diversion nature offers you is more exciting than any invented by man, yet it is close at hand and costs you nothing. In many suburbs you may look out of the window in the morning and see a woodchuck nibbling its breakfast in a dewy field, or a rabbit scampering across the lawn, purposefully headed for the vegetable garden. You may watch spiders spinning silken traps, or see an exciting tug-of-war between a robin and an earthworm. In woodlands and meadows, in zoos and museums, there is even more for you to observe. No television, radio, or motion picture producer could invest in his productions the millions of years that nature has spent in preparing these thrilling spectacles for you.

The Best Approach To Exploring Nature

What is the best method of exploring nature? The answer depends on the individual child, for children vary in their approach to nature's activities just as they differ in countless other ways. One child is full of curiosity about plant and animal life from the time he is an infant. Another is absorbed in fanciful ideas, while still another has a mechanical bent, remaining oblivious of natural wonders until you bring them to his attention.

And so exploring nature is not always a simple matter: It is not just "knowing all the answers" or pointing out each tree or bird that you see. A background of information is invaluable, to be sure, but you must pass it on in such a way that you do not overwhelm the child's own modest discoveries. Awareness is essential, but it should not be carried to a point where your child considers you slightly eccentric. On the whole, the successful approach lies in encouraging his inquisitiveness and providing opportunities for him to satisfy his curiosity.

We Learn from Nature

Children with a practical turn of mind particularly enjoy hearing about ways in which man has put nature's "inventions" to use. Outstanding among these devices is camouflage, applied so effectively by many birds and other animals for their own protection. This principle pointed the way for the change from army uniforms that made soldiers conspicuous targets to the deceptive, neutral earth and leaf tones used in battle nowadays.

Another debt we owe nature is the inspiration of bird flight, which has been carefully studied in advancing our own conquest of the air. Fish that swam in prehistoric seas, and many other creatures, have benefited from streamlining—another principle that we have put to use only recently. Wasps were adept at making paper from wood fiber centuries before human beings learned the technique. Our recent invention of radar is an old story to bats, which have a somewhat comparable system for getting their bearings as they fly sightless through treacherous passageways. These are just a few of the lessons that the practical-minded child—or any child—will enjoy having pointed out to him as he becomes acquainted with nature's ways.

Overcoming Fear

Exploring nature teaches children to overcome many baseless fears. Occasionally you find a boy or girl showing more timidity than enjoyment in encounters with animals. The reason for this may be difficult to trace, for a child sometimes has experiences of which his parents are not aware. I saw a case in point one day in a woodsy stretch of a large city park where children were playing unsupervised. A big boy, hand outstretched, started to chase a little fellow, and was fairly hissing with menace:

"Spider! Spider!"

The smaller child was screaming in fright. My curiosity aroused as to the size of the creature inspiring his terror, I approached the older boy and asked if I might see the spider. He gave me a delighted conspiratorial smile and showed me what was in his hand: a small flower!

"I just wanted to scare him," he explained. "He didn't come close enough to see what I really had."

Meanwhile something remarkable had happened. The younger boy had not only stopped crying, but was coming slowly toward us. My interest in the "spider" had aroused his curiosity and was giving him courage to at least see what the "dangerous" creature looked like. It was strong evidence of the influence of older people on a youngster—to his advantage or detriment.

As we spend time with children out-of-doors, we become familiar with the fears they may have of little-known creatures. Once we realize that these fears exist, it is usually not difficult to set at rest any timidity that is really baseless. The remedy is simply to give the youngster an understanding of the dreaded animal.

"The Child Is Father of the Man"

We contribute a great deal to a child's future happiness by giving him a sympathetic acquaintance with as much wildlife as possible. The point is brought home to us when we meet an adult who is agitated by any number of groundless fears.

I remember, for example, a visit to our woodland cabin by a woman whose usual haunts were in New York. All day long she had been enjoying the trees and flowers, the river, and glimpses of bird life; but in the evening a screech owl's tremulous wailing whistle suddenly shattered the quiet. All our explanations about its being "only an owl" proved futile. Our visitor had been quite unnerved by the unearthly sound, and it was obvious she could hardly wait to return to what to her was the calming environment of the big city.

A few evenings later another visitor—this time a little boy of no more than five—heard the wail of the screech owl.

"What was that?" he asked.

We told him, hastily thinking of interesting facts that might dispel his fears. But we need not have bothered. As soon as he heard it was an owl, he said wistfully:

"I wish he would come close so I could hold him and pat him."

It is pleasant to think how rich life will be for this child, growing up with an acceptance of all the sounds and sights that have a rightful place in nature's scheme. But he did not come by this attitude through chance. His parents have been giving him a knowledge and understanding of wildlife since he was three. They have told him nature stories and taught him nature lore and hobbies that have widened his world and made it more enjoyable. All this will certainly contribute to a healthful serenity in later years.

You will find it easy—and delightful—to do the same for your child or children. You are building for the future when you instil in your child a true appreciation of nature and outdoor activities. No one who has this heritage is likely to become a neurotic adult. His conception of the universe and our own earth and the life on it, including himself, is on too grand a scale to permit petty man-made problems to shatter his nerves.

Famous People As Nature Lovers

It is true that some children show a deep interest in flowers and birds and beasts without any special encouragement from adults; but if they can share their interest with their parents, the whole experience becomes more vital and the bonds of family affection are strengthened. Many leading citizens, who are not only famous but have also been successful in their personal lives, have happy childhood memories of nature exploring with their parents.

Theodore Roosevelt's closely knit family had a wealth of such shared interests, and when he was President of the United States his letters to his children away at school were filled with nature news. When spring came to Washington, he reported that "not only are the song sparrows and robins singing, but white-throated sparrows which will soon leave us for the North." The oncoming of fall was noted with: "The Virginia creepers and some maple and gum trees are scarlet and crimson. The oaks are deep, red brown." He told of watching a mother bird bring worms to her babies, of feeding elk at the zoo, and countless other incidents about animals and plants.

Mary Mapes Dodge, who won world fame with *Hans Brinker*

and the Silver Skates and other writings, fondly recalled her
father as a companion on nature jaunts. One of her most vivid
recollections in adult years was of a trip with him to the Botanical
Gardens in New York where some plant experiments were explained. The next day, with her father's interested approval, Mary
started "a little botanical garden" at her bedroom window—a
sweet potato in a hanging vase, and seeds planted in old teacups
filled with different kinds of soil.

Herbert Hoover was an outstanding geologist and mining
engineer before he became President of the United States. He
was an "outdoor boy" from babyhood on, and only the worst sort
of weather could keep him in the house. His parents took him
often to his grandfather's farm where he could herd cattle, plant
corn, and tend chickens. Though his father died when the boy
was small, his mother found time in her busy life for picnics and
other outdoor excursions. It was on these outings that Herbert
started collecting rocks—the introduction to his absorbing lifelong
interest in geology. By the time he was seven he knew how to fish,
forecast storms, and track animals; he loved learning about the
ways of birds, snakes, and all other small creatures of the woods.

As a friend of the Hoover family puts it, "Bert read his fairy
tales in stones, the everlasting hills, the dawn of creation, the
fashioning of a universe." This heritage of nature appreciation
has been passed on to Herbert Hoover's sons and grandchildren.

In all countries, men and women have achieved eminence after
evincing an early and continuing interest in the world around
them, and particularly in nature's ways. Their awareness of nature
has brought greater contentment and happiness into their own
lives. Indeed, they have enriched the lives of all of us with those
achievements of the inquiring mind that has been trained by
close and habitual observation.

Why Nature Is Important to Your Child

Modern schools have excellent programs of nature study; but
even the best programs cannot take the place of family participation in nature interests. On the other hand, any child whose parents

enjoy nature with him finds this of real help with his schoolwork. He will readily discuss ideas that are presented to him at school when he knows his father and mother are interested.

Actually it is not always simple to keep up with the rapid strides made by children. It seemed I had barely stopped smiling over my three-year-old's comments, such as, "I know bees make honey, but I don't see *how* they get it into jars," when he was coming home from the first grade asking, "What is the difference between rodents and other kinds of animals?" A year later he was likely to interrupt lunch with such posers as: "If dinosaurs were so big and powerful, why did they all die?" Suddenly we had arrived at questions that still puzzle many a scientist.

The important place that nature has in the life of a young child has been sensitively analyzed by Arnold and Beatrice Chandler Gesell. Here is what these eminent experts on child behavior say:

"There is nothing new under the sun, but to childhood all is novelty. The most commonplace things teem with novelty.

"Children are in a stage of sense experience when this warm glow of contact through eye and ear and touch may be transmitted into the life of spirit; when light, shadow, sound, motion, and touch weave a tangle of lovely associations around commonplace experiences and build up a deep appreciation of life and things. Thus the truths of nature become unconsciously associated with emotional response, which deepens and safeguards them. The child learns more through unconscious absorption than through didactic prescription, and in nature study daily contact with the beauty, motive, and unceasing effort everywhere shown by plant and animal gives an impulse to individual character and sets standards of behavior.

"The child who stands on tiptoe to peep cautiously into the new-found bird's nest, who feels the velvety softness of growing things beneath his feet as he hunts out the tiny wild flowers in the spring, who sows his own garden seed and waits to see the first young green push its way through the dark, moist soil is building up a reverence for life, a sense of kinship with it, which will uphold him in his later and deeper understanding of its meaning."

CHAPTER 2 How to Understand the Birds

OST CHILDREN, as soon as they are old enough to take an interest in their surroundings, delight in birds. A bundle of feathers with bright eyes and a perky air of self-confidence is an appealing figure whether trilling on a summer day or seeking food in wintry gales. As the child matures, he looks more inquiringly at the graceful songster with which he has become familiar, and one day may startle you with the question:

"What makes a bird a bird?"

Taken off guard you might answer: "A bird has feathers and wings and is able to fly."

But there you stop in confusion. Some birds, such as the ostrich and penguin, do not fly! A fuller explanation will take this into account. Birds are warm-blooded, feathered, egg-laying animals that have backbone and wings, although the wings do not necessarily serve as flying aids. Naturally, you will have to expand this description to make it clear to a child—but it will fit the tiny, speedy hummingbird, the earth-bound ostrich, the majestic eagle, the comical puffin. It will fit the feathered creatures of woodlands, prairies, oceanic islands, high mountain slopes, lakes, deserts, jungles and barnyards. It will stand up under such a challenge as I had from a three-year-old:

"But, Mommy, you called the chicken a bird. It's a chicken!"

By strongly emphasizing feathers I finally persuaded her that even the stalwart barnyard fowl deserves to be ranked with the birds. Feathers are about the only feature which birds do not share with any other kind of animal.

Feathers for Clothes

Bird plumage is often so beautiful that we are likely to overlook its practical value. What clothes are to people, feathers are to birds: undergarments, overcoat and raincoat all in one.

Watch a chicken caught in a rainstorm and you will have a perfect illustration of the "raincoat." The chicken droops its wings and tail, making the best possible use of the feathers—for rain flows off them as it does from your slicker. Examine one of the feathers and you will find it has three distinctive parts: the quill (or central stem); the barbs attached to the major part of the quill; and a soft fluff. This fluff, snuggling against the body at the base of the quill, plays the part of warm underclothing.

Why Protective Coloring Is Important

Feathers often serve birds as camouflage. We quickly recognize this in many wild birds. The value of protective coloring in chickens is less obvious to us because we usually see them in a barnyard. Were a hen living in a state of nature, wandering in grassy fields with her chicks, her neutral color would blend with her surroundings. It is the rooster who is decorative, having lovely iridescent tail feathers and, sometimes, colorful neck plumage.

Wild birds offer many convincing examples of the safety value of camouflage. The female Baltimore oriole, for example, is a dull orange-yellow while her mate is a brilliant combination of vivid orange, black, and white. Among the cardinals, the male is a rich red; the female's plumage is light brown with only the faintest tinge of red. The name "rose-breasted grosbeak" is appropriate for the male of this species, as he displays a deep rose patch on his white breast; but his mottled yellow-brown and white mate looks rather like an overgrown sparrow.

In each case we see the same principle at work: The mother birds that must look after the eggs and babies do not attract notice. Meanwhile the arrestingly colored males can remain at a suitable distance from the nest, distracting the attention of squirrels or other possible enemies.

You may notice an interesting phase of protective coloration in birds that are "molting." When the males of certain species lose their bright feathers after the mating season, they develop new ones of somber hues. By fall the male scarlet tanager is the same dull yellow green as his mate; both male and female bobolink become sparrow-like in appearance; and the bright yellow body-feathers of the goldfinch have given way to others of dull yellow brown. So garbed, the male birds are fairly inconspicuous until the time comes again for them to be gaily attractive to the females.

New Feathers for Old

If late summer happens to be the time that your boy or girl starts to show a more than casual interest in birds, the subject of molting makes the most dramatic theme to explore. Some species lose their worn and faded feathers in August, and by September have a completely new plumage. Among the exceptions to this schedule are waterfowl, which begin to molt in June. By September they have passed through two molts, during which they took on and discarded a dull plumage.

Unless there is a definite change in a bird's coloration during molting, the process is not easy to observe, since the change is gradual. Starting with one certain feather—usually this is the innermost primary wing feather—it continues over the wings until all are replaced. The feathers of some kinds of birds develop all over the body at the same time, while on others the development comes in patches. Ducks, grebes, loons and other swimming birds which do not depend on flight as their only means of locomotion, molt all feathers at the ends of the wings (the primaries) within a very short time.

Feathers do not grow haphazardly over a bird's body, but are arranged in definite lines or patches (called "feather tracts") between which there are bare areas. However, the overlapping of feathers of the adjacent tracts keeps the skin completely covered in healthy birds. You may see a chicken looking "half-naked" as the result of arrested feather development. This never happens to wild birds unless they are diseased.

Most birds molt only once a year, but the brilliantly colored males that have dull winter coats must change again to regain their beauty in the spring. Hence such birds as the scarlet tanager and the goldfinch undergo a spring (prenuptial) as well as fall (postnuptial) molt. The spring molt is usually not complete, however; the wing and tail feathers serve both plumages.

Some birds change appearance between winter and spring without undergoing a second molt. They do so merely by "feather wear"; that is, the feather tips which have given the general tone to the winter plumage wear away and expose the bright colors of the breeding plumage. The robin is a notable example. His breast becomes redder as spring advances because the gray feather tips are wearing off. In other birds yellow, brown, and gray most frequently edge the feathers in winter plumage. As these colors disappear, black, brown, or red is revealed.

Molting consumes energy. While it is growing a new set of feathers, a bird neither sings nor fights, staying in seclusion except when it must seek food. It is for this reason, rather than because of an early departure for southern climes, that you see few birds in late August and early September. As soon as the birds have completed their molting they regain their vitality and are ready to migrate or to face the rigors of a northern winter.

The Versatile Beak

The child who is always asking "Why?" will be fascinated by the endless variety of bird beaks. In almost every case, beak formation gives us the clue to a bird's eating habits, diet—and even its surroundings. The duck, for example, has a wide, flat bill that equips it for feeding on water insects and plants. After seizing food in its beak, the duck holds the food until the water strains out of the sievelike edges. Given the same conditions, the sharp, horny beak of the hen would be quite useless. The hen's beak resembles a pick rather than a scoop, and it strikes efficiently into the soil for insects or seeds.

Another bird with a sharp, seed-eating beak is the sparrow. As for the woodpecker, its beak is virtually a chisel. You may spy one of these birds drilling for insects, or come upon the evidence where a woodpecker has left a series of holes in a tree trunk.

These are but a few examples of the close relationship between the style of a bird's beak and the kind of food that it eats. Children will get the point at once if you tell them the delightful Aesop fable of the stork and the fox. The stork, having been served soup in a shallow dish by his host, a fox, gets his revenge by inviting the fox to dinner and serving it in a narrow-necked vessel down which its own long bill fits perfectly.

Getting food for the adult and feeding the young are the two basic uses of the beak. But it has other important functions: It is a tool for gathering nesting material and digging nesting sites and it often serves as a weapon of attack or defense. It also enables many birds to do an effective job of preening and smoothing their plumage and keeping it clean.

If the hen you watched during a storm could be observed after the rain stopped, you might see her using her beak to oil her feathers. There is an oil gland on her back, just at the base of the tail feathers. She presses the gland with her beak to force out oil; then she rubs the beak over the surface of her feathers and passes it through them. Now her "oilskin slicker" is ready for the next downpour. A number of other birds, including waterfowl, use this same oiling method.

The parrot's curved bill is unique in construction and use, as it is a first-class climbing aid. The upper mandible, or beak, is movable, being connected to the bird's skull by a hinge. When the parrot climbs, it uses this mandible as a hook to support its body while its feet find a new resting place.

Feet Are Versatile Too

Versatile as the beak is, the bird's feet are equally valuable tools. Wading birds, such as flamingoes and herons, have extremely

THE FLAMINGO—LONG AND LUGUBRIOUS

"Long" is the key word for the flamingo: long body, long bill, long neck, long legs, long toes. Its weird habits include: sleeping in its famous one-legged stance, eating with its head upside-down, and roosting on its foot-high cone-shaped nest.

long toes which distribute their weight and keep them from sinking into soft mud. Short-tailed birds—the murres, for example—use the feet as rudders during flight. Diving birds, such as grebes, use their feet to propel them under water.

Whenever you see a bird scratching for food, you are noticing another use for its feet. Birds of prey, such as eagles and hawks, seize their victims in their long, powerful talons. Many birds use their feet to gather and place nesting material; with other birds, the feet are fighting weapons. The parrot uses a foot to grasp and bring food to its mouth, much as we use a hand. So we see that a bird's feet serve many purposes aside from the most obvious one of supporting its body.

Sharp Eyes and Ears

Are the bright eyes of a bird as efficient as their alert and shining appearance leads you to believe? They really are: Birds are much more sharp-sighted than we are. Not only do birds have keen vision, but some of them are remarkably well adapted for seeing objects both far away and at close range. Thus a hawk flying so high that it would appear as a mere speck to us, may look down and see a rabbit or even a mouse on the ground! The hawk has two centers of vision, and as it swoops down from the heights, its vision shifts from one center to the other so that its eyes are adjusted for short-range work when it seizes its prey.

Yet most birds, despite their sharp eyes, do not have bifocal vision like the hawk. One consequence is that they do not detect telephone and telegraph wires, and many birds are injured or killed every year by collision with such obstacles.

Among birds there is quite a bit of variety in the color of the iris; it may be brown, gray, blue, yellow, white, pink, purple, green, and even red. The red-eyed vireo takes the first part of its name from this striking feature. The hen, which is ideal for bird study, has a yellow iris. It is equipped with an eyelid that shuts out vision, coming up from the bottom of the eye, however, rather than down from the top. It also has another kind of eyelid —a film that moves across the eye from the inside corner to the outer side.

You may escape questioning about a bird's hearing ability because their ears are fairly well hidden. Then suddenly this very fact may be the basis for a query from your young observer: "How can that bird hear? I don't see any ears!"

Except for the owls, which have noticeable "ear tufts," the ear of a bird is no more than a hole, rather well covered with feathers, on the side of its head. Yet a bird's hearing is just as remarkable as its sight—perhaps even more remarkable. Walking in a field or forest you may notice how the snapping of a small twig will startle and put to flight a bird that is a considerable distance away. And when you see a robin cocking its head and realize it is listening for an earthworm under the surface of the ground, you develop a well-deserved respect for birds' hearing.

How Birds Fly

"How *do* birds fly?" is a question that most children ask at some time. The child may accompany his query with a leap into the air, arms outstretched, and a faint hope that he too can "take off."

BIRDS ARE BUILT FOR FLIGHT

It helps your inquisitive child to understand the mechanics of flight if you point out that the bird's streamlined form is of great advantage in flying. Besides this, it has an extremely light structure: Its bones and the shafts of its feathers are hollow and, as is easily seen, the size of its wing is greater in proportion to its body than an arm is to the human body.

You can then go on to compare the child's framework to the bone and feather structure of the bird, which has a bone corresponding to his upper arm and another to the bone between his elbow and wrist. Have the child extend his thumb upward, hold his first and second fingers in a horizontal position, and fold the other two into his palm—somewhat as he would do in making a pretend-gun out of his hand. This will give him a rough comparison with the structure of a bird's wing.

The bird has a winglet corresponding to the child's thumb, and a second and third digit similar to his extended fingers. These are sometimes extended upright, but may also be held horizontally. While the child's arm, hand, and fingers are covered only with skin, the bird has flight feathers also—one sheath on the "forearm," and another series on the "hand." The number of feathers varies in different birds.

FLIGHT TECHNIQUES

There are four types of bird flight: flapping, gliding, static soaring, and dynamic soaring. In flapping flight the "arm" wings help to lift most large wings into the air, while the "hand" wings produce propulsion through the air. Speed or forward motion is gained with each downward stroke of the wings; lift is obtained on up-and-down strokes. In this up-and-down motion the wing tips move through a much greater arc than the wrists would. (In airplane flight lift and speed are produced by the propeller *and* the wings.) In small birds, such as the finch, the whole wing flaps as a unit, producing speed and lift at the same time. During the upstroke, the wing is folded.

When a bird glides, it loses altitude to keep its forward-pushing motion. In static soaring, the bird takes advantage of up-air currents which offset the loss of altitude suffered during its gliding flight. For dynamic soaring a bird such as the albatross will use the force of the wind. Wind force increases with altitude; hence the bird, after descending most of the way, levels off with the slowing down of the wind near the surface of the water, and then ascends again, once more making use of the air currents.

Birds use their wings differently depending on the kind of flight, such as horizontal, soaring, descending, gliding, hovering, taking off, and climbing. Various types of birds have wings of different shapes and proportions, and each employs each wing in the distinctive manner appropriate to it.

An important feature of the bird's flying mechanism is a sinew with elastic qualities. On the downward thrust of the wing, the sinew holds the feathers in a tight overlapping position. When the wing comes up, the tension of the sinew relaxes and the feathers part and rotate. This allows air to flow between them as an aid in flight.

It gives us pleasure to understand how birds fly, but all the analysis in the world cannot dim the initial thrill of seeing birds in flight.

The Mystery of Migration

There is no more fascinating way of arousing interest in flight than having your child catch a sight of migrating birds—perhaps a flight of geese in military formation, or a close-massed flock of grackles racing like a dark wind-blown cloud. Even after years of research and experiment, scientists speak of the "mystery" of bird migration, for they still do not completely understand it. Yet, puzzling as this semiannual pilgrimage of countless birds is, it is no more puzzling to me than the way in which my daughter took note of it before she reached her second birthday. On three different occasions we were having a late afternoon walk along streets brightening with rows of electric lights and alive with home-bound traffic, when the little girl in the stroller looked up and pointed in great excitement:

"Look, birdies!"

And there they were—large flocks of them, high above the city's hubbub, traveling in steady and sure flight toward their winter destination. The wonderful instinct that keeps birds on their course in long-distance travel has been called a "sixth sense," and it seemed that a similar sense must have prompted this mite to take her eyes from the noise and excitement on the ground at exactly the right time to catch the nature news high in the sky. Now that she is older we have fun deliberately watching for the "birdies."

Not all birds migrate. Some you will know as "permanent residents" in your neighborhood. The migratory birds that arrive in the spring and remain through the summer are "summer residents." Fall migrants that remain through the cold season are "winter residents." Other birds you may see only briefly as they pass through to nesting grounds or winter quarters. These you know as "transients." Migratory birds thus are different things to different people, for *your* summer residents are winter residents in other regions and your transients somewhere become winter and summer residents.

A confusing fact about migration is that certain well-known migrators do not travel as far south, or north, as we think. According to popular belief, the robin, that noted herald of spring, winters in the warm comfort of the South. It is a bit disconcerting therefore, when taking a winter walk, to see a robin hunting food amid frozen surroundings, especially if the boy or girl with you asks:

"Don't robins go south in winter?"

The majority of them *are* reveling in southern sunshine. Many are along the Gulf coast, some are in Mexico, and enormous flocks are in Florida, feeding on holly and mistletoe berries. But a few elect to remain in northern climes with only the friendly evergreens to shield them. You may also see occasional members of other species, such as the bluebird, song sparrow, meadow lark, redwinged blackbird, and cedar waxwing, braving the northern winter.

Sky Lanes of the Birds

Because the expressions "traveling north" or "flying south" are used repeatedly, children are apt to believe that the birds migrate unfailingly in these directions. However, this is not an accurate picture, as some fly southeast, others southwest. Certain species have followed fixed travel routes until they have become well-defined pathways, or sky lanes, for these birds. Some travel north by one route and return south by another, perhaps leading over an entirely different part of the country. Or else one route may be over land and the return route over water. The golden plover is an interesting example of these birds that have a "double migration route." In the spring it travels from South America to Labrador in as direct a line as possible, through the middle of the North American continent. In the fall it goes eastward to the Atlantic, and much of its return flight is over water. On this longer course it must fly 2,400 miles.

Flying Hours

There are also variations in the time of day for migratory flight. Some birds are on the wing by day, others by night, while still others are active day and night. Warblers, thrushes, and woodcocks are among the night fliers; geese, crows, swallows, robins, hummingbirds, blue jays, and bluebirds are a few of the daytime travelers. As for ducks, you may see them on the wing day or night.

How Fast Do Birds Fly?

Long ago, birds were credited with a speed that approaches the speed of a modern airplane. The theory was that most birds performed the greater part of their journey in one night! In recent times the speed of many birds has been "clocked" accurately with the aid of airplanes and motorcars. We now know that a hundred miles an hour is an exceptionally fast rate, achieved by only a few birds, such as certain swifts.

In making their migratory flights most birds apparently move at a rate somewhere between twenty and fifty miles an hour. The great journeys made by some species are accomplished by the birds moving for long hours at a steady rate rather than by great bursts of speed over short distances. When we compare the speed of an individual bird with the time it takes a flock of that same species to complete its migratory journey, we realize that the birds do not fly continuously night after night or day after day. They may pause for extended rests or for favorable weather conditions.

WHERE BIRDS MIGRATE

In the autumn several familiar species of smaller birds go as far as Central and South America. Bobolinks, for instance, leave the fields and meadows of northern states traveling southward in leisurely fashion through the West Indies and along

THE BOBOLINK—MIGRATOR EXTRAORDINARY

Every winter the bobolink journeys some five thousand miles from its United States haunts to Brazil or Argentina, where it relishes their summer weather in the winter months. The bobolink is welcomed where it devours weed seeds, detested where it destroys rice crops.

eastern Central America. Even when they reach the northern parts of South America they are not satisfied but continue until they come to the wide open plains and marshes of southern Brazil and northern Argentine.

In contrast to these we have some birds that migrate for only short distances. The chickadee is one; the crow is another. Such birds may move southward from your community in the fall, only to be replaced by other chickadees or crows moving down from points farther north. Thus while you seem to have the same birds the year round, they are actually different individuals.

We can sum up some of the puzzling aspects of bird migration by saying that in its simplest form, migration is merely a journey away from, and back to, a nesting ground, and apparently made without any relation to temperature.

How to Keep a Bird Calendar

If you live in a region where the four seasons are clearly defined by sharp weather contrasts, the study of bird migrations will provide you with an especially enjoyable hobby. By keeping a bird calendar you can note the comings, the goings, and the passings through of different species. Your calendar can be quite simple: a large ruled sheet of paper, divided into four columns. Head the first column "Date," the second "Bird's Name," the third "Where Seen," the fourth "Time of Day." You may simply fill in information about birds that come near your home, but the record becomes far more lively when you widen the range of observation by means of bird walks.

Some children enjoy such a project as an individual enterprise. Others are more stimulated if the calendar is a family affair with scope for friendly rivalry. Who will have the fun of recording the first robin of spring? Who will see a bluebird this year? Who will trace a song sparrow by its lilting melody or look for a hummingbird near its nest? Interest becomes keener when you keep calendars year after year, trying to better the record of observation with each new calendar.

How to Be a Good Neighbor to the Birds

There are a number of ways to bring wild birds close to your home where you may enjoy them and study them. One of the most effective overtures of friendship is to provide a birdbath. Songbirds as a rule seem to be attracted by water. Some of them even relish taking a bath when it is raining; but during hot dry spells when many natural sources of water dry up, your birdbath will serve a really essential purpose.

There are also times when birds have trouble finding drinking water. The simplest way to provide a bath and drinking fountain is to set a shallow pan filled with water on the ground, on a post, or on a ledge. In placing the pan, keep in mind the danger from cats. These enemies must not have any nearby hiding place from which to launch a surprise attack against the birds. A birdbath of concrete comes near to being ideal because its dull surface blends well with the browns, greens, and grays that surround it, and its rough surface makes perching easy.

FEEDING THE BIRDS IN WINTERTIME

You can also attract birds by building houses and shelters for them. But probably the greatest service you can render is to furnish winter food. Though completely self-reliant in warm weather, the birds that remain north throughout the year are often desperate for food during the winter months. Birds have an exceptionally high body temperature, and so long as they have sufficient food to keep this temperature normal they do not suffer from the cold. But if a scarcity of food results in a lowering of the body temperature, the birds suffer severely and may even freeze to death.

You can provide food for them in a number of ways. If you have a yard, simply trample down the snow at some suitable spot and sprinkle crumbs and seeds. Or else you may tie pieces of suet to trees or posts. A feeding tray fastened to a window makes a good, safe feeding station and also gives you a wonderful opportunity to watch birds at close quarters. You can even photograph them without much trouble. Cut a circular hole at the bottom of a board that fits into the window frame where your feeding tray is placed. When you wish to take pictures you can raise the window, insert the board barrier, and direct your camera through the hole. Birds will partake of your food offering without the least alarm as they let themselves be photographed.

Feeding trays, moreover, have their uses beyond country or suburb. A businessman in Topeka, Kansas, who decided to put a tray of sunflower seeds at his office window sill, reported that the following day it was visited by a chickadee, a downy wood-pecker, a junco, and a brown creeper.

One other excellent type of feeding station is a *covered* plat-form attached to a post. The covering keeps the food dry and the elevation protects the birds while they are eating. There are many other efficient types of bird feeders that you can buy or make and place on porch, window sill, or around the yard.

What Birds Feed On

Insect-eating birds, such as chickadees and woodpeckers, welcome suet when their usual food is not available. Seed-eating birds are not greatly tempted by fat, but they thrive on stale

THE GROUSE—SPORTSMAN'S FAVORITE

These handsome game birds are great favorites with hunters. Grouse are hardy creatures, accustomed to living through the rigors of severe winter. When their usual insect diet is not available, they get by on twigs and buds.

bread, crackers and cake broken into crumbs, sunflower seeds, squash, and cracked corn. Nuts are a special treat to many birds, and a number of them are fond of peanut butter. It is worth while to remember the ground birds, such as pheasant, grouse, and quail, if they live near you. A spot by a hedge or a clump of trees makes a good feeding place for them. During a winter of extreme snow and sleet, you may help them to survive by supplying corn or other grains in a simple lean-to shelter.

Birds as Songsters

Spring is the time to enjoy the singing of birds, for it is during the nesting season that their choral symphony is in full swing. Most of the singing is instinctive and probably an attempt on the part of the male to intimidate other males. What makes this seem likely is that the males of some species reach their nesting grounds well ahead of their female audience. "Singing for fun" is characteristic of certain caged birds whose only companionship is that of human beings. Then there are species that have a second singing period after the postbreeding molt; but this lasts only a few days.

A frequent question I have received in letters from children is: "Do birds sing when they are flying?" Unfortunately it is not possible to give the eager correspondents a simple yes-or-no answer. As a rule, singing usually takes a bird's undivided attention, but some birds—the bobolink, for one—do sing while flying as well as when perching. Other birds, besides singing from a perch, indulge in occasional songs of "ecstasy" as they bound into the air and seem about to burst with their hurried, twittering notes. The meadow lark and goldfinch are just two of the species which carry on in this delightful fashion.

Other Bird Sounds

Aside from its song a bird can produce several other kinds of sounds. Some of these are very useful in the baby stage, as when the young greet their parents from the nest with what is unmistakably a hunger call. Some babies can follow the parent around

THE GOLDFINCH—ECSTATIC SONGSTER

Like their famous relatives the canaries, goldfinches are inspired singers. They sing while perching and sometimes bound into the air with an ecstatic outburst of twittering notes. The goldfinch flies in graceful curves that are a pleasure to watch.

shortly after hatching; the youngsters of these species make a *peeping* sound which prevents them from getting lost. As the bird matures, it develops a "vocabulary" of some variety. It has a call, especially useful during migration, which keeps it in touch with the rest of the group. It can also give a call of alarm and one of warning.

While some birds have won a reputation as excellent songsters, others, such as the brown pelican, are noted for being virtually silent. Then there are birds that make sounds which take the place of song. An example is the ruffed grouse with his drumming.

The male grouse produces his music by standing stiffly erect with his tail down and fanning the air with his wings. He may select a given location, say a log, for his performance, going to the same spot and facing in the same direction every time he drums. This habit reminds us of some songbirds that become greatly attached to favorite perches from which they sing.

When you hear your child trilling happily at his play, you may tell yourself with some satisfaction that he is "singing like a bird." Strictly speaking, however, such a feat is impossible! The human voice is produced in the larynx. A bird's voice comes from a different structure called the syrinx, located at the base of the windpipe. (In Greek mythology, Syrinx was a nymph who was transformed into a tuft of reeds from which the god Pan made his pipes.)

IDENTIFYING BIRDS BY THEIR SONG

"What bird is that?" is a frequent question from youngsters who are becoming interested in identification.

If you are able to recognize the songs of the birds, you are well on the way to the right answer. Some songs are as characteristic as the bird's physical appearance: The interested observer and listener soon recognizes such tunes as the *conk-a-ree-e* of the red-winged blackbird and the rollicking medley of the bobolink. The best time of the year to begin your study of bird songs is very early in spring, before migrants arriving in large numbers create a confusion of voices. The best time of day to listen is the morning or late afternoon. Concentrate at first on the songs of the more common, hence more familiar, birds of your region. This will make it easier for you to distinguish individual calls and melodies in the chorus that arises later on when the season is at its height.

Certain birds make recognition quite simple for you by calling their own names—for it was their calls that gave them their names to begin with! Among the better known of these are the bobolink, chickadee, phoebe, bobwhite, and whippoorwill.

HOW TO RECORD BIRD SONGS

While you may not be able to write out bird songs in musical notation, you should find it easy to jot down many songs in words or syllables. This is instructive—and amusing too, for naturally any two listeners may arrive at varying interpretations of the same song. Here are three versions, for example, of the song of the white-throated sparrow: *Old Sam Peabody, Peabody, Peabody;* or, *Sow wheat Peverly, Peverly, Peverly;* or, *Sweet Canada, Canada, Canada.*

Some interpretations have been published so often, however, that we may now consider them as standard. Thus the scarlet tanager is supposed to say *chip-churr* and the nuthatch *ank, ank.* Though the robin has a variety of sweet songs, its apt early morning serenade is *wake-up, cheer-up, cheerily-up, wake-up.* A cardinal may join in with a shrill *whoit, whoit, whoit, whit, whit, whit, whit.* As for the song sparrow, it suggests in a lyrical mood: *maids, maids, put on your teakettle—ettle, ettle, ettle.* Some songs are longer and have more variations; we write their lyrics in couplets. The interpretation of the brown thrasher's song is a good example:

> *Shuck it, Shuck it; sow it, sow it;*
> *Plow it, Plow it; hoe it, hoe it!*

On occasion birds may vary their phrasing just enough to confuse us. However, an excellent way to become familiar with bird songs is through recordings. In many stores—and libraries as well —you can find such collections as "Bird Songs" and "More Bird Songs," both recorded by Albert R. Brand.

To become a skillful imitator of songs and calls requires a great deal of practice. The chickadee is a good bird to imitate, as it is a particularly responsive bird. If you can get the chickadee to answer your imitation of its call, you will be sure of a fascinated and admiring audience in your child.

How to Make Birds Feel at Home

One of the most satisfying outlets for the energies of a young carpenter is building a bird house. As he uses his tools he gets a practical grasp of the essentials of construction work. Later on, if he keeps an eye on the house after it is set up, he will learn a great deal about the habits of birds and their likes and dislikes. As he sees them in and about "his" house, he will experience a feeling of pride and protective tenderness.

But remember that birds are often very "choosy," inspecting and passing up, or simply ignoring, an ideal-looking residence designed for them and nesting nearby in a hollow stump, post, or tree. To be a successful bird-house "proprietor" you need to be familiar with the habits and wants of the birds you wish to attract, and to make a building especially suitable for them. This certainly improves your prospects of attracting "tenants." You can still expect surprises, for birds like to do things their own way. One summer a neighbor of mine proudly drew my attention to wrens settling in a home he had built for them. The following year he sheepishly admitted that other wrens were using the house as a foundation. They were nesting on the roof!

The Hobby of Nest Collecting

In doing their own nest building, birds choose from a wide variety of materials. The chipping sparrow goes exploring for fine roots, the robin prefers mud and grass, the ovenbird fancies the spore stems of mosses, while the Baltimore oriole favors milkweed, bark, and long moss. If their favorite materials are not to be found, birds are ever resourceful in finding substitutes. My son's nature collection includes a chipping sparrow nest that is neatly lined with pig bristles! Orioles are noted for their fondness for yarn if any happens to be available. And there are many other examples of the ingenuity which birds lavish on their nests.

Spring is the season for providing nesting places. To enjoy the hobby of collecting nests, you ought to wait until fall; for in this way you avoid removing a nest when there is still a chance that the birds may have a further use for it.

Many birds are masters at the art of concealment, and you will need all your powers as a "nature detective" to find nests before most of the leaves have fallen. Some birds, such as the hummingbird, use a camouflage technique to protect their nests. Another favorite device, used by the warbler, for example, is to nest in thick foliage. Still another precaution, favored by some owls, is to build high in tall trees.

When your child collects deserted nests for a home exhibit, he can give them quite an impressive setting with a few leafy twigs and a background taken from the original location of the nest. To complete the exhibit appropriately, add a label giving the species, time, and place of the collection.

Baby Birds

THE CHICKEN AND THE EGG

The best-known bird's egg by far is that of the chicken. It is such a common sight on grocery shelf and breakfast table that it really requires an effort of imagination on a child's part to think of the egg in connection with bird life.

Yet if, in this day of incubators, children could watch a hen with her brood, they would soon realize she is one of the best of bird mothers. When she takes her chicks into tall grass she clucks constantly so that they will not stray away from her. Finding a bit of food, she calls them quickly and they understand just what she means. Should a hawk appear overhead, she gives a warning cry which sends the chicks scurrying for cover. If a rat or other enemy threatens her brood, she will fight to the limit of her strength to protect the chicks.

A newly hatched chick wears an odd little "bump" on the tip of its upper mandible, or beak. This is the "egg tooth" that the baby used as a pick to break its way through the eggshell. After the egg tooth has served its purpose the chick has no further use for it and it soon disappears.

How Many Eggs Are Laid

There is an almost endless variety in bird's eggs. There are big eggs and little eggs; white, colored, and spotted eggs; eggs that differ in shape and length of time required for incubation. And so you need considerable information to answer the simple question: "How many eggs does a bird lay?"

We have no unconditional reply to this question. Each species has a *usual* number that makes up a full set; but differences will still crop up. Northern thrushes, for example, normally lay four eggs, while tropical thrushes lay only two or three. If a nest is robbed, the bird will often lay additional eggs to replace the stolen ones. There is an historic case of a brown woodpecker—known as the flicker—laying seventy-one eggs in seventy-three days!

Fantastic as this may sound, it points up the fact that constant nest-robbing has virtually turned domestic fowls into egg-laying machines. A domestic hen may lay more than two hundred eggs a season if they are promptly taken away, thus assuring "continuous performance." On the other hand, if the eggs are left in the nest to be incubated, her production will stop after fifteen or twenty eggs.

The best you can do, then, in giving actual numbers of eggs that different birds have in a clutch, is to say that in a full set of eggs there may be as many as twenty or as few as one.

THE AMAZING HUMMINGBIRD

The smallest of all birds, with the tiniest of eggs, the hummingbird has other claims to fame. Aside from flying backward or remaining stationary in mid-air, it can move its wings so rapidly that they become invisible. This incredibly rapid motion produces the sound that gives the "hummer" its name.

THE SIZE OF EGGS

"Which bird lays the biggest eggs?" and "Which lays the smallest?" are welcome questions because we have direct and definite answers to them. The ostrich, largest of birds, lays the largest eggs; the hummingbird, smallest of birds, lays the smallest eggs.

However, it does not always follow that the larger bird lays the larger egg. A bird whose chicks come forth in a well-developed state, lays relatively larger eggs than a bird whose chicks are less well developed.

Among the well-developed babies are those of our friend the chicken, the grouse, and the spotted sandpiper. When they hatch they are already covered with a soft down. Their eyes open immediately and in no time at all they can toddle about and follow their mother. Before long they learn to pick up and eat their own food. We term this kind of bird "precocial," a word related to "precocious." Birds that hatch in a more helpless state are naked or at best have a scant covering of down. They are blind at first and are dependent on their parents for at least a week—usually much longer. Such birds are known as "altricial," from the Latin word for "nourishers."

"BABY SITTERS"

The length of time needed for incubation varies with different species. The English sparrow takes twelve or thirteen days; the robin, thirteen or fourteen days; the fish hawk, about four weeks. In some families the duty of sitting on the eggs is shared by both parents; in others, it falls entirely to the lot of the mother. There is one curious family in which the eggs, once they have been laid by the female, become the sole responsibility of the male. He incubates the eggs unaided, though the mother stays nearby and shows continued interest in her family. These birds are the phalaropes, found in many parts of North America.

BRINGING UP BABY

Helpless baby birds require an extraordinary amount of care, and perhaps because it helps to build in themselves a sense of the security of parental care and affection, children greatly enjoy hearing about the devoted family life of birds. How proud the mother hen is of her chicks as she struts about the barnyard, clucking loudly to call attention to her brood! In the wilds, where danger constantly threatens, the mother bird's behavior may be quite the opposite—she does everything possible to make her brood inconspicuous. A grouse, sensing an intruder, will go to the extreme of chirping pitifully while thrashing along the ground as if hurt. This serves two purposes. Her cry warns the young to remain quiet or escape from the danger, and her movements divert attention from her little family.

How Bird Babies Are Fed

Bird babies have enormous appetites. Until they are able to take care of themselves, their parents must find and bring them food. The fledglings usually feed on insects, even though many of them will grow up to be seed-eaters. In species where the young are most helpless—the mourning dove, for example—the parent first swallows the food and then feeds it to them in partly digested form. That is why one of these birds, unlike so many other bird parents, is never seen flying back to the nest with food in its bill.

Children occasionally have the good fortune to watch baby birds being fed. More often the children see pictures of the birds at feeding time, and they may notice that feeding techniques vary with different birds. The most common method is for the parent to push its bill down the baby's throat—a method that prevents any live insect from escaping. With pelicans and certain other species that regurgitate food, the process is reversed: The baby puts its head in its mother's throat pouch or takes food from her bill. The babies' need for water is satisfied by the moisture in their solid food.

Parents often continue feeding the young after they have left the nest; but at this point the feeding methods are no longer so painstaking. The swallows are particularly interesting to observe at this stage of development. While in the nest, the young bird has food carefully placed down its throat. But once the fledgling is able to hop away from the nest, it must be on the alert with bill opened upward, for the parents merely drop food to it without pausing in their flight. When the young swallows start to fly, this catch-as-catch-can feeding continues while the parents and the young birds as well are in full flight.

Proper manners, as taught to our children, are out of place as far as baby birds are concerned. Usually the aggressive one that stretches its neck farthest and cries the loudest is the one that is fed—until another member of the family becomes more "grabby." However, the parent, with a kind of rough justice, usually looks into the youngster's mouth after each feeding; if a morsel has not been swallowed instantly, the older bird snatches it back and turns its attention to another baby.

GETTING READY TO LEAVE THE NEST

Some babies—those of chickens, for example—are covered with down and able to run about when newly hatched. The parents may keep them under their wings, "brooding" them over a period of five or six weeks. Other kinds of birds also "brood" while the babies are in the nest, but never after they have started to fly. Brooding protects the young ones from the cold—and from excessive heat as well, as it prevents their being overheated in a nest unprotected from the sun.

As the baby birds develop feathers, their responsibilities grow. They preen their feathers and begin to exercise, concentrating on stretching their wings. Often they practice "taking off" before leaving the safety of the nest.

Though birds fly by instinct, the first flight generally requires considerable parental coaxing. It may be no more than a flutter to a nearby limb or it may be, as in the case of swallows, a sustained and graceful performance. Song sparrows and others are ready to try their wings only a week after hatching, while the wandering albatross has to be forced out by its parents to make room for a new brood—nearly a year later. But whatever the amount of time involved, the youngsters have flourished on the solicitous care of their parents, and are now ready to face life on their own.

CHAPTER 3 The Delightful Hobby
of Bird Watching

WATCHING FOR BIRDS can give sparkle to an otherwise ordinary walk through a park— it can offer an inducement for extensive hiking—and it can add zest to your auto trips. If you do not try it, you will miss a world of fun. For children, it is one of the most delightful of pastimes.

The best way for you to carry on bird watching depends largely on the age of your children. Obviously you cannot expect a child of kindergarten age to adapt himself to an excursion in the woods where you hope to see the less common birds in their natural surroundings; a young child is too restless to maintain the necessary quiet. Also, since he is more interested in what birds do than in what they are called, the most ordinary bird will appeal to him just as strongly as a rare species. Thus you may find it best to start your observations with the "everyday" birds around your home.

A small child loves to answer easy questions. And questions can provide the motivation here if the presence of birds on the lawn or in the park is not motivation enough. You might start with some of these queries, leaving out bird names unless the child is ready for them: Do the birds walk (as blackbirds do), run (like robins), or hop (like sparrows)? Do they keep together in flocks (like waxwings, for example), or do they prefer to be alone? Do they seem to talk to each other, or do they concentrate

49

on feeding? Do they hunt worms or look for seeds for their food? You can proceed from these questions to others that will come to you naturally enough as you read what this book has to say about birds. All you need is a start. Your child's rich imagination will carry you the rest of the way.

How to Get the Most Out of Bird Walks

Once boys and girls have become interested in watching birds at home, they are usually eager to go farther afield. Then you will enjoy your trip a lot more if you are forearmed with some general knowledge: What birds may be found where?

For example: In orchards and gardens you are likely to find bluebirds, mockingbirds, screech owls, downy woodpeckers, chicka-

THE BRILLIANT SCARLET TANAGER

With his striking red body and black wings and tail, the male tanager is one of the most brilliant birds of North America. The female, olive-colored, is not nearly so pretty, but she's the one that gathers twigs and weeds to build the nest in an oak or orchard tree. Here she lays three or four bluish-white eggs.

dees. In open meadows, look for bobolinks and crows; in damp meadows, red-winged blackbirds. Along rivers and by lakes and ponds you may find kingfishers, swallows, and phoebes. At woods' edges there are white-throated sparrows, field sparrows, wood peewees, scarlet tanagers, and some owls; in deeper woods, barred owls, ovenbirds, hermit thrush, ruffed grouse.

Swamps and marshes are the places for herons, bitterns and rails, while near large ponds and lakes you may expect ducks, fish hawks, and bald eagles. Seashore and mud flats are the setting for sandpipers and avocets.

This greatly shortened list of birds and their customary home grounds suggests how you may "line up" the birds of your locality before starting on a bird walk. You will have an idea of where to look for certain types of birds, so that you can map out a plan of action.

The best time to go is early morning; soon after sunrise bird activities slow down and do not resume until late afternoon. On early-morning walks, avoid traveling east, as the low-lying sun in your eyes makes it hard to see birds. Hawks, ducks, and water-fowl are active throughout the day and you may often observe them when other birds are quiet.

There is no special season for bird watching. The great attraction of spring is the birds migrating north; summer offers nesting birds and the appearance of the young; fall is the time for the flocks to wing south; winter is almost best of all with the hardy birds showing themselves boldly as they seek food among snowy surroundings.

An interested pair of eyes is the only essential equipment you need for bird watching. But good field glasses or binoculars are really valuable in identifying species and they greatly enhance the pleasure of a trip for any child old enough to use them.

You can get more out of a bird walk, also, if you bring along a pocket guide of birds for occasional reference and also a note-book for making brief entries about birds that you cannot identify on the spot. Thus you can note size (comparing your bird to a robin or other familiar species) ; you can mention whether the tail is outstandingly long or short; you can list the bird's color and any conspicuous markings; you can describe its actions (walking, hopping, up-and-down or zigzag flight, posture on tree trunk) , and, of course, the kind of surroundings where you saw it. With this information handy, you can consult reference books with a good chance of identifying the unknown bird.

Some Bird Neighbors

ROBINS MEAN SPRING IS HERE

If you have a birdbath, robins are very likely to be among those patronizing it. They enjoy bathing and are friendly and trusting. The robin is so well known that it is commonly used as a basis for comparison with other birds that are described as "larger than," "smaller than," or "about the size of," a robin. Its length is about ten inches from the tip of its bill to the tip of its tail.

In most of the United States (aside from the Gulf Coast), and in Canada, robins are "summer residents"; their return to familiar nesting sites is a sign of spring. You are likely to see them then, hurrying about in search of building material. (Robins never walk; they run.) They pick up coarse grasses, rootlets, and other serviceable bits in their bills and fly to the home base. Here they add their plunder to former collections. After putting it down they hop on it and rapidly work it with their feet until it is wedged tightly in place. Even as they do this, they turn their bodies from side to side, squatting down against the nest. In this way they form a depression that is really "made to measure." Both male and female share in the construction work.

The female robin lays from three to five greenish blue eggs in the compact little home. Mother and father take turns sitting on the eggs to keep them warm day and night. When the young robins appear in about two weeks the parents continue their devoted care, feeding them insects and guarding them to the best of their ability from such enemies as cats, squirrels, and snakes. By late June the robin family may be really sizable, for there is likely to be a second brood in the nest. The young of the first brood now go each night with the adult male to some favorite roosting place. The mother, busy caring for her second lot of triplets or quadruplets, is not forgotten by her mate, who may return each day to help her with her duties.

If you glimpse a robin still dressed in "baby clothes" you will notice that, unlike adults with their solid black-and-orange coloring, it has a spotted breast. Here you have a clue to the robin's relationship to other birds. Many of us know that adult thrushes have spotted breasts and we can correctly assume that robins and thrushes belong to the same family. The bluebird is another famous close relative.

Sparrows Are Pleasant Neighbors

The sparrow family has been discredited to some extent in the United States and Canada by a species of weaver bird that was imported a hundred years ago from England and became generally known as the English, or house, sparrow. This "sparrow" spread over the continent and in many places it drove away the more attractive bluebirds and purple martins.

"Only a sparrow," may be your child's attitude toward this bird family—it is easy for youngsters to acquire the general prejudice against these birds. As he becomes acquainted with sparrows, however, he will find that some of them are surprisingly attractive and that some sing sweet, melodious songs. The white-crowned sparrow is probably the most handsome, with a striking black and white crown, a gray breast with no throat markings, and an erect posture. It is found all over North America but it is much more common in the West than in the East.

The song sparrow is noted more for its song than for its appearance. Its cheerful *Tea-tea-tea! Polly-put-the-kettle-on*, heard frequently in early spring, is most distinctive. The marking that distinguishes it from other sparrows is a large brown spot centered on a streaked breast. It has a long rounded tail which pumps up and down as it flies.

You are most likely to see little "chippy," the chipping sparrow, in suburban areas. It seems to prefer lawns or pasture lands to wilder country and it often nests in dooryards, hedges, and shrubbery. It is among the smallest of sparrows (about half as long as a robin), and its reddish crown, black bill, and white line over the eye and a black one through the eye are its distinguishing marks. Though this sparrow spends most of its time on the ground, it often perches on some lofty spot to deliver its song—a rapid succession of metallic-sounding *chips*.

JAYS

If you travel from coast to coast, there are few places where you will lose sight of the jay family. Of its various members the blue jays are most common, most widespread and probably the boldest. Their striking markings make them easy to recognize, and anywhere from the Atlantic Coast to the Rocky Mountains you may see them along highways and byways. In bright blue plumage marked with stripes and patches of black and with clear white, they fly with a regular series of wing flappings. Or else they strut and swagger on the ground, scolding loudly at any bird, man, or beast that seems likely to interfere with their activities. Usually they have a raucous cry, but they can also produce flute-like notes as well as a noise resembling the sound of nutcracking. Sometimes they imitate the cry of the red-shouldered hawk.

In the West, the Steller jay is slightly larger than the blue jay, and you can distinguish it by its black head, throat and breast and its long black crest. The "California" jay (also found in Florida) has a blue cap, back, wings, and tail.

CROWS

The chances are your child has been able to recognize a crow for a long time, if only from seeing pictures of this black bird in connection with scarecrows ever since he was of nursery school age. The crow is also one of the easiest birds to "spot" in fields and woods because of its large size and its intense black coloring, identical in male and female. You are likely to see crows near farms; unfortunately, their taste runs to such crops as corn and wheat as well as fruit.

Crows are also fond of the eggs and fledglings of thrushes and meadow larks, game birds, and even poultry. That is why the crow is in great disfavor with farmers and with the champions of songbirds. But "Peck's bad boy" of the bird world though it may be, the crow is a prime favorite with children. And we must admit that with all the damage crows cause, they do make up for it by eating beetles, caterpillars, and slugs—all of them menaces to gardens, orchards, and grainfields.

CARDINALS FOR COLOR

You can recognize a male cardinal as easily as the crow, for it is almost as intensely red (the color we associate with cardinals of the Church) as the crow is black. There are very few red birds in North America, and the cardinal is the only one with a crest. Even its heavy bill is red, though around the base there is a patch of black that extends back through its eyes and

THE COLORFUL CARDINAL

The male cardinal is an eye-filling red from bill to tail tip, with the exception of a touch of black at his big, efficient-looking beak. His "windswept" crest makes him even more conspicuous. In wintertime he presents a colorful contrast to snowy landscapes. But his musical call makes him a welcome visitor in any season.

down its throat. Though the female has the crest and red bill of the male, her plumage is light brown.

Cardinals are not commonly seen in New England or on the Pacific Coast, but in other sections of the United States you may come on them anywhere—in suburbs, towns, or open country. As a rule they are "permanent residents" of whatever area they live in, and in the northern part of their range they endure many a severe winter while creating scenes of striking beauty: crimson feathers against a snowy-white background.

GOLDFINCHES—OUR WILD CANARIES

You may call them "wild canaries" as you see a group of goldfinches chattering and twittering on a lawn. They suggest these pet birds because of their yellow coloring, their small size, and their pleasant song. Actually they are closely related to the canary and also to native sparrows.

In flight goldfinches are recognizable by their long bounding motion, which may remind a youngster of a roller-coaster ride. At each dip they seem to call *Per-chick-o-ree, per-chick-o-ree.* They travel around in small groups during breeding season. Goldfinches may be found in fields and meadows throughout temperate North America. Like the cardinals, they are usually permanent residents of one region—although some goldfinches travel a bit south to escape the most severe winter weather.

CHICKADEES

If you furnish a winter feeding station for birds, you are quite likely to have chickadees among your patrons. The easiest way to recognize this plump little black-and-white bird is by its black cap and bib. In the South there is the Carolina chickadee, only four and a half inches long; and in the West, a chestnut-backed chickadee with a dull brown, rather than black, cap.

Chickadees are commonly found around farms and country homes. In warm weather they seclude themselves in the woods, nesting in holes in trees; in winter they are out scouting and seem especially grateful for "handouts" from human friends.

Hummingbirds—Smallest of the Birds

Most children, loving tiny things as they do, are delighted with hummingbirds, the smallest birds in the world. Those found in the United States and Canada range from about three and a half to four and a half inches in length.

West of the Mississippi the hummingbird may be lured near homes by an abundance of flowers and any small stream of water. On the west coast it nests in porch vines and is frequently satisfied with birdbaths or lawn sprinklers for its water supply. The ruby-throated hummingbird, the only one that frequents the East, is not quite so sociable; but it may be attracted to a garden by brightly colored tubes of sugar water. You can make a hummingbird feeder with a medium-size vial. Wrap this with red ribbon or crepe paper and fasten it with a thin wire to a twig in the garden. Fill the vial with a mixture of one part sugar to two parts water.

Hummingbirds usually nest in fruit and shade trees, and their well-camouflaged home is so small that it could easily be covered by a fifty-cent piece. The female builds the deeply cupped nest by herself. While she is busy molding and shaping it with her feet and bill, her mate disappears from the scene.

Newly hatched hummers look more like black insects than birds, and watching a mother feed them is quite an experience. She gives them food in a series of stabbing motions as she jabs her long beak, filled with nectar and insects, down their throats. She not only feeds them well; she is ever ready to defend them and will even attack an enemy as large as a hawk if it comes near.

Hummingbirds have exceptional flying powers. Some move their wings so fast that it is quite impossible for the human eye to see them. Hummers are among the very few birds that can fly backwards (the phoebe and the oriental sunbird are the others), and they can "stand still" in the air. They get their name from the hum of their wings which can be heard during their rapid darting flight as well as when they hover.

Meadow Larks

When you walk through meadows or marshes you may be startled by a large brownish bird rising out of the grass in front

THE MEADOW LARK — AN AMERICAN SYMBOL

This large pudgy brownish bird has a lovely flutelike song and likes to nest in the long grasses of meadowbanks along streams. A useful bird, it preys on great quantities of pernicious insect pests. It is found in so many parts of our land that it might well replace the eagle as an American symbol.

of you. If you notice a striped head and white outer tail feathers as it flies away, the chances are you have flushed a meadow lark. This bird seems to have great faith in long grasses for protection (even nesting among them on the ground). You may walk up to within a few feet of a meadow lark before it will take wing. In the fall, meadow larks of the North gather in flocks and migrate to southern swamps.

BALTIMORE ORIOLES

The Baltimore oriole is a striking example of how our familiar roles may be reversed in the bird world: The male is noted for his beauty, the female for her skill in home construction. You can easily sight the brilliant orange and black plumage of the male even when he flits among tree branches. His olive-yellow mate looks confusingly like the female orchard oriole and somewhat like the female scarlet tanager; the only time it is easy to identify her is when she is with her handsome husband.

You may best appreciate the female's building prowess after the family has migrated southward and you see the nest hold up through wind, snow, and sleet. She works with such plant fibers as the inner bark of milkweed, as well as string and other available materials, weaving them skillfully together. The nest, a large one, is very unusual in being fastened to a branch at its rim, with the bottom hanging free. Vireos are the only other birds that build this type of nest, but theirs is less than two inches deep on the inside—much smaller than an oriole structure.

Cowbirds Follow Cattle

You can find cowbirds in pastures and woodlands. Often small flocks of them follow cattle. They find good hunting by catching insects that infest the big animals; the birds alight on the cows' backs to obtain their prey. The cowbird, smallest of our native blackbirds, is undistinguished in appearance. In a good light you can see that the male's head is a rich brown rather than black, while the female and young have gray-brown plumage.

Though ordinary enough in appearance, the cowbird has an extraordinary—and most dishonest—way of providing for its young. It does not build a nest! Instead, the female merely deposits an egg in the home of a warbler, song sparrow, or other bird, biding her time until the owner of the nest is away.

In due course the foster mother hatches the cowbird egg with her own eggs. The cowbird is invariably larger than its legitimate nest-mates. It can therefore poke its head over theirs to be first in line whenever the mother appears with food. The result is that the intruder grows faster and often pushes the little ones out of the nest to die of starvation. Occasionally a victimized bird discovers the fraud in time and destroys the impostor egg, or else abandons the nest to build a new one and lay a new clutch of eggs.

The yellow warbler has an ingenious way of dealing with the cowbird's maneuvering. If she discovers a strange egg, she simply builds another nest over the first one. If still another cowbird egg is "planted" in the second nest, she builds a third on top of that. Warblers have been known to build up to five nests in this way!

MOCKINGBIRDS DON'T ALWAYS MOCK

The name of this justly famous songbird is misleading in a way. Individual birds may "mock" the notes of other birds and even the bark of a dog or the meow of a cat; but occasionally the birds stick to their own notes. Aside from its imitations, the mockingbird has a lovely liquid song that deserves appreciative recognition in its own right. Mockingbirds not only have song fests by day; they are most eloquent on moonlit nights.

While the mockingbird is primarily a southerner, some birds venture to feeding stations as far north as New England. The mockingbird has an over-all grayish tone and in flight shows flashes of black and white in its wings. The mockingbird is about the size of a robin, though not so plump, and it has a long tail.

THE MOCKINGBIRD—EXPERT AT MIMICRY
Though moonlit nights inspire the mockingbird to a hauntingly beautiful song with exquisite variations, it has a great gift for sardonic mimicry of other birds. Its lifelike imitation of a hawk's shriek is as convincing as "the real thing."

WHIPPOORWILLS—THE INVISIBLE SINGERS

Like the mockingbird, the whippoorwill is noted above all else for its voice. While you may frequently hear its call, you will rarely see the bird itself. It usually lives in a river valley or in a meadow if water is nearby, stays close to the ground, and does not become active until the sun goes down. Then it starts to feed on insects during low short flights, between which it gives the oft repeated call *whip-poor-WILL, whip-poor-WILL.* The bird's brownish plumage makes it practically invisible when it is resting on dry leaves.

WOODPECKERS—GOOD CREEPERS AND CLIMBERS

The name of the "redheaded" woodpecker appeals so strongly to children that this bird almost seems to be the outstanding member of the tribe. However, this woodpecker is only one of many: There are at least 375 varieties. The woodpecker is found in all parts of the world except the Australian region and Madagascar. There are twenty-four species in North America. The downy woodpecker which is at home in our woods and parks is probably the most widespread and common. One of the smallest of the family, it is a plain black and white except for the red patch the male wears on the back of its head. It is also one of the friendliest, and an eager visitor at winter feeding stations if you provide suet for it.

Woodpeckers are well adapted for creeping and climbing, as they have two toes directed forward and two backward to assist them in clinging to an upright surface. The stiff-pointed tail feathers serve as a prop. Their other notable adaptation is the strong sharp bill with which they can chisel away wood to expose grubs. This bird's specialized tongue is also useful: it can be extended some distance and has a horny spearlike tip on which the food is impaled and then drawn into the woodpecker's bill.

OWLS—BIRDS OF THE NIGHT

Even before a child hears "The Owl and the Pussycat," his imagination may be captured by this dignified bird. Since owls are creatures of the night they are seldom seen; but their hoots, shrieks, and other distinctive calls often betray their presence in a neighborhood. Most owls are woodland birds, though some make their homes in steeples, towers, barns, and other outbuildings; some owls prefer marshes and plains.

Many people have mistaken ideas about owls. One of these notions is that owls cannot see in the daytime. It is true that their sight is keenest at night, when they do their hunting; but they can use their big staring orbs from sunrise to dark if they wish. These eyes are placed in their sockets in an odd manner, being fixed in such a way that the bird cannot look from one place to another by merely rolling its eyeballs. In order to see to the side, it must turn its head in that direction. As a result, its efforts to keep an object in view may make the owl seem to be "unscrewing" its head.

Owls vary greatly in size according to species. Whereas the screech owl is no more than ten inches long, the great horned owl may reach a maximum of twenty-three inches. Both of these have conspicuous ear tufts. The great horned owl seeks wild, heavily forested regions. The screech owl frequently lives near dwellings, in shade trees of village streets or suburban lots. On occasion it will accept the hospitality of a bird-box home. Its plumage is rather odd: its color—gray or reddish—offers no clue as to sex, age, or season. Some owls simply have reddish-brown feathers while others have grayish-brown ones.

Hawks—More Friends Than Foes

You can perhaps best recognize the large and varied hawk family by actions and sounds. Hawks are solitary birds except during the migration season. Ordinarily you may see one of them soaring in wide circles high overhead, scanning the ground below for a possible victim. When it spots a quarry it swoops down, strikes the prey with its feet and tears it to pieces with its bill. Its loud, startling cry seems very suitable to its fierce nature.

Because of the many similarities among different species, it is not always simple to tell them apart. Sometimes you can identify the red-tailed hawk by the feature which gives it its name, even when it is flying quite high above you. Its tail is frequently slanted in flight, and especially on a sunny day the red tones on the upper

THE RED-TAILED HAWK—BETTER THAN ITS REPUTATION

With their sharp eyes and ability to fly swiftly and tirelessly, the rapacious hawks are ideally adapted to be birds of prey. Though falsely accused of making off with poultry—it is sometimes called "the chicken hawk"—the red-tailed hawk specializes in mice and other creatures harmful to crops.

surface are surprisingly evident. The red-tailed hawk is of medium size, its body length ranging from nineteen to twenty-five inches. Its wing-spread may be fifty inches or more. The Cooper's hawk is slightly smaller. It looks very much like the sharp-shinned hawk, the adult males of both species having blue-gray plumage above and whitish below with reddish-brown cross stripes.

Many hawks perform a valuable service in farm areas by eating great numbers of mice and other destructive small mammals. In spite of this, there is a popular notion that all hawks are the farmer's enemies.

"But don't chicken hawks steal the farmer's hens?" your child may ask.

Strangely enough, it is not the chicken hawks that do the stealing. Or if they do, it is an exceptional case. The two kinds widely known as chicken or hen hawks are the red-tailed hawk and the red-shouldered hawk. Both of these eat mostly mice, gophers and other mammals, insects, and reptiles. Only rarely do they attack poultry.

The Cooper's hawk, however, is one that the farmer may definitely class as bad from his point of view. The sharp-shinned hawk also kills chickens as well as many wild birds. The chances are that the larger and more strikingly marked red-shouldered and red-tailed types attract the most attention, while the smaller and less noticeable Cooper's and sharp-shinned hawks actually carry out the sneak attacks on poultry yards. So, ironically enough, birds that are really allies of the farmer are classed as foes.

BALD EAGLES

"Is the bald eagle really bald?"

Inquisitive children ask this question so often that you ought to have a ready answer handy. Actually this bird has a fine crop of feathers on its head; but because they are white, in contrast to most of its plumage, they do not show up when seen from a distance.

Because of its strength and daring and its air of majestic dignity, the Americans chose the bald eagle as their national emblem when they first formed an independent nation. Some people find fault with this selection on the ground that eagles often get their food by snatching it from terrified smaller birds that have procured it from river, lake, or ocean. This banditry charge is true, but it is difficult to watch the enormous-winged creature soaring through the air without thinking of it as a noble bird.

The golden eagle of the West is somewhat larger than the bald one and has been known to grow as long as forty-three inches. It has sometimes been accused of carrying off children in its enormous claws. However, there is apparently no verified case of this happening, and experiment has shown that six pounds is about the greatest weight the golden eagle can carry.

DUCKS ARE NATURAL COMEDIANS

A duck's short legs are placed far apart, making it walk with an amusing waddle, and its voice is as comical as it is raucous. No wonder that this bird inspired the universally popular cartoon character, Donald Duck. Water, not land, is the duck's proper element, and in a pond it swims and dives expertly.

Standard Oil (N. J.)

k News

A BABY ROBIN'S APPETITE IS AS HUGE AS ITS MOUTH

Mother and father robin have to work overtime to keep their young fed. Still, their efforts get results. Completely helpless when hatched, the babies develop rapidly and are well feathered and able to leave the nest when only two weeks old.

ONE OF THE BEST OF BIRD MOTHERS

When the hen leads her brood through thick grass, she keeps up a steady *cluck-cluck* so they can tell where she is. She calls her chicks to her when she finds food, sounds a cry of warning if an enemy approaches, and courageously holds him off as long as she can. At rest, she lends her down-clad babies the warmth of her wings.

VULTURES—NATURE'S STREET CLEANERS

These are the birds that actually merit the name "bald," as the head and neck of both black and turkey vultures are bare of feathers. When you see one of these birds of prey, in the flesh or in pictures, you are more likely to be repelled than attracted; no one is apt to speak fondly of a vulture. Nevertheless it is extremely valuable as a scavenger, and in certain towns of the South, vultures form a dependable street-cleaning department.

GULLS—THEY ROOST ON WATER

You are most likely to see gulls along the seashore and in bays and harbors. But, as many of them nest on the islands of inland lakes, it is not impossible to glimpse them in a wide variety of places. The herring gull, abundant along the Atlantic Coast, is one of the largest types and has a gray back and wings that are tipped with black. The California gull closely resembles the herring gull. Some kinds, such as the laughing gull of the East and the Franklin gull of the West, have a black head.

Gulls are as buoyant as cork on the water and they often rest and roost there. They are a valuable aid to sanitation along water fronts, especially in harbors where garbage is dumped. They often gather in tremendous numbers at such places and seize the refuse as it is thrown off scows. It is exciting to watch them vie for offal discarded from a returning fishing craft when the catch is being cleaned. In addition they devour the bodies of dead creatures of the sea which have floated to the surface.

Making Wild Birds Feel at Home

Rescuing a helpless animal is one of childhood's greatest thrills. Most youngsters are thoroughly delighted at an opportunity to care for an injured older bird—or a baby bird that has become separated from its parents.

This is an endearing trait in children, but before you let them make the attempt, you ought to know how hard it is to feed wild birds—especially the young ones. Baby birds often starve to death because people have no conception of the enormous quantities of food the fledglings require. These figures tell the story: A house wren was seen feeding her three babies 111 spiders and insects within four hours! Chipping sparrows brought their three youngsters thirty-seven grasshoppers in an hour and a half. Most amazing of all, a baby robin, just ready to leave its nest, was able to eat the equivalent of fourteen feet of earthworms in a day!

Fortunately, you can supply substitutes for natural foods if a young bird suddenly becomes your responsibility. Sparrows, robins, bluebirds, waxwings, and many others, will flourish on a well-balanced diet of meal worms, hard-boiled egg yolk fully grated, bread with milk, and berries.

Remember, before rashly adopting a bird "orphan," that young ones sometimes become separated temporarily from their family and cry loudly trying to attract their parents' attention. If you find one of these lost youngsters on the ground, you do best to place the bird gently on the branch of a tree rather than take it home. If the hour is late, your wisest course may be to take the baby home and wait until early next morning to return it to the place where you found it.

THE RAVEN—FRIEND OR FOE?

These blackbirds, immortalized by Edgar Allan Poe in his famous poem, are twice as big as crows. They are very intelligent and can be trained to talk and to perform simple stunts. But out in the fields, ravens are a nuisance and their raids are very costly to farmers. Their notes are loud and coarse.

If you succeed in raising a young bird, you will want to give it its liberty as soon as it is able to shift for itself. In fact, there are many species which cannot be legally kept in captivity without a permit. Crows are one of the exceptions to this ruling, and they may become fascinating pets. If they are taken as young birds, they attach themselves firmly to a household and shun the efforts of other crows to draw them away. They enjoy the companionship of humans and can learn to talk like parrots. Unfortunately, some people mistakenly believe that splitting a crow's tongue helps it talk. This is a cruel thing to do, and futile as well; the crow does not use its tongue to produce sounds.

You will find tame crows at a number of zoos. The Philadelphia Zoo used to keep one near the main entrance, where it would greet arrivals with a cheery "Hello"; and there was another whose favorite exclamation was, "Wow! Cold out!" even in midsummer. A crow named Deacon was one of the first features of the Children's Zoo at the Bronx Zoological Gardens in New York City. Someone had found the bird, a forlorn little orphan, under a tree. The crow repaid the good care he received from zoo officials by playing the gracious host to countless boys and girls.

Like crows, some owls make fine pets. An elderly friend of mine delights in reminiscing about a great horned owl he had when he was a boy. He found it as a small ball of down under a huge nest in the woods near his home and immediately became the bird's foster father. He named it Jack and took full charge of its diet of raw fish, flesh, and fowl, keeping it healthy and happy until it was full-grown.

"Jack was an affectionate bird," he recalls. "Often he would sit beside me and I would ruffle his feathers just behind his head. He would bend forward, his eyes almost closed, and every few minutes there would be a succession of deep baritone hoots." Such gentle, trusting companionship can mean a great deal to a child.

CHAPTER 4 Birds of Farm and Zoo

Most children who live in rural areas are accustomed to chickens, ducks, and other domesticated birds as part of the daily scene. To city dwellers these creatures may seem even more remote than the wild birds, which at least make their home in parks of metropolitan areas. But whether farm birds are intriguingly distant or familiar to the point of being commonplace, they repay close observation.

We think of chickens as being very timid, in fact, "chicken-hearted." Yet they become exciting personalities when two roosters engage in a duel. The two antagonists face each other with lowered heads, then each strikes out with his wing spurs, tears his opponent with his leg spurs, and tries to seize him by the back of the neck with his beak. Roosters are unbelievably tenacious fighters, going after each other with brutal abandon. Though roosters fight it out for barnyard supremacy, they display equal spirit against rats, skunks, hawks, and other marauders.

Chickens have a varied and eloquent language all their own. The rooster's crow is unmistakably boastful, challenging. When a hen is setting, she sounds irritable; when her chicks have hatched, her voice takes on a triumphant note. When she is enjoying the sun in the company of other hens, she sounds pleasantly chatty; when frightened, she squalls. Listening to these notes and others as well, and interpreting them, is an interesting pastime for youngsters.

TURKEYS—THE PILGRIMS' PRIDE

The turkey gobble is possibly the most famous of all bird sounds. The tom "gobbles" aggressively as he struts and displays his beauty to a flock of hens. He lifts his beautiful tail feathers in a semicircular fan, sticks out his breast, and makes a handsome ruff by raising the iridescent plumage about his neck.

The Bronze Turkey: There is a bronze breed of turkey that has a very close resemblance to the North American wild turkey.

From its neck halfway to the middle of its back the plumage is bronze, glittering with green and purple tones. Each feather is tipped with a narrow black band. The breast plumage is the same. As for the lower back, it is black except for a bronze edging on each feather. The long quills on the wings are crossed with black-and-white bands, and each feather of the fan-shaped tail is banded with black and brown and at the end has a black bar tipped with white.

The hen's plumage is similar in color—except that her breast, neck, and wings are not so brilliant, being dimmed by a line of white at the tip of each feather. The warty, wrinkled skin over the head and neck of both sexes is colorful: bluish white on the crown, grayish blue about the eyes, and the rest red. In the male the colors are more vivid.

Turkey With Trimmings: Turkeys have several distinctive "trimmings." The wattle (as in chickens) is a hanging fold below the throat. Above the beak is the "caruncle," a fleshy, pointed knob which on the gobbler is long enough to fall over, and hang below, the beak. When the bird is angry, both these parts swell and turn a more brilliant red.

On all toms, and occasionally on a hen, you will see a "beard"—a bunch of black bristles hanging from the center of the breast. These hang limply when the birds are feeding, but when a gobbler struts, he thrusts the beard forward.

How the Turkey Got Its Name: Despite the Thanksgiving lore absorbed at school—or perhaps because of it—your youngster may raise this point: "Did the Pilgrims *have* to go out and shoot turkeys? Didn't they raise them on their farms?"

The answer is rather complex. When the early Spanish explorers came to Mexico they discovered a breed of turkeys with white-tipped tail feathers and took some of them back to Europe. About a century later, the Pilgrims brought domesticated descendants of these turkeys to eastern North America. There, as well as farther to the west, turkeys with brown-tipped feathers were to be found in a wild state. Thus the Pilgrims had the white-tipped turkeys in captivity, but they filled their larder by hunting brown-tipped ones as well.

Apparently this Western bird was given an Oriental name in the course of its travels from continent to continent. When it first appeared in Europe it was confused there with the guinea cock, an African bird that was imported by way of the Turkish dominions. While the two kinds of birds were later distinguished from each other, the name "turkey" was kept for the American bird.

The Sun Dance: Turkeys, wild or domesticated, have a curious custom—a "sun dance." While dawn is still faint in the sky, the birds gather and begin high-stepping flip-flop motions. As they jump up and down with wings lifted, the hens call *quit, quit,* and the males accompany them with a high-keyed rattle. No sooner does the sun show above the horizon than the dance ends as abruptly as it began.

DUCKS, TAME AND WILD

In your study of wild bird life you may find that water birds are on the whole less accessible than land birds. The duck is an excellent representative of the water dwellers that you can observe at close range by visiting a barnyard. When you see a duck on shore you may have a good look at its legs, which partly explain its prowess in the water. You will notice that the duck's short legs are set wide apart and far back on its body. The three front toes are joined by a tough skin or web. These admirably adapted legs and feet make perfect paddles in the water.

Domesticated ducks have modest needs in the way of shelter;

a low open shed to protect them from snow and driving rains is sufficient. Their thick feathers and down form an almost weather-proof coat which shields them from the foulest weather.

The Muscovy Duck: Ducks are raised more commonly for meat than for their eggs, though some breeds are good egg producers. There are ten outstanding varieties of ducks that are widely bred for meat, eggs, or both. One of the most interesting to observe is the "Muscovy" variety, which despite its name is native to Latin America. It cannot quack in the familiar manner of most ducks. Instead, it makes a hoarse, raucous hissing sound; and it has the further peculiarity of wagging its tail from side to side like a dog. The Muscovy duck is a better flier than other domestic ducks, and it is not unusual to see one perched on top of a barn. Muscovys are almost completely self-supporting. They make their own nests, hatch their young, and raise them with no more than a feed of corn once or twice a day.

Fresh-Water and Salt-Water Ducks: As the ancestors of our domestic breeds, wild ducks are among the better known of bird families. You may have some conflicting stories to straighten out about them. Your boy may say:

"Ducks are good divers."

His pal contradicts: "I've watched them! They never do anything more than stick their heads under water and raise their tails. I don't call *that* diving."

Actually both boys may be right; there are two groups or sub-families of ducks, each with different habits. One group lives in rivers and ponds, the other in bays and the open sea. The pond and river ducks do very little diving. They dabble along the shore and probe down into the mud where the water is shallow. The sea ducks, however, are expert divers. They may go under water 150 feet or more!

The canvasback is probably the most familiar of the sea ducks. One of the best known of the river and pond group is the mallard. Many varieties of domestic ducks are descended from this bird.

GEESE—AND HOW TO KNOW THEM

"What's the difference between a duck and a goose?" is a question that might readily occur to any boy or girl. There is much about either animal that suggests the other, and it is true that they both belong to the same bird family. Still, a duck is a duck and a goose is a goose! The goose is more of a "landlubber" than the duck and feeds more on land vegetation. Its beak is harder, and less flat in appearance, than a duck's. The legs of the goose are not placed so far back on its body, so that geese are able to walk and run more freely than ducks.

While male and female ducks are easily distinguished by the usual sex difference in coloration, geese are alike in color. (The gander, however, is larger than his mate. He shares the responsibility of incubating the eggs and helps to care for the goslings.) Finally, geese usually have longer necks than ducks. All these distinctions add up to a difference which your boy or girl will easily notice.

Domestic geese have largely lost their power of flight, but in other ways they suggest their wild relatives. They honk to each other in expressive goose language. Mother and father bird are devoted to each other and to their young. They proudly take their goslings to the pond for the first swimming lesson and gently push them in with their bills if they hesitate.

It is not uncommon for a wild goose that has been injured or become overtired to join a domestic flock along the path of its flight. But usually after a season "the call of the wild" is so strong that it will join any flock that happens along—unless the farmer has clipped its wings.

"Silly Goose!": Have you ever called your child a "silly goose"? This widely used expression is strangely inappropriate, for geese usually seem to know just what they want and how to go about getting it. Some people contend that geese are among the smartest of all animals.

A goose named Simon who lived on a farm I often visited well deserved this reputation. He appointed himself guardian of the small boy of the family, he would take no nonsense from the dog, and he "policed" the barnyard in such a way that we liked to imagine him in a cap and badge. Even the adults of the family hesitated to do anything out of the ordinary routine for fear of provoking Simon's displeasure.

Geese react resourcefully under danger. A goose is quick to dive under water if it is wounded. Then, with its body just below the surface and only its bill exposed, it heads for shore where it tries to hide among the brush and grass.

Both goose and gander will defy a suspected enemy by opening the mouth and hissing violently. Nor is this loud "talk" a bluff. A gander is able to seize many smaller adversaries in his strong hard bill and beat them to death with his wings.

The Canada Goose: There are several species of wild geese on the North American continent, but probably none are more widely known than the Canada goose. At one season or another this bird

THE CANADA GOOSE—ANYTHING BUT SILLY

Most observers are agreed that the goose is the most intelligent of all our domesticated birds. The Canada goose is perhaps the most famous of all the wild varieties. It is greatly admired for its fabulous long-distance migrations covering thousands of miles. A large bird—about three feet long—it is noted for its loud honks.

may be found from the Atlantic Ocean to the Pacific, and from the Gulf of Mexico to the Arctic.

In the northern part of its range, when the days grow shorter and a hint of frost warns that winter is approaching, the leaders of the flocks spur their followers to action. These leaders are usually old ganders that have trekked down the continent and back many times.

The birds soar skyward. High above the ground they form two lines which join to form a large V, with the lead-gander at the forward point. His strength enables him to make the initial break in the air mass. He starts off with spirited honks and is frequently answered by the birds behind him as if by way of assurance that "all's well!"

As a rule, migrating geese rest at night. As sundown approaches, the leader looks for a suitable lake and glides down to it in a long incline, followed by the flock. However, if no safe landing place is found, a flock of Canada geese may stay in the air for more than twenty-four hours. It has been calculated that they sometimes fly a thousand miles without a stop!

THE GRACEFUL SWANS

The swan belongs to the bird family that includes the duck and the goose. Swans also favor the V formation in which migrating flocks travel. Both the male and the female swan are noted for their lovely white plumage and their tranquil grace in the water.

In olden times the striking beauty of the swan was a favorite theme of many myths, legends, and fairly tales, and to this day every child is familiar with the classic story of the Ugly Duckling. Anyone who has ever seen a swan can understand its hold on the imagination of noted composers and masters of the ballet. The famous ballerina Pavlova, who scored her greatest successes in a composition called *The Swan,* was very fond of swans and kept them as pets for many years.

PIGEONS

Their Courtship Antics: While watching pigeons, you have probably wondered at their occasionally odd antics. Sometimes you may see one pecking at another bird's head and pushing it around for apparently no reason at all. But there is a reason, and a compelling one: The "pusher" is a cock bird and the "pushed" is a hen. The pecking and pushing are part of the cock's breeding display. The cock coos much louder than the hen, and while he is performing his courtship dances the hen usually feigns indifference and walks away from the male who is striving so hard to make an impression.

Where Pigeons Are Found: You may encounter pigeons on farms or in city parks. They have adapted themselves so successfully to city life that they are often a distinct nuisance in cluttering and soiling buildings. And sometimes their cooing outside the windows of a humdrum business office can take on a weird unearthly quality! But children love these birds, and "feeding the pigeons" has become almost a national sport.

There is nothing novel about this, for pigeons have been popular domestic birds for many centuries: There were pigeon fanciers in ancient Rome. All our present domestic varieties have been developed from the rock pigeon, a wild species found in many parts of Europe and Asia.

There are vast numbers of pigeons in America, but they also dwell in all parts of the temperate and tropical regions of the world, existing in the greatest quantity and variety in the Eastern Hemisphere, particularly in the Australian and Malayan regions.

The Homing Pigeon: This remarkable variety was developed during the Middle Ages, when there was a lack of dependable means of communication. A warrior or traveler would take several of these pigeons when setting out on a journey. After a few days' travel, he would attach a letter to one of the birds, which on being released would fly straight back to his family at home. Later he would send back more letters with the other birds. Today, champion homing pigeons can fly at the rate of almost a mile a minute, keeping up that amazing pace for several hours!

THE OSTRICH—OUTRUNS A HORSE, BUT CANNOT FLY

A giant with small wings and long legs, the ostrich can dash off at sixty miles an hour at the first sign of danger. Twenty-five miles an hour, though, is nearer to its normal rate of speed. At bay, the ostrich lashes out with its legs with a force that can break a man's leg.

At the Zoo

OSTRICHES—THE WORLD'S LARGEST BIRDS

Even when birds are extremely rare, children may become acquainted with them through pictures and stories or, better still, see them in the flesh in some of our larger zoos. You may find the great bird of Africa, the ostrich, in many zoos—though not all of them are able to accommodate very large or rare species.

The ostrich is the largest living bird: A full-grown male measures about eight feet from its toes to the crown of its head. Its wings are so small in relation to the size of its body that a child readily realizes that the ostrich is a flightless bird. But nature has compensated, as it so often does when an animal has some lack or defect, by developing other traits which help in survival. We see this compensation in the case of the small-winged ostrich; it has tremendously powerful legs on which it can travel as much as thirty miles an hour.

The Huge Ostrich Egg: In keeping with its size the ostrich lays eggs that are about eighteen times larger than a chicken's egg. A family group of ostriches is made up of a cock and several hens. The hens all lay their eggs in one large depression scooped out of the sand. One of the hens covers the eggs during the day, but the father takes over the task at night.

The Maligned Ostrich: When you go to see the ostrich, your child is almost certain to ask about the bird's reputation for stupidity. The ostrich gets this reputation because of the widespread notion that it believes itself hidden when it sticks its head in the sand. Though this story is well entrenched in people's minds, it is completely false. This fable is probably based on the fact that when an ostrich chick is alarmed, it flops to the ground and extends its long neck flat along the surface.

PEACOCKS—NATURE'S GORGEOUS SPECTACLE

Even when he is not "displaying," the peacock is a handsome bird. But if you are lucky enough to catch him in the act of courting, you can see one of the most beautiful sights of the bird world.

The male and female may be walking quietly side by side when suddenly there is a rattling of quills as the male shakes out the feathers of his train. With a few stiff-legged steps he puts himself ahead of his companion. Then, with a dramatic sweep of the long feathers which trail behind him, he wheels in front of her, lifts and spreads his gorgeous fan. This fan is not made of his true tail feathers, which are stiff and blackish and entirely concealed. The true tail feathers support the fan when the long brilliant feathers are held erect.

This unforgettable performance will bring home to your child just what we mean when we say that somebody "struts like a peacock." Incidentally, the other members of the pheasant family, to which the peacock belongs, are also given to the display habit. All the males are noted for their colorful plumage and dazzling displays. A curious final detail: the voice of the peacock is not in keeping with its appearance, being shrill and unpleasant.

PENGUINS—BIRDS THAT SWIM BUT CAN'T FLY

The penguin is a prime favorite with children because of its comical and ingratiating appearance. Penguins are paradoxical creatures: though they cannot fly, they are accomplished swimmers! Aside from diving into the water to catch fish for food, they love to swim for the fun of it.

Laying Eggs on Ice: The largest kind of penguin, the "emperor," has an average weight of seventy pounds. Unlike some other species, it is a true antarctic bird. The female lays her egg on ice; then, to prevent its freezing, she tucks it in a fold of skin between her legs and crouches low over it. The male has a similar fold of skin, and the parents take turns shielding the egg so that it never comes in contact with the ice long enough to freeze.

Where Penguins Live: Most of us have the impression that all penguins are native to the ice barriers along the coast of Antarctica. There are sixteen or more species of penguins, and it is true that most of them live in the frozen wastes of the far South. However, some penguins live near the tropical belts, with one species actually at the equator, on the Galápagos Islands.

STORKS AND MORE STORKS

You may see at the zoo a grotesque-looking bird which, according to a sign, is a stork; but it appears quite different from the storks that have been described in stories and fables you have read.

A close look at the sign may then reveal you are looking at a jabiru stork. This is one of twenty or more different kinds of stork. It stands between four and five feet in height, and is striking in appearance because its white plumage forms a strong contrast to its bare head and neck, which are black. Its homeland is South America. To Africa belongs another type of stork—the "shoebill," with its bill as prominent as its name suggests. Exquisitely soft "marabou" feathers are taken from the marabou stork of Africa and India. Oddly enough, it is among the ugliest of birds, with its head bare of feathers and a large bare pouch hanging from its throat. Also found in Africa and Asia, as well as in Europe, are black storks, handsome birds with red legs and beak.

The "good luck" bird, the stork associated with children (Dutch children for many generations have chanted a verse to this stork asking for a little brother) is white. In Denmark, Germany, Holland, and Turkey, where white storks breed, people eagerly attempt to persuade them to settle on their housetops. It is an old custom for the Dutch to erect large wooden boxes or platforms above their chimneys as a nesting site. Once a nest has been used by a pair of storks, they return to it year after year. They repair it by adding sticks and reeds, and after a number of seasons, the nest may be several feet high. During breeding season they make a loud clapping noise with their beaks, but aside from this they are silent. They display great affection for their babies; and the Hebrew name, *chasidah,* given this stork, signifies "kindness" or "mercy."

CANARIES—FAVORITE PETS

The companionship of one of these cheerful songsters has been a boon to many otherwise lonely people. For several hundred years canaries have been the most popular of all bird pets. Today we have about fifty different domestic kinds, each with distinctive coloring and markings. Aside from the familiar yellow canaries, you may see others with blue-gray, white, cinnamon-brown, and a number of other tones.

Keeping a caged pet makes it very convenient for you to observe at close range many phases which are common to both domesticated and wild birds. A canary begins to molt about the middle of July and continues to exchange old feathers for new until the end of summer. If the bird starts losing its feathers after this normal molt, the chances are that it is being subjected to cold drafts or to extreme variations of heat and cold.

Where Canaries Come From: Originally canaries came from the Canary Islands off the west coast of Africa. (The islands in turn get their name from the Latin word *canis*—"dog"—because of an unusual breed of large dogs.) But the islands stopped exporting the birds many years ago, and canaries are bred extensively in America and Europe. The wild canary's upper plumage is olive green; its breast is golden yellow.

Singing and Sex Differences: The canary's popularity is based on song rather than looks. There are many variations in voice quality and type of song, with the "roller" canary rated as the outstanding songster of the canary family. A first-rate roller sings from ten to fourteen different notes in connected or "rolling" phrases, performing with his beak closed. The general style of singing is inherited, but the breeder trains the young males to establish their song properly by exposing them to the influence of a tutor bird for about three months.

Male canaries are the leading singers; but this is not necessarily a guide to the sex of an individual bird, as some females also sing. An experienced breeder verifies a bird's sex by holding the canary in his hand and gently feeling its abdomen. The casual observer can be guided by these points: The male is usually slightly larger than the female; its head is somewhat larger; the eye is not only larger, but bolder as well; and the male's call is louder and more musical.

PARROTS—MASTERS OF MIMICRY

The parrot has a very special appeal for us because of its talking ability, which bridges the gap in a way between "dumb" animals and humans.

Children are often disappointed when they realize that instead of conversing with them, the parrot is merely imitating sounds, copying words or laughter as it might mimic a bird melody if it were a song bird. But this disappointment may be softened by the discovery that the parrot is exceptionally intelligent for an animal. (Do you remember Long John Silver's parrot Captain Flint in *Treasure Island* with his repeated cry of "Pieces of eight! Pieces of eight!"?) A favorite method of teaching a parrot is to hide from its view and repeat several words frequently, slowly, and always in the same tone.

Members of the Parrot Family: Parakeets, which are related to the parrots, vary in size—but most of them are small, some no larger than a sparrow. Though parakeets can also learn to talk, it is not so easy to understand them, for they speak very rapidly and in high-pitched voices. Distinguishing between the parrots and the parakeets is something of a problem, as there is no sharp dividing line between the two groups. All of them are birds of the forest; they are poor walkers but good fliers and climbers; all eat fruit and seeds.

Other relatives are the macaws (largest and most brightly colored of the family), cockatoos, cockateels, lories, lorikeets, conures, and the interestingly named lovebirds, noted for their affectionate nature. The Amazon parrot is a popular cage bird, especially the species with blue markings on its face. It is a very efficient talker, though the African gray parrot is considered the champion in this respect.

How Birds Began

Sometimes children are even more fascinated by the remote and somewhat mysterious past than by the wonders they see around them. So, do not be surprised if your air-minded son or daughter turns to you with such questions as, "When did birds start to fly?" and, "Why?"

THE FLYING REPTILES

Fortunately, and in a way that seems almost miraculous, scientists have looked back over the ages and reconstructed an understandable picture of life as it went on long before history was recorded. Let's pretend to look through their magic spyglass at the world that existed about 150 million years ago. What do we see?

Dinosaurs of many shapes and sizes are wandering over the land, crocodiles are swarming in the rivers, and lizards are running over dry, sandy stretches. In addition to these weird creatures on the surface of the earth, we see others soaring overhead; but they do not seem to be flying so much as *gliding*.

It does not take us long to realize that these air-borne animals have a big advantage over the earth-bound monsters, for they can swoop earthward, seize a victim, and then soar up to a perch and devour their prey at leisure without danger of attack from enemies. As we look closer, we see that these strange gliders are not birds: They have no feathers. Aside from their flying powers, they are not unlike the reptiles on the ground.

We look again. This time we see another flying creature. This one has feathers! It is a bird.

The Earliest Known Bird

Most boys and girls take delight in impressive-sounding, mouth-rolling words, and your child will enjoy learning the name that has been given to this earliest known bird: Archaeopteryx (*arck-ee-op'-ter-ix*) . This word combines two Greek terms meaning "ancient wing."

Archaeopteryx had teeth in its upper and lower jaws and was equipped with a long tail. It was its feathers that took it out of the realm of reptiles. In time the teeth were to disappear and the mouth formation was to change until it became a hard beak more adapted to pecking than biting.

Very gradually, over a long period of time, the flying reptiles disappeared while birds grew more numerous and varied. After Archaeopteryx there is a lapse of millions of years in the known history of birds. By the time their story is resumed by fossils of a much later age, they had become specialized and diverse: They were more akin to modern birds than to Archaeopteryx. Scientists believe that some of the birds that enliven our earth today have existed in their present form for over a million years.

CHAPTER 5 Animals
in the Wild

A DVENTUROUS YOUNGSTERS are thrilled at the thought of stalking wild animals. It may suggest to them mighty gorillas hidden in trackless jungles or lions prowling over African plains—or perhaps a man-eating tiger that is terrorizing a village in India. They may think of our own North American deer and bears, or even the smaller foxes and wildcats.

Though the animals that occur to them may be of many different kinds, one thing is certain: Each will be four-legged and have fur or hair. For most children—and many parents as well!—only this type of beast is an "animal."

True, these beasts *are* animals, but they are only one type: the mammals.

Aside from mammals, we find in the animal world many creatures without four legs and fur. Among them are birds, fish, snakes, frogs, spiders, and worms. In fact, all living things that have feeling and the power of voluntary motion may properly be termed animals.

"What is the difference, then," the inquiring young mind wonders, "between mammals and other kinds of animals?"

To be considered a mammal, an animal must have three quali- ties. It must be warm-blooded, which means that its blood remains at nearly the same temperature no matter how hot or cold its surroundings may be. It must have hair or fur on its body. And a baby mammal is always nourished by milk furnished by its mother.

Opportunities to observe wild mammal life at first hand are much less common than those for bird study. At an early age children become familiar, to be sure, with a variety of beasts in their story books—the bears in "Goldilocks," the wolf in "Red Riding Hood," the fox in "Chicken Little"—but this acquaintance is based on fantasy rather than facts. When the youngster begins to grow away from his make-believe world and shows an interest in animals as they really are, he has considerable misinformation to discard as well as facts to learn.

Many Kinds of Mammals

A useful way to simplify the story of the mammals for an older child is to group these animals into their main divisions.

One group consists of flesh-eating ("carnivorous") mammals, such as wolves, foxes, lions, and tigers. A second group is made up of rodents—mice, squirrels, beavers and others with long, sharp front teeth. The third group, the hoofed animals, includes deer and cattle.

Strange water mammals known as manatees and dugongs are in a class by themselves—so are the flying mammals we call bats. Whales are probably the best known of the group known as "cetaceans."

All toothless mammals such as the anteater are included in one group. Finally there are the marsupials, made up chiefly of mammals with pouches in which to carry their babies. The opossum is the one American representative of this group, but the kangaroo of Australia is perhaps the most widely known of the pouched animals.

Flesh Eaters and Plant Eaters

On the basis of their food habits mammals may be divided into two general classes. There are plant eaters (herbivores) and flesh eaters (carnivores). In trying to distinguish one type from the other, a child would pretty much take for granted that the flesh eaters are larger and stronger. But that is not always the case.

Teeth and claws are a better basis for distinguishing between the two groups. You can point out that the flesh eater has sharp enlarged canine teeth, shearing side teeth, and strong, sharp claws.

"Good" and "Bad" Animals

Perhaps you have noticed a tendency on the part of a young child to label certain animals "bad" and others "good." If you query the child you are likely to find that the "bad" animals are those which eat other animals. This habit may well be frightening to a child, who does not see the connection between his own appetite for steak and the needs of a carnivorous animal devouring prey in order to sustain life. It is a good idea to point out, at some appropriate moment, that the food habits of both flesh eaters and plant eaters are inborn and not a matter of choice, and that moreover the flesh eaters seldom kill except when they are hungry or defending themselves from attack.

Watch a dog gnaw a bone and you have an excellent illustration

THE TIGER—FEROCIOUS JUNGLE PROWLER

In the zoo the tiger looks like an overgrown pussycat; in jungle regions it is a fierce beast of prey. When attacking, it may spring fifteen feet or more. Its stripes are a useful aid in stalking; the light-and-dark pattern blends with the alternation of sunlight and shadow in the jungle, concealing it from its victims.

of a carnivorous mammal in action. Not only are his incisors sharp and the canine teeth long and strong; the molars are especially designed for cutting.

All members of the cat family are meat eaters. Jaguars and pumas, the largest cat animals on the American continent, are a menace to game and livestock in some areas. You can study their hunting tactics at close range when you watch a house cat stalking a bird. The cat does not run down its prey as a dog would; instead it creeps along stealthily until it is within striking distance, when it takes a final vicious leap. The hunting technique of the big wild cats is exactly the same.

The weasel offers solid proof that you cannot judge an animal's eating habits or its disposition by its size. Though small and slender, the weasel is one of the most aggressive and ferocious of flesh-eating animals. Completely fearless, it sometimes kills animals several times larger than itself and may satisfy its appetite merely by lapping up their blood.

Hunting for Animal Tracks

When your child becomes interested in the activities of wild mammals, you can join him in a fascinating hobby: hunting for footprints and identifying them. In bygone days the Indians were expert trackers—but for them it was not a hobby. The game they secured by their expert knowledge of tracking often meant the difference between starving and having enough food.

Today a knowledge of animal tracks is no longer necessary for survival, but it can help satisfy the child's desire to play nature detective. What child is not thrilled at reviving this once-important Indian activity—especially if he realizes the early significance of tracking!

How to Identify Tracks

You may start track-hunting by going to likely places such as muddy stream banks and finding tracks there, identifying them later—or you may first obtain a background for field study from books and observations near home. In your own back yard you may find the tracks of dogs, cats, and squirrels.

TRACKS NEAR HOME AND IN THE WILDS

The footprints of cats and dogs are excellent "first studies" in tracking. At the left are the tracks of a domestic cat; next to them are the tracks of a lynx—similar in form but more than twice as large. The tracks at the far right of the drawing are those of a dog; next to them are the footprints of a wolf. It is almost impossible to distinguish one from the other, except for size. A wolf has a larger foot than a dog of normal size (the wolf is five feet long, weighs one hundred pounds).

A dog's tracks practically duplicate those of a wolf or coyote except that the wolf tracks are usually larger. The tracks of a cat are similar to those of the wildcat and mountain lion except for size. In these tracks only the pads and claws make an imprint.

FLAT-FOOTED ANIMALS MAKE THESE TRACKS
Tracks made by an animal that walks on its toes are quite different from these, all of which show the soles of the feet. At the left is the track of a black bear. In the center are footprints made by a running raccoon. At the right are tracks of a running skunk. Skunk tracks are rare in winter—the animal hibernates then.

Bears, skunks, and raccoons make plantigrade tracks, which means that they are practically flat-footed, and the greater part of the foot shows in the tracks. Deer, sheep, moose, and elk make hoofed tracks.

Another clue for identification is that tree-climbing animals normally place their front feet side by side when they jump, whereas animals that stay on the ground rarely show the front feet paired in this way. However, the hind feet of both tree-climbing and ground-living animals are generally paired.

Raccoon tracks are particularly intriguing, for this animal's hind foot is long with a well-marked heel and five comparatively short toes that make an impression remarkably like that of a small human foot.

COLLECTING TRACKS

Children are eager collectors. If they wish to carry their interest in tracking still further, it is sometimes possible to bring tracks home—in plaster. Making plaster casts of tracks is not a difficult process. Pamphlets or books in your library should provide detailed instructions for preparing such casts.

There are other ways to collect tracks—photographing them or sketching them. Neither you nor your child need be an artist to try this; a very simple sketch will picture a footprint quite graphically.

HOOFS ARE PLAINLY INDICATED IN THESE TRACKS

At the left are footprints of the whitetailed deer, such as you might discover in summer along the edge of small ponds or lakes. At the right are moose tracks. Those made by a full-grown moose are longer, larger and more pointed than those of all other hoofed animals. Tracks of the moose are not uncommon in Maine.

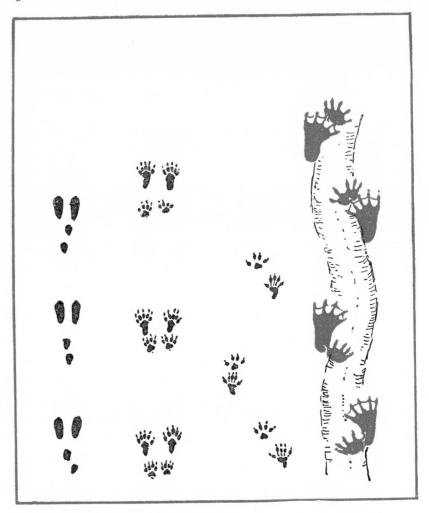

FOOTPRINTS IN FIELDS AND NEAR STREAMS

Tracks are best seen after a light fall of snow, or on dry, flat ground if the animal's feet were wet. At the far left of the drawing are footprints of a cottontail rabbit. Next to them you see the imprint made by a bounding gray squirrel. Next is the track of a field mouse, and at the far right is the trail left by a beaver. It is distinguished by the webbed hind feet and the mark made by the broad dragging tail.

TRACKS TELL A STORY

Tracks can reveal exciting incidents, such as a fox overtaking a rabbit, or a weasel pouncing on a squirrel—or they may depict peaceful animals wandering in search of shelter and food. After a fresh snowfall tracks are particularly clear and easy to follow.

Sooner or later tracks lead you to the haunts where mammal parents bring up their young. Altogether, tracking helps furnish an answer to your child's question: "What do mammals do?" It becomes apparent that securing food and raising families are their major concern.

How Mammals Talk

Most children get their first inklings of animal communication when they become familiar with the sounds made by dogs or cats. The dog barks and squeals with pleasure; he growls when he is angry, whines when he is afraid, and howls for the sheer pleasure of hearing his own voice.

THE FEEBLE CALL OF THE MIGHTY BULL MOOSE
Standing about six feet high at the shoulder, the bull moose makes a majestic appearance with its formidable antlers. (Some of nature's most tearsome duels have been fought with these antlers.) Yet the bull moose cannot produce anything more impressive in the way of sound than a subdued, coughing grunt.

The cat mews in friendly conversational tones; it purrs with contentment and yowls when it is hurt, it howls and screams in a fight. Its love serenade is shrill and agonizing—to the human ear.

The mammals of our forests and plains come near to duplicating some of these sounds, and they have other kinds of vocal expression as well. Some mammals roar, some whistle, some scream, some yap, some bleat, others are virtually silent.

One of the more unusual sounds is sufficiently well known so that even children hear about it. This is the call of the moose. Many hunters practice it diligently in the hope of luring one of these massive creatures within gun range. The hunters learn to imitate the female, whose call is like the bawl of a domestic cow. The bull moose, for all his size and strength, usually emits nothing more than a feeble, coughing grunt.

CRY DANGER!

To a child it is especially touching to note that frequently the calls and cries of wild animals serve to alert their family to the approach of danger. When the marmot, standing like a sentinel at a lookout post, gives his shrill warning whistle, not only the marmots but mountain sheep and other creatures as well take cover. A bear, a wolf—or a man!—may be approaching.

Shrill, also, is the whistle of the marmot's cousin, the woodchuck. With more abandon than good sense, it whistles and grinds its teeth while trying to escape from an enemy. Gray squirrels give the alarm with a kind of flat rasping bark finally prolonged into a whining snarl.

Even the customarily silent mammals find their voices when they are wounded. The scream of a white-tailed deer struck by a bullet can be heard half a mile away, and a rabbit often gives a piercing squeal when hit. But mammals do not always depend on their voices to express emotion. The cottontail rabbit thumps the ground with a hind foot when he senses danger. The beaver slaps the water with its tail. As for deer and sheep, they stamp with a fore foot when they are frightened.

A museum staff guide has often proved to me that animal sounds have a powerful appeal for children. As he takes visitors through mammal exhibition halls, he demonstrates the cries of the appropriate creatures in a thoroughly uninhibited manner. These calls are enjoyed not only by the group of visitors assigned to him, but by fascinated children who seem to appear from nowhere, all eager to hear *what animals sound like.*

How Mammals Fight

Warfare in the animal world is not limited to sporadic outbreaks when some creature or other decides to attack its neighbors. Instead, the warfare is constant and unceasing. The need for food drives the meat eaters to prey on other animals, and there seem to be a few that kill for the sake of killing. Among some groups, the males fight it out to win a mate or establish themselves as leader of a herd. Among the most dramatic of mammal battles are those between animals that wear antlers or horns—such as moose, deer, elk, and goats.

A Duel Between Moose

The instinct of boys for pounding and pummeling each other seems mild indeed compared to a clash between two bull moose. Hostilities may start with a moose striking its antlers against small trees in a way that broadcasts his defiance to all within hearing. Another male rushes out to accept the challenge—and the battle is on! Heads lowered, the two giants rush at each other. The impact of the collision may knock one down; if he regains his footing, they charge again.

Each moose tries to stab his enemy with the sharp brow tines that are the vicious part of the antler. The wide flattened areas are useful for defense in warding off blows. Frequently it is a fight to the death for one of the contenders. Sometimes the ending is tragic for both: Their antlers may become so firmly locked together that they are powerless to move, and death by starvation is their fate.

Special Battle Techniques

Mountain lions, jaguars, and other members of the cat family have four long pointed teeth (canines) as weapons, as well as sharp claws that can be withdrawn into the fleshy foot pads when they are not needed. When your child sees a fight between two tomcats he can feel that he has witnessed real jungle warfare; they use their teeth and claws in the same way as the big cats.

Squirrels, woodchucks, rats, and other rodents have dependable weapons in their chisel-like front teeth, though rabbits rely chiefly on their strong hind legs with which they can kick savagely. When rabbits fight, each one tries to leap on top of his opponent and kick downward. A deer avoids trouble whenever possible, but if it is cornered it defends itself by striking at the enemy with its front hoofs. The bucks also fight with their antlers.

Horses, burros, and some other hoofed mammals are able to kick with both front and back feet. The grizzly bear has strong, sharp teeth, and its huge front paws can be deadly to an enemy.

Not-So-Secret Weapons

Some mammals have specialized defensive weapons. The skunk can discharge a notoriously evil-smelling scent that overpowers the enemy with nature's poison gas. Foxes, wolverines, weasels, and some other animals have scent glands more or less like the skunk's and use odor as a defense weapon. But none of these scents is so potent as that of the black and white "wood pussy."

Porcupines, like the skunk, are not aggressive; they are slow-moving and stupid. Their quills, however, are splendid equipment for defense. Trapped by an enemy, Porky contracts his skin muscles, causing the quills to stand erect. Then he bunches himself up, raises his tail, flails anything within reach, and drives many of his barbs into the flesh of his opponents. Contrary to popular belief, the porcupine never shoots or throws his quills.

Keeping a Mammal Chart

Man has constantly expanded his knowledge of the world around him by keeping records. You and your child will find your interest in nature stimulated if you keep records of your observations. A chart of personal findings on mammals has many

THE PORCUPINE'S REARGUARD ATTACK
Sluggish in its movements and reactions, the porcupine is nevertheless no easy
prey for other animals. It uses its quills only as a last resort and does not shoot
them, but attacks by a backward rush, driving them deep into its foe's
flesh. Estimated number of quills for an individual: 25,000!

attractive features. It is quite different from a bird calendar, as
the four-footed creatures are neither so numerous, so varied, nor
so easily seen as the birds.

You may arrange your chart by calendar months or by species
of mammals seen, but in either case you will want to record the
time and place of your observations. You can start it when you
take country walks with your son or daughter and continue it
through the years until the child is old enough to jot down later
discoveries.

Motoring in Search of Mammals

In many regions you can carry on your search for mammals
quite successfully by car. In fact, where small children are involved,
this method is far more practical than hiking. In some of the
national parks, or in places where roads run through field and
forest, you may observe a variety of mammals—especially if you
drive slowly and travel either in the morning or late afternoon.

One of the greatest thrills my family had during a tour of the United States came in Zion National Park in Utah when a bobcat bounded across the highway. The animal was so close to our car that only a quick use of brakes prevented our hitting it. Shortly afterward we learned from a ranger-naturalist that though bobcats were fairly numerous in the park, one of these animals is not likely to be seen by visitors more than once in twenty years.

Vivid Details

You need not limit your record to animals actually seen; you can also include evidences of them. Have you seen footprints of deer? Have they led to trees scraped by antlers? Have you found a woodchuck's hole, the burrowings of a mole, or the dug-up turf and smooth incline at the water's edge which proclaims an otter's playground? An account of your experiences may include pictures, tracks, or tufts of hair—an endless variety depending on your inclinations and opportunities. Whatever form your findings take, they become a continuously enriched account of your awareness of the world of nature.

How Mammals Survive the Winter

The rigors of cold weather and the scarcity of food create hardships for mammals in wintertime. However, this is unlikely to impress us as much as the plight of the birds, as mammals are so little in evidence all year round.

One of the few mammals that we are likely to see during all four seasons is the gray squirrel. On cold winter days children can appreciate the practical value as well as the beauty of this creature's fur coat. He may often be seen scampering over the snow; only on the most frigid days does he curl up in his tree-trunk nest and cover himself with his bushy tail. He has some food tucked away and hunts industriously for more whenever weather permits.

Even hardier than the squirrel is the cottontail rabbit, which has no cozy retreat. A pile of brush is usually the only protection he seeks. When his favorite grass is no longer available, he nibbles

HAMSTERS BELIEVE IN SAVING FOR A RAINY DAY

Lilo Hess (Three Lions)

A pet hamster hoards just like a wild one. In its native Europe and Asia, the hamster lives in a burrow, complete with a number of capacious storerooms crammed with grain. These caches are so large that people have been known to rob them.

A SHARED DELIGHT

Bunny's pleasure in receiving a juicy carrot is equaled by the child's joy in feeding it. Children eager to keep their pets happy and healthy must treat them with consideration. Though a rabbit's long ears may have the appearance of convenient handles, they should not be used as such. The rabbit should be picked up by the nape of its neck and its haunches at one time.

Eastman Kodak

A VERY TAME WILD ANIMAL

Because gray squirrels make themselves at home in city or suburb, they offer many children a wonderful opportunity to observe the ways of a wild mammal. Except for their habit of begging, park squirrels behave like their relatives in forests, building nests in treetops or in hollow trunks. The squirrel's amazing leaps among the branches are possible only because of its bushy tail, which aids it in balancing and landing.

Eastman Kodak

CAMOUFLAGE IN A DAISY FIELD

The spotted back of a fawn blends perfectly with these surroundings. Camouflage is the young deer's best protection; and a mother deer teaches her youngsters to stay quietly in one place so they'll be safe while she ventures in search of food.

THE DEER—TIMID CREATURE OF THE WILD
These shy, graceful, and swift-footed animals were hunted by the Indians long before the white man's arrival on the shores of America. Despite centuries of intensive hunting, deer are probably more numerous in this country than ever before, thanks to the protection of our modern game laws.

the tender bark of small trees and shrubs, dead leaves, weeds, and flower stalks.

White-tailed deer also endure rugged times. Their winter home is a reasonably sheltered area in a woods. A group of a dozen or more band together and choose a suitable spot—called a "yard"— for their headquarters. From this home they make paths to places where they can find food: tender bark and shrubs, lichens, acorns, and moss, for which they dig under the snow.

Wild Mammal Neighbors

SQUIRRELS—NATURE'S ACROBATS

Of all the wild four-footed animals, the gray squirrel is probably the one most commonly observed by children. He dwells in wooded regions, and also in city parks and suburban areas as

well. In fact, these attractive rodents seem to prefer the hazards
of civilization to the dangers of the wilds, and their habits vary
little whether they live in town or country.

Young Squirrels: Watch for young squirrels about the middle of
May. A mother bears four to six infants during March, and she
may have a second litter during the summer. She gives her young
devoted care. They are born blind and hairless. When they are
about six weeks old they begin to climb around the tree branches
and nibble at buds and leaves. At eight or nine weeks they have
a full coat of fur and are about half grown.

In a year they have almost reached full growth and are able to
leap among the branches with astounding agility. The bushy tail
is a great help in balancing and making easy landings possible.
There is endless entertainment in watching the acrobatics of a
gray squirrel. I recall observing one of them leap from a branch of
a tree to a long attached wire, and then slide down the wire like
a fireman using his pole for speedy descent. The lure was a
well-stocked bird-feeding station at the end of the wire!

During cold weather squirrels generally live in a hollow tree,
but later in the year they find a suitable location, usually thirty
feet from the ground in the crotch of a tree, and there they
construct a nest of dead leaves and sticks. The shape of the nest is
a clue to the tenant's identity. A bird's nest is flattened at the top;
the squirrel's is rounded. Red squirrels also build nests—sprawling
but comfortable ones of bark, twigs, leaves or moss.

Squirrels and Food: As you watch a squirrel bury a nut in the
ground, you may well ask yourself: Will he ever find it again? It
would be a mistake to think that all the nuts that are buried get
dug up afterward. This is especially true in the wilds where food
is plentiful; and for this reason the squirrel makes a valuable
contribution to replanting the forests.

However, in regions where winter food is scarce the clever
little rodent recovers more of the stored nuts. It is believed that
the squirrel is guided to the right locality by memory, and to the
exact spot by a keen sense of smell which can penetrate through
several inches of snow

Aside from nuts, squirrels enjoy the seeds from apples, pears, and other fruit, mushrooms, corn, and wheat. Sometimes they raid birds' nests for eggs or fledglings, though they are guilty of such raids less often than red squirrels. An overabundance of peanuts is unhealthy for squirrels, but a few added to tree nuts or other foods are a nourishing addition to their diet.

RABBITS—NATURE'S INDESTRUCTIBLES

If you are familiar with the story of Peter Rabbit's adventures in Mr. McGregor's garden you have an excellent basis for understanding this rodent's fate in life. He is the Pursued; his daily routine is one escape after another. In addition to being a victim of almost every flesh-eating mammal and bird, he is also a favorite target for sportsmen.

How Rabbits Survive: Yet although they are the prey of countless enemies, rabbits are fast breeders and continue to exist in great numbers. As we observe them we see two further features which help account for their survival: the long ears that detect the enemy's approach from a distance, and the long, muscular hind legs which propel a rabbit away from danger with remarkable speed.

A further aid to the rabbit's flair for self-preservation is its extremely keen sense of smell: Its nostrils twitch constantly to catch every scent in the air. The rabbit's whiskers serve as trusted feelers, its eyes are large and bright. It has strong front cutting teeth, and with its split upper lip makes most efficient use of them.

In summer, the rabbit's fondness for cabbage and lettuce makes it the plague of gardeners. It also feeds on grass, clover, and other herbs. During the winter, when green leaves are scarce, it gnaws bark from trees and nibbles buds from shrubs.

There are many varieties of rabbits. Aside from those living in the wild state, there are others raised by thousands of people either for a hobby or for extra income. I once knew a rabbit that began its career as an Easter pet. Later on its young owner kept it at his family's store, where the rabbit was trained to snip with its front teeth the cord used to tie packages. This novel performance stimulated business considerably!

TWENTY FEET AT A BOUND
Jack rabbits are among the swiftest animals in creation. They may hit forty-five miles an hour in escaping from attack, and single bounds of twenty feet are not uncommon! The jack rabbit's long ears, reminding us of those of a jackass, inspired its popular name. They are capable of extraordinarily keen hearing.

Rabbits and Hares: It is sometimes confusing, especially to a child, to hear a rabbit called a hare. Ostensibly "hare" is just another word for "rabbit." Yet actually this is not the case. Rabbits resemble hares in appearance, though they differ in some of their habits. Hares are larger in size.

Rabbits are born blind and hairless and completely dependent on their mother's care. She pulls fur from her own body with her teeth and paws to line the nest. When she goes foraging for food she covers the young with fur and grass. This serves as a blanket and also as camouflage. Our tame rabbits are all descendants of wild rabbits of Europe.

The babies of the hare are born with their eyes open and are able to take care of themselves in three weeks or less. The jack rabbit is a hare, despite its common name, which is derived from its long jackass-like ears. Its shoulder height is as much as twelve inches and it can make leaps of from twelve to twenty feet with its long powerful hind legs.

MICE AND RATS—PETS AND PESTS

Among parents and children there are two schools of thought about mice. As far as the adult is concerned, these rodents are pests to be exterminated whenever possible. As the child sees it, mice are engaging, clever pets that can be kept without entailing a great amount of work for their owner.

The House Mouse: The house mouse, originally a native of Asia, is responsible for much of the dislike visited on the whole tribe. Through its ability to stow away wherever food is kept, this creature infiltrated into Europe and later on came to this country. Although this mouse usually makes its home in houses or barns, it sometimes nests under cornstalks or in grain fields.

Indoors it uses the space between plaster and outer walls for runways, or else it travels between ceiling and floor. With its strong gnawing teeth it can easily cut through wood, cardboard, or almost any obstacle but metal. The mother mouse makes her nest out of cloth, paper, or whatever pliable material she can find.

The Harvest Mouse: Wandering across country fields you may catch sight of a mouse which resembles the house mouse so closely that you might think it was the same creature. However, the outdoor species is probably a harvest mouse, content to find its food under natural conditions. It works the year round for its living, seeking in summertime greens, fruits, berries, and a variety of seeds. It stores some seeds in its nest or underground, and in the winter it tunnels under the snow, if need be, to its hidden supplies.

Other Members of the Mouse Family: If you part the grass in the fields and find hard-packed little roadways about an inch wide, you have probably come upon the meadow mouse's "communication system" between burrows. Again, in wintertime, the tiny animal footprints you find in the snow often prove to be those of the meadow mouse.

The most attractive and interesting of wild mice is the white-footed or deer mouse. Look for it in the woods where a log, a broken rock, or merely grass provides its shelter. It is an excellent

THE WHITE-FOOTED MOUSE
More attractive than many other members of its family, the white-footed mouse
is an appealing creature with a strong bump of curiosity. This mischievous little
mouse lives in the woods, and eats berries and nuts. It has a musical voice and
often chirps. It's a native animal, unlike the house mouse, which came to this
country at about the time of the American Revolution.

climber and occasionally makes its home in a bird's nest that
has been deserted.

BEAVERS—SOCIABLE BUILDERS

In many areas where it was once threatened with extinc-
tion the beaver, now protected by law, again enlivens the landscape. When you are in the vicinity of beaver homes you can play
a game that never fails to arouse youthful enthusiasm in nature
exploring:

"Who will find one first?"

Competition ends when you or your young companion catch
sight of a beaver home—a rounded mass of sticks and mud rising
like a miniature island out of a lake. This is where a beaver family
lives!

The Beaver's Home: You can see the exterior of a beaver lodge and admire the structure of the dams they build to cause water to flood around it; but you cannot investigate the interior.

If you could look inside you would see that the home is made up of one large room or several smaller ones. In either case you would notice openings in the floor. The beaver comes and goes through these, reaching land by an underwater route. As the areas in the lodge around the floor openings are wet and cold, the main floor is slightly raised, somewhat like a step. The sleeping quarters are snugly lined with wood fibers, chewed fine, or with grass. In wintertime the mud plaster of the lodge freezes, and the walls become so strong that even a bear cannot break through.

The Beaver's Building Methods: A popular myth about the beaver's building technique is that he uses his large flat-ribbed tail as a

THE EAGER BEAVER

Beavers' work is never done. They are forever gnawing trees into neat lengths, building canals for floating their logs, assembling tons of material for constructing dams, or else putting together one of their snug housing developments, complete with a hole on top for ventilation. Mostly, beavers do their work at night.

trowel to pat down mud. Actually he works with his fore feet—sometimes with the side of his head—to push and poke mud into place.
Another belief about beavers is that they use their tails as "trailers"
to convey grass, earth, and stones to the building site; but such
claims have always lacked proof.

We do know that beavers carry these materials in their front
paws or in the mouth. The tail does seem to be useful in helping
a beaver steer and propel its body in the water. Another use for
the tail, as we have learned, is that by slapping it against the
surface of the water the beaver is able to warn his companions
of approaching danger.

The Sociable Beaver: Beavers form sociable family circles. They
enjoy being together, and when a family outgrows its lodge they
may construct new homes along nearby shores until a large settle-
ment develops. If, on the other hand, overpopulation results in a
food shortage in the immediate neighborhood, the generation of
two-year-olds starts off in search of a building site for a new colony.
When young beavers are not occupied learning the serious business of tree-cutting, engineering, and building, they like to play
and frolic, sometimes getting underfoot while the adults are at
work.

Muskrats Are Also Builders

Muskrats also use mud in building their homes, but they
mix it with roots and stems of plants, for they live in marshes and
shallow water areas. Beginning the construction of a lodge in
shallow water, they pile layer upon layer of rushes and mud until
the heap is large and reaches a height of four or five feet above
the surface of the water. Then the muskrat, working under water,
chews and digs into this stack from the bottom, until he hollows
out a space above the water line large enough to house himself and
his family.

Near towns and villages you are much more likely to run across
muskrat homes rather than beaver lodges. Muskrats seem to be
undisturbed by the sights and sounds of civilization, whereas the
more retiring beaver prefers wilder regions. Muskrats make use
of swamps and streams as nature provides them, and they also take

advantage of man-made ponds. Despite their ingenuity, however, they have never learned to construct their own dams, as beavers do.

Otters—Shy But Likable

Few creatures are as wary of man as the otter. Even when your nature trails extend far beyond cities and town, you may fail to catch a glimpse of this attractive animal. But though otters remain unseen, you can still find evidence of their whereabouts by looking closely along the banks of streams and lakes. There will be footprints in the mud that borders their favorite fishing waters.

Otters Outswim Fish: Otters are remarkably swift and agile in the water: They catch the fish they delight to eat, literally out-swimming them! Yet young otters are anything but "born swimmers." They live quietly at first, feeding on their mother's milk. When they are old enough she takes them for their first swimming lesson. By way of encouraging a baby she has it climb on her shoulders; then she dives into the water, often swimming with the baby still clinging to her. Lessons may continue throughout the summer until the young otters are as big as cats. Painstaking practice finally turns the pupils into first-class swimmers.

The Otters' Playful Habits: An otter family keeps together for at least a year, and all its members, parents as well as youngsters, know how to have fun the way boys and girls do. A pastime the otters favor, for example, is for two of them to pull at opposite ends of a stick, tug-of-war fashion. They romp and roll like puppies, clawing up the turf and throwing the clods about. Their greatest fun comes from sliding. They love to chute-the-chute on their stomachs down steep river banks into the water, and will keep this up in one place until it becomes very slippery. In wintertime they toboggan down snow-covered hills.

Moles—Nature's Excavators

You do not have to go far afield for evidence of moles. All too often unsightly ridges appear in your garden or lawn which proclaim that these strange, near-blind underground mammals have been tunneling there. But though they live near human dwellings, moles are seldom seen. This endows them with a rather mysterious quality for a child, who quite naturally wonders how an animal can dig up the ground while it is actually under it.

How the Mole Burrows: When the mole is digging, it braces itself with one of its short powerful front paws while the other pushes the soil upward—this is how the ridges that disfigure your lawn are created. To make deeper tunnels, the mole scoops the earth under its body and pushes it as far back as possible with its back feet. Every now and then the mole turns a somersault and then proceeds in the opposite direction, shoving the accumulated pile of dirt along until it comes to a vertical tunnel excavated on a previous occasion. Here the mole forces the dirt up into the open, forming the proverbial "molehill."

The mole's nest, lined with grass and leaves, is some six to twelve inches below the surface of the ground. A main passageway leads from the nest to a series of tunnels extending in all directions. Most of these tunnels lead in turn to hunting grounds where worms and grubs abound; but one tunnel is reserved for an emergency exit when danger threatens.

PRAIRIE DOGS—MASTER ENGINEERS

The chubby rodents known as prairie dogs—they were misnamed by early pioneers in the plains region—are also remarkable excavators. We do not have a clear picture of just how they carry out their elaborate digging operations, but we know that each prairie dog family has a burrow of its own consisting of a main shaft which goes straight down about fourteen feet. Horizontal tunnels branch out from the shaft to the animals' sleeping quarters.

Other vertical shafts rise from some of the horizontal tunnels and are probably used as safety zones in case the lower levels are flooded. The burrows are grouped together in large colonies, sometimes called "towns." There is reason to believe that some of these towns once had a million or more inhabitants!

Tall Tales: Many fantastic stories have been told about a cozy alliance between prairie dogs, burrowing owls, and rattlesnakes for sharing the same burrows in friendly fashion. It is true that these mammals, birds, and reptiles do inhabit the same western regions; but that is all there is to the alliance. The owls dig holes for themselves—though they may put a prairie dog's burrow to use under favorable circumstances; and a rattlesnake may occupy the burrow of either animal. It is a most unwelcome intrusion, however, probably resulting in the loss of the young of the rightful home owners.

THE WARY MARMOT

Prairie dogs are related to the golden-mantled marmots which are so numerous in some of our western national parks— where they have lost much of their fear of people. Even so, you may see a group eating while one animal stands guard. Whenever this lookout senses danger it gives a single sharp whistle and all scurry for cover. Nevertheless, marmots combine some curiosity with their caution, and if you are able to give a near-imitation of their whistle, you can frequently get quite close to one for better observation or for picture-taking.

THE STRIPED GOPHER

Still another prairie dweller that makes excellent burrows is the striped gopher. Some, apparently used only for shelter, are short. There are also longer burrows that end in nests where the young are born. Adjoining rooms serve as storehouses for a large supply of winter grain.

Prospectors prize the gopher and other burrowers as good "pardners" because the dirt thrown up around the opening of a tunnel by the animal provides them with underground soil samples. The prospector pans such dumps for gold traces.

RACCOONS—INGRATIATING AND INQUISITIVE

If you have a camper son or daughter you may be startled one of these days by the introduction into your home of a bright-eyed pointed-faced creature with long, bushy fur. This will be a raccoon that your youngster has adopted during the summer and could not bear to leave behind. Provided there is enough space

for a roomy pen, it is possible to keep a raccoon in captivity successfully—though not all raccoons lend themselves to a domestic
routine.

Not a Finicky Eater: The raccoon relishes many different kinds of
food. It prowls the woods at night, raiding birds' and squirrels'
nests for babies, eggs, or even adults. The black markings across
the raccoon's face, suggestive of a bandit's mask, seem most appropriate for such nighttime excursions! The raccoon enjoys fish,
catching them by a nimble technique which involves lying in wait
at the edge of a stream and hooking out with its paw to seize
victims that swim within reach. It also pounces on bugs and
reptiles, and enjoys all kinds of fruits and vegetables.

Raccoons have a fascinating way of using their front paws as
hands. If a raccoon is allowed in a house it must be watched closely,
as it can open latches and will unhesitatingly try to climb on anything at all. The curiosity of this animal is boundless.

"THE BLACK-MASKED LITTLE BEAR"
This is the name the American Indians gave the raccoon in their stories. Centuries
ago they learned to admire the raccoon's ingenuity, curiosity, and genial play-
fulness. The raccoon eats a large variety of animals, catching them with appropriately versatile techniques. It is said to wash all food whenever possible.

OFFENSIVENESS IS THE BEST DEFENSE
The skunk is a peaceable, friendly creature. When menaced, however, it resorts
to a nasty spray that can be smelled for half a mile—though only the equivalent
of two or three drops is emitted! Skunk's fur, of excellent quality, is often
marketed under the tactful trade names of Alaska sable and black marten.

Skunks—Friendlier Than You Think

There is another wild mammal an enthusiastic young
camper may wish to bring home: the skunk. As it is best known
for the obnoxious odor it can give off, this animal is likely to meet
with a frosty reception. It may be, however, that the camp coun-
selors have already had the skunk's scent glands removed. Most
owners of skunks do have such an operation performed on their
pets, and this is best done while the creature is still quite young.

A skunk makes a friendly, easygoing pet. A small cage will do
for its headquarters; but if the cage is out-of-doors the sides must
be carried well below the surface of the ground. Skunks are expert
burrowers and can easily dig their way to freedom through an
ordinary earth floor. They can be housebroken, and they often
render excellent service in catching mice.

OTHER PETS

Guinea Pigs: If you adopt a skunk, a raccoon, or a related wild animal, you will have a lively hobby to share with your youngster. That old-time favorite among mammal pets, the guinea pig, is perhaps a more conservative choice. Given proper care, it is practically odorless, and easy to feed. However, its habit of breaking out in a shrill whistling sound may be disconcerting if you live in a city and must keep your pets in an apartment or a garage.

Hamsters: Hamsters are comparative newcomers to the ranks of furry pets. These rodents look like fat-faced stubby-eared squirrels, but are smaller. They have no specialized tastes in food and are free from unpleasant odors. Friendly and winning in their ways, hamsters retain some of the interesting habits of wild creatures—such as hoarding food until they are ready to consume it. Many a hamster has a routine of packing food into the cheek pouches that extend over its shoulders. It carries the food to a hiding place and tucks it away; then at night—for it tends to indulge in nighttime activity—the hamster digs up the buried food and nibbles away contentedly. It is not, by the way, a native American, but an import from Eurasia.

BEARS—NOTED GOURMETS

Nursery stories present such an appealing picture of Mother Bear, Daddy Bear, and Baby Bear that a child is all too likely to think of this closely knit family group as being true to life. Let's look at the facts.

The mother-and-baby bear relationship does really exist in nature, but as far as Daddy is concerned, we shall have to remove him from the scene if we are to be faithful to the facts. He actually goes off by himself, taking no responsibility for feeding, protecting, or educating the young: The mother does it all. In this respect bears differ from wolves, foxes, and coyotes—in each of those families the father does his full share when it comes to bringing up the children.

The Playful Bear Cub: Bear cubs are not handicapped by the father's absence, as the mother takes care of their needs in the

THE BEAR'S ROUNDHOUSE PUNCH
Black bears are not large as bears go, and their top weight is about three hundred pounds. They are fond of berries and—of course—honey. Bears pack a tremendous, often lethal, wallop in their forepaws; but the "bear hug" is now generally dismissed by scientists as a fable.

most competent fashion. At birth the twin cubs of a black bear are blind, almost hairless and not much larger than rats. By the time they leave the winter retreat where they were born, they have become saucy, fun-loving creatures with fluffy hair and sharp claws. They box and wrestle, play hide-and-seek, and try all sorts of tricks on their mother.

Sometimes she loses patience with them and boxes their ears. For all that, she guards them jealously and the only time she is ever really dangerous to human beings is when her cubs are with her.

You may see black bears in some of our national parks; their desire for food from tourists has overcome their natural shyness. One lesson they learn well in the wilderness is to be ever wary of humans and other possible enemies. Mother bear teaches the cubs to swim and to climb trees to escape danger. She shows them how to tear apart rotted stumps and mop up swarming ants with the tongue. She demonstrates how to catch mice, how to slap a frog out of water, and how to raid a tree in which bees have stored honey.

The Bear's Sweet Tooth: Bears are noted for being gourmets. Black bears live chiefly on vegetables, but they also dig for roots and bugs and catch grasshoppers and crickets. They enjoy all kinds of fruit, blueberries being their favorite; and like all bears, they are so fond of honey that they will risk the vengeance of furious swarms of bees to tear open and rob a bee tree.

Some black bears add meat to this diet, but it is said that when other food is plentiful they will not show the slightest interest in freshly killed deer or sheep. Grizzly bears are flesh eaters: They hunt deer and wapiti (an especially large deer), and will even attack cattle and horses. Small game is their usual prey, however, and a grizzly will hunt mice tirelessly, digging them out of the grass with his huge paws.

The Bear's Long Sleep: It is probable that in prehistoric times great cave bears, like the "cave men," made good use of dens and caves for shelter and safety. Nowadays bears are chiefly interested in dens as places to sleep in during the winter months.

A female bear chooses a particularly snug retreat, for it is during the long, cold-weather rest period that her babies are born. In the spring she leaves her winter headquarters, taking her cubs with her. From then on, all outdoors is her home. Black bears and grizzlies usually seek out a natural cave or partially uprooted tree that will shelter them—but if need be, they dig a hole under some steep embankment.

Foxes and Wolves

Unlike the bears, foxes remain together in family groups. While the young are growing up, both parents take care of them in their underground den. The red fox digs its own burrow, often supplementing the living room with a pantry and then building a tunnel to connect the food storage room with the main burrow. Though a fox family leaves its cozy home during warm weather, it may return to the same winter address year after year.

JUST AS FOXY AS HE LOOKS
Many are the centuries-old tales that center about the cunning of the fox. The red fox is perhaps the slyest of the tribe—the terror of the hen coops, but a model husband and father. The beautiful silver fox fur is highly prized—a sad end for Brer Fox. Besides man, his enemies are the lynx, wolf, and fisher.

Gray foxes do not regularly dig homes; they dwell in natural cavities in rocks or in hollow trees.

The Wolf's Home: The wolf is also partial to dens. Sometimes a wolf digs a short burrow in the ground; a large hollow log or an excavation under a tree stump will also serve his purpose, and in rock-strewn regions he often adopts a natural cave.

Coyotes are more ambitious when it comes to constructing a home. Not content with general living quarters among secluded rocks or brush, the mother digs a nursery den, and she may also have a separate resting den where she can retire to "get away from it all." Not to be outdone, the male digs a den of his own to use while his mate is caring for the young.

LYNXES AND BOBCATS—MORE BALLYHOO THAN FEROCITY

The oversized bobtailed cat known as the lynx is frequently heard but rarely seen. This animal prefers night prowling to daytime hunting and is therefore hardly ever seen by man; but its yowls are all too familiar to campers in northern regions and visitors to some of the national parks who are trying to doze off to sleep. Though its call sounds terrifying, the lynx usually seeks no larger game than the hare or smaller rodents. On rare occasions a lynx may leap from a tree branch or ledge to kill a deer or an antelope.

Bobcats, unlike lynxes, are not confined to the North. Bobcat trails may be seen in Arizona deserts or on Canadian snow-covered plains. "Fighting like a wildcat" suggests the most vicious kind of battle but, like the lynx, bobcats usually prey only on rabbits, other small rodents, and ground-nesting birds.

DEER—APPEALING CREATURES

Thanks to the classic story of Bambi, many children take a sympathetic interest in the white-tailed deer. The young deer, or fawn, makes an interesting contrast with some other mammal babies, such as the blind and helpless bear cubs. As infants, deer are weak and wobbly, but they can see immediately and before long they are anxious to explore their surroundings. The mother, or doe, scolds them, warning against such activity; if necessary, she bunts them on the head to make them stay put.

A fawn's spotted coat blends effectively with its surroundings. This enables it to protect itself by merely lying still and relying on camouflage. Once the mother has taught this lesson to her fawns, she can leave to seek food; but she returns several times a day to nurse them. If an enemy is nearby, she will deliberately attract attention to herself to save the fawns.

The Buck's Antlers: The father of the deer family, the buck, is a handsome, impressive animal. The buck's crowning glory, his antlers, are shed every year, and he proceeds to grow a new pair. Considering the thousands of antlers discarded every year, your child might well expect the woods to be carpeted with them. Some antlers are found, to be sure; but many are eaten by porcupines, mice, and rabbits for their mineral content, while others disintegrate after sufficient weathering.

Adventures In Park And Zoo

The mammals of American field and woodland have first claim on our children's interest; these animals are part of the American scene, and their colorful variety always suggests some fascinating detail to absorb our attention. Yet, somehow, there is a greater enchantment about the exotic animals of faraway places. Thrilling as it is to see a shy, graceful creature like the deer in our native woods, we often feel it would be a more exciting experience to stalk elephants and other big game in Africa.

Such expeditions are out of the question for most of us. But not altogether. There are little safaris we can make close to home. A visit to the zoo is a delightful way to make the acquaintance of strange animals from every part of the world. Throughout the United States and Canada there are a number of fine zoos and zoological parks where animals from Asia, Africa, Australia and the other continents may be seen in the space of a single afternoon.

SHOWMEN AND SHOW-OFFS

Every zoo has sights and sounds that take us completely out of the daily round of humdrum living. But to get the most fun out of a visit to the zoo, you must have one or more youngsters along with you. You will enjoy their reactions, their curiosity, their astonishment. For a visit to the zoo is *fun*—as much fun as the circus, and often very much like the circus if you see the animals at feeding time, or in the spring when frisky babies enliven many cages.

Some animals, the natural showmen and show-offs, are entertaining at all times. The sea lions with their graceful diving, their awkward waddling, their hoarse yawps, their bent for deadpan horseplay, and their efficient if not elegant eating habits, are great favorites. All children are delighted with the tail-swinging antics of the monkeys and some of their droll attitudes which caricature humans. The huge elephant with his fantastic trunk and his dignified, patient look; the tigers and leopards with their air of sleek power, and drowsy laziness; the giraffes with their incredibly long necks and the camels with their bumpy backs—all these and many other inhabitants of the zoo are natural-born showmen and show-offs that children love to watch.

Your child's enjoyment of a visit to the zoo stimulates him to learn more about the animal world. Many exhibits have labels or placards giving specific information about the animals. And before going on a visit, you can prepare yourself at home with some background reading—one of the purposes of this chapter is to supply you with it. Thus you will be well equipped to furnish details about the animals or offer interesting information at the strategic moment.

MONKEYS—HIGH-SPIRITED PERFORMERS

It is a good idea to make the Monkey House the first stop on your zoo tour: There is a special appeal in these volatile animals and their endearing ways which often remind us of human beings in miniature. The monkeys also show to good advantage because cages are less confining for them than for the great apes such as the gorilla and the orangutan.

The Rhesus Monkey: As you watch a family of rhesus monkeys chasing each other, chattering and occasionally screaming, it is easy for you to picture them in their native jungles of India. They behave there pretty much the same way, quarreling and screeching at each other one moment, then suddenly quieting down and grooming each other's fur. Thousands of rhesus monkeys are brought to the United States each year to be placed in zoos or to be used for medical research.

Swinging by the Tail: The woolly monkey is one of the largest of the species native to South America. When you see one at the zoo, it is interesting to contrast its antics with the gambols of the rhesus. You can observe the woolly monkey swing daringly from branches or bars by its tail. No matter how long you watch the rhesus, it will never duplicate this feat. The point is that the woolly monkey is one of the species that has a prehensile tail—a "grasping" tail that functions in effect as a fifth limb or extra hand.

Only the monkeys of Central and South America have a pre-hensile tail. The species with the longest tail of the monkey tribe

RAUCOUS BUT AMIABLE
The well-named howler monkey, a talented climber and swinger, relies on its prehensile tail, which in effect serves as a fifth paw, or hand. At the zoo, the howler performs amazing acrobatic feats, every now and then pausing thoughtfully to pick tidbits out of a crony's hair.

live in India, and of course this tail is not prehensile. As for the howler monkey, its prehensile tail is "different"—the fur is missing from the inner portion near the tip.

It is curious that many of the larger monkeys are afraid of the water; not so the rhesus, which is a good swimmer.

As for tastes in food, monkeys thrive on a leafy diet and on such fruit as apples and bananas. Those living in the natural state augment this diet in one way or another. The South American squirrel monkey, for example, eats insects, and possibly young birds.

Despite their general reputation for amiability, not all monkeys are good pet or exhibition material. One of the most attractive species, the lion-tailed monkey, is likely to turn savage if removed from its native forests in western India. Even the Indians, who have a way with animals, cannot keep the lion-tailed monkey in captivity successfully.

THE BIG APES

Gorillas—Shy and Retiring: When you see the gorillas behind the bars at the zoo, they impress you as fierce and vicious. Sometimes a gorilla acts that way as well—spitting at its admiring audience and carrying on as if trying to pull the cage apart. In their natural surroundings, however, the disposition of these animals is quite different. While they may occasionally attack men or animals in self-defense, they are by nature shy and retiring and prefer to stay clear of trouble whenever possible.

On their native grounds, gorillas roam about in small family groups in search of the vegetables, roots and fruit on which they feed. Though they can stand upright as humans do, and their babies often walk that way, older gorillas always walk on all fours.

Their great strength notwithstanding, gorillas—like many wild animals—have rather frail health. In the wild state they are distressed by jungle-bred worms which bring on intestinal troubles; in captivity gorillas are very susceptible to colds and pneumonia.

Chimpanzees—Intelligent and Comical: The chimpanzee is as widely known for its intelligence as for its comical antics. It can be taught all sorts of tricks and—what is more impressive—it often shows actual reasoning powers. Like the gorillas, chimpanzees dwell in Africa and they also live on fruit and vegetables. They are, however, much smaller than gorillas. An adult male rarely attains more than 175 pounds, while a gorilla may reach six hundred or more.

Chimps can walk upright but—again like the gorillas—they usually travel on all fours with their hands curled into fists. Though their hands resemble those of humans, chimpanzees lack manipulative powers—particularly in the thumbs.

Orangutans—Slow and Deliberate: "Man of the Woods" and "Wild Man" are alternative renderings for the orangutan's Malay name. This big ape of Borneo and Sumatra lives almost entirely among leafy branches and, despite its bulk, swings with great agility from one tree to another. Though it is capable of moving speedily, it is usually slow and deliberate. A big male orang weighs two hundred pounds or more.

ELEPHANTS—LARGEST LAND ANIMALS

Children love elephants. This animal is interesting to observe for many reasons: its huge size, its amazing trunk, its tusks from which ivory is obtained, its status as a living relic of the great mammoths that roamed the earth many ages ago, and its wise, benign expression that reminds us of some distinguished elder statesman.

Having been told that the elephant is the largest land mammal, a child may be puzzled by its tough, wrinkled skin.

"I thought all mammals had fur or hair," he may tell you. "But the elephant's a mammal and look at *him*."

Indeed, this skeptical attitude is well taken, for adult elephants are almost completely devoid of hair. You have to look closely to see even a bit of it on their hide. A young elephant, however, is covered with a fuzzy coat. Several other beasts, such as the adult rhinoceros and hippopotamus, follow this pattern of being nearly hairless.

The Elephant's Trunk: Elephants at the zoo are particularly fascinating because we are allowed to feed them and thus see in action the amazing "nose" which serves them as arm, hand, and fingers. The size and muscular strength of an elephant's trunk make it possible for him to carry heavy, bulky objects; the finger-like tabs that project from the end of the trunk enable him to pick up an object as small as a peanut and swing it through a great arc into his mouth. At the end of an African elephant's trunk there are two tabs of about equal length. An Indian elephant has only one tab.

Elephants of Africa and India can also be distinguished by size. As a rule the African species grow considerably larger than the Indian variety and their ears are much larger. In the jungles of west Africa, however, there are elephants that are an exception to this rule. These elephants are often described as pygmies or dwarfs, as they average considerably less in size than most African elephants.

A LOT OF ANIMAL
The African elephant, weighing five or six tons, is bigger than its Indian cousin—
in fact the largest of all land animals. It grows to a height of eleven or twelve
feet, and has two tusks that average about ten feet in length and 250 pounds
in weight. It has been claimed that the powerful but delicate trunk contains as
many as forty thousand muscles! Indian species has smaller, less fanlike ears.

Training an Elephant: You see the Indian elephants far more
frequently in zoos and circuses than the African species; the Indian
animals, aside from being smaller, are obtained more easily and
can be trained more rapidly. For thousands of years the natives
of eastern India have been skilled in the training of elephants,
and the knack has been handed down from father to son.

An important factor in their success lies in the use of the human
voice: The trainer first wins his charge's trust by softly chanting
an "elephant song," after which he bribes the beast with its
favorite foods. (Wild elephants eat leaves and grass—perhaps half

a ton in a single day!—but they relish sweet fruits and other dainties. In the zoo they are fed mostly on hay and grain.)

Besides drilling some elephants for circus performance, the natives of India train others for use in hunting and for carrying heavy materials—an important consideration in a land lacking machinery. In ancient days elephants played an impressive role in warfare as forerunners of the modern giant tank. The most famous instance of their military use was in Hannibal's great victory over the Romans at Cannae after he had brought these huge creatures across a pass over the Alps. In time elephants fell out of military favor because they were too easily terrified by the noise and violence of battle.

Elephants have always excited a great deal of interest and many curious beliefs have grown up about them. One of these is that elephants are afraid of mice! There seems to be no scientific evidence for this notion. Another fallacious idea is that elephants live a century or more. Scientists believe that the life span of these giant mammals is about the same as that of human beings—from sixty to eighty years.

Hippos—"River Horses"

Next in size to the elephant is the grotesque African hippopotamus, which may achieve a weight of four tons—or more! It is perhaps this creature's very ugliness that makes it appealing to children. Though the hippo performs no stunts. they watch it with absorbed interest.

The Hippo in the Water: The hippopotamus spends a great deal of time in the water, which must always be provided in its enclosure. In the wild state the hippo seeks out the calm waters of a tropical river where it browses on water plants as it swims or floats. (The name hippopotamus means "river horse.") When frightened, a hippo takes to flight by sinking to the river bottom, where it can walk easily and quickly. Ten minutes is about the longest it can stay under water, and when it comes to the surface it usually spouts a column of air from its nostrils.

A mother hippo often rides her baby on her back in the water, and the young one clings there even when they go below the

THE MONUMENTAL HIPPO

This four-ton river horse is anything but glamorous—yet, despite the hippo's ugliness, children enjoy observing it, perhaps because of its great size and mild manner. Its enormous mouth and tusklike teeth are exercised exclusively on vegetation. The African natives hunt it for its flesh and its tusks.

surface! Once your child realizes the extent to which hippos are water animals, he may see the advantage of their peculiarly placed eyes, ears, and nose. All these features are at about the same level on top of the animal's huge flat head. Thus the hippo need keep only a small part of its head above water in order to see, hear, and breathe at times when all the rest of its body is submerged.

THE UNPREDICTABLE RHINO

Like the elephant, the rhinoceros is native to both Africa and India. You can tell the African "black" rhino by its two horns; the large Indian rhino has only one horn. Rhinos spend much of their time sleeping and browsing on twigs. They have remarkably keen senses of smell and hearing and they are quickly alert to danger. They may charge an enemy with surprising agility or do a right-about-face and gallop away. Poor eyesight makes their actions especially unpredictable. They were once much more plentiful than they are today, for hunters have greatly reduced the numbers of these "nose-horns" (the literal meaning of "rhinoceros").

THE BIG CATS

Tigers and lions appeal strongly to the average child because of his affection for pussy cats. A small cub appears as gentle and playful as a kitten, and even an adult—particularly a tiger—suggests a giant "tabby."

Lions and tigers are the two biggest members of the cat family. Some kinds of tiger grow considerably larger than others. The Bengal tiger, one of the best known, may be twelve feet long and weigh more than five hundred pounds. The Siberian tiger, which is even larger, also has longer, heavier hair to protect it in the cold northern forests where it lives.

Tigers—"Ten Pounds of Meat a Day": A mother tiger has two to four babies in a litter. In a zoo, tiger babies are sometimes raised by human foster parents who feed them milk from nursing bottles. In captivity they sleep, purr, play, and chase their tails like the kittens that are so dear to the hearts of children. In the natural state young tigers start killing small game by the time they are seven months old. They stay with their family about two years.

The usual diet of a tiger is wild game, such as deer, but many prey on sheep, cattle, and other domestic animals. Occasionally a tiger turns man-eater and becomes a serious menace to the community. Well-fed tigers in a zoo are usually peaceable and contented. It takes about ten pounds of meat a day to keep them that way!

LIONS—NOT SO LIONHEARTED

A lion may also become a man-killer, but it is more usual for him to avoid humans whenever possible. By day, lions like to rest quietly in shady places; at night, they are on the alert, seeking such game as zebra and antelope. The clichés "king of beasts" and "brave as a lion" help keep alive the idea that lions are the most daring and courageous of all the animals. But, though they look the part, they do not really live up to it.

According to Frank Buck, the famous "Bring 'em Back Alive" animal collector, a tiger is often self-confident enough to take on a more powerful foe—a water buffalo, for example—but a lion rarely

LEO THE LION
Lions like each other's society more than tigers, and groups of ten or twenty
traveling together are often seen in African game reserves. There they look on
undisturbed when visitors' cars go by.

tries to overpower any animal that is a match for it. Mr. Buck
discovered, furthermore, that lion cubs are more tame than tiger
cubs, and that older lions are more amenable to the company of
humans than tigers are.

A male lion is far more handsome than his mate, because of
the great ruff around his neck. A lioness may have as many as six
cubs in one litter. They are completely helpless at first, as their
eyes do not open for about a week. Sometimes they suffer from
the once-common childhood ailment of rickets, and teething may
give them a great deal of trouble.

Giraffes—Walking Skyscrapers

Children are naturally fascinated by the giraffe, the world's
tallest animal, because of its long neck. A youngster who already
knows something about anatomy may wonder whether this un-

THE TALLEST OF THEM ALL
The giraffe has many interesting features aside from its long neck. It sleeps standing, and it can go without formal drinking for weeks, getting enough moisture from foliage. Its spotted coloring blends admirably with its surroundings, and its fleet legs make a quick getaway possible when danger threatens.

gainly animal has more than the normal number of vertebrae from head to shoulders. It does not, however. It has the usual seven neck vertebrae—they are simply longer than those of other mammals.

The long neck makes it possible for the giraffe to feed on the leaves of trees. It can manage to reach its head down to a pool for drinking water, but it depends for most of its liquid nourishment on the moisture on leaves. As you may have guessed, the giraffe can cover ground speedily with its long legs, and has been known to go over thirty miles an hour! The giraffe reputedly is silent, but at times it does produce a sound somewhat like a cow's moo.

DESERT TRANSPORT WITH BUILT-IN COMMISSARY
The camel was domesticated thousands of years ago—it is pictured on ancient pottery and Assyrian friezes. The hump is not part of the camel's backbone, but a reserve supply of fat which is gradually absorbed as needed. The camel also keeps a water reservoir in its innards to provide for emergencies.

CAMELS—AVID WATER DRINKERS

The camel is another one of those animals that interest children because of a physical peculiarity. At some zoos children need not content themselves with looking at a camel; they may ride on the animal as well. Thus they can come to know something of the sensation of a desert traveler as he progresses over the sands on camel-back. Of course the youngsters do not have a chance to appreciate how this useful animal weathers a sandstorm in its natural surroundings. The camel can close its nostrils against the flying sand, and in addition its double row of eyelashes offers excellent protection for its eyes. A one-humped dromedary in good form can travel nearly a hundred miles a day.

Going Without Water: The accomplishment for which camels are most noted—the ability to do without water—seems more improbable than ever if you see them drinking. When a supply is available, a camel will drink six or seven gallons of water a day! A camel bearing a heavy load cannot go without drink for much more than three days; but records show that some animals have survived for several weeks without water. At such times the camel draws upon moisture stored in its stomach walls and actually "drinks from the inside." The one-humped camel is still a valued beast of burden in Africa and the Arab lands.

The Two-humped Camel: The two-humped Bactrian camel grows a far heavier coat than the dromedary. Its native land is Central Asia, where many people depend on their camels not only for transportation but also for food (they drink the milk and eat the meat) and for clothing (made from the hair). In the spring a camel looks disreputable as its winter coat peels off in ragged patches. Flabby humps are a sign of poor physical condition, as the hump provides a storehouse of reserve nourishment which the animal draws upon when food is scarce.

ZOO BEARS—SURPRISINGLY TIMID

Children enjoy watching bears because they are reminded of their beloved teddy bears. At the zoo, aside from the familiar native North American black bear, you may also see several more spectacular or unusual species.

The Alaskan Brown Bear: A large zoo may be able to exhibit the biggest bears in the world—the Alaskan brown bear. Some of them weigh fifteen hundred pounds or more. Despite their great power and tremendous claws, they are timid rather than daring and attack only when cornered or wounded. As in the case of other bears, the cubs are amazingly tiny compared to the adults. A baby bear weighs about a pound and a half at birth.

The Polar Bear: Some polar bears are as heavy as the Alaskan brown bear, though the average male is not over nine hundred pounds. This bear does not have the timidity of most species. It is a hunter that preys upon fish, seals, walrus, and it will stalk a

THE POLAR BEAR DOES NOT SEEM TO MISS ITS ICE FLOES

At first thought it seems astonishing that this native of the Arctic regions can thrive in temperate-zone zoos. Apparently the polar bear is not uncomfortable so long as it has a chance to immerse itself in a refreshing pool. This animal has a keen sense of smell in detecting food or enemies.

man in the same way that it pursues the large mammals. The polar bear mother, like all bear mothers, is a conscientious guardian and teacher of her cubs. She frequently offers them a unique towing service in the water, allowing them to grip her tail with their teeth!

The Grizzly Bear: You may look with some awe at the grizzlies, as they have won a reputation as the most ferocious of all bears. Books about the lives of the American pioneers and frontiersmen contain many accounts of struggles with grizzlies. If wounded or fearful for their cubs, they may kill a man—but they do not go out of their way to hunt him. Grizzlies live chiefly on fruit, berries, insects, fish, and small mammals.

THE GIANT PANDA—CHILDREN'S FAVORITE

Few zoos are in a position to exhibit so rare an animal as the giant panda, but wherever it is shown, this strikingly marked black and white mammal makes an immediate hit with children. Not until 1937 was a giant panda captured alive. It was a baby, and had many of the appealing ways of a human baby. It romped

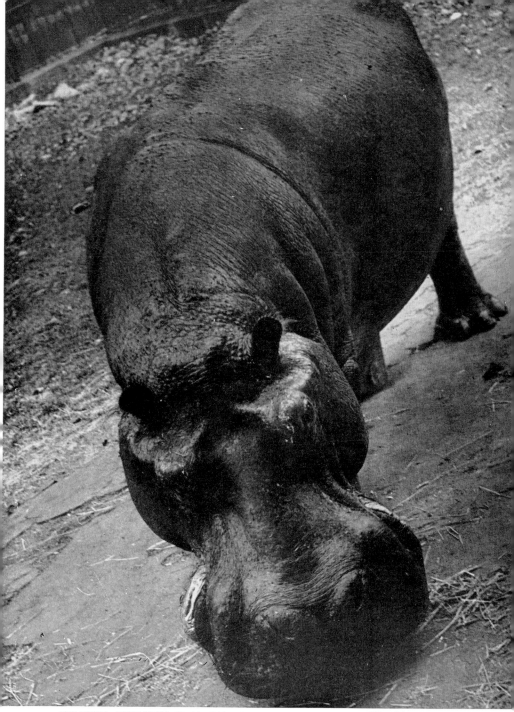

THE HIPPO—FOUR TONS OF AFRICAN ANIMAL LIFE   *Three Lions*

Never winner in a beauty contest, the hippopotamus can take a runner-up's award
for size. It weighs up to 8,000 pounds, is the second largest animal that lives on
land today (the elephant is first). A zoo must provide a hippo guest with an
enormous swimming pool, for it is most at home in water. It is a vegetarian.

Harold K. Whitford

BEAR TWINS PLOT MISCHIEF

Black bear cubs are as full of fun and ready for rough-and-tumble play as small boys are. They are born while the mother is "denned up" and at first weigh little more than half a pound. By the time they leave the den early in the spring, they are roly-poly and ready not only for play but for learning lessons as well.

STERN TEACHER AND LOVING PARENT

Mother bear anxiously guards her young, and painstakingly teaches them the secrets of food-hunting as well as how to escape from danger by climbing trees. Even a heavy adult bear can run swiftly and dash up a tree with agility that is really amazing.

"THE BLACK-AND-WHITE BEAR"
In its toddler stage the giant panda is playful and appealing—one of the zoo's outstandingly popular performers. But the grown-up giant panda, which weighs about three hundred pounds, does not relish captivity and is apt to be surly, not to say downright bad-tempered.

in a play pen, took milk from a nursing bottle, and when it was tired it whimpered like a human infant. It was named Su-Lin, which has been translated as "a little bit of something mighty cute."

Since the time of Su-Lin's introduction into the United States, more than a dozen giant pandas have been captured and brought from their homes in western China to zoos in the United States and Europe. An unfortunate aspect of the pandas' scarcity is that when one of them dies, it is not easily replaced. Although this animal's appearance reminds us of a bear, it is more closely related to the raccoon. In the wild state the panda is believed to live on bamboo leaves and stems; in a zoo corn-meal mush, nourishing if less exotic, forms a large part of its diet.

Oddities from Australia

Among the most remarkable creatures in our zoos are several near-extinct Australian animals. Even in Australia these believe-it-or-not leftovers from prehistoric times can generally be seen only in zoos.

The Platypus—Scrambled Mammal: The strangest of these strange creatures is perhaps the platypus, which has a bill like a duck's and grows to a length of about eighteen inches. It is considered a mammal because it feeds its young on its own milk, and because it has hair and is warm-blooded. But the platypus lays eggs, and the temperature of its blood changes to some extent, depending on the weather. Most curious of all, the nursing technique of the mother platypus is highly unorthodox: Milk oozes from special pores in her skin and clings to her fur, from which the babies lap it up. The platypus is considered one of the most primitive of mammals—in some ways it is very close to the reptiles.

THE CURIOUS KANGAROO

As a relic of prehistoric times, the kangaroo has traits that are off the beaten track in our own prosaic era. Its offspring, only an inch long—or less!—at birth, is not strong enough to suck milk. However, the milk is pumped automatically to the infant. The largest kangaroos are about five feet high.

The Kangaroo's Built-in Baby Carriage: Children have always been intrigued by the kangaroo and its built-in baby-carriage features. This animal is the largest and most spectacular of the marsupials—a kind of mammal remarkable for having small, undeveloped babies that spend their first weeks—or months—in a pouch on the mother's abdomen.

Usually a kangaroo mother has only one baby at a time and the infant stays in the nursery pouch for five or six months. After that the baby pokes its head out and often hops out to explore on its own; when it gets tired or hungry, it quickly dives back again.

The kangaroo can jump over a five-foot fence with ease, and may even leap more than twice that height. In Australia, the animal has been trained to be a skillful boxer. It is a vegetarian, and lives about ten or fifteen years. Smaller types of kangaroos are known as wallabies.

THE AUSTRALIAN TEDDY BEAR

The koala fascinates children by its droll resemblance to a teddy bear as well as by its gentle, wistful expression. On its native grounds the koala, a leaf-eater, lives in tall trees and leaps sure-footedly from branch to branch, as far as five feet at a time. Zoo keepers must feed it its natural diet of eucalyptus leaves.

The Koala—Nature's Teddy Bear: The appeal of the koala is much the same as that of the giant panda—it looks like the work of a toy designer. In fact, some people believe that the koala inspired the long-popular "teddy bear." (The "teddy" part of the name is supposed to have been in honor of Theodore Roosevelt.) Like the kangaroo, the koala is a marsupial. A newborn baby is less than an inch long, and it stays in the mother's pouch for about two months. After emerging, the baby clings to the fur on the mother's back, riding there until it becomes quite a heavy load.

Sea Lions and Seals—Nature's Clowns

It is the easily tamed and trained sea lions that you usually see in zoo and circus. They are born show-offs. In the zoo their feeding-time antics never fail to draw a large and admiring crowd. Children and grown-ups alike chortle with delight at the nonchalant way in which the sea lion holds his mouth wide open and catches the fish thrown to him by the keeper across the length of the pool. The sea lion is also an expert circus performer, balancing a large ball on his nose, "answering" questions, and "playing" musical instruments.

"What is the difference between a sea lion and a seal?" you may wonder as you watch the frolicking acrobatic water mammals at the zoo.

Though many people use the names interchangeably, sea lions differ somewhat from true seals. To recognize a sea lion, look for ears at the sides of his sleek head. They are small but distinguishable. True seals have no external ear structure. Sea lions are also unique in their ability to turn their hind flippers forward and under, making possible a fairly rapid if awkward progress over land.

Under natural conditions sea lions spend considerable time on shore, and there the babies are born. The mothers take them to shallow water to teach them how to swim and catch fish. Sea lions live only along the Pacific coast. The common seal is found along the shores of both the North Atlantic and North Pacific Oceans. The common seal (known also as the harbor seal) is notably tame and friendly with humans, and has a strong sense of curiosity.

WALRUSES—TIMID GIANTS

Most children will look forward eagerly to seeing a walrus in the flesh if they are familiar with Tweedledee's nonsensical recitation about the Walrus and the Carpenter in *Through the Looking-Glass.* Everyone knows the famous passage in which the Walrus pompously declaims:

> *"The time has come," the Walrus said,*
>   *To talk of many things:*
> *Of shoes—and ships—and sealing-wax—*
>   *Of cabbages—and kings—*
> *And why the sea is boiling hot—*
>   *And whether pigs have wings."*

The walrus is a mighty creature often weighing a ton or more and reaching a length of about ten feet. Its name is derived from the Scandinavian for "whale horse," an allusion to its size and the fact that it lives both on the land and in the sea. The walrus gives no lively performance as seals do; its appearance is a show in itself. The bristly whiskers and the male's fantastically elongated upper canine teeth—they sometimes reach a length of thirty inches!—enhance the formidable impression made by the walrus.

For all their size and power, walruses are rather timid and try to avoid trouble. They live in herds, and if one member is attacked, all the rest rush to its defense. They can fight fiercely if they have to, making good use of their tusks, and a mother never hesitates to show fight if an enemy approaches her "baby." The walrus has an unearthly bellow that is in keeping with its appearance.

BATS AND NATURE'S RADAR SYSTEM

Each season half a million people visit Carlsbad Caverns in New Mexico. They are almost as interested in the bats they may see there as in the cave itself. Each afternoon hordes of the flying mammals come out, literally darkening the sky as they set out in quest of food. It is estimated that there are millions of bats in this colony! They are the little brown bats, of which there are more than two dozen kinds in the United States.

Bats are not good zoo exhibition subjects because they sleep in the daytime. Aside from roosting at Carlsbad and other, smaller, caves, the little brown bat takes refuge in hollow trees and under the roofs or eaves of houses. Your child may shudder, as many adults do, at the thought of a bat's approach. It is a pity that so many superstitions have grown up about these creatures of darkness. Despite their sinister appearance they are really useful animals, as they eat large numbers of insects—catching them in mid-flight.

Occasionally bats do become entangled in a human being's hair. Such incidents are accidental—never intentional. As a matter of fact the bat rarely flies into things, thanks to its own special radar system. As it flies it emits high-pitched squeaks—far too shrill to be caught by the human ear. The sound waves hit any nearby solid objects and bounce back, a signal to the bat to swerve aside.

A Four-foot Wingspread: The "flying fox," the world's largest bat, lives in India and on tropical islands of the Pacific. Its wingspread measures more than four feet from tip to tip. The flying foxes live on fruit and leave their tree roosts at night to fly to orchards or wild fruit trees, often traveling many miles to their goal. Because of their potential danger to fruit, none of these bats may be brought into the United States, even for a zoo.

Blood-sucking Bats: The vampire bat is the one kind of bat that really deserves a place in horror tales; it actually lives on the blood of animals and humans. At dusk these vampire bats, which dwell in Mexico and tropical South America, begin their hunt for cattle, wild creatures, or human beings who are susceptible to attack through living in unscreened homes.

A bite from the vampire bat's sharp teeth is not painful—nor would it be harmful except that sometimes this bat is infected with a disease that is transmitted to the victim and usually proves fatal. The vampire laps the blood as it flows from the wound.

Mammals in Maps, Games, Stamps, and Art

Your visit to a zoo is an end in itself because of the pure pleasure it yields in direct, enjoyable experience. Yet such visits can take on lasting meaning in a child's life if you can unobtrusively associate each animal with its natural home. In this way the child's mind forms a clear idea of the wildlife of different countries and continents. Some zoos group the animals in exhibits—such as the *Plains of Africa*—where mammals that are natural neighbors are seen together; but in many zoos it is necessary to point out these associations yourself.

Of course, the *how* and the *when* of imparting such information will depend on the child's age and interest and receptivity. The best method is doubtless one that involves some active participation by the child. Keeping a scrapbook of animal pictures is fun at almost any age, and it provides a good starting point for talking and learning about animals.

Mammal Maps

Most children are fascinated by a map that pictures a continent in outline with its animals or plants shown in the approximate area where they are most commonly found. Elaborate maps of this kind are available; but children will enjoy making simple maps of their own—perhaps after an expedition to the zoo—which will mean more to them because they have created the maps themselves.

Animal Lotto

One of the pleasantest ways for very young children to become familiar with animals is to play games involving them, such as Animal Lotto. In this game more than fifty mammals, with identifying names, are pictured on master cards; the players try to match them by drawing individual pictures of the animals from the "stock pile."

Place Cards for Parties

For a four-year-old's birthday we used an idea for place cards which enabled the youngsters to seat themselves without assistance. From colored cardboard we cut silhouettes of elephants.

kangaroos, giraffes, and other animals, in duplicate. Each child was given one of these, and the duplicate was set as his place card on the table. When refreshment time arrived, there was much excitement over matching up the animals, and the children had a happy sense of accomplishment in recognizing each silhouette.

ANIMALS ON STAMPS

For older children a stamp collection helps create a link with animals of the world; many countries depict their characteristic and famous animals on stamps. The elephant, camel, leopard, giraffe, horse, tiger and antelope are but a few of the animals represented. A child's interest in animals may create a desire to collect stamps, or, contrariwise, stamp collecting may develop a desire on the child's part to know more about the animals.

ANIMALS IN ART

The limitless field of art suggests another way in which two different interests may mutually stimulate one another. Almost every youngster enjoys drawing familiar animals, and many children favor some animal that they will draw tirelessly, again and again. Aside from this, the great world of art opens up an enormous field of animal drawings, pictures, and statues that will delight children. Very often these works of art will impinge on other interests of a child. Think of the rock paintings of prehistoric man, Egyptian sculpture, Assyrian reliefs, Chinese jade figures, the art of the North American Indians, the Aztecs, the Negroes of Africa. All have used animals in their art. An interest in art will intensify a youngster's interest in animals and give him a source of lifelong pleasure.

CHAPTER 6 Animal Friends
and Helpers

Most children look upon their cats and dogs
as affectionate companions, bound to them
by strong ties of love and loyalty. On a farm, they quickly take
full charge of colts, lambs, calves, and kids, giving them infinite
care and consideration. Young animals—or small ones—seem to
be a child's natural playmates. It often comes as quite a surprise
to a boy or girl to learn that these friendly, docile creatures are
descended from wild beasts that once feared man or fought with
him.

The story of how animals were tamed has been an important
one to all mankind, not merely to children. No one knows when
the first wild animal was domesticated. Certainly it was long,
long ago, before the building of the pyramids. It happened in
what we call prehistoric times.

In those times, our ancestors were mostly wanderers on the
face of the earth. Some had learned to garden and raise crops
but others had not. Famine was always at their heels. They had
to be constantly on the move in search of the wild beasts from
which they took their food and clothing. Stone-tipped spears,
bows and arrows, and crude axes were the weapons with which
they fought for their livelihood in the primeval forest.

Somehow, in some way, ancient man captured animals. Perhaps
he started with those that haunted the outskirts of his camp,
waiting to feed on his leavings. He tamed them, fed them and
bred them. Little by little, this new practice of his worked a
tremendous revolution in his way of life. Flocks and herds meant
a sure supply of flesh for food and pelts for clothing. With these

things and garden crops, he could settle down at last and make permanent towns and villages. Civilization, long postponed by the never-ending quest for enough to eat, could at last begin.

Man has not been satisfied merely to raise animals as he found them in nature. He has carefully selected and mated stocks, developing in his animals the qualities that serve him best. He has bred meat animals that give more meat, fur bearers that give more fur. He has created different varieties of dogs—over three hundred are known today— for practically every conceivable purpose. Still, if he lets some of his animals go—cats, for example— in a few generations they become wild creatures again.

There is plenty of food for thought and talk when you take your children on a family excursion to a farm and see domestic animals in their proper setting, or encounter a cat, a dog, or a horse on city streets. Today they are our friends and helpers. We take them completely for granted. But in a distant yesterday, they were prowlers and fighters whose conquest was one of the greatest victories of all time.

Dogs

Dogs are "sniffers." They depend on their sense of smell much more than on the other senses, and with good reason. The soft damp skin that covers the dog's nose carries all scents to the wide nostrils, which can be lifted in any direction. The upper sides are slitted. This enables the nostrils to quiver, making them even more sensitive to odors.

You will notice that a dog investigates strangers by sniffing. If the scent he detects has pleasant associations, he accepts the stranger as a friend. On the other hand, the dog may immediately turn hostile if the scent is distasteful—that is, if it suggests a person who has been unkind, or perhaps the odor of another dog.

A dog will frequently rely on his nose where another creature would use its eyes. If he loses something—a bone, say, or a toy— he does not look for it; he sniffs until he locates it. A foxhound stays on the trail of a fox for many miles, guided by a scent which may be several hours old. This ability has been put to good use in several breeds. An outstanding example is the bloodhound, which does an extraordinary job of tracking down lost or straying people when all other means have failed.

Your youngster will be better equipped to take care of his pet if he is aware that the nose is an index of well-being. When the nose of a dog—or of any other moist-nosed animal—becomes dry, it is a sure indication of illness.

KEEN EYES AND EARS

We admire a dog's eyes as "beautifully soft" or "soulful" rather than "keen." The fact is, though, that dogs are sharp-sighted, despite their reliance on their sense of smell when it comes to locating misplaced articles. Dogs even see fairly well in the dark, though probably inferior to cats in this respect. We have an interesting contrast in breeds in the hunting dog, which stays on an old or recent trail guided solely by scent, and the greyhound, swiftest of all large dogs, which hunts by sight.

In most dogs the iris is a rich brown—though puppies usually have blue eyes—and the pupil, as in human eyes, is round.

There is a considerable range of difference in the shape and appearance of the outer ears of dogs. This might lead us to expect a great deal of variation in hearing ability. Actually, however, most breeds of dogs enjoy an acute sense of hearing. Whether the animal has long or short earflaps, the act of "pricking up his ears" is typical of an alert dog. As the hound lifts his long ears they form tubes, thereby bringing sound more effectively to the inner ear.

DOGS ARE GOOD RUNNERS

Most dogs are strong runners, although running ability varies quite a bit from one breed to another. Dogs have long muscular legs and when they are running their lithe bodies extend full length. The feet are adapted for running, as they are protected by thick fleshy pads. Another aid in running is the fact that the dog's claws do not draw in as the cat's do; this gives the feet additional protection.

The legs and feet of dogs and cats have interestingly contrasted qualities, for the cat is a jumper rather than a runner. The cat's legs are delicate, but its hips are very powerful. These factors, plus the lightness of its foot pads, make it an admirable jumper. But the cat's claws, excellent though they are for grasping and fighting, are pulled in and thus afford no protection to running feet.

DOGS HAVE HEARTY APPETITES

Nowadays we generally feed our dog pets daintily with bits of food cut up in approved civilized fashion; but they are still capable of gulping down large chunks. A friend of mine who takes his dog with him on hunting trips has learned to be alert in picking up a rabbit after the kill; on several occasions the hound arrived first and swallowed the rabbit whole! Not only can dogs swallow in bulk; they digest the food without any trouble.

Your child may point to the dog as an example of why *he* need not chew his food. In that case you can explain the interesting difference in the shape of the teeth which drastically alters the case. Where we have molar teeth fitted for grinding (and hence chewing), the dog has molars that are more suited for cutting. Watch him work on a bone, gnawing first with the back teeth on one side and then on the other. His canine teeth, like those of the wolf, are his chief weapons.

HOW DOGS TALK

A dog has feelings of affection, anger, fear, jealousy, sorrow, and joy; he can express all of them by his voice. He whines when he is afraid, growls when angry, and sometimes yips for sheer joy. His bark is expressive of defiance or excitement. He has still another medium of expression in his tail: It wags when he is happy and wants to express friendliness, stands stiff when he is angry, and droops between his legs when he is dejected or ashamed. Sometimes in the theater you see "talking dogs"—animals that have been taught to answer questions with barks that approximate responses. Actually any intelligent dog needs little training before you can say of him, "He all but talks."

WHEN A CHILD FEARS DOGS

Parents who are dog enthusiasts are often disconcerted to find that their children fear these animals. Experiments tend to prove that a child's timidity with animals is explained by some prior unpleasant encounter, or by his associating an animal with some frightening experience—possibly entirely unrelated to the animal. At the same time I cannot help also crediting a very simple theory—that the generally unpredictable actions of dogs and their sudden movements are enough to make some youngsters wary and hence distrustful of them. There is also the matter of size: To a toddler, even a spaniel must appear as large as a lion does to an adult.

As a very young explorer in the world my son had a caution toward dogs and cats that might have been interpreted as fear. We had no hint of any plausible reason for his attitude, but we never ridiculed or lectured him about it. We did give him every opportunity to see that we considered these animals good friends, and by the time he was five he wanted nothing so much as a dog of his own.

Some people believe that a dog, through its sense of smell, or some instinct, knows whether a person is afraid of him; and that the animal has one attitude toward a brave soul, another toward a timid one. Presenting a bold front is undoubtedly the best approach when dealing with a strange or unfriendly dog—all the more so as there is evidence to indicate that an animal cannot detect well-concealed fear.

A doctor of circus animals once confessed that throughout his career he had to struggle with actual terror whenever called upon to treat a sick tiger or leopard or other creature capable of great violence. Luckily he was able to mask his fear by keeping his voice stern and his actions incisive. In this way he remained master of the situation. But, the doctor added, if animals had any way of "sensing" fear in a human being, he would surely have been found out, and his career ended before it had fairly started.

THE WILD STRAIN IN OUR DOGS

There is a widespread belief that the wolf was the dog's ancestor, but we now know that this theory is only partially correct. Dogs and wolves may have had a common ancestor some fifteen million years ago, and scientists believe that the four earliest breeds of dogs probably developed from this animal.

We can clearly trace some of the modern dog's outstanding traits to its wild ancestors. When a dog gives chase, he usually barks—a throwback to the wild pack that barked or bayed to keep together while hunting. Similarly, the modern dog's habit of turning around a number of times before lying down makes no sense to us, but he owes this characteristic to his distant ancestors—it was the way they made themselves a comfortable place for lying down in brush, grass, or reeds. Your dog gains nothing by such actions in a modern home, but he repeats them instinctively just the same. Sometimes when a dog is gazing at the moon or when he hears music he will emit a series of mournful howls. This too may be a reversion to the past—to the time when the "pack" was called together, perhaps to hunt by moonlight.

How Man Tamed the Dog

The friendly association of human beings and dogs goes back through countless ages. It must have started in some such way as this: In the course of their hunting excursions the early cave dwellers found litters of puppies and brought back the appealing creatures to their primitive homes. The puppies did not grow up wild like their parents—for they were fed and sheltered by people, and in return defended their cave from enemies. The cave was their home, the humans were their masters.

Primitive man could not fail to appreciate the dog's keen senses of smell and sight: He could take the animal on hunting trips to uncover game where he himself might not suspect it existed.

As the centuries passed, men gradually changed their way of living. A crude cave was no longer a good home, and hunting was no longer the only means of supplying food for the family. Yet the desire to keep a dog in the household did not change. All over the world they had become established as friends and helpers, and were bred for all sorts of special purposes.

The ancient Greeks bred dogs small enough to sit comfortably in ladies' laps—with a view to keeping the owner's stomach warm!

In England there was a need for quite a different kind of dog. Almost a thousand years ago a breed was developed there with a retreating nose, an undershot jaw, and menacing teeth. It was to become known as the bulldog, for its special purpose was to fight bulls—a ferocious sport that enjoyed great popularity for hundreds of years. The peculiar formation of the bulldog's snout enabled him to breathe easily while biting and gripping a bull.

The Scottish terrier is another good example of special breeding. Its shaggy eyebrows evolved from breeders' efforts to provide these small hunting dogs with protection against dirt as they dug into fox holes and carried out other hunting chores.

Even dog styles had a practical purpose at the time of their origin. Poodles, used as retrievers, had wool left on their chest to protect them against cold while the flanks were shaved to streamline them for swimming. Ear-cropping became the fashion in the eighteenth century to guard the floppy ears of hunting dogs against being torn in the underbrush.

Today, in our highly mechanical age, dogs are still being bred and trained for specific purposes, performing tasks which no machines have been able to take over. One of the most interesting ways to study the specialized dog breeds is to read stories about dogs. Fortunately there is an abundance of them that you can read together with your child, who will be delighted with them. Aside from the ageless classics, good adventure tales about dogs are constantly being written.

THE ST. BERNARD

In his *Book of Famous Dogs,* Albert Payson Terhune gives a touching description of Barry, a St. Bernard that rescued as many as forty travelers from death in the snow during the first ten years of his life.

Until a great tunnel was cut through the Alps in relatively recent times, travelers had to make their way on foot over the snow-clad mountain slopes. Frequently they lost their way or were overtaken by a blizzard. The rescue of such unfortunates presented a baffling problem, especially to the monks of the monastery of St. Bernard situated at the crest of the mountain pass. We can only guess at how much these good men of nearly a thousand years ago understood of "natural history," but we do know that they solved the problem effectively.

What they did was to secure strong, oversized yellowish dogs (whose ancestors may have come from Central Asia), and to breed them carefully for many generations. This resulted in the breed we know as the St. Bernard. Not only are St. Bernards still used in Europe to find people lost in the snow and bring them aid; these dogs are beloved pets in many homes of our own country. Their gentle and benign character makes them perfect companions for children.

SEEING EYE DOGS

In almost any city or town in America you may chance to see a remarkable man-and-dog-team walking along quickly and confidently. Before you are fully aware of the implications, the boy or girl with you may exclaim:

"There's a Seeing Eye dog!"

It seems incredible that up to the last few decades there were no Seeing Eye dogs. And there might still be none if not for the extraordinary pioneering work of Dorothy Eustis a generation ago. Mrs. Eustis happened to own a particularly wise and faithful German shepherd dog. The animal's joy in serving his mistress started her on a long road of research, breeding, and training to develop superservice dogs.

After establishing a school that graduated dogs thoroughly trained to work with policemen, help patrol penitentiaries, and aid in war maneuvers, Mrs. Eustis carried on a work that had already been started in Germany—educating dogs to be the "eyes" of blind people. Her pioneering eventually led to the establishment of The Seeing Eye organization.

THE GERMAN SHEPHERD

The chances are that the Seeing Eye dog you will encounter on your walk is a German shepherd. Your young companion is likely to inquire, "Are shepherds *always* used for Seeing Eye dogs?"

As a matter of fact they are not—though it is true that most of the dogs graduated by The Seeing Eye are shepherds. The ability not only to assimilate education but to use *reasoning power* as well is inherent to some degree in most shepherds. Other breeds may respond brilliantly to training, but there is a difference.

The French poodle, for example, one of the outstandingly intelligent dogs, has a keen memory and is remarkably quick. The poodle could learn the routine of guiding a blind person in considerably shorter time than it takes the German shepherd. But the poodle would then probably carry out any command given by his master, regardless of consequences. The shepherd, on the other hand, makes his own decision—to hold back if a "forward" command means trouble.

How Seeing Eye Dogs Are Trained: Another almost inevitable question is, "How are the dogs taught to do their work?" This query is constantly being put to the members of The Seeing Eye staff. A complete answer would literally fill volumes, but we can get some idea of the thoroughness of the program from a knowledge of the work and study required to become a teacher in the organization.

The apprenticeship is a lengthy one. First the newcomer must spend several months working as a kennel assistant, feeding and cleaning the dogs and turning them out to exercise. Only then is he ready to start primary work in obedience training. He studies voice culture in order to learn the best inflections to use in speaking to the dogs; he learns hand and body movements that supplement spoken commands in the early training stages.

Only after the student teacher has mastered the technique of command does he start actual work with dogs—some of them partly trained, others completely undisciplined. His next step is to experience the actual sensations of a sightless person: For a month he constantly wears a lightproof shield over his eyes. He is then ready to work with human pupils.

A blind person who is eligible for a dog-guide must live at the headquarters of The Seeing Eye in Morristown, New Jersey, during the period of training with the dog that is to become his guide.

As for the training of the dogs, members of The Seeing Eye staff will tell you that their method stresses kindness. The principle is sound for training any kind of dog; for kindness and patience are the basic ingredients that spell success with a German shepherd pup just as much as with your faithful old Rover.

Dogs in the Home

With more than a hundred breeds to choose from, the wise parent will give careful consideration to the type that is best for his household. In all fairness to yourself, your child, and the pet, you want to select an animal that you can take care of properly without overtaxing your time, purse, or housing accommodations.

Training a dog pet can be a fascinating project. There is much in the training of dogs that duplicates the upbringing of a child! Good health is important: A tired, nervous creature will not respond to the best trainer. Patience, consistent rules and actions, determination—all these are essential to successful training. Like a child, the dog does his best for someone who understands him and whom he likes.

The age of a dog is less important than we are led to believe by the saying, "You can't teach an old dog new tricks." Nine-year-old dogs have been taught tricks and even trained as dependable hunting companions. It is true, however, that the earlier training is begun, the easier it is likely to be.

Cats

Most children love cats, and they recite the nursery rhyme "I love little pussy" with genuine feeling. But as they grow older, they find that their feline companions have many critics and even enemies. Some people feel that cats should be done away with because, given a chance, they kill birds. Others, who doubtless have in mind abandoned "strays" that try to make a living from garbage cans, claim that cats are dirty animals. Another charge is that cats are incapable of loyalty and affection.

But cats have their defenders as well—many people champion them with fiery zeal. And, as they can prove, cats are devoted to their masters if they are treated kindly. They also render valuable service in preying on the rats and mice that must be kept in check. And cats are wonderfully adaptable; if they have to, they can live by their wits in the manner of jungle beasts, though they can be kept happy and healthy in a city apartment.

SEEING IN THE DARK

The ability of cats to see well in the dark long ago gave them a touch of the macabre: People came to associate them with the nighttime activities of witches and hobgoblins, particularly on Halloween. Because of this reputation, children are especially interested to know just how cats' eyes function.

Back of the eye is a reflecting surface which catches and reflects any available bit of light. The resulting glow enables the cat to see in situations where our eyes are inadequate. The startling green glare given off by a cat's eyes is due to this reflection, its eye being almost completely covered by the pupil. During the day the pupil is narrowed down to a mere slit. In adult cats the iris is usually yellow; in kittens it may be blue or green.

SENSITIVE FEELERS

Cats, like dogs, have moist noses, and their senses of smell and hearing are keen. The hairs in a cat's ears, far from being obstructions, are sensitive aids in catching sounds. Cats can detect vibrations beyond the range of the human ear. They are often critical of musical performances, removing themselves as far as possible from shrill radio music or singing practice in the home.

The hairs on a cat's face—its whiskers—are also valuable as "feelers." A set of whiskers contains between twenty-five and thirty hairs. If you look at them closely, you will note that they are set in four lines above and at the sides of the mouth, where they are connected to sensitive nerves. Feelers are useful to hunters, especially night hunters, as Pussy is when in its natural state; the hairs supply information about the underbrush or other terrain through which the animal is moving.

THE CAT AS A HUNTER

Stalking and pouncing on prey come as naturally to a cat as breathing. Where the dog uses sheer power and speed, the cat resorts to stealth and cunning. Having discovered the haunts of a possible victim, the cat crouches motionless until the right instant to spring. The weight of the marauder's body knocks down the rabbit, mouse, or other victim—which the cat then seizes with its sharp hooked claws and its strong canine teeth to make the kill.

If you look into Pussy's mouth you can see the equipment of a real prowler of the jungle. There are two big sharp tushes in each jaw. Its molars are sharp-edged wedges, perfectly adapted for cutting up meat. Its tongue is so rough it can rasp juices from meat.

Under the conditions of modern civilization cats are often expected to be split personalities: alert hunters ready to pounce on any rodent that shows itself, and at the same time restrained and even friendly neighbors to all birds, tame or wild. Actually cats are intelligent enough to refrain from molesting birds if they are properly trained toward that end while still young. The most successful training method seems to be that of association— creating situations where the cat can observe its mistress or master being friendly with birds and expecting the cat to help in protecting them. Punishment as a means of curing bird-hunting cats is usually quite unsuccessful.

Cats are Model Mothers

It is a rare cat mother that shirks her responsibility to her kittens. As a rule, even before they are born she shows her solicitude by looking for a dark secluded spot for their entrance into the world—just as in the primitive state a cat sought a dark cave for the event. Though kittens are active almost immediately after birth, they do not start to open their eyes until after five days or so. Within ten days the eyes are fully open.

Meanwhile the mother nurses the kittens and industriously washes them from nose-tip to tail with her rough tongue. She allows them to romp and play boisterously—even to the extent of frolicking over and around her; but if they go too far she will box their ears soundly.

When they are older she gives them lessons in hunting, if circumstances permit, showing all the tricks at her command for catching mice and other prey. She will even instruct them in the fine art of backing down a tree trunk—an important accomplishment for a cat. Instinct prompts cats to climb, but many a cat that has had no coaching may reach the top of a tree and then be too terrified to descend. Often a fire company or the S.P.C.A. must come to the rescue!

CHILDREN AND CATS

When a cat—and this is even truer of a kitten—is brought into the home, training is usually desirable in more than one respect. Not only must we teach the little animal how to fit into the family program; we also need to instruct the children of the family how to handle and treat their pet.

A frightened cat or one that has been excited or angered by teasing, may inflict serious scratches on a child. It is not difficult to teach even a small child to pick up a cat properly—by approaching it from the back or side and placing one arm under the cat's forelegs and the other around its body underneath the abdomen. The best way to pick up a little kitten is by placing your hand under its body. Grasping the scruff of its neck will not hurt a cat, but it is not a sensation that the animal enjoys; it is best to resort to it only for disciplinary reasons.

CAT LANGUAGE

Children will quickly learn something of the cat's own language: the happy purr, the soft mew of contentment, the begging meow of hunger, the frightened yowl, the shrill battle cry when the cat is involved in a fight. The cat's body is just as expressive as its voice. A lashing tail (in contrast to a dog's happy wag) is a sign of angry excitement. At such times the cat's ears lie back—and if it is badly frightened, its hair stands on end over its entire body and tail.

WHERE CATS CAME FROM

Though we can trace back the cat family millions of years to prehistoric times, there is much about the ancestry of domestic cats that remains a mystery. Many conflicting theories have been advanced from time to time regarding their origin.

The striped tabby pattern is a strong indication that the forebear of our pets of today was either the European wildcat or the African wildcat, for both of these species have a striped pattern.

But which of the two was the original ancestor is a question that has been hotly debated. The most generally held opinion favors the African or Kaffir cat, which was tamed by the ancient Egyptians. For centuries the domestic short-hair cats have mated haphazardly, and as a result there is more variation in their size and form than in any other breeds.

PERSIAN CATS

The Persian, or long-hair, cat is generally believed to have originated somewhere in East Asia. Though its long silky coat and fluffy tail give the Persian infinite grace, it is not so lithe in build as the short-hair cats. Its body and legs are both short and compact. "Refined" seems the most suitable adjective for the Persian. It is characteristically unaggressive, lofty in its bearing, and has a soft, well-modulated voice.

SIAMESE CATS

The Siamese cat is a comparative newcomer to America, the first of the breed having been imported from England little more than fifty years ago. Only a few years before that a famous pair named Pho and Mia were first brought to England from Siam. The Siamese cat is distinguished by its form—its hind legs, being longer than the front ones, give the body a slight tilt upward from the shoulder to pelvis, and its head is long and wedge-shaped with a flat forehead.

The Siamese cat also has a peculiar coloration, which varies with three distinctive types. The seal point Siamese has cream or fawn-colored body fur, with face, ears, legs, and tail a seal brown. Its slanted eyes are a deep sapphire blue. In the blue point Siamese, the body color may be cream or pale blue with the points (or markings) a deeper blue. As for the chocolate Siamese, it has a deeper body tone and rich brown markings.

The acrobatic ability of Siamese cats, combined with their great mischievousness, gave rise to the legend that their ancestry was part monkey. The legend is completely fanciful, but it is amusing to recall it as you watch a Siamese climbing, leaping, twisting its tail and in general performing "monkeyshines."

THE MANX

One of the oddities of animal life is the Manx—a cat without a tail! This breed, whose ancestors hailed from the Isle of Man in the Irish Sea, has a particularly mild and trusting nature and as a pet is especially easy to train and manage.

Pet Shows and Pictures

Once your children are interested in the different breeds of cats and dogs, attending a pet show becomes a worthwhile family excursion. At such an exhibit you can see fine specimens of many breeds and observe the fascinating results of specialized training. If you live in a neighborhood where a number of children own dogs and cats, it is possible to stage a strictly home-style pet show guaranteed to provide fun as well as an added incentive for the young masters and mistresses to have their pets well groomed and trained.

Making a cat or dog picture album is an activity anyone can enjoy. It is fun to watch the magazines for suitable pictures, and even the youngest member of the family can join in the game. The resulting album can be either extremely simple or else elaborate, depending on the amount of time you can give as adviser to the "art and production department."

Horses

If there was ever the possibility of a waning of interest in horses in this machine age of ours, that prospect vanished when television brought Western movies with their hard-riding cowboys into the home. Life on a ranch with horses became the dream of countless city-dwelling girls and boys, and children who had the opportunity to ride felt a new appreciation of that privilege.

Fortunately it is not necessary to live on a ranch to have a personal acquaintance with horses. There are numerous farms where we may see different breeds of horses, and rodeos and horse shows are held throughout the country. In some cities there are the magnificent steeds of mounted police, as well as riding horses in the parks. In at least a few communities, the plodding horse of the milkman still survives.

Horseback Riding

A resident of a large city had a young daughter who regularly "galloped' rather than walked along the street. This was a real worry to her parents, as the girl had a heart condition which ruled out strenuous activity. After many attempts to dissuade her, her mother happened to ask *why* she galloped. Her daughter's answer was a matter-of-fact "I'm riding my horse." Mother and doctor then got together on the happy solution of providing limited riding lessons which actually benefited the girl's health.

When a boy or girl is given an opportunity to ride, an understanding of the background of the horse is genuinely valuable; for some of the animal's qualities and reactions are easily traceable to its wild ancestors. When startled, a horse shies in the way a wild horse would from a suddenly discovered enemy. The wise rider, therefore, speaks in a confident and encouraging voice to his shying horse instead of scolding or hitting him.

When a horse lays his ears flat back, it is a warning that he is angry. The ears may also be an indication of a horse's character. The horse with ears drooped or turned back is likely to be treacherous, whereas quick-moving ears are a sign of a particularly sensitive nature. A good horse has ears pointed upward or forward. He also has a broad space between the eyes, and his head is high between the ears.

A Horse's Teeth Tell Its Age

The child who feeds a horse discovers that it is wise to offer lumps of sugar in an open palm rather than grasped in his finger tips. A horse can crop grass even more closely than a cow, thanks to his large incisor teeth. These teeth might easily nip the fingers with the sugar.

It is by these incisors that an experienced horseman can estimate the age of a horse. As the teeth develop, annual growth rings are formed in them. (The effect is somewhat like that of growth rings in a tree trunk.) As the teeth wear with age, these rings become clearly visible. The time-honored warning not to look a gift horse in the mouth is based on this revelation of the animal's age by the state of its teeth.

Behind the incisors is a bare space which allows for the placing of a bit, and behind this are six molars on each side of each jaw. When a male horse is about three years old, canine teeth appear behind the incisors—four in all. In a mare these canines are generally small or completely missing.

How Horses Run

Would-be cowboys and cowgirls thrill to the pounding of hoofs as horses gallop across the plains. They may notice that during a gallop the horse is completely off the ground for a moment after each spring forward. The animal makes each spring from one of his fore feet and lands on the hind foot of the opposite side of his body. Just before this "pair" of feet touches the earth the other two are coming up again, so that the body is in the air with all legs bent beneath.

When a horse is walking, two or more of his feet are always on the ground. The order of their progression is right hind foot, right fore foot, left hind foot, left fore foot. In a canter the same rotation of feet is used, but the motion is of course much more rapid. When the horse trots, each diagonal pair of legs is alternately raised and put forward.

The Horse's Wild Relatives

A well-groomed horse is sleek, glossy, and thoroughly "civilized" in appearance, but an animal that has been running in the pasture all winter long presents a very different picture. Like all wild horses, which grow a thick covering of hair during cold weather, he has a shaggy coat. They shed this hair in the springtime.

Wild horses still exist in limited numbers. These include the so-called tarpans of Mongolia and Central Asia, which, though smaller than domesticated horses, are strong and of stocky build.

There are still herds of half-wild horses on our western prairies— descendants from horses brought to Mexico by Cortez and to Florida by De Soto. Some of these imports from Spain strayed from their masters and roamed far and wide over the new continent. Eventually members of the two groups met and mated, and before long thousands of unbridled horses added a colorful

note to the American scene. Comparatively few survive in the
wild state today; and of this remnant, many are captured by
ranch owners, branded, and then released. We generally speak
of these animals as "mustangs."

As for "broncho," this is not a name for a special breed, but
rather a generic term applied to any wild American horse that
is captured and trained for man's use. Today's bronchos are
usually born of domesticated horses, then turned loose and
allowed to run wild until they reach the age of usefulness.

The African zebras, members of the horse family, have resisted
all attempts to domesticate them. By way of contrast Shetland
ponies, which still run wild on Shetland and other islands about a
hundred miles north of Scotland, are valuable pack animals and
trustworthy pets.

Where Horses Came From

The distribution of horses in the modern world follows a
long history of wanderings and migrations. The family started
in North America with the "Dawn Horse"—the original ancestor.
This was a creature about the size of a fox, with several toes on
each foot. Over a long period of time gradual changes took place
in later ancestral horses, notably in the lengthening of the legs
and the steady enlargement and greater specialization of the
middle toe. At the same time the other toes grew smaller and
smaller, finally vanishing and being replaced by the enormously
enlarged middle toe, which had taken on the proportions of the
hoof as we know it today.

Even before the Ice Age, some of the ancestral horses had been
leaving North America for other continents, and the true horse
of the Ice Age migrated also. Then, while the branches that had
gone to Asia, Europe and Africa flourished, the original North
American family died out. Thus there were no horses on the
North Amecian continent until the Spanish explorers brought
them back.

Thoroughbreds and Other Popular Breeds

Even when many groups of horses still lived in the wild
state, men in diverse lands were busy breeding the animals for

specialized uses. To these efforts we owe such breeds as the German coach horse, the Belgian saddle horse, the American saddle
horse. Especially notable breeds were developed in England,
among them the thoroughbred, which became so famous as a
horse of high quality that people began to use the term incorrectly, saying "thoroughbred" when they meant "purebred." (A
purebred animal is one which has known and recorded ancestry
and represents but one breed.)

Thoroughbreds excel in running, and the finest race horses
are of this breed. All our thoroughbreds nowadays are descended
from three horses brought to England more than two hundred
years ago—two of them Arabian steeds, the remaining one
Turkish.

Arabian Horses: Originally Arabian horses were creatures of the
desert and, as such, needed little food and water. So great was
the dependence of the Arabs hundreds of year ago on their
horses that they bred the animals with great care, raised them
virtually as members of the family, and trained them like children. The result after several generations was one of the most
remarkable triumphs of domestication—a truly great breed, outstanding in appearance, intelligence and performance. Not the
least value of the Arabian horse lies in its contribution to new
breeds—the thoroughbred, for example.

THE HUMBLE DONKEY AND MULE

Children know donkeys as amusingly stubborn creatures.
Though these relatives of the horse often do display rather difficult temperament, they are valuable as beasts of burden in arid
regions, and for the breeding of mules (a mule being the offspring of a male donkey and a mare.) Donkeys are descended
from wild asses which were tamed and used in Egypt before the
horse became domesticated. In its size, short hair and other less
noticeable features, an ass bears a closer resemblance to the zebra
than to the horse. It even has a tendency to show stripes on the
legs.

Mules are larger than donkeys, and shaped more like horses.
Still, with their long ears, small hoofs, and large heads, they rather

resemble donkeys. They are also considered valuable as pack animals, being noted for their sureness of foot and their great powers of endurance. As a rule, they cannot reproduce their kind.

Cattle

About the first thing a toddler learns about cattle is that "cows say moo," and that cows give milk. The cow thereupon becomes an impressive figure, milk being the most important and most frequent item in a child's diet. Even a child of five is more likely than not to tell you gravely that "milk gives vitamins." His older brother is interested in cows too—but mainly because they are the pawns in our televised folklore of ranchers and rustlers.

Cows for Milk

Man has developed all the varieties of domesticated cattle from wild species of Asia and Europe. It took many generations of selective breeding to achieve such marvels as the Holstein cow, which can produce its weight in milk in two weeks, and the Jersey, which gives more than five thousand pounds of rich milk in a year! Other noted dairy breeds are the Guernsey, Ayrshire, and brown Swiss cows.

There are certain features by which you can recognize a good milch cow. These include: the head high between the eyes, which should be clear, large, and placid; a large mouth with a muscular lower jaw; a deep wide chest, hips much broader than the shoulders, and a large, well-supported abdomen. As you would expect, the udder should be large and its four quarters of equal size.

Cattle for Beef

Aside from the cattle bred for milk production there are the breeds designed as beef factories. Among the best known of these are the Hereford, Aberdeen-Angus, Galloway, and Short-horn. You can see many contrasts between them and the milch cows. The beef cattle are big and full across the back and have thick, short necks. (You will notice that the milch cow has a thin, fine neck.) The shape of the body is markedly different in these groups: The milch cow's body is oval and the outline of her body sags in front of the hips, whereas the meat animal tends more to a square-shaped body and its back is straight from neck to tail.

How Milk is Produced

Most city children do not get to see cows very often, so it is not surprising that they develop some strange notions about how cows give milk. For one thing, the supply of milk seems as constant as water flowing from a tap. Another misconception has turned up since the homogenizing process became widespread; many children believe that milk is originally produced in that state. And I am probably not the only one who has heard a small child wondering what kind of cows give *chocolate* milk!

Despite the way in which man has disrupted the animal's natural processes, a cow still produces milk as nourishment for her own offspring. Her supply of milk is of course most abundant soon after a calf is born. Under normal conditions she would go dry as soon as the young one could turn to other feeds, but a domestic cow that is milked continuously may give milk for almost a year. The quantity decreases, however, after six to eight months, and the cow must be bred again to renew the milk supply. A wise dairyman does not expect cows to produce constantly, and gives them a rest of at least six weeks every year.

How Cows Eat

If your child watches a horse and cow grazing, he may observe as he looks on that the horse is pulling his head in whereas the cow is pushing her head forward. These distinctive eating habits are no accident; they are determined by each animal's mouth and teeth formations.

A cow has eight front teeth on her lower jaw, with only a horny pad above them. While grazing, she runs her tongue out, seizes a clump of grass, and closes her upper lip tightly over it. A forward thrust of her head then causes the teeth below to cut or tear the grass from its roots. Thus she always eats "away from herself."

The horse cannot gather grass with his tongue, but he can use his flexible upper lip to grasp it. He has both upper and lower teeth and, taking the grass between these two rows, he cuts it by pulling his head back. Thus a horse always eats "toward himself."

There is another striking difference in the eating habits of horses and cows. A horse chews as it grazes. The cow uses a different technique, due to the fact that instead of one stomach, she has four! She swallows the grass exactly as it is cut, and the unchewed food goes directly into her first stomach. Later the food progresses to the second stomach, where it is formed into cud balls in a convenient size for chewing. When the cow lies down, this food is brought back to the mouth. She chews her cud contentedly with her grinding teeth until it is ready to be swallowed. It then passes to her third and fourth stomachs, where it is digested.

Mammals equipped to eat in this fashion are known as "ruminants." They include sheep, deer, antelope, and camels. In the wild state, the ruminants' technique is a definite protection, for they can graze rapidly in the open (where flesh-eating beasts might prey upon them), and then retire to a sheltered area to continue their meal in comparative safety.

How Cattle Express Themselves

Though their domestication goes back through countless generations, cattle still reveal traces of their wild ancestry. Their vocal expressions are akin to those of cattle still living in the wild state. The bull gives a sullen roar when he is angry. The cow moos gently to her calf, and the lowing sound so characteristic of late afternoon in dairy farm country is the call of the herd—the call which kept members of a group together when they were in the natural state.

Though the adult cow gives the impression of being the most phlegmatic of creatures, few animals are more frolicsome than a calf. Even cows sometimes forget their dignity, kicking up their heels exuberantly as the tail is held aloft. In bulls the instinct for battle is still strong. Those living in the wild state use their vicious horns not so much against other animals as against rival bulls that attempt to displace them as master of a harem.

GOOD HEARERS AND SMELLERS

Cattle have a keen sense of hearing, benefiting from the fact that they can turn their ears in any direction. Their sense of smell is also excellent: The moist, sensitive nose is equally well adapted for picking up the scent of an enemy or deciding if food is properly edible.

TAIL-SWITCHING

As the cow is such an emphatic tail switcher, an observer might read into the action those meanings which apply to the tail movements of a dog or cat. However, the tail has nothing to do with a cow's emotions; it is an efficient fly-brush and swatter, and without it a cow would be miserably at the mercy of these ubiquitous insects.

Goats—They Don't Eat Cans

Children are usually amused as well as impressed by the fact that goats will eat anything, but one young girl I know was more impressed than amused. Lying on the grass reading one fine afternoon, she was so absorbed in her story that she paid no attention to a gentle tugging at her braided hair. Suddenly she realized that a goat was thoughtfully chewing one of the braids!

This seemingly fantastic willingness to "try anything once" in the way of food begins to make more sense when a child realizes that in the wild state goats must subsist on the most meager resources. As moss, lichens, and bits of vegetation are the best fare to be found high on the rocky mountain slopes where goats live, it is hardly surprising that they are not very "choosy" about what they introduce to their digestive systems. There is a popular fallacy that goats eat tin cans. What they really enjoy eating is the glue from the paper labels on the cans.

GOATS ARE USEFUL ANIMALS

By means of selective breeding, man has developed goats to serve him in more ways than one. He uses the Angora and Cashmere for their hair, which is woven into very fine fabrics. Another type, the short-hair goat, yields a good meat supply, and still another group is valued for its milk.

These three kinds of goats have served people all over the world, and today milk goats are found in every part of the United States. Many belong to commercial dairies, but probably half of our goat population is made up of "back yard" residents. A great point in their favor is that they can eke out an existence even when the food supply is at its scantiest.

Goat milk is superior to cow's milk for two reasons: Goat milk is digested more quickly and completely, and it is safe without pasteurization. Its taste, slightly different from that of cow's milk, is preferred by some people but is displeasing to others. Goats do not get tuberculosis and they are as nearly disease-free as any domestic animal.

A goat becomes an affectionate pet if it is well treated. When a goat is angry, it shows its feelings by shaking its head. It defends itself by butting with its head and striking an adversary with its sharp horns.

Sheep—They Came Down from Mountains

Like goats, sheep are mountain animals. Even when they are domesticated they thrive best in cool dry surroundings. In the wild state they lived in less rugged localities than mountain goats do, but on the other hand sheep were able to subsist on pasturage that was too thin for cattle.

The sheep's great wool coat, originally developed as a protection against cold, has been particularly exploited in the Merino breed of Spain which produces exceptionally fine wool. In England, where mutton is a staple food, such breeds as the Dorset and Shropshire are valued for their flesh, although their wool is also used to good advantage.

OBEDIENCE SAVES THE SHEEP

Most children are familiar with the figure of speech that puts people blindly following a leader on the same level with "a lot of sheep." This scornful phrase implies that the unquestioning obedience indicates a lack of intelligence; yet in the case of sheep the instinct for following has often saved their lives.

MARY AND HER LAMB HAVE A BLEATING CONTEST

One delightful nature hobby that not enough people have discovered is taking out-of-door pictures. Animals and children are natural subjects. But so, too, are trees and flowers in bloom, a winter landscape, or brooks breaking open in the spring.

"SMILE INTO THE CAMERA, PLEASE"

Children can begin a fascinating lifetime hobby with a camera. A visit to a zoo or a farm provides exciting opportunities for the young photographer. Later, birds and other wildlife—in their natural haunts—are fine game for the picture hunter.

David W. Corson from A. Devaney, I'

PUPPY LOVE, STRICTLY SPEAKING

A cat and a dog can become fond of each other if they live together and neither is made to feel the less favored. A cat can also be trained to treat birds as friends.

When sheep lived in the wild state, they gathered habitually in flocks to feed, with a sentinel always on guard. When this leader spied an approaching enemy or picked up his scent, he signaled with a bleat of alarm, then started off with the whole flock immediately at his heels. Over difficult terrain, leaping from precipices when necessary, leader and flock made their way until they reached a safe retreat.

The bleating sound for which sheep are noted is their means of keeping in touch with each other. In time of danger they are silent; but they have a special bleat when they catch sight of an enemy and another one when they come upon water.

Sheep have keen senses. Their large ears move alertly toward the direction of any sound. They can pick up the faintest scent. Their excellent eyes alter according to the light conditions. In sunshine the eye is just a narrow slit, showing a yellowish or brownish iris; in a dim light the pupil grows larger until it absorbs practically the whole eye.

How Sheep Feed

The teeth of sheep and goats are alike. There are six rear grinding teeth on each side of the upper and lower jaws, and eight incisors on the lower but none on the upper. Thus equipped, sheep can crop short grass close to its roots. Because the close cropping by sheep may ruin pasture and because sheep droppings render grass obnoxious to cattle, sheep herders and cattlemen have had bitter conflicts. In any event, sheep and goats manage to be well fed where cattle might starve. Man probably could not invent a more efficient self-powered lawn mower!

Pigs—Smarter Than You Think

"*Dirty* pig!" exclaims the tot just learning the names of animals.

It is a pity that pigs' habits are so generally misunderstood, for actually they are rated with the most intelligent, valuable, and interesting of domesticated mammals. The notion that they enjoy filthy surroundings is largely the consequence of man's carelessness in keeping them.

The truth is that a pig will keep its own bed clean and neat under the most discouraging conditions. The wild hogs of India, for example, make themselves quite respectable nests which resemble grass huts—thatched on top and with openings at the side.

The fact that pigs like to wallow in mud is advanced as further evidence that they like dirt. The real reason for their wallowing is that the pig, being only sparsely covered with hairs and bristles, is a constant victim of flies and other insects. It has no tail, as a cow has, to swish these tormentors off, and so its only hope of cleaning itself free of pests is to take a mud bath.

Your child probably shares the general view that the pig's nose is singularly ugly. Be that as it may, the nose has many uses and is even comparable to the elephant's trunk in its value to its owner. The fleshy covering of the nostrils is a sensitive-feeling organ which, especially in the wilds, aids the pig to locate bulbs, acorns, roots, and other foods. Besides guiding the pig to food, the nose also serves as a digging tool. Bony plates under the flesh give it remarkable strength.

"Pig eyes," small but gleaming, reflect a good brain, though tame pigs rarely have a chance to show how intelligent they are. Wild pigs have large open ears; those of tame breeds vary, some being sharp and forward-opening, others lopped. The distinctive feature of the male pig's teeth is the upward curve of its upper canines. These tusks, especially in the wild boar, make formidable weapons.

Pig Talk

Though the squeals and grunts of a pig are anything but musical, they are interestingly intelligible to the human ear. You recognize the hunger squeal easily enough by its querulous tone, and the terrified squeal of fright is equally unmistakable. It does not take you long to distinguish between the grunt of well-fed satisfaction and the habitual grunting that echoes wild animal ways. Continuous grunting was once the means by which the pig herd kept together.

PIGS ARE BIG EATERS

Wild pigs eat almost constantly when food is available, storing up fat to sustain them during the winter months. Tame pigs, too, will eat almost anything, and they are much more efficient than other animals when it comes to converting plant food into flesh. In our own country, meat-producing breeds have become more popular than the lard hog breeds which inspired the old rhyme beginning, "To market, to market, to buy a fat pig." The pure American breeds include the black and white Poland China and the chestnut or reddish Duroc-Jersey.

CHAPTER 7

Fish and Their
Fabulous Neighbors

"HOW DO THEY stay in the water?" "How do they breathe?" "Can they hear?" "How long can they live?"

These are but a few of the questions that will occur to your child as he observes the goldfish or tropical fish in an aquarium at home or elsewhere. For fish are interesting, question-provoking creatures. Schools have recognized their popular appeal by making aquariums classroom projects. Newspapers have daily columns telling how to take care of tropical fish; whole magazines deal with the subject; and shows displaying the most unusual kinds of fish are attended by eager youngsters as well as grown-ups.

The common goldfish is the most popular among children, and even a young child can be taught to care for a few of these hardy, handsome creatures in an ordinary fish bowl before you enlarge the collection with tropical specimens.

So attractive are goldfish and the colorful natives of tropical waters, that interior decorators often plan space for aquariums in formal settings as well as in recreation rooms. But beauty is by no means the whole charm of these creatures. As we watch the fish behind glass walls, so tranquil and completely undisturbed by captivity, we have an experience comparable to donning a diving helmet and going into the sea to observe underwater life. Much of what we see and learn applies as well to the life of fish which cannot be observed so closely.

Now for some of the questions that a youngster, especially one learning to swim, may ask about fish.

"How does it just *stay there*?" he may inquire when he sees a fish motionless in the water. "Why doesn't it sink to the bottom or come to the top?"

THE SWIM BLADDER

The ability of some fish to stay quietly in one place is due to a unique organ known as the "swim bladder." It is in the forward part of the body and is filled with gas—a mixture of oxygen and nitrogen. Most fish (including the goldfish) that have skeletons of true bone possess this organ; they need very little fin movement to stay at a given depth. When they die, their bodies rise to the surface.

Sharks and some other kinds of fish have skeletons of gristle. They lack the swim bladder and consequently they can remain suspended in one position only by continuous muscular effort. When these fish die, their bodies sink instead of rising.

How Fish Breathe

A fish has very small nostrils which you can see if you look closely on either side of its snout. The nostrils lead to a little sac where the sense of smell is located—but they have no connection whatever with breathing. When you see a goldfish constantly opening and closing its mouth, it is seeking air or oxygen and not food. Though they live in water, fish need oxygen just as people do; but they need it in a different form. Most fish "drown" in the air just as a human being will under water if he is submerged too long.

HOW THE GILLS WORK

Instead of breathing through nostrils and lungs, a fish is equipped to breathe with gills. You can see its gill covers—flat, bony flaps—just back of its head, one on each side. When the fish opens its mouth, allowing water to flow in, the gill covers are pressed against the body so that water will not enter from behind them.

Then you see the gill covers move outward as the water is forced out through the gill slits when the mouth closes. As the water passes through, the oxygen that it contains is absorbed by the tiny blood vessels making up the gills. (At the same time these blood vessels give off carbon dioxide and other body wastes.) The new oxygen thus obtained is then circulated through the body.

What Fins Are For

As you watch your goldfish swimming you may get the idea that its fins are an important element in its forward movement. And you are right, though nowadays scientists do not attach as much value to the locomotion value of fins as they once did. Experiments have shown that a fish can navigate even without its fins.

You will note seven fins on the common goldfish. Just behind its gill covers it has a pair of fins called the pectorals. Farther back is another pair called the ventrals—or, if quite far forward, called the pelvics. On its back the fish has a dorsal fin, which it sometimes lifts and shuts down like a fan. On the underside, toward the tail, is the anal fin. Finally, at the end of the tail is the caudal fin; we often call it the tail fin.

How Fins Help Fish To Swim

How the different kinds of fins aid a fish's movement depends on their shape and location. The caudal or tail fin helps the fish propel itself as it presses its tail against the water first to one side then to the other. The shape of this fin seems to be related to the swimming speed of different species. On swift swimmers, such as the trout, the caudal fin is strongly forked or moon-shaped; on slow swimmers this tail fin is blunt or rounded.

The dorsal fin acts as a keel: It prevents rolling. The anal fin serves the same purpose and in some species it is also used to give the fish a powerful upward sweep.

Pectoral fins appear to serve chiefly as brakes for fish with bony skeletons—this is particularly true of perch—and these fins also have a slight balancing effect. In fish with other than bony skeletons—and this makes an interesting contrast—the pectorals have a powerful balancing action but are of little use as brakes. Sharks, for example, are apparently unable to make a sudden stop. As for the ventral fins, they contribute further to keeping the fish evenly balanced.

The fins of the common goldfish are by no means standard equipment. Many fishes do not have ventrals. Some, like the cod, have three dorsal fins; others have two; others, one. Some have two anal fins; others, one.

Fascinating Fins: Certain kinds of fish have fascinatingly specialized uses for one or more of their fins. The front ray of the first dorsal fin of the angler fish is perfectly adapted as a rod and lure with which it fishes for smaller creatures to eat. A number of fish have fins modified into sucking pads, and some use specially adapted pectoral fins for walking on the bottom of the sea—or even on land!

MOVING THROUGH THE WATER

The fish's mastery of motion in the water is wonderful to behold. It can dart forward with tremendous speed, starting from a complete "standstill"; it can progress a fraction of an inch with scarcely a motion; it can move straight up or down or backward. There are three types of swimming motions, and most fish use all three. These are: a sinuous movement of the whole body, the movements of the fins, and the propulsion resulting from water being shot through the gill chambers.

THE COD—PROLIFIC, USEFUL, STREAMLINED

The codfish, which produces in the neighborhood of eight million eggs at a time, is the most valuable of all fish, as far as man is concerned, because of its cod-liver oil. The body of the cod, by the way, is admirably streamlined for speedy progress through the water.

Swimming Speeds: When your child sees his goldfish cover the length of its aquarium with one quick swish of its body in what seems like no time at all, he may get the impression that fish always move with notable speed. It is true that many species are capable of extremely rapid bursts of speed, but over long distances they average a much slower rate of speed. Salmon may go at a rate of twenty-five miles an hour, whereas carp are not known to exceed seven and a half.

How the Goldfish Gets Its Color

Goldfish owe much of their attractiveness to their golden sheen. "Is there really any gold in a goldfish?" a youngster looking at his aquarium may ask. The goldfish scales do resemble this precious metal, but of course there is no trace of gold in their shiny covering. Color in fish is mainly the effect of pigments which for the most part are scattered in the surface layers of the skin and are visible through the scales.

The ancestors of goldfish were olive in color. They belonged to the carp family and lived in the streams of China. Hundreds of years ago some specimens were found with golden tones on their sides, and breeding was started with these. The gold predominated in some of their offspring, and selective breeding continued until fish completely golden in color were achieved. About seventy-five years ago a sailor brought back goldfish to America from the Orient. They have been popular pets here ever since.

VARIETIES OF GOLDFISH

Today we see many fancy varieties, such as fantail, fringetail, telescope, and lion-head. The breeding of specially selected fish produces these highly ornamental creatures, though great numbers of "common" goldfish appear along with them. This type characteristically has a long body, forked tail, and small head. It may be all gold or marked with black and silver. It is hardier than its ornamental relatives and if it is transferred to a pond with ample food, it may grow to be a foot in length.

Fish Use Camouflage Too

The color of fish is often a definite camouflage, comparable to protective schemes on many birds and mammals. You may see a hint of protective coloration in a goldfish, as the orange tones of its back fade to pale lemon-yellow below. In general, fish are darker-colored on the back than on the underside. As the darker color blends with the river or pond bottom, fish tend to be less noticeable to an observer from above. Yet when fish feed near the surface their light underparts blend with the sky, so that they are not too likely to be seen by enemies swimming below.

Perch, pike, and other species that live among weeds are protected by their vertical stripes. An extreme example of camouflage is the "leaf fish" of the Amazon River which is colored like a dead leaf and has a projection from its lower lip that resembles a leaf stalk. Even its actions reinforce the illusion: In stalking its prey it drifts along like a dead leaf.

How Fish See and Hear

"Goldie winked at me. I saw him!" my exuberant youngster exclaimed one day during a close scrutiny of the aquarium.

He was disappointed when I pointed out that a fish has no eyelids and therefore cannot wink. However, fish do have eyeballs and when one of these is flicked downward you get the impression of a wink. The lack of eyelids also means that whether the fish is awake or asleep, its eyes are wide open.

Fish do not have keen sight. The part of the eye that takes in light is round—whereas in land animals it is flattened. Fish are near-sighted because of the shape of their eye lens.

"Can the fish hear us?" is another challenging thought to children who enjoy talking to their charges at feeding time. It is doubtful that they can, but they do seem to be aware of hand clapping or the sound of tapping on the aquarium walls.

The fish has no outside ear—or even openings where you would expect to find ears. It does have other sense organs, however, through which it can get some of the same impressions that we receive through our ears. In fact goldfish, minnows and others learn to react to whistles and certain other sounds at feeding time,

Fish Scales

The scales of a fish look a good deal like the shingles on a roof. Each of the scales grows separately from the skin, but they are set at an angle so that they overlap and form a complete covering for the body. Naturalists sometimes call this scaly covering the "outside skeleton."

Some fish, the catfish for one, do not have scales. Among the species that do have scales, a newly hatched fish of the bony group lacks the protection of scales for its skin; but it does not take long for them to develop. Some kinds of scales—those of the eel, for example—are so tiny that you can hardly notice them. A curious feature of some members of the tuna family is that they are only partly scale-covered.

TELLING THE AGE OF FISH

As the fish grows, its scales grow too. You can tell the age of many of the bony fish by the markings on their scales; by examining the rings you can tell how many birthdays they have passed. Of course you will not want to do this with your goldfish pet: Its scales should never be touched, let alone pulled out of the skin. A protective slime covers the scales and if this is rubbed off by dry hands or in any other way, death may result for the fish.

Children enjoy studying the scales cleaned from a fish destined for the family dinner. Any youngster who knows how to count will get a thrill looking at the scales through a magnifying glass, checking the number and nature of the rings, and reporting the age of the main course for dinner!

"It Was *That* Big!"

Among fish, size is not so standardized as among mammals. The goldfish is an outstanding case in point. In an aquarium it remains small, whereas, given the freedom of a pond, it increases its size many times over. Such factors as the temperature and acidity of the water and the type of food available limit the length and weight a fish can attain.

Most of the really big fish are found in the ocean—though there is a huge species, the arapaima, that lives in the rivers of Brazil and attains a weight of four hundred pounds. Among the giants of the sea is that popular American food staple, the tuna. These giants vary in size depending on the regions to which they are native, but a weight of a thousand pounds is about the maximum. Another big fish is the spectacular swordfish. Few sports are as adventurous as deep-sea fishing, and many a boy or girl, thrilled by pictures or films, looks forward to taking a marlin or sailfish with rod and reel.

Fish Migrate Too

"What happened to the fish when the water froze?" children often ask as they prepare to go skating over ice that was a rippling lake or stream only a few weeks before.

There is more than one answer to this question. Some fish—the common sucker, for example—burrow in the mud and may be frozen and thawed without being any the worse! Others remain active if the water under the ice is deep enough. As for carp and some other species, they move en masse to deeper water at the beginning of winter.

Children accept the seasonal travels of birds rather casually because they can witness some phases of their migrations each year; but they are likely to be surprised to find that many fish migrate too. Even their parents often do not realize how wide-spread the migration habit is among fish. Except for the fish living in ponds, a great many may make migratory journeys in the course of their lives. Sometimes the individuals in a traveling "school" are counted by the million.

Spawning Migrations

Aside from the journeys of fish to deeper waters for the winter, some species of fresh-water fish travel many miles in search of food. There are also salt-water migrations by fish that swim away from their feeding grounds to deposit their eggs. A famous example is that of the North Sea herring migrating in the autumn to coastal waters off France. There they spawn and go northward again. When the young hatch they swim to the surface to feed and are gradually swept north by the main currents until they reach the North Sea. There are still other migrations that take fish from the salty ocean to fresh inland waters to deposit their eggs.

How to Keep an Aquarium Successfully

A home aquarium may be a simple matter of keeping one or two goldfish or it may be a full-scale hobby involving a variety of fishes. Tropical and toy fishes are more difficult to raise than the goldfish, but even this hardy pet requires certain favorable conditions in order to survive.

The goldfish needs adequate amounts of water—about a gallon for every inch of fish in the tank. It must be given food in proper amounts; overfeeding is a far more common trouble than insufficient food. The water must be kept clean—yet the fish must not be subjected to a sudden change in temperature when fresh water is provided. The tank must have the right amount of sunlight, not too much, not too little. Several hours of hot summer sun may kill the occupants of a small tank.

Plants are attractive in an aquarium and give the fish a sheltered place to rest and possibly to lay eggs. Contrary to general opinion, they are not essential, however, and too many plants are harmful rather than beneficial.

The popularity of goldfish has put goldfish breeding on a substantial commercial basis. A goldfish hatchery near Frederick, Maryland, covers 150 acres and turns out about five million fish a year!

How Long Fish Live

Properly cared for, the common goldfish may reach an age of twenty-five or thirty years. Many species of fish have a long life span, but in the natural state they are not likely to live to a ripe old age: They have too many enemies, and some—such as the Pacific coast salmon—die after spawning. However, records of fish in ponds or aquariums tell us of catfish that lived sixty years, halibut that rounded out thirty, and trout that flourished for eighteen years.

Fishes in the Brook

Not long after most children learn the "little fishes in the brook" rhyme, they have a strong desire to join Daddy when he goes to catch fish. There is something about dangling a hook in water and wondering what it may bring up that has a universal appeal for youngsters. If you have access to remote country streams you have a perfect setting for introducing your child to the sport of fishing.

But even without your efforts you may find him tying a bent pin to a string, getting ready to try his luck at a pond in the park. Though fishing may be inconvenient to supervise, it is a hobby well worth encouraging. A five-year-old always seems to be letting his cap fall into the pond, with himself on the verge of following the cap. But give him a few more years and the wholesome outdoor sport of fishing is something you and he will be thankful for.

How To Plan A Fishing Trip

When you plan a fishing trip you can get helpful information from several sources: a fishing-tackle dealer, your county agent, a local game warden, or your state fish and game commission. You will want to know the lakes and streams where there are fish, the open season for fishing, the minimum size at which a caught fish may be kept, and whether you need to have a license. Often a grown-up requires one but a child does not.

More Fishing Fun For Children

Children's needs have been recognized by an organization known as Better Fishing, Inc., which has arranged for them to have exclusive rights to certain lakes, ponds, and streams throughout the United States. A sign, "Fishing for Children Only," marks these spots which are reserved for fishermen under fishing license age. Sportsmen in local communities stock the waters with trout, catfish, bass, and pike; and many of these people teach children how to fish and also encourage good sportsmanship and conservation.

Better Fishing, Inc.* carries out a nation-wide program during

---

*Its headquarters are at 509 South Wabash Avenue, Chicago 5, Ill.

the summer school-vacation time. This is climaxed by a Boy and Girl Better Fishing Rodeo Day, when prizes are awarded to the boy and girl from each participating municipality who bring in the heaviest fish. More than three million children have thrills and fun in this contest every year.

Shiners and "Pumpkin Seeds"

A COMMON CATCH

One fish that father and son are likely to encounter in any country stream is the shiner; this is among the commonest of little fish in the brooks of America. It belongs to the same family as the minnow, and they look very much alike, wedge-shaped as seen from above, rounded in front and tapering to a point in back. However, shiners are lighter in tone than minnows. A delicate olive-green covers the shiner's back, bordered at the sides by a line of blue-purple, with a silvery sheen on the bottom that seems to reflect the varied hues of a rainbow.

Because they are small, shiners are the prey of many kinds of fish. Were it not for the countless eggs that this species lays, it could never survive. Shiners live on water insects and the eggs of larger fishes. You are rather likely to see them traveling in schools—a large group of little fish swimming against the current.

THE PLUCKY SUNFISH

Another attractive little resident of brooks and ponds is the sunfish — known also as "tobacco box," "pumpkin seed," "sunny," and a variety of other names. Pumpkin seed is a good description of the fish's general form because, viewed from the side, its outlines strongly suggest the seeds you find when you carve a Halloween jack-o'-lantern.

Sunfish are perhaps best known for their gameness: Though small, they are fierce fighters. Not only do sunfish put up a real battle when caught on a hook—the males fight each other to win a desired mate. It is not a fight to the death, but each fish tries to mutilate its rival's fins.

Fishing for "sunnies" with angleworms and any available equipment has always been a popular sport for boys. Furthermore, as summer approaches, sunfish eagerly take a dry fly; fathers find fishing for "pumpkin seeds" an excellent way of introducing their sons to the techniques of dry-fly fishing.

Catching Fish for Observation

It is satisfying to catch fish for food or for the sheer fun of it, but taking them for observation makes an interesting hobby. You need a barbless hook for this purpose, and the simplest solution is to file the barb off a regular or fly-tied hook. When you catch a fish of the right size, remove it quickly with wet hands and drop it into a wide-mouthed gallon jar of water. You can then study the actions of this underwater creature at leisure.

Another method is to securely cover with wire mesh the top of the jar in which the fish is captive, and place the jar on its side in shallow water with about an inch of air between the water and the top side. Then you can watch the fish for a day or more; if your youngster enjoys drawing he may wish to sketch the captive.

CATCHING FISH WITH A NET

An old and widely used method is taking fish with a net, which you can employ if it is not against the law in your locality. A dark-colored net, deep and tapering toward a rounded bottom, is best.

This is how to use the net: Walk into a shallow pond or stream and hold the net as you would a hoe. Walk slowly, keeping your shadow from falling in front of you and thus frightening the fish away. When you see a fish, twirl the net rapidly in the air so that the opening will cut the water first. Then, with a downward swoop, cover the fish and drag the net briefly shoreward along the bottom. As you lift the net from the water, twist it again so that the opening faces upward; then immediately transfer your catch into a jar or bucket of water.

KEEPING RECORDS OF FISH

Keeping a chart of fish found in your region can be as rewarding as a bird or mammal record. To prepare a chart devoted

to fish, you can set up five columns with headings for name and
brief description, spawning grounds, feeding grounds, natural
food, and accepted bait. You may, if you wish, add columns for
the date and place of specimens caught, and another in which a
small sketch may be made. Such a chart is fun to keep up and in
time becomes a lively textbook for children in learning about
native fish.

VISITING FISH HATCHERIES

A trip to a state or national fish hatchery is entertaining
and a child can learn a great deal from observing the fish in all
stages of development and discovering how streams and lakes are
stocked. Most hatcheries have regular visiting hours for the
public, and if none are located near your home, you may discover
one during a vacation trip. Signs along the highways will often
direct you to hatcheries, and a travel guidebook usually lists them
in the region it covers.

Family Life in the Fish World

Duels between rival males are not the only drama to be observed
in the lives of sunfish. They belong to the interesting group of
fish that make nests for their families.

The male sunfish selects a spot in shallow water close by the
shore and excavates mud and sand there to make a saucer-like
basin. He clears the place of pebbles by jerking them away with
his tail fin or by taking them in his mouth and carrying them
away. Measured across, the finished nest is about twice the length
of the fish.

The female sunny, recently won by right of conquest, deposits
her eggs in the nest and then takes leave of home and mate. But
the male does not share her irresponsibility. He stays close to
the nest and bravely defends it from enemies until the eggs hatch.
Then the male too resumes a carefree life so far as his family is
concerned. There are fish that carry parental duties still further.
The male bullhead, for example, continues to guard the baby
fish many days after they hatch.

THE SUNFISH IS A SCRAPPER

Despite its maximum length of eight inches, the sunfish leads a full and adventurous life. Fierce and courageous, the males fight duels during the courting period. But they also have their tender side, building nests and guarding the eggs after their fickle mates depart. The sunfish has lovely shimmering colors and is an exceptionally graceful swimmer.

FISH THAT DON'T LAY EGGS

Not all fish lay eggs. Some species, ranging from the great tiger shark to the tiny guppy, give birth to young that are in an advanced state of development. A guppy produces at least twenty-five and perhaps as many as fifty offspring at a time; but the parent fish eat many of their young, and only a small proportion survives.

Some Famous Fish

TROUT—FISHERMAN'S FAVORITE

Trout live in cool mountain streams or lakes, where they feed on a variety of insects that lay eggs on water; the trout also greedily snatch the emerging insects as they hatch. These feeding habits make fly-fishing for trout an exciting sport as the fisherman lures his victim with imitations of its favorite food. In small streams trout rarely exceed half a pound; but in larger rivers and lakes where food is abundant they often reach from five to ten pounds.

How Trout Build Nests: One female trout lays hundreds of eggs. For her nest she seeks water with a gravelly bottom, perhaps where the brook she inhabits flows into a larger stream. There the mother fish shapes a depression with her tail and carries away larger stones in her mouth.

After she has laid her eggs in the nest and the male has fertilized them, she moves a little upstream and repeats the whole process. The gravel and sand she displaces are carried along by the current. Most of the discarded material is conveniently deposited over the first nest, protecting the eggs it contains. The mother trout makes several nests and lays eggs in all of them before she is finished with the job.

Legal Protection for the Trout: In spite of the enormous quantities of eggs laid by trout, these fish were in serious danger of extermination once motor highways began opening wilderness country to ever-increasing numbers of fishermen. Aside from being destroyed by their natural enemies, such as other fish that eat the eggs and young, the trout were caught by these fishermen who gave no thought to size or season or how many fish might be left in a stream.

The passage of effective conservation laws prevented the disappearance of trout from native waters by regulating the seasons for trout fishing, the number a fisherman may catch and the size a fish must be before it can be taken.

SALMON—THEY LEAP WATERFALLS

Many children have heard about the travels of the salmon, for this fish has become a symbol of determination to reach a goal. Pacific salmon swim hundreds of miles to their spawning grounds in North American rivers; the Atlantic salmon go hundreds of miles to reach theirs in rivers of Europe or of America.

If you had the opportunity to be at a waterfall where salmon were making their way upstream, you might see them putting their noses out of the swirling water as if "sizing up" the situation. They turn their heads against the falling water and twist their bodies like bows, then straighten out again. They bring every muscle into play as they try to progress.

Sometimes they succeed by practically climbing the cascade, at other times they top it with a single leap. No matter what their method, they never give up. If need be, they wait for days—even weeks!—until a change in the volume of water provides a better opportunity to scale the barrier.

Pacific salmon rarely survive spawning to return to the sea. Their usual fate is to die after breeding.

EELS—VERSATILE CREATURES

"Is that a *fish*? Looks like a snake to me!"

With some reason the children are dubious when Daddy displays an eel as the morning's "catch." But despite its elongated, snakelike form it is a true fish, having gills for breathing and fins for swimming.

Eels and Snakes: The well-known figure of speech, "slippery as an eel," makes a good point of contrast between this fish and the snake. The skin of a snake is never slimy; that of an eel is always slimy. The eel's skin is thick and flexible, with the scales lodged in it instead of on the outside. Quantities of tiny glands in the skin produce a sticky mucus. These factors, combined with the creature's suppleness, give it the ability to slip through anyone's fingers.

Eels Love Privacy: Eels live in all kinds of waters, in mountain lakes and streams, in salt-water pools along the shore, and in stagnant ponds. Clean water or foul—it makes no difference to the welfare of these hardy fish. It might seem strange, therefore, that we do not see them more frequently. The fact is, however, that eels are secretive creatures, and much of the time they lie buried in mud. If something seriously disturbs them in their hiding place, they come out in swarms; they live in groups.

Vast Migrations: Like salmon, eels make astounding migratory journeys—but they reverse the salmons' procedure. Instead of leaving the ocean for fresh water, they travel from ponds and lakes down rivers to the depths of the ocean—and there the females eject their eggs.

The two species of eel—one European, the other American—that spawn in the same area in the Atlantic, travel in opposite directions. The young whose parents come from American rivers take about a year to travel from their ocean breeding place to this continent; the offspring of European species take three years to reach their destination in Europe.

In the course of its travels the eel has a notable advantage over most fish. It has specialized gills that can store a certain amount of water. This makes it possible for the eel to leave a stream or pond and wriggle over land to another body of water some distance away.

Fish That Are Different

THE FISH THAT WALKS

The fish family has its share of fantastic creatures. In some ways their real-life qualities are more amazing than those of mythological monsters of legend and myth. The climbing perch is the commonest of these believe-it-or-not fish. It can survive out of water for several days, and its pectoral fins are strong enough to support its body by acting as legs! This perch may be said to walk rather than wriggle, and it has been found on low tree trunks.

"FLYING" FISH

Perhaps more generally known than the walking fishes are those that leave the water and glide above its surface. If you travel in tropical waters, such as those around Bermuda or the West Indies, you frequently see some of these gliders in action. Most expert of the group, the "flying fish" travel through the air about three feet above the water at forty miles an hour, and may go as much as four hundred yards at a stretch. All the "flying fish" —they glide rather than fly—live in the ocean, with the exception of one little "butterfly" fish of Africa which makes brief excursions over its fresh-water home.

A FISH OUT OF WATER

One of the most remarkable oddities of the fish world is the climbing perch, which can survive for several days out of water. Equipped with pectoral fins that are sturdy enough to act as legs, the climbing perch "walks" on land and has even been known to climb low tree trunks.

SEA HORSES—NATURE'S ECCENTRICS

The sea horse, despite its name, is a fish, and strictly a swimming fish at that; but its method of swimming is amusingly different. Children delight in seeing a group of them in a public aquarium, moving through the water with an appearance of great dignity—head upright, fins at the back. Any onlooker is bound to be convulsed with laughter when the sea horse rolls its eyes; for a sea horse can look straight ahead with one eye and backward with the other at the same time.

But these features by no means exhaust the eccentricities of this odd little fish. (It averages about three inches in length.) The eggs of the sea horse are incubated in a pouch that belongs to the *male*—not the female. The mother sea horse transfers her eggs to the pouch as soon as they are produced; and there they stay until they hatch.

THE SEA HORSE—AS ODD AS ITS NAME

The ways of a sea horse are strange indeed. It is a fish—not a horse; but it has a horse-shaped head and a tail that reminds us of a caterpillar's. It swims upright, and its eyes move independently of each other. The eggs of the sea horse are carried in a pouch—by the male! Bony plates cover the body of this fish.

The dried bodies of sea horses are prize discoveries for boys and girls at a beach, where the animals are often stranded by the tide.

Shocking Fish

Another unusual fish you may encounter at the seashore is the little electric star gazer, which spends much of its time buried to its eyes in sand. Only if you happen to step on one is its hiding place quickly revealed: Its power to give an electric shock is its means of defense.

There are other fish, larger than the star gazer, that are also equipped with "batteries," but they are not native to our country. One of these is the electric catfish of Africa, another the electric eel of South America which not only uses its powers of shock to defend itself, but also as a weapon for securing food.

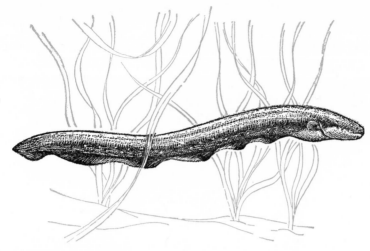

EELS WITH BUILT-IN BATTERIES
The electric eel of South America carries a formidable electric charge with enough current to light several bulbs. This creature, which may reach a length of as much as seven feet when full grown, uses shock tactics to immobilize its prey, devouring its victims at its convenience. It is toothless, so has to swallow them whole.

Just as zoos give you an opportunity to see strange mammals, so public aquariums present some rare and exotic fishes. A trip to one of these aquariums is the best substitute for a trip underseas.

SHARKS—NOT SO FEROCIOUS

The "ferocious" shark, like the pirates of old who captured the imagination of adventure-loving children, represents a terrible menace of the sea. Any story of shipwreck immediately takes on an element of terror when "shark-infested waters" are mentioned.

Yet it is claimed sometimes that sharks never attack humans but eat only small forms of oceanic life. If you watch native boys fearlessly diving after coins tossed by tourists in the harbor of Nassau in the Bahamas, you may conclude that there is a sound basis for this theory. Frequently the fins of sharks which abound in nearby waters may be seen cutting the surface close by the divers—yet the sharks never molest the boys. The probable explanation is that the noise and excitement and the evident vitality of the divers discourage the sharks.

The "Man-Eater": Actually the biggest member of the shark family, the whale shark, is quite harmless to humans, eating only small fish, jellyfish, and shell creatures. By way of contrast, the great white shark, which is found in all warm seas, comes legitimately by its other name of "man-eater": It will devour almost anything it can find, including humans as well as other sharks. The victim need only be disabled or too small to defend itself.

Neighbors of the Fish

WHALES—BIGGEST MAMMALS OF THEM ALL

Whales are the biggest animals in the world. Fully grown, one of them may weigh ten times as much as an elephant! The heroic whale-hunters in the palmy days of Nantucket and New Bedford created one of the imperishable epics of American history when they sailed the seven seas in search of this mighty prey.

The enormous size of the whale is bound to impress a child. He is likely to be even more amazed when he learns that whales are mammals—though they live in water, as fish do. "How come, then, that they're mammals?" he will surely demand.

Whale "Babies": One proof that whales are mammals is the fact that the babies are born alive and are nourished by their mother's milk. Whale calves are undoubtedly the biggest babies produced by any kind of animal, although their size depends on the size and species of the parent. Occasionally it has been possible to record birth weights, and we have a record of an eighty-foot blue whale that bore a four-ton baby! The whale mother nurses her calf by means of a special compressor muscle that injects into its mouth milk which looks exactly like cow's milk.

Whales Have Hair: Like land-dwelling mammals, whales are warm-blooded; this means that the blood remains at pretty much the same temperature regardless of how warm or cold the animal's surroundings may be. But how about the remaining test of a mammal: Does the whale, with its bare skin, meet the mammal requirement for having fur or hair? Well, it does have some hairs —just a few!—sprouting under its chin. Its ancestors of long ago doubtless had a great deal more hair.

How Whales Breathe: But here is another unorthodox feature of the whale. We know that mammals, unlike fish, do not have gills. How, then, does the whale manage to breathe in its ocean home? Like the land mammals, it must take oxygen into its lungs.

This mammal of the sea has nostrils at the top of its head, making possible a quick intake of air when it comes to the surface. When the whale is below the surface, special muscles close the nostrils firmly against water. There is also a passageway at the back of the mouth which directly connects the nose passage with the windpipe. Thus water cannot reach the whale's lungs even when its mouth is open. Ordinarily a whale comes up for air every few minutes; but it can stay below the surface twenty minutes or more by making use of oxygen stored in its blood.

"There She Blows!": During an ocean voyage you might see the last phase of the whale's unique breathing operation. The exclamation "There she blows!" on shipboard calls attention to one or two fine sprays, looking like steam erupting from the water. They indicate the spot where a whale has just risen to the surface and exhaled! The blast of air sent out of its nostrils is very warm and saturated with water vapor. The blast condenses as it strikes the colder air, forming the columns of spray that have led people to insist—incorrectly—that whales spout water.

How Whales Swim: If you are looking at a picture of a whale that shows its whole body, it will be interesting to see whether your child can notice an important difference between the whale's tail and the tail fin of a fish. The former flattens out into a broad paddle, lying in a horizontal plane. This is just the opposite of the fish's tail, which is always expanded vertical-wise. While the fish helps move itself forward by lashing its tail to the right and left, the whale propels itself forward with an up and down motion.

What Whales Eat: After learning the story of Jonah and the whale, a child may ask, "Do whales really eat people?"

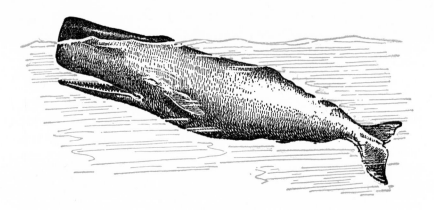

THE BREED OF MOBY DICK
The sperm whale, with a maximum length of sixty feet and a maximum weight of
sixty tons, is not among the largest whales! Its nose may yield as much as a ton
of spermacetti, an oil which has many uses. Its head is about one-third the length
of its whole body. Moby Dick (in Herman Melville's classic) was a sperm whale.

Strangely enough, this largest of creatures lives on very small
animals. Only one species—the sperm whale—is capable of swallowing a man whole. Others would be apt to choke on any large
prey. The sperm whale's teeth are usually only on the lower jaw;
its diet consists chiefly of fish and squid.

Of course, the "killer" whales and the species known as por-
poises have teeth; but the largest whales are equipped, instead,
with enormous strainers. These are made of whalebone plates
which, despite their name, are not bone at all but material resembling that of human fingernails. The whalebone plates,
bordered with a horsehair-like fringe, grow from the roof of the
mouth. When the whale swims with its mouth open, quantities
of shrimp and other small creatures are enmeshed; when the
whale closes its mouth, the water is forced out but the victims
cannot escape from the trap.

MERMAIDS—GLAMOUR GIRLS OF THE SEA

Fairy tales, cartoons, and sometimes decorative motifs introduce most children to the fantastic, lovely ladies known as mermaids. Many primitive peoples the world over have legends about

mermaids. Babylonian art dating from about 1800 B.C. depicts mermaids, and only a century ago Barnum featured a "stuffed mermaid" in his side show! The inquiring mind of a child plays, naturally enough, with the idea of mermaids—even if "no such animal" is alive now, did it ever exist? If not, why were mermaids "thought up"?

The sea cow, a creature which, like the whale, is a sea-dwelling mammal, probably gave rise to the mermaid legend. The sea cow's head is shaped much like that of the seal; its body is plump but somewhat fishlike. Its startling feature is its face, which suggests an oversize, ugly human. It is believed that when early navigators saw sea cows raise their heads above water, they were struck by the animals' part human, part fishlike appearance. As they did not have binoculars to help them see more clearly, they reported these creatures as glamorous mermaids!

SPONGES

Boys and girls can learn something of life on the floor of tropical seas by examining the natural (not synthetic) sponges. The sponge, when it is alive and growing at the bottom of the sea, looks more like a plant than an animal. There are many varieties of sponges, but not all of them are used commercially as some skeletons are too thin or scratchy or brittle. Sometimes the skeletons become detached and float in on a beach. However, the sponges destined for commercial use are obtained by divers or by workers who pull them from the ocean floor with tongs fastened to long poles.

CORALS—SEMI-PRECIOUS ORNAMENTS

Another sea animal that children may know from its skeleton is the coral. As in the case of sponges, there are many varieties of corals. Aside from the type used for making necklaces and ornaments, there are the reef-building, "stony" kind. These are responsible for the well-known coral isles of the Pacific, as well as the great coral reefs such as may be found near the Bahamas and off the coast of Australia. The Great Barrier Reefs off Australia are more than a thousand miles long and have caused many a shipwreck.

Architect of the Seas: Any child's imagination is bound to be stimulated by the amazing explanation of how the tiny soft-bodied coral polyp produces these gigantic structures. A newborn coral polyp is active at first and swims freely; but soon it fastens itself to a rock or to the sea floor. Using carbonate of lime obtained from food and water, it forms a little platform under its body and a hard wall (called the skeleton) around itself.

What happens to most kinds of corals is that these new polyps remain attached to the parent and in turn produce new buds. As the older ones die, young polyps build on top of their skeletons and thus the structure grows until an island or reef is formed.

THE BASHFUL SNAILS

Observing a snail's daily activities need not be the only pleasure your child derives from his unusual pet. He can also train the animal to be less shy. I knew one friendly snail that would come out of its shell when summoned by a sharp clicking sound, and would proceed to eat from its owner's fingers.

When a snail has enough confidence to come out of its shell, your child will be able to observe its eyes, which are located at the ends of tentacles attached to its head; he can also study the horny jaws that cut up the plant material it eats. If the snail learns to eat from his finger, he can feel the tiny teeth on the tongue which give it a sandpaper texture.

How to Take Care of a Pet Snail: A glass terrarium furnished with moss and ferns makes an excellent home for a snail. You will need a wire covering for the enclosure, as snails can crawl up any-thing—even a slippery piece of glass. They owe this ability to a substance they secrete as they travel. Snails require little food, usually thriving on cabbage or lettuce leaves, carrot pulp and the like.

At the Seashore

If you could take your child on an exploring trip around a coral reef, you would find many fantastic forms of life such as the giant plantlike sea anemones, and such shellfish as the bright pink crab that camouflages itself with bits of sponge. Such an expedition is out of the question for most of us, so it is fortunate that a number of these tropical wonders can be seen much closer to home—in tide pools along the shore, and on rocky coasts and sandy beaches.

Looking for these creatures and learning something of their way of life can become a delightful summer hobby. You will find that a magnifying hand lens is a valuable piece of equipment to help the youngster enjoy his discoveries to the fullest. Children of six or over can use a microscope to good advantage.

Stinging Hydroids

You can often come across hydroids as you examine a tide pool. These are tiny creatures that—like the giant sea anemones of the coral reefs—resemble flowers. When they are magnified, the hydroids are revealed as animals. Like the corals, they are known as polyps. Each individual is attached to a delicate stalk, and it has numerous threadlike tentacles that are equipped with stinging cells. Small creatures that come close are paralyzed and drawn into the opening that serves the hydroid as a mouth. Many hydroids are quite transparent, and for this reason they are especially interesting to observe.

Flower-like Sea Anemones

In the tide pools, too, you may find sea anemones, much smaller than those of tropical seas yet larger than the hydroids. When undisturbed, they expand into flower-like forms; but they can contract quickly into an unattractive jelly-like mass. When they are in this form you will note their resemblance to jellyfish; actually the two animals are closely related.

Shellfish—They Aren't Really Fish

A child running barefoot along the seashore is likely to have an unpleasant encounter with these creatures, for their sharp edges can inflict painful cuts. He soon learns to watch out for mussels, clams, and all shellfish that are exposed to view during low tide. He will surely wonder, too, how these animals can be fish when they are so different from salmon, trout, or other "regular" fish.

SEA ANEMONES—ANIMALS OR PLANTS?
These anemones are animals, though they look more like plants; their "petals"
are really tentacles encircling an odd sort of mouth. There are about one thousand
different kinds of sea anemones, some having as many as ninety-six tentacles, some
equipped for stinging. If menaced, these queer creatures contract into a jelly-like
mass. They have no skeletons, and are classed as polyps.

The fact is that the term "shellfish," though constantly used,
is incorrect; the proper name for these animals is "mollusks."
Every kind of mollusk—there are something like eighty thousand
species!—has a soft body enveloped in a mantle which in most
cases manufactures or secretes a hard shell. There are two siphons
in the mantle; one of them brings water to the animal, the other
carries the water away after it has passed through the gills.

The mollusk's shell is sometimes described as a skeleton—a
skeleton without a backbone. Instead of being an internal structure, the skeleton is carried on the outside of the body.

The Clam's Pearly Lining

One of the best-known mollusks, the clam, has a shell made up of three layers—a thin one on the outside, a thick strong middle layer, and a smooth pearly lining. When a bit of sand or other foreign matter gets lodged within the shells, it becomes coated like the lining and in time may become a true pearl.

Squatters' Rights

We find mollusks not only in the sea, but in fresh-water lakes and streams and on land as well. Some of them—the periwinkle, for example—have a single shell; others, such as clams and oysters, have two shells hinged along the back. Shellfish give the deceptive appearance of leading a peaceful existence, though the fact is that life is a constant struggle for them. They are devoured by a variety of animals, and they often vie with each other for living space.

Oysters settle as a rule in fairly deep water, though sometimes a colony is located on a mud flat that is exposed to the air during low tide. In such a situation you may see an invasion take place. Mussels, which multiply with a great rapidity, may move in and smother the oysters out of existence by sheer weight of numbers. But, once the mussel colony is established, it may in turn be invaded by a host of barnacles which soon take over the territory for their own.

One of the mollusks' worst enemies is an innocent-looking snail with the sinister name of oyster drill. It plays great havoc in oyster beds boring holes through the oyster shell and feeding on the soft underlying flesh.

The Self-effacing Crabs

You have to keep a sharp lookout to catch a glimpse of these notable creatures of the seashore. Some are expert at disguising themselves by putting seaweed or bits of sponge on their back; some hide themselves almost completely in the sand as they lie in wait for prey; and some are very small.

The Rock Crab: It should not be too difficult to discover the rock crab, which is common on most rocky shores. Full grown,

SEASHORE SCAVENGERS
Crabs are useful as scavengers. They have five pairs of legs, the front pair being pinching claws for seizing food and fighting, the last pair fin-shaped for swimming, and the legs in between adapted for walking. Their eyes are on long stalks equipped with antennae. Nature explorers young and old find crabs fun to watch.

it is a little over five inches wide, and is commonly reddish purple in color. Like all crabs, the little fellow has five pairs of legs. The first pair are adapted as pinching claws, and in some crabs the last two pairs, shaped like fins, serve effectively as swimming aids.

It is amusing to watch crabs walk—they move sideways instead of forward or backward. Shore crabs are rather slow in their movements; the swimming crabs are considerably more active.

Spare Parts: If a crab accidentally loses a claw, it can grow a new one. During its lifetime it also replaces its shell, not because of a mishap, but because its body gradually grows too big for the shell. When the original shell starts getting too snug, the animal pulls itself free, and until it grows a new covering it is known as a "soft-shell" crab.

Lilo Hess (Three Lions)

THIS ISN'T LOVE—IT'S WAR

Some kinds of fish have a strong feeling of possessiveness for a certain territory, and will savagely fight an intruder. The beautiful Siamese fighting fish is a noted example of this type. The two shown here have their jaws locked in combat. Little sunfish, which you may commonly find in country streams, are also valiant fighters.

PORTRAIT OF A BUTTERFLY-IN-THE-MAKING

New Y
Zoological Soc

The two-inch caterpillar of the tiger swallowtail is particularly startling in appearance because of two colorful spots on its head, which look like hypnotic eyes. Just back of its head it is equipped with a scent organ which it can thrust out to produce a disagreeable odor that drives off birds that would otherwise make a meal of it.

THE AGGRESSIVE LOBSTERS

If you make a habit of observing the activity among the seaweed in shallow waters, you may have an opportunity to see a struggle between a lobster and a crab, although such encounters are rather infrequent. The crab—even a large one—apparently has little chance against his opponent: A lobster's claws are extremely powerful. One of them is very broad and is used for crushing; the narrower one cuts food to bits. Its mouth can crush as well as bite. It is also probable that the lobster has an advantage over the crab because its feelers, especially a second pair, are longer than the crab's. With them the lobster can investigate holes and crevices and is extra-sensitive to danger as well as possible prey.

THE LOBSTER IS HELPLESS WITHOUT ITS COAT OF ARMOR
Though the lobster has a great fighting asset in its brutal claws, its tough shell has enormous defensive value. At the times when the lobster has to shed its shell for a new one, it is helpless against the onslaught of its enemies. The lobster is valuable as food, and our yearly catch is worth upwards of one million dollars.

Shell Hobbies Are Fun

SHELL COLLECTING

Sea shells delight children who live inland as well as those who have the seashore close at hand. They may collect them as stamps and coins are collected through purchase at stores, by order from catalogues, and through trading with correspondents the world over.

Shells have a multiple appeal. Some, such as the giant conch shell, intensify the sounds they pick up in their spiral interior and thus bring to a child's ear "the sound of the sea."

DECORATIVE USES FOR SHELLS

Shells have a further appeal because you can make art objects with them. If your child is an enthusiastic collector, he may call on you for ideas to put quantities of shells to use.

One project that serves the purpose is making shell book ends. You start these with two triangular blocks of wood, each attached to a heavy wood base about six inches square. Then you apply a coat of ready-mixed putty, nearly a quarter of an inch thick, to the outer surfaces that are to be decorated. While this is still soft, press shells into it just far enough to be held firm. With good cutting tools your wood blocks may take varied shapes, while the shell groupings and designs are limitless and the wood and putty may be painted as desired.

SHELL HANDICRAFTS

Some shells are suitable for making belts, necklaces, bracelets, and earrings. A small child needs help in making the holes where stringing is necessary, for shells crack easily. The most effective way to puncture them is with a fine-pointed electric drill. You can buy shellcraft hobby packages in which the preliminary work has been done; this greatly simplifies the assembling of shell "jewelry."

A child who gathers sea shells takes a far livelier interest in his collection if he thinks of a shell as a fortress created by a soft-bodied creature. The shell served the mollusk as a protective covering during its lifetime, and after death remained as a memorial to the little creature that lived in it.

CHAPTER 8

Snakes and Frogs
and Their Relatives

HE CHANCES ARE that snakes either fascinate you or arouse your intense dislike. Few people are neutral, and children are quick to adopt their parents' admiration or profound distaste for the crawling reptiles. However, some children are so fond of snakes that they will bring them home for pets regardless of how their families receive the creatures. Under such circumstances one conscientious mother said to me:

"*How* can I make myself like snakes? They revolt me, but my boys are always bringing them home and have so much fun with them that I don't like to object."

My suggestion was not to try to force a liking for snakes—but merely to try to understand them. Snakes are probably the victims of more erroneous beliefs than any other group of animals. Some popular misconceptions, and the true facts about them, are:

1. *False:* All kinds of snakes are venomous. *True:* Most snakes are harmless.

2. *False:* A snake thrusts out its tongue as an act of hostility. *True:* A snake uses its tongue as a sensory organ to explore its surroundings.

3. *False:* Snakes have no fear of people and are constantly on the lookout for victims. *True:* Most snakes do not display an aggressive disposition toward people; if possible, they creep away and hide at a human's approach.

4. *False:* Snakes can sting as well as bite. *True:* No snake can inflict a sting.

5. *False:* Snakes have great hypnotic powers. *True:* Only the

snake's unblinking stare, caused by its lack of movable eyelids, gives us the idea that it is trying to hypnotize its victim.

6. *False:* Snakes spring from the ground to attack a victim. *True:* No snake jumps clear of the ground to strike.

7. *False:* Snakes are slimy. *True:* Snakes are completely covered with dry scales.

8. *False:* Snakes have yellow blood or no blood at all. *True:* Their blood is red and practically the same as that of a mammal.

When you get to know the truth about snakes, and understand why they behave as they do, you may find yourself regarding them with interest rather than horror.

Reptiles — Past and Present

Snakes are reptiles, a name scientists have given to a group of animals that includes lizards, turtles, crocodiles, and alligators. The name was suggested by the Latin word for "creeping."

Reptiles were the most important animals on earth millions of years ago. Porpoise-like species lived in the ocean while batlike reptiles flew in the air. The land was dominated by reptiles called dinosaurs. At first they were no larger than rabbits; later they developed species far bigger and heavier than the largest elephant. We do not know for certain why these mighty creatures disappeared—changes in the earth's climate may have been the cause. Whatever the reason, the importance of reptiles dwindled and warm-blooded mammals became the outstanding animals.

THE COLD-BLOODED SNAKES

All reptiles are alike in being covered with scales or bony plates, and all are cold-blooded. (They derive their heat from external sources, whereas warm-blooded animals derive theirs from within their bodies.) We find, however, that reptiles vary greatly in the way they live and in the places they inhabit. Many of them dwell only in regions where summer conditions prevail all year; but there are some snakes that have to adjust to a climate with extreme variations of heat and cold.

Sleeping Through the Winter: Though cold does not endanger a snake's life until it reaches a few degrees below freezing, a lesser drop in temperature is enough to cause sluggishness; and a sluggish snake does not have the energy to procure food. The solution in cold climates is to hibernate in a well-sheltered rocky crevice or in the ground below the frost line. In this way the snake is protected from a fall in body temperature that would be low enough to cause death. The animal can survive hibernation without eating, provided it is in a healthy and well-fattened condition at the beginning of its long rest.

THE SNAKE'S BODY—MORE THAN A TAIL

Many children, and countless adults as well, think of a snake as a long tail attached to a head. This is far from a true picture—there is a very efficient body between head and tail!

This body contains a stomach capable of amazing distension and digestive powers, a liver, kidneys, and other organs too. The snake's heart differs from a mammal's in having only three chambers. (A mammal's heart has four.) The right lung is quite elongated, much more developed than the left.

THE SNAKE'S TAIL

The length of the tail differs according to the species. However, if you scrutinize a snake's underside, you will see that the tail has a definite starting point. There a distinctly enlarged scale—sometimes divided into two overlapping parts—covers the orifice through which wastes pass. This marks the beginning of the tail.

Another way of distinguishing the tail from the rest of the body in most snakes is that the underside scales are large and each of them extends across the whole undersurface of the body— whereas the scales on the underside of the tail are almost always arranged in two columns. A zoologist dissecting a snake observes a still more obvious division of tail and body, for the long series of ribs ends where the ribless tail begins.

THE SNAKE'S HEAD

There are two reasons for the snake's fixed gaze: It has no movable eyelids, and its eyeballs are capable of only slight motion. This results in its "stony stare" and the false belief that snakes hypnotize their prey.

The Snake's Hearing Aid: Though snakes have no ears, they might be said to have a sense of hearing as sounds are transmitted to them through ground vibrations. Tests have been made with cobras to illustrate this point. After the snakes' eyes had been bound with adhesive tape, someone walked toward the animals. Immediately they reared and faced in the direction from which the footsteps were approaching. By way of contrast, the noise made by blowing a bugle brought no response.

This inability to hear sounds carried through the air tends to disprove the Hindu snake charmer's claim that music charms serpents into dancing. The truth seems to be that the snakes merely follow the continuous movement of the musician's arms or knees as he plays his reed instrument.

You can quite easily see the snake's nostrils. There is one on either side of the snout, and they function in the normal manner.

Molting—How Snakes Shed Their Skin

Your child may be thrilled by the discovery of a discarded snakeskin in the course of his summer wanderings. If he visits the zoo he may see just how this molting takes place. The snake loses its lustrous appearance before shedding; its bright colors are dimmed. Even the eyes become milky and the color of the eyes is obscured.

This goes on for a week or two; then the snake's normal coloration returns and it is ready to molt. It finds a rough, hard object and rubs its nose and chin against it until its skin breaks. Once the head is freed, the snake wriggles its body until the whole skin peels off, inside out.

Why Shedding is Necessary: Molting is necessary because the skin to which a snake's scales are attached, cannot grow. After the skin has stretched as much as possible to accommodate the growing snake, it must be discarded. Actually a new layer of skin forms beneath the old one before molting takes place. There is no regular interval for shedding: It depends to a great extent on the age and vitality of the reptile. Young snakes shed more frequently than adults, and healthy individuals more often than those in poor condition.

How Snakes Move

If you discover a snake on hard, packed soil, you will notice that it moves very slowly. But once it gets off this smooth surface into long grass or on rough ground, it will whisk out of sight with surprising swiftness.

Observe a captive snake and you will see the reason for this change in pace. When it is placed on a large piece of glass, it will slip and slide ineffectively; but if it is transferred to loose sand, it is immediately able to make progress. This it does with sideways movements, keeping the full length of its body against the ground.

You will observe that the creature leaves in its wake a series of slightly curved piles of sand; these prove to be pivots the reptile has raised in pushing its body forward. Next watch a snake on rough grass. Here it will travel with even greater ease—each blade of grass serves as a pivot.

"Legs" Without Feet: To produce this undulating movement—apparently its most usual method of traveling—the snake depends largely on its muscles and ribs which, in effect, are footless legs. The ribs are attached to the backbone and also to the muscles and the slightly overlapping scales on the underpart of the body.

When the muscles are moved forward, the scales are carried forward also. When the muscles are pulled back, the lower edges of the scales press and catch against any roughness on the surface over which the snake rests, and push it forward, using the rough spot for leverage. The snake does not move muscles all along its body at the same time; instead, it brings them forward gradually, and the scales move in waves.

Side-winding: Another method snakes occasionally employ is to curve the body into an S form and then straighten it out again, pushing forward a little in the process. Some desert snakes have developed a specialized method called "side-winding" which is practically indescribable except that the body is thrown into great

SIDEWINDING FOR DESERT TRAVEL
Most snakes move forward with the body flat against the ground. Not so this desert rattler, which progresses in S-shaped loops—a motion known as sidewinding. This is an effective technique for crawling on sand and it is used not only by the American rattler, but by snakes in the deserts of Africa and Asia as well.

loops and seems to be flowing sidewise. Using these motions a snake does not waste energy building pivots; yet it does not slip backward.

Snake Tracks: Snakes leave trails in sand or dust that are just as revealing in their way as mammal footprints. Experts not only identify the kind of snake by its trail—they can tell the approximate rate of speed at which it was moving when the trail was made.

How Snakes Breed

It is often said that some snakes lay eggs while others bear living young; yet actually all species reproduce by means of eggs. The difference between egg-laying and "live-bearing" consists in this: The live-bearing female retains the eggs in her oviduct *until the embryo is fully developed.* When the offspring are "born" they are covered by a thin membrane which soon bursts. Only about one-fourth of the known species of snakes follow this procedure.

Snake Eggs

When a female of the other species is ready to deposit her eggs, she finds a sunny sandbank or rotting log in which to burrow a hole. There she lays her eggs—the number, size, and shape depend on the species. Usually they are elliptical, with flattened ends. When first laid, the eggs are covered with a moist and sticky skin which gradually becomes tough and leathery. They absorb water and thus continue to grow after leaving the mother's body until they have increased about one-third in size.

THE EGG-TOOTH

Projecting from the middle of the upper jaw of the full-grown embryo is an egg-tooth with which it slits the tough egg skin when it is ready to emerge as a perfectly formed young snake. If you rub your finger over the nose of a baby snake you may feel this egg-tooth, which remains until the baby is about a week old.

How Snakes Kill

It may well be that the horror snakes arouse in many people is evoked by their methods of killing. A tiger's prey is just as dead as a snake's victim; but constriction and poison somehow seem more sinister means of inflicting death than fang and claw.

Snakes get their food in three different ways. For the first and most primitive, the reptile seizes its prey by throwing its coils about a victim—without constriction—and then swallows it alive. Constriction is a second method, suffocating the victim until its heart and lungs can no longer function properly. At one time it was believed that constrictors crushed the bones of any creature within their grip; today we know this theory to be erroneous.

Poison is the third method of killing. There are several types of poisonous snakes; those known as vipers and pit vipers have the most effective poison apparatus. The group includes rattlesnakes, copperheads, water moccasins, bushmasters, and the tropical fer-de-lance.

How Poison Fangs Work

All these snakes have hollow fangs in the upper jaw, firmly anchored to the bone above, which they can move to thrust the fangs forward for a strike. When they are not in use, the fangs can be folded back against the roof of the mouth.

As a child, you may have been told that the mere pressure of a snake's fangs against a solid substance brought forth the venom.

It is not quite so simple as that. The snake has its poison supply in two sacs—one in either cheek. Each sac is connected to the fangs by a duct that runs under the eye and over the bone to which the fangs are attached. When the viper strikes, muscles that surround the poison sacs, contract and force the venom through the ducts into the fangs, from which it flows to the wound just made in the victim's flesh.

HEARTY EATERS

The ability of snakes to swallow objects larger than themselves is one of their most spectacular traits. The larger snakes, such as pythons or boas, sometimes devour a goat or small deer whole. Such a feat would be impossible without a number of special body features with which nature has provided them.

Let's look at their jaws, for example. An extra bone hinges the upper jaw to the lower, allowing them to spread far apart. Also, the lower jawbones are held together only by elastic ligaments and they can separate at the chin to further increase the size of the mouth. The teeth point backward and thus present no obstacle to objects taken into the mouth. Even the snake's sides are adapted to the task—they have great elasticity and can stretch to many times their normal dimensions!

THE MOVABLE WINDPIPE

Despite all these helps, you might still expect a snake to choke to death swallowing anything large enough to force its jawbones wide apart. The snake overcomes this difficulty by being able to extend a portion of its windpipe forward—even a few inches beyond its open mouth if need be! By this means it can breathe during the long slow process of forcing down a meal apparently far too big for its size.

Some species of snakes can live on three or four big meals a year; others may eat a moderate meal every week or ten days.

The Ways of a Rattler

Children are understandably curious about the hows and whys of a rattler's rattle. How does a tail tip turn into a rattle? Why do some snakes have rattles? How does the rattle work?

The rattle is made up of a series of horny sections or "buttons" on the end of the spinal column. They are loosely interlocked, and when the snake vibrates its tail they click against each other. Many other kinds of snakes also vibrate their tails, and if they happen to be lying among dead leaves the resulting rustle sounds like a rattle. However, the rattlesnake's vibration is distinctive. It is a half metallic, half insect-like sound, somewhat like the dull buzz of the bumblebee.

THE RATTLE RINGS

At birth a rattler has a bulbous swelling at the tip of its tail. When the snake molts, the tip of its old skin cannot be pulled over this enlargement, so it remains and forms the beginning of a rattle. As successive molts take place, the tip of the skin that cannot be shed forms an additional segment or ring. The rings form around a bone known as the "shaker," made up of the last seven or eight vertebrae which fuse together soon after the snake is born.

THE DANGEROUS DIAMOND-BACK RATTLER

The diamond-back, so called because of the distinctive diamond-shaped pattern on its back, is one of the relatively few harmful snakes in the United States. Practically all the deaths by snake bite in this country (estimated at about a hundred a year) are caused by diamond-back rattlers, prairie and timber rattlers, and water moccasins. If proper treatment is given, their bites rarely prove fatal.

The old theory that a ring is added each year has been disproved. Sometimes several molts take place in a year and rings are added; it is also possible for the snake to molt without a new ring being created. This irregularity, not to mention the fact that rings are often broken from the end, makes it impossible to reckon a snake's age by the size of its rattle. If a rattle is unbroken, however, you may approximate the animal's age by allowing one year for each two rings.

What the Rattle Is For

Many snakes have the habit of vibrating the tip of the tail when they are excited, but the rattler is the only kind equipped with a "noise-maker." We do not entirely understand the purpose of the rattle. The once general belief that this reptile always rattles before striking is no longer credited. Apparently it does use its rattle, as a rule, to try to frighten enemies dangerous to its own safety.

As for the theory of "warning" prospective prey, some observers have decided that this snake sounds its rattle to startle birds, rabbits, or other possible victims into momentary inactivity, thus gaining time for a strike. Other people claim that it never rattles before attacking. There are many reports of rattlers that never rattled at any time, and habitually struck without warning.

Kinds of Rattlesnakes

There are no less than fifteen different species of rattlesnakes in the United States and they live in many localities. The deadly diamond-back of the southeastern states frequents neighborhoods where water is plentiful, the timber rattler lives in woodland mountain regions, the prairie rattler haunts the Great Plains of the West; another species is found in desert wastes.

Rattlers are among the more important kinds of snakes in our country that bear live young. The mother gives her offspring no care—but none is necessary. They are able to fend for themselves immediately, and have been seen eating ten minutes after birth!

Spectacular Deadly Snakes

A visit to the snake house at a zoo gives you a first-hand acquaintance with species you would never welcome as house pets, though they are well thought of by zoo keepers.

THE GOOD-NATURED BOA

One of these deadly creatures is the boa constrictor—a big reptile of South America that reaches a length of eighteen feet. It is quite hardy in captivity, and many specimens are good-natured and easily fed with birds and small mammals. Though most South American Indians dread this boa and believe it to be poisonous, it is not. As a rule this boa seems anxious to keep away from humans, but it will occasionally appear in a native village, apparently attracted by the domestic fowl.

Still greater in size than the boa constrictor is a water boa known as the anaconda, native to the river valleys of nothern

THE ANACONDA — GIANT AMONG SNAKES

A huge boa fossil of about fifty million years ago, unearthed in Egypt, is supposed to have been fifty feet long. Our modern anaconda (or water boa), the largest of New World snakes, has a length of over twenty feet. It lives in South America and though it spends much of its time in the water, it is also an expert tree climber. The anaconda is not poisonous. It will seldom attack humans without provocation.

South America. Reliable records show that this species sometimes attains a length of twenty-eight feet. The anaconda is the largest snake in the New World.

Pythons—The Largest Snakes

Among the most fearsome-looking reptiles are the pythons, which have been imported from Asia or Africa. There are giants among them: a twenty-five-foot Indian python may weigh more than two hundred pounds; the reticulated python, not quite so thick in body, may be nearly thirty feet long. The large pythons eat a variety of animals, but their taste runs to fairly large mammals.

"Snake-charming" showmen frequently use relatively small specimens of the rock python in their acts, as these snakes become very docile in captivity. Nevertheless, there is always some danger. If the snake accidentally throws a complete coil about the body of the performer, it will begin to constrict and throw new coils. The "charmer" must quickly straighten out the reptile or be in real danger of strangulation. Anyone who closely watches a snake charmer with a python or boa, will observe that every movement of his hands and arms is made solely to prevent the snake from forming a coil.

The Cobra's Double Personality

A child who has been reading colorful stories of the Orient in which cobras play a sinister part, may well be disappointed when he sees this snake in the zoo. When it is not excited, this dangerously venomous reptile looks quite commonplace. Alarmed or angry the cobra presents a far different picture, weaving its raised head back and forth with its hood erect.

The Cobra's Terrifying Hood: The hood is actually only the skin of the neck stretched taut. The cobra has a series of ribs on the sides of the vertebrae of the neck, and when it is excited it uses powerful muscles to draw these ribs forward, thus stretching its skin and forcing the scales wide apart.

Seen from in back when its hood is spread, the Indian cobra gives the impression of having eyes on top of its head. But what the observer sees are merely markings; the eyes are at the sides of the head, little of which is visible when the hood is open. It is a mistake to think that cobras can be identified by the erection of the hood; other snakes—such as the harmless hognose snake—possess the same ability.

While people most frequently think of India as the home of cobras, these snakes also dwell in Africa. The king cobra, which may grow as long as eighteen feet, is the largest venomous snake known. It is very aggressive and its poison is deadly. The common Indian cobra, which rarely attains a length of more than six feet, also causes many deaths every year.

Some Common Harmless Snakes

THE GARTER SNAKE

We have many kinds of garter snakes in the United States and they are well distributed all over the country. The "common" variety (often called the garden snake) is found in the eastern states up into Canada. You cannot be sure of recognizing it by its color, which varies in different individuals.

The ground or major body color may be olive, brown, or black. There is usually a stripe of yellow, green, or whitish hue down the center of the back. Along each side is a similar stripe, subdued in tone, which may be broken up into spots. The underside is greenish white or yellow. A full-grown specimen is about thirty inches long.

Where Garter Snakes Are Found: You are most likely to come upon garter snakes in summer along the banks and edges of streams where their favorite foods—toads, frogs, earthworms, and insects—are plentiful. In the fall they are likely to gather on rocky ledges or stony hillsides. Here each finds a crevice or makes a burrow, which may extend more than a yard underground, where it sleeps through the cold weather.

HOGNOSE SNAKES—HAM ACTORS

The garter snake and the hognose snake both make excellent pets—though the hognose variety has bluffed its way into a bad reputation. When it is frightened, it immediately swells its body, flattens its neck like a cobra, and hisses in a vicious manner. These fearsome actions have earned it such names as "spreading adder," "blowing viper," and "blow snake."

However, the hognose has no poisonous power whatever. If it succeeds in bluffing its enemy, it quickly calms down and crawls into seclusion. If the bluff fails, "hognose" plays dead, rolling over on its back and becoming completely quiet!

How the Hognose Got Its Name: This snake has a remarkable nose. It is equipped with a hard, trowel-shaped shield that plows efficiently into loose soil and often roots out toads that are buried near the surface. Its diet is made up exclusively of toads and frogs.

The Maligned Milk Snake

This snake is the subject of one of the most fantastic of all snake myths. According to the fable, the milk snake milks cows. Not only is this feat physically impossible, but no milk snake in captivity could ever be persuaded to drink milk. This snake's presence in barns and stables is explained by its liking for mice and rats as food. Thus, instead of being a menace, the milk snake is an ally of the farmer.

Though the milk snake's ground color is light gray, it is covered with so many brown or dark gray spots that either of these may seem to be the predominating color. The underside is white with square black spots and blotches. A fully grown specimen ranges from thirty inches to three feet long.

King Snakes—Cannibals

The common king snake is an impressive-looking creature, for it may attain a length of six feet. In the natural state it is a cannibal; in fact it is noted for its attacks on other snakes—even rattlers. It is black and decorated with yellow spots and bands. Strangely enough, some king snakes in captivity show no interest in snakes as food, while others will eat nothing else. King snakes are nevertheless easy to feed as a rule, and are inclined to be docile with their keepers. There are fourteen different kinds of king snakes, and they are found throughout most of the United States.

WATER SNAKES—HARMLESS AND DANGEROUS KINDS

Children who go fishing are very likely to encounter this dingy brown reptile, which haunts dams, wharves, rocks and bushes near water. Because of its protective color plan it may escape notice until it moves suddenly. Like the hognose snake, it puts on a great show when cornered, flattening out its body and striking fiercely.

However, the water snake has no venom and its teeth can inflict only harmless wounds. It makes a good pet. While it will eat almost anything, it particularly likes fish. Its usual size is from thirty inches to three feet. Water snakes are found over almost all of eastern North America.

From southern Virginia to Florida and the Gulf states, you must be extremely cautious about water snakes; for this section is the home of the deadly water moccasin, which has a superficial resemblance to the harmless water snake.

How to Recognize a Poisonous Snake

A child who is determined to be not only an observer of snakes but also a collector of them, should be well coached in safety rules. Of first importance is knowing the character of all snakes in your locality. If there are poisonous species among them, it is essential to distinguish them from the harmless ones. *Collecting poisonous species should be left to the experts!*

The poisonous snakes of the United States fall into four groups: rattlesnakes, which have been found in every state; copperheads, which are distributed from New England to Texas and in all the southern states; water moccasins, found chiefly in the southern and southeastern states; and coral snakes, which live only in the deep South, from North Carolina to Texas and parts of Arizona. While this broad distribution sounds forbidding, there are many areas within these regions where you will find only harmless species.

WHAT POISONOUS SNAKES LOOK LIKE

The rattlesnakes vary considerably in size and general appearance, but all of them are identified by their "rattles." You can distinguish copperheads by hourglass-shaped markings on the back. Usually, but not always, the top of the head is bronze or copper colored.

Water moccasins have markings resembling those of the copperhead, but they are not noticeably copper colored. The inside of the mouth has a whitish color. Unlike most snakes, which try a hurried retreat at the approach of an enemy, water moccasins stand their ground and fight any intruder in their territory.

Coral snakes are brightly colored, with red, yellow, and black rings encircling the body. They closely resemble certain harmless species, and considerable concentration is needed to distinguish the harmless types from the deadly poisonous coral species.

WHEN YOU ENCOUNTER A SNAKE

If you accidentally come upon a snake and are frightened, just bear in mind that the snake is doubtless as anxious to get away from you as you are to avoid it. Remember that it has no "power of hypnotism." This has been proved many times by experiments in which birds, guinea pigs, and other animals were placed in cages with a snake and where they acted entirely unconcerned about their reptile companion. If you can think of a snake as "just another animal," it will be easy for you to remain calm and move away from your unwelcome discovery.

If you are actively interested in snake collecting, you ought to be thoroughly familiar with first-aid treatment for poisonous snake bite and have a snake-bite kit along on all field trips if there are poisonous species in the vicinity.

You will also want to have a "snake stick" for capturing live specimens. A two-pronged metal fork attached to a pole, or a cut stick with a forked end, may serve your purpose. You can pin down the snake behind the head until you are ready to pick it up and transfer it to a bag.

Snakes As Pets

When a youngster has captured a harmless snake and is keeping it as a pet, he may wish to build a cage especially for his prize. However, an ordinary rectangular fish tank will serve the purpose effectively for a small specimen such as a ribbon or garter snake. To accommodate a king snake or one of the other big fellows, the cage should be at least equal in length to the reptile's body. This will make it possible for the snake to coil and uncoil and move about comfortably.

A cage should have a water dish large enough for the snake to crawl into. A big ash tray is convenient and large enough for a garter snake. Cover the floor of the cage with moss, gravel, or slightly moistened sand to make cleaning easier. The cage should be wiped out regularly with warm water and soap, and the floor covering changed. All waste matter and uneaten food must be removed daily.

There is no harm in exposing a snake to direct sunlight provided that shade is available at all times. Sun that does not feel excessively hot to your hand may be dangerously hot for a snake; a reptile's body absorbs heat and becomes warmer and warmer, as would a piece of iron lying in the sun. A rock or block of wood placed in the cage helps furnish shade, and it is also useful to the snake for rubbing against when it sheds its skin.

Proper Diet for a Pet Snake: A captive snake that has eaten well from spring through fall may safely go through several winter months without eating. But if you have a local specimen that refuses food for nine or ten weeks during warm weather, it is best to give it its freedom. Forcible feeding by an inexperienced person is sure to be fatal to the snake.

Of course it is necessary to know which snakes will eat what. Thus, garter snakes thrive on frogs, tadpoles, and earthworms; larger species, including black racers and pilots, eat rats, mice, rabbits, and gophers. King snakes may eat other snakes, as they do in the natural state, or they may prefer rodents. Very small species such as the green snake eat earthworms, grasshoppers, and other insects. The insect-eating snakes need more frequent feedings than those that feed on rodents.

You may be told that snakes will not touch dead animals, but zoo keepers have found that these reptiles will consume dead prey as readily as living victims. The keepers sometimes teach them to eat raw meat by first serving it mixed with chopped earthworms, then gradually reducing the quantity of worms. When dead food is used, it is moved right in front of the snake to attract its attention.

Captive snakes are likely to be frightened by sudden movements of your hand. "Slow and easy" is the best rule in dealing with them. When you lift a snake, give its long, slender body adequate support; the animal is not comfortable when it is dangled by the head or the tail.

If snakes capture your family's imagination, a generally satisfactory program is to try keeping one or two during the summer and then to release them so that they may hibernate under natural conditions in wintertime.

Turtles

Of all reptile pets, turtles are probably the most commonly enjoyed. Your child is apt to bring home one of these creatures from camp or from an outing to ponds or fields; or they may be bought in pet or novelty stores.

Unfortunately thousands of turtles are entrusted to the care of people who understand little about their way of life. If your child has a turtle, you and he will certainly want to know more about it. And even if you don't have a turtle pet, you will agree that it is a fascinating animal to watch and study if you are at all interested in nature's ways.

Armor Plate for Defense

At first glance a turtle may give the impression of an inanimate piece of armor; when it is uncertain of its surroundings, it cautiously keeps every bit of its body under its hard shell. Once the turtle feels safe, however, you will see the snakelike head project from the front of its shell, the pointed tail poke out from the rear, and two wide legs appear at each side. Then you will notice

THE PAINTED TURTLE AND ITS ATTRACTIVE SHELL

Encased in armor, turtles have sturdily maintained themselves against their enemies for many millions of years. They are wary and unsociable creatures—at least when they suspect the presence of an enemy. The painted turtle, with a shell about six inches long, has vivid markings of red and yellow on its blackish or olive upper shell. It feeds on water plants and animals, eats them only under water.

that even the soft body is covered with rough, coarse skin and often with many scales.

You can appreciate the effectiveness of this protective covering when you realize that turtles have survived for many millions of years with no means of fighting countless larger animals that might attack them. Their success is strictly due to defense equipment. (A noteworthy exception, of course, is the big snapper with its vicious hooked beak.)

The Protective Shell: The upper shell (the "carapace") varies in shape depending on the species of turtle. This shell grows attached to the turtle's backbone; in a few species the carapace is quite flat, in others it is rounded.

The lower shell (the "plastron") also varies in shape and size and is attached to the breastbone. There is also a great deal of variation from one species to one another as to size and color of the turtle's body. Other oddities include the tail of the snapping turtle, which bears a saw-toothed armor of plates, and the front and rear "trap doors" which the box turtle can pull up against the carapace to enclose the body completely!

A child may wonder how a creature encased so completely can manage to breathe. The turtle's shoulder and hip bones do most of the work in contracting and expanding the lungs. The constant pulsation you can observe in the throat is caused by air being swallowed.

Sight, Smell, and Teeth

Like snakes, turtles lack movable eyelids. However, turtles have a protective membrane which comes up from the lower edge to cover the eye. Some species have nostrils no larger than pinholes, and their poor sense of smell is not surprising. Others, better equipped, have a keen sense of smell.

Though a turtle has no real teeth, its mouth has sawlike cutting edges. It does not bother to chew food but simply tears it to pieces.

How to Take Care of Turtle Pets

We naturally avoid the big snapping turtles, but the small ones are good pet material because they are hardy and usually easy to feed. (This is also true of musk turtles.) The kind you are most likely to find in pet shops is the Troost's turtle, which is green with yellow markings.

Keeping a Turtle Pet Comfortable: To keep water turtles healthy, you must give them some means of getting out of water to dry and sun themselves. If they are lodged in a tank or aquarium, a stone island or floating piece of wood will answer the purpose.

Instead of an aquarium, you may use a dry cage or box to advantage. In that case you must furnish it with a dish of water deep enough to serve as a swimming pool, and so arranged that the turtle will find it easily accessible. The rest of the floor of the cage may be covered with stones, sand, gravel, or moss.

The water, especially in the aquarium-type housing, should consistently be between 75 and 85 degrees. Chilling at night must be avoided. (Most pet turtles come from southern states, and they need a little extra warmth in order to thrive in northern regions.)

While turtles should have an abundance of sunshine (or even bask under a sun lamp), they must also have a shady retreat. Too much heat can kill them.

Menus for Turtle Pets: Most water turtles prefer to swallow their food under water. Small bits put on a broom straw will often arouse an indifferent pet. Raw, lean meat or fish scraped or chopped fine is usually acceptable; but small worms, insects, tadpoles and other little creatures are the natural food of young turtles and are excellent if available.

A good way to supplement the home diet is to mix a bit of bone meal and a drop of cod-liver oil frequently with meat. Lettuce and other greens or raw fruits and vegetables add variety to the menu. Baby turtles may be fed as often and as much as they will eat; but a good feeding about twice a week should be enough. A straight diet of "ant eggs" or house flies is not satisfactory.

Turtle Ailments and Remedies: Turtles are often afflicted with softening of the shell and swollen, closed eyes. Recommended remedies are a warmer cage, more sunlight, and a more balanced diet. Swollen eyes should be carefully wiped twice a day with cotton dipped in warm boric-acid solution. When a turtle refuses food for a long time, its appetite may improve if you give the animal more warmth and sunlight. In winter there is a natural tendency for turtles to eat less frequently and to be less active.

Some Common Turtles

Ponds are the most likely places to encounter turtles, though aside from the species that frequent ponds there are also sea turtles and those that live exclusively on land. "Tortoise" is a general term that covers all types. "Turtle" is usually applied to sea or fresh-water forms; "terrapin" is the name (of Indian origin) for certain American fresh-water species.

You may find a wood tortoise in the damp woods, far away from water. Its upper shell—one of its distinguishing features—may reach a length of six and a half inches. It is made up of many plates ornamented with concentric ridges. With the exception of the top of the head and the limbs, all the fleshy parts of this creature are brick-red. It thrives in captivity and will soon learn

THE GIANT TORTOISES OF THE GALAPAGOS ISLANDS
In contrast to the six-inch painted turtle, the giant tortoise reaches a length of
four feet and weighs as much as five hundred pounds. It was once a favorite source
of meat for Pacific whalers that touched at the islands off Ecuador. Though these
giant tortoises may live to well over a hundred years in the natural state, they
have been subjected to relentless extermination by man.

to accept food from your fingers. Tender vegetables, berries,
insects, and chopped meat form an acceptable diet.

Another turtle that you can tame with very satisfactory results
is the spotted turtle, found in many ponds and marshy streams.
Its black upper shell is decorated with numerous spots, whence
its name. The spotted turtle enjoys perching on a log for long
stretches of time, but its feeding is done under water.

You may recognize another pond turtle—often called the painted
terrapin—by the red mottled border of its shell. This is a good
aquarium pet but it is much too aggressive to be kept with other
creatures.

Snapping turtles, so intriguing as babies, may attain a weight
of forty pounds as adults, with a shell fourteen inches long. Be
on the watch for them in slow-running streams, ponds, or marshes.

The "alligator snapper" of the South sometimes weighs a
hundred pounds.

The mud turtle and the musk turtle are really water dwellers to all intents and purposes; the only time they come to shore is to deposit their eggs. They find their food in muddy bottoms of ponds and streams, and eat only under water. The musk turtle, which has two broad yellow stripes on either side of its head, gives off a strong odor on being handled. The head of the mud turtle is ornamented with greenish yellow spots.

The box turtle, unlike the mud and musk turtles, lives entirely on land. It is easy to recognize this species by the hinges on the front and rear of the lower shell by which it can "box" itself completely within its armor. This turtle grows to a length of about five inches.

After the wintertime hibernation a turtle deposits her eggs in a shallow hole in earth or sand. As a rule there are five or six eggs, though some species lay more—the snapper, for example, usually produces about two dozen.

Chameleons and Other Lizards

If you take a casual look at a lizard, it will remind you very much of a snake. Outwardly there is not much difference between them—except that most lizards have legs. Nevertheless, a legless lizard is a lizard, not a snake.

One definite difference you can observe between the two groups is in the structure of the lower jawbone. In all snakes the lower jaw is made up of two bones joined at the chin by a more or less flexible ligament. The lizard also has a lower jawbone on either side, but these are attached firmly at the center of the chin.

Another visible difference is that lizards generally have movable eyelids—something no snake possesses.

The Secret of the Chameleon's Color Changes

At a fair or circus, boys and girls frequently buy a souvenir in the form of a little lizard which they are told is a chameleon. As it happens, true chameleons are seldom seen in our country; they are animals of the Old World, belonging especially to Africa. But another kind of lizard, often called the "American chameleon," also has the ability of the true chameleons to change color frequently. It is this American lizard that is usually peddled at amusement places.

Most children are apt to overrate the chameleon's ability to change color; they take the excessively simplified view that the animal speedily alters to the color of whatever object it stands upon. Chameleons do, to a great extent, harmonize with the foliage on which they rest; but several other factors are involved.

Light and temperature are important influences in changing the animal's color—and so are excitement and fright. Not only does the tone of the body change, but strange patterns come and go on the skin. How does this happen? To put it briefly: Beneath the reptile's skin are a number of tiny branched cells containing pigments of various colors. Whenever the chameleon contracts or expands these branches, the position of the pigments is changed. Those that travel to the surface of the skin are partly responsible for the color the animal suggests.

All-around Eyes and a Quick Tongue

The true chameleon has a versatility that can be positively startling. It can roll one eye upward while the other rolls down— or turn one eye forward and the other backward! Its tongue is a "secret weapon" that shoots forward to a distance of seven or eight inches. On its sticky tip the chameleon snares insects that apparently were well out of harm's way.

How to Keep a Chameleon Pet

Old World chameleons rarely eat in captivity and seldom live longer than five or six months when they are kept confined. The so-called "American chameleon" is not so remarkable an animal, but it does make a better pet.

The American species should be kept in a warm sunny place and fed crickets, cockroaches, or live flies. If it loses interest in eating, you may revive its appetite by moving food slowly in front of it. Your chameleon needs water; but do not put it in a pan or cup in the cage. Instead, sprinkle the water about the cage so that the little creature can lap up the drops just as it drinks dew from leaves in its natural state.

LIZARDS OF THE SOUTHWEST

Children who live in the southwestern United States, and others whose vacation travels take them over some of the arid stretches of this region, may encounter a variety of lizards. There is the whiptail or race runner, a striped species that is active all day in open areas; the collared lizard, a scrappy fighter that has been known to attack rattlesnakes; the big chuckwalla, which may grow as long as sixteen inches; and the banded gecko, a lizard active chiefly at night.

THE RESOURCEFUL FENCE LIZARD
This lizard, about six inches long, has a very lengthy tail. If a pursuer grasps the tail the lizard is able to shed it, later growing a new one to replace the one it lost. In some lizards the tail is four or five times the length of the rest of the body!

The only poisonous lizard found in the United States is the Gila monster—a colorful figure strongly marbled with coal black and some other marking, often pink, yellow, or white. Its stout body may grow to a length of twenty inches, although eighteen inches is pretty much the average. Its bite can quickly kill a small mammal and seriously affect a human being.

Lizards are able to grow a new tail when they have lost the

THE ONLY POISONOUS LIZARD OF THE UNITED STATES
The attractively colored Gila monster is large for a lizard—about twenty inches long or so. It lives in our southwestern desert lands, and has the useful trait of being able to store food in its tail! The Gila monster moves sluggishly as a rule, but strikes quickly when injecting its venom. It rarely bites, and its poison is not fatal to humans. It lays its eggs in the sand, where the sun hatches them.

original one through some mishap. The true chameleon, however, lacks this regrowing ability.

Alligators and Crocodiles

A child is likely to see these giant reptiles only in zoos, for their natural range in the United States is limited to the swamps and lagoons of the Carolinas, Georgia, and Florida west to Texas. If he (or his parent) looks at these animals only casually, he is sure to ask this natural question:

"What's the difference between an alligator and a crocodile?"

How Alligators and Crocodiles Differ: If you look closely, you will quickly perceive a decided difference in the shape of the snout. You will see that the alligator's snout is wide and more rounded than that of the crocodile.

There is also a difference in the teeth. In the case of the crocodile, the fourth tooth on either side of its lower jaw fits into notches on the outside of the upper jaw—so that even when its mouth is closed, the vicious fangs show. The usual effect is to give the crocodile a fiercer and more belligerent appearance than the alligator. Nor are looks deceiving here, for on the whole alligators are timid and try to escape any encounter with human beings, whereas crocodiles are sulky and ferocious by turns.

In the zoo a keeper will often step among and over alligators while cleaning their swimming pool—but he does not take such chances with his crocodile charges. At the circus you may see the "strong man" wrestle with the lazy and slow-moving alligator— never with the quick and active crocodile.

Both alligators and crocodiles spend much of their time in water. Their nostrils, located on top of little bumps at the end of the snout, take in air as the animals float just under the surface of the water. They can even feed under water by shutting off the food tube from the tube that leads to the lungs.

Unlike most reptiles, alligators and crocodiles are able to make noises with their mouths. The young produce a curious grunting sound, while the bellowing of the old bulls may be heard a mile away.

ALLIGATORS LOVE SUNSHINE

Alligators love to bask in the sun, reserving most of their feeding activities for night-time. They favor temperatures of between 75° and 85° Fahrenheit; a temperature over 100° would be fatal to them. An alligator occasionally uses its powerful tail to knock down its prey. As a rule, it tries to keep away from human beings.

Alligators in the Home: An alligator is an unlikely but not impossible pet. It is not suited to captivity and seldom lives more than a couple of years away from its natural surroundings. However, it is occasionally possible to obtain young 'gators and—judging from inquiries to zoos and museums about their care—a number of people do cope with the problem of keeping an alligator in the home.

A little alligator, like other reptile pets, must be kept in a consistently warm temperature with plenty of sunshine, and with shade always available. Its cage must be kept dry and clean and furnished with a pan of water. Feeding it once or twice a week is enough. Raw fish or bits of meat should be offered on a moving stick, preferably to one side of the 'gator's head.

Frogs

Naturalists call the frog an "amphibian"—a creature that lives a double life. This is a good name for the frog, as it divides its time between land and water. It has characteristics in common with fish: It is cold-blooded, and it lays its eggs in the water. In other respects it is akin to reptiles, which are also cold-blooded but are able to live on dry land. Thus the frog, along with the toad, newt, salamander, and other amphibians, is a "connecting link" between the two great cold-blooded groups—fish and reptiles.

THE HOBBY OF COLLECTING FROGS' EGGS

For generations children have sought frogs' eggs, and successful hunters still bring them home to observe their development in an aquarium. Collecting eggs should not be encouraged, as it makes inroads on the frog population. However, the ability to recognize eggs adds interest to a springtime expedition to a pond or quiet stream.

If a child is serious about exploring nature and particularly anxious to watch tadpole development, it is important to know what species he is collecting; the time required for development of the eggs varies widely according to the species of the parent frogs. Wood frogs take on adult form the same season the eggs are laid; green frog tadpoles usually do not grow into frogs until the following summer; bullfrogs may remain in a tadpole state for two or three years!

How the Eggs Develop

We find frog eggs laid in a transparent protective jelly. The shape of the jelly mass is one clue to the species; the date it is discovered is another. The eggs of leopard or wood frogs, for example, may be found by the first of April; those of the green frog do not appear until a bit later, and the bullfrog may not lay before July. The leopard frog's egg masses are in the form of a flattened sphere; those of the wood frog are round masses.

In the earliest stages, as the original single cell gradually divides into many, you can follow the egg's development only with the aid of a magnifying glass. It is only when the embryo begins to lengthen that it can be easily seen with the naked eye. After five or six days the embryo has a tadpole form, but it is still inside the jelly mass. About the ninth day the tadpole breaks loose from its protective covering.

How a Tadpole Grows

The Development of the Head: At first the tadpole is so shapeless that the only way to know head from tail is to observe the direction in which it swims—the head naturally goes first. But soon the head grows larger. Instead of a mouth the tadpole has a V-shaped raised sucker by which it attaches itself to water weeds. Later this gives way to a small round mouth provided with horny jaws. As the tadpole grows, the mouth gets wider and larger.

How the Tadpole Breathes: When you observe the tadpole you see little tassel-like gills appear on either side of the throat. Blood passing through the gills is purified by coming in contact with the oxygen in the water. Later the feathery gills disappear as a membrane grows down over them, and they function inside the body instead of externally. Water taken in through the nostrils passes through an opening in the throat, on over the gills, and out through a little opening, or breathing pore, at the left side of the body. This breathing pore may easily be seen in larger tadpoles.

The Legs and Tail Develop: A tadpole's flat tail, bordered by a fin, is a valuable swimming aid. But in a matter of weeks—the time depends on the species—the first sign of legs foreshadows the decline of the tail's usefulness. The hind legs appear first as mere bumps but soon push out completely with five webbed toes.

Meanwhile the front legs show just in back of the head, the left one pushing out through the breathing pore. The front feet have only four toes apiece and are not webbed; they are used for balancing, whereas the back feet serve for thrusting forward. While these changes are taking place, the tail is becoming absorbed by the body.

First Amphibian Landing: Young frogs do not always wait for the completion of their adult form before venturing on land. In late spring or early summer you may see one hopping about, still wearing its stumpy little tail. From then on the frog is primarily a land animal, though the members of most species stay near water, ready to jump in at a sign of danger or simply to refresh themselves.

The frog puts its tongue to good use. Hinged to the front of the lower jaw, the tongue can be thrust far out of the mouth to capture insects on its sticky surface.

Biggest and Smallest Frogs

The bullfrog is the giant among North American frogs. Eight inches is about its maximum length. Its head is usually a bright green, the upper part of its body green also but shading to gray and brown, and its underside is yellowish.

Other identifying features are its large eardrums and the conspicuous folds of skin which run from behind the eyes around the eardrums to the front legs. The bullfrog's deep voice is probably better known than its appearance. You may hear its sonorous *jug-o'-rum* repeatedly near lakes and ponds on summer evenings.

Just as the bullfrog is a typical "voice of summer," the little tree frog, commonly known as the peeper, might be called the "voice of spring." The spring peeper—or, more prosaically, Pickering's hyla—is one of the tiniest of froglets. Fully grown, it is about an inch long!

THE BULLFROG—OGRE OF THE LILY POND

This largest of American frogs is a menace to practically every creature that shares its pond home. It eats smaller frogs of all kinds, fish, the nymphs of dragonflies, other water insects, worms, and practically anything that fits in its huge mouth

Lilo Hess (Three Lions)

THE "REAL THING" IN CHAMELEONS

Although certain American lizards are popularly known as chameleons, the true chameleon, pictured above, is a native of Africa. One of the most fantastic of animals, it has a long, grasping tail, strangely shaped limbs, eyes that move independently of each other, a head ornamented like some huge prehistoric dinosaur's, plus the ability to change color from moment to moment, to match its background.

TWENTY THOUSAND EGGS AT A TIME

The bullfrog gets its name from its sonorous call. Though the female lays as many as twenty thousand eggs at one time, the tadpole takes quite long (three years) to develop into an adult. Protective coloration and unusual jumping ability safe. guard the frog against most enemies; but the demand for frogs' legs as a delicacy has made inroads on our frog population.

Under the throat of the male is a thin membrane that swells to surprising proportions as he blows air into it, then closes the openings to his nose and forces the air up and down his gullet. As early as March you may hear the din raised by a number of peepers going through their vocal gymnastics.

There are several reasons why the spring peeper is able to elude most observers. Aside from its tiny size, it changes color to blend with its background. In less than half an hour the dark cross on its back can alter to a mottled effect, and its body tone can change from a pale yellowish brown to leaf-green, earth-brown, or even the brighter tones of flower petals!

Another point is that the spring peeper spends a great deal of time in trees, which it can climb easily because of its marvelously adapted toes. Each toe ends in a rounded disk that secretes a sticky substance so effective that a peeper can walk up a vertical pane of glass.

Toads

Though most children delight in catching frogs, many hesitate to touch a toad. They have heard the old myth that a toad is sure to produce warts on the hand that touches it. While this much-maligned amphibian does have warts on its back, it has no power to transfer them.

Basis for the "Wart" Myth: The so-called warts are really glands which secrete a disagreeable-tasting substance. The elongated swollen glands above and just back of the ears exude a milky poisonous substance when the toad is seized by a hungry enemy. This protective feature is entirely successful in some cases, but many toads become victims of snakes and other animals.

THE TOAD EATS ITS SKIN

Unlike the slippery, slimy frog, the toad has a perfectly dry skin. It is cold to the touch because toads, like all amphibians, are cold-blooded. Though the toad sheds its skin periodically, you will never find one of these skins as you may a snake's skin. The skin is promptly swallowed by the toad that sheds it!

HOW TOADS DRINK AND BREATHE

The toad has a very absorbent skin. When it is thirsty it never drinks by mouth; instead, it stretches out in shallow water and absorbs moisture through its skin. Consequently, if pools are not available and if the atmosphere is dry, the toad will die in a short time.

The toad's breathing technique is also curious. You may notice a steady pulsation in a toad's throat that results from its swallowing air. Lacking ribs, it cannot inflate its chest to draw air into its lungs as we do.

HOW TOADS DEFEND THEMSELVES

The toad is a favorite prey of many larger animals. It cannot fight back, but it is resourceful in trying to save itself. Toads and frogs use the same means of defense: Both are jumpers capable of making long rapid jumps. The popular game "leap-frog" is a tribute to the extraordinary jumping ability of the frog, which has larger and more muscular hind legs.

TRUTH AND FICTION ABOUT TOADS

There is no truth in the quaint superstition that "it rains toads" and that "toads cause warts." The truth about toads is interesting enough—for example, a toad eats its skin after shedding it; it "drinks" by absorbing moisture through its skin; and it digs holes with its hind feet, retreating into one of these hideouts on the approach of enemies. It stays in concealment by day, becomes active at night.

With both of these amphibians protective coloration is specialized to the point of transforming color tone to blend with the background. A toad also has a clever way of disappearing. Instead of squatting where it can easily be seen, it kicks backward until its body is covered with earth. At the approach of an enemy, the toad quickly jerks its head back letting earth tumble over its head as well.

The toad also knows how to become inconspicuous by flattening out its body and, when actually trapped, it will "play dead."

Finally, if all these ruses fail and it is seized by an enemy, it emits a terrified noise.

Where to Find Toads

These amphibians are rarely out in the open during the daytime, and a child's best chance to observe their habits is to keep one as a pet. They go abroad mostly at nighttime, hunting for slugs, worms, and insects; most of the day they remain in hiding.

Toads frequent cool damp places; in suburban areas you may discover one under a porch or dug in under a sidewalk. In the fall they burrow deep into the ground to hibernate. When they awaken in the spring they make their way to a pond to breed and lay their eggs.

How Toads' Eggs Develop

The eggs of the toad, like frogs' eggs, are laid in a transparent jelly-like substance, but they can be identified by their form. The toad's eggs are laid in long strings, instead of in masses like the frog's eggs. Changes in toads' eggs take place rapidly. Tadpoles may emerge only four days after the eggs are laid; only a few weeks later the tadpoles have developed into adults.

The toads are still very small, however, and continue to grow as adults—in contrast to frogs, which attain much of their adult size while still in the tadpole stage. The final size achieved by a toad varies with the species. One kind, native to the Southwest, sometimes measures six and a half inches in length; a little green toad that lives on the grassy flatlands of the Southwest is no more than an inch and a half long.

Salamanders

A most likely time to make the acquaintance of the little amphibians known variously as salamanders, newts, or efts, is shortly after a spring or summer rain. If you are walking along a country road or woodland path, you may not even have to look for them: They are out in the open enjoying the newly fallen moisture.

At other times you may find them under stones or rotting logs, in wet crevices along a brook, and even in the water. All salamanders must stay in places where their skin will not become too dry—though some prefer more water than others do.

Frequently when a child discovers a salamander he calls it a lizard; and it does strongly suggest the small reptile. However, there are several distinguishing features. The salamander's skin may be moist, slimy, or even dry and rough; but it is never covered with scales, as is the skin of a lizard. No salamander has claws, whereas you will find these on the toes of a lizard.

THE RED EFT

There is quite a bit of variety in the appearance of salamanders and in the pattern of their lives. The red-backed species

THE ELUSIVE TIGER SALAMANDER

This salamander gets its name from its colors (yellow splotches cover its brown body), and reaches a length of ten inches. Like most of its kind, it is an elusive creature, burrowing by day, and coming out at night to forage for food. All salamanders have smooth skins, in contrast to the scaly bodies of lizards.

does not even conform to the usual amphibian program of a land-and-water existence and spends its entire life on land.

One of the most commonly seen salamanders is the red eft. It begins its adventurous existence in a pond or stream, where it hatches from an egg laid on a water plant. The next few months it dwells in the water; it is an expert swimmer, has gills, and breathes like a fish. By the middle of August the eft has lost its gills, developed legs, and in all respects is ready for life ashore. About this time it takes on a bright orange hue.

For the next two and a half years the red eft lives on land, usually frequenting damp, shady places and hiding under leaves or moss. Then, though it may have wandered far away from water, it starts traveling purposefully until it reaches a pond or stream.

After returning to its native element the eft undergoes more changes: Its color becomes olive-green above and buff below, while its tail develops a keel that extends along its back. Only now does it seek a mate, and its remaining years are spent as a water animal. In this final water stage the red eft is frequently called a newt—a common name for this type of salamander.

The Care of Amphibians

Collecting frogs or other amphibians and keeping them for a while is a fine seasonal hobby for children. However, it is important to first inquire of the conservation department of your state for regulations about which kinds of frogs may be collected and when.

How to Catch a Frog

A stout collecting net is a useful aid in catching the elusive frog which you are most likely to find in a swamp or shallow pond.

Extend the net slowly and quietly toward and under a prospective captive. With a quick upward and outward movement you may succeed in snaring the frog. It should then be transferred to a suitable container, such as a wet burlap bag, for carrying home.

LIVING QUARTERS FOR THE AMPHIBIAN

You can turn an aquarium into a satisfactory home for small specimens of frogs, toads, or salamanders. A screen top made secure around the edges will prevent their escape. For frogs and salamanders the aquarium should be about one-third full of water, with stones piled high at one end to give the amphibians a place to land. Toads need far less water; for them, the bulk of the cage should be dry.

It is important to bring home some water from the pond where the frogs are caught, using it for them while they are in your care. Tap water is often purified with chemicals that are fatal to these animals. The water in the amphibian's quarters must be changed often and kept perfectly clean; uneaten food particles should be removed daily.

HOW TO FEED AN AMPHIBIAN PET

Live insects—such as flies or bugs—and earthworms are a good diet for most amphibians. Sometimes a captive will nibble at small bits of food, and you can experiment to find the diet that appeals most to it. If it does not respond to your attempts, it should be given its freedom near the locality where it was found.

Sometimes it may prove practical to grow your own insects; this is what a boy of my acquaintance did who was keeping a dozen salamanders in a large terrarium. In it he placed a bottle containing a few pieces of banana. Fruit flies bred rapidly there, and as they started to fly out they were snapped into the ready mouths of the salamanders.

Frogs and salamanders should always be picked up by placing your hand under their body. They are then less apt to get away, and such handling is far less injurious than encircling them with warm, dry skin. The heat of the human hand can kill a very small amphibian. Thus we see that even in the case of seemingly petty details we have to bear in mind the basic physical make-up of the amphibian, and the possible consequences of not heeding its requirements.

CHAPTER 9 The Wonderful Ways
of Insects and Spiders

T O MOST PEOPLE a fly is something to be
swatted; mosquitoes often take the joy out
of country life; and ants call to mind all the troublesome aspects
of a picnic! Altogether there is plenty of reason for children—and
parents as well—to feel that insects are above all else a terrific
nuisance.

There is another way of looking at them, though. The lives
of some species are as fanciful as fairy stories, and those "curiosi-
ties" of nature which so delight all of us are found in striking
abundance among the insects.

Some of them are skillful engineers and manufacturers. Bees
and ants live in societies complex enough to rival those of mankind. One insect, the doodlebug, always walks backward! The
queen of a tropical species of termites may produce ten million
offspring in her lifetime. There are wasps that keep their food
fresh over a period of time—just as successfully as we keep ours
in a refrigerator—by injecting a fluid which paralyzes the nerves
of their victims without producing death. Then the wasps store
the bodies until they are needed as food.

Many of our common, everyday insects become objects of
wonder if we examine their way of life; and, as they live in city,
town, and country, we can enjoy hours of fascinating observation
without troubling to go far afield.

What is An Insect?

People have a habit of referring to every small, creeping animal as an insect. However, many creatures that are so called do not belong to the classification of insects. Spiders are not insects—nor are worms and centipedes. How, then, do we really determine what is or isn't an insect?

An insect in the adult stage has three pairs of legs—no more, no less. It also has three distinct parts to its body—the head, the thorax, and the abdomen. And all insects have a shell-like covering to protect their bodies.

How Insects Are Able To Move

Insects have no inside bone structure to help them move as our bones help us; but movement is possible for them because each end of their muscles is attached to the hard outer covering that serves as an "outside skeleton." A muscle, for example, which acts to move a leg forward has one end attached to the hard covering of the leg and the other end attached to the covering of the thorax in front of the legs. When this muscle contracts, it pulls the two solid attachments closer together—and the leg moves forward.

It might seem impossible for a creature encased in a rigid covering to bend. However, the insect has joints in places where the body wall is flexible. That is why the creature can bend, somewhat as a knight of old could bend because his suit of heavy armor was jointed.

The Lowly Bug

Frequently the term "bug" is mistakenly used for "insect." Though all bugs are insects, in the scientific sense, not all insects are bugs. Bugs belong to a specific group that varies within itself in many respects; but all bugs are alike in having piercing, sucking mouth parts. The group includes the giant water bugs (also known as electric-light bugs because the adults often fly about electric lights), squash bugs and bedbugs.

MILLIONS OF KINDS OF INSECTS

The creatures that rightly bear the name "insects" are included in an astoundingly huge number of species. We already know of hundreds of thousands of different kinds, and scientists believe that the total number of kinds will eventually be reckoned in the millions! There are more species of insects than all other species of animals added together. More than any other kind of creature, *insects may be regarded as man's competitor for mastery of the earth.*

The destruction of farm crops, stored products, and wooden buildings by insects, and their injury to the health of human beings by spreading disease, is beyond calculating. However, millions of dollars are being spent every year on research, quarantine and control: The menace of insects is far less frightening

HUGE HORNET COLONIES
As many as fifteen thousand hornets may live in a single paper-covered nest. They have sentinels posted at the door to warn of the approach of intruders. Hornets are irritated by the presence of marauders and all too ready to sting near their nest. However, they are much less likely to sting when away from it.

to us than it was to our parents. Despite all the havoc that insects wreak, they are actually of enormous value to us in some ways.

Insects play a vital role by pollinizing many plants on which we depend for food for ourselves and our domesticated animals; and many birds as well as fish would disappear if they were deprived of insect food.

How Insects Develop

THE MAGIC OF METAMORPHOSIS

The child who observes a crawling caterpillar change into a winged butterfly is enthralled by a mystery which seems one of nature's greatest wonders. This is, however, only one of several patterns of growth that we find among insects. It involves four different forms. Butterflies, moths and others that grow this way are said to have a "complete metamorphosis." (The word is from the Greek and means "change of form.")

The first form is the egg; the next is the larva. Then comes the pupal stage, a period of relatively quiet resting. Finally the pupa develops into the adult. The larva of a butterfly we commonly call a caterpillar; the term for the pupa is "chrysalis." The larva of a fly, you may know as a "maggot"; that of a bee or a beetle, as a "grub."

INCOMPLETE METAMORPHOSIS

Another type of insect growth is called an "incomplete metamorphosis" because the insects do not go through any striking change in form during their growth after the egg stage. They do, however, gradually change their proportions. The young of this group, known as "nymphs," are like adults in most respects. They eat the same food and are much the same in appearance and behavior. The grasshopper is a well-known member of this group.

In the case of some water-dwelling nymphs, such as the young of the dragonfly, we see a great change when the gilled nymph becomes an adult; but the metamorphosis is still considered "incomplete."

The silverfish illustrates still another type of growth. It has no metamorphosis; the general body form does not change noticeably from the time it leaves the egg until it is fully grown.

All insects shed their skeletal coverings a number of times while they are still growing.

How Insects See, Hear, and Feel

EYES WITH THOUSANDS OF FACETS

Occasionally among published photographs you may see a strange-looking object suggesting a mosaic of diamonds. It proves to be the compound eye, greatly magnified, of an insect. The photograph makes a curiously intricate pattern of what are, in effect, many tiny eyes set close together, somewhat like the cells of a honeycomb. An adult insect has one of these compound eyes on each side of its head.

The six-sided areas into which the eyes are divided are known as "facets." The compound eyes of ants and other insects that live on the ground have only a few facets, and their vision is not sharp. The eyes of dragonflies and other keen-eyed species may have thousands of facets!

There are also many species with simple eyes—three of them— situated between the compound eyes. The simple eyes are so tiny, however, that you will need a magnifying lens to find them.

Insects can perceive mass and motion, light and darkness and, to a certain extent, they can distinguish colors.

EARS ANYWHERE AND EVERYWHERE

Whenever hearing equipment has been discovered in certain kinds of insects, it has been found on rather unconventional parts of the body. The grasshopper, for example, has an oval membrane sensitive to sound, and it is located on the side of the first abdominal segment. Crickets, ants, and katydids have hearing organs on their front legs, and the male mosquito hears through its antennae, or "feelers."

THE INSECT'S DETECTING EQUIPMENT

The antennae vary in shape and degree of complexity according to species. The segments which make up the antennae vary in number—and in form as well. The grasshopper's antennae may have more than twenty segments, whereas the common housefly has only three stubby segments. An insect uses its antennae to investigate its surroundings, and in many species these feelers are related in some degree to the sense of smell. The antennae are attached to the head—in front of, or between, the eyes.

How Insects Eat and Breathe

When we learn about the mouth parts of insects we realize that there is no more dramatic example of the way nature varies the forms of its creatures to suit special needs.

Crushing and Sucking: The sharp strong jaws of the ground beetle are excellently adapted to crush and eat caterpillars. The big brown squash bug and others use a sucking tube to take juice from plants; bedbugs have a similar mechanism for taking blood from animals. As for butterflies and other insects that extract nectar from flowers, they use a long tube, or tongue, which at other times is tightly coiled beneath the head.

Grasshoppers Bite Their Food: The grasshoppers and other biting insects have an upper lip and an underlip, with two pairs of jaws between them. If you look at a grasshopper through a magnifying lens you will see that the upper pair of jaws (the mandibles) are somewhat heavier than the lower pair (the maxillae).

On these lower jaws and on the lower lip there are feelers or tasters called "palpi." The taste buds—comparable to our own—on the tips of the palpi enable the grasshopper to taste its food before biting it. Though mandibles function somewhat as human jaws do, they work from side to side instead of up and down.

Breathing Without Lungs: Insects do not breathe the way we do. If you examine almost any insect closely, you will discover a series of tiny openings along the sides of the body. These are the "spiracles" or breathing holes through which air passes into the insect's body.

The spiracles lead into a system of thin-walled tubes which distribute the air throughout the body. As the insect's blood comes into contact with these tubes, it becomes purified as your blood does when it bathes the air tubes of your lungs. In the case of grasshoppers and a number of other insects naturalists have discovered that some of the spiracles are used exclusively for inhaling the others only for exhaling.

The Delicate Structures of Legs and Wings

We have already learned that an insect's body has three main parts: the head, the thorax, and the abdomen. Each of these three parts is made up of ringlike segments that have grown together. The thorax, or middle region, is made up of three segments, each bearing a pair of legs. (You will recall that all insects have three pairs of legs.)

The insect's front legs are attached to the first segment. The front wings—if there are any—and the middle legs are attached to the second segment. The hind legs—and the hind wings, if they are present—are attached to the third segment.

If you spread apart a grasshopper's four wings, you will find that the upper ones are long and narrow, while the broad lower wings rest, folded like fans, beneath them. If you feel their texture you will discover that the lower pair are far more delicate than the upper wings which protect them.

Once insects acquire wings they stop growing. You may see little flies and big flies, but they belong to different species; the little ones are never going to "catch up" and be big ones.

The legs of all insects are jointed and made up of about ten segments—though the number and size vary with different kinds of insects. On many insects the last segment bears one or two claws.

Some Popular Insects

BUTTERFLIES—INSECTS WITH GLAMOUR

These lovely winged creatures seem a special gift of nature to children. Many a boy who has been oblivious to outdoor beauty is captivated by the sight of a colorful butterfly perched on a bright flower. Some children go further than merely admiring the appearance of butterflies; they become absorbed in the hobby of collecting them. Taken in the caterpillar stage, these insects may be observed through their metamorphosis into winged adults. Later on the adult insects, captured and mounted, make home exhibits that are a delight to the eye.

The collector must handle his delicate captives with care. (There will be more about this later on.) Even with careful handling, some fine colored dust comes off the butterflies onto his fingers. If he could examine this dust under a powerful microscope, he would see that it is made up of tiny scales. These cover the insect's wings, overlapping like shingles, and they are often responsible for the striking pattern and brilliant coloring.

There is wide variety in the size, shape, and habits of different kinds of butterflies. The caterpillars are equally varied: They may be hairy, naked, or covered with spines. Most caterpillars eat their own special choice of leaves and will starve to death if they are given the wrong kind.

The Beautiful Black Swallowtail: This swallowtail is one of the loveliest butterflies you are likely to find. It lives in almost all parts of the United States and frequents gardens, sipping nectar from the blossoms. In meadows it is most likely to be seen on thistles or the orange-flowered milkweed. Two projections from the margins of its hind wings, which are responsible for its popular name, make it easy to identify. Its color is velvety black, with rows of yellow spots; the hind wings have metallic blue splashes.

The female is larger than her mate, and though she has more blue on her wings, the yellow markings on his hind wings are more vivid.

COLLECTOR'S PRIZE

The tiger swallowtail butterfly has wings that are beautifully striped in black and yellow. It gets its name from the tail-like extensions of its hind wings. While it visits many flowers, it is partial to thistle and milkweed. The caterpillar of this butterfly is famous for a repulsive stench it produces to discourage enemies, particularly hungry birds. It is also noted for two large eyespots at front end.

From Egg to Caterpillar: A black swallowtail deposits her eggs on the leaves of carrots, parsnips, or parsley. Each egg looks like a tiny drop of honey. By the end of ten days, the honey-colored eggs have turned almost coal black, and spiny little caterpillars make their appearance. Each caterpillar at once eats the shell of the egg from which it hatched, then continues feeding on the leaf where it was originally placed.

As the caterpillar grows it sheds its skin from time to time, and with each molt it changes its size and coloring until it has become a "carrot worm." Now it is about two inches long and strikingly colored in green, black, and yellow. If you poke a finger at one of these creatures, it will thrust out brilliant orange horns that give off a disagreeable smell. This odor proves a most effective defense against birds.

The Chrysalis Emerges from the Silken Halter: If you bring one of these caterpillars indoors or manage to keep it under close observation in some other way, you will in due course see one of those wonders of nature that never seem commonplace no matter how often you may observe them. One day you will see the caterpillar spin a button of silk against a solid support. (Out-of-doors, the lower edge of a fence rail is a favorite place.)

The caterpillar grasps this button firmly with its hind prop-leg. Then it spins a strong loop of silk, fastening both ends to the same support, and finally it thrusts its head inside the silken halter. Thus supported, it starts to shed its last caterpillar skin, and we see a soft pale-green pupa, or chrysalis, beginning to emerge.

Now comes a moment crucial for its survival: The chrysalis releases its hold on the little silk button, relying completely on the halter for support while it pushes off its shrunken skin and inserts its hooks into the button. Sometimes the chrysalis falls to the ground during this delicate maneuvering—with fatal results. The possibility of sudden death adds a poignant touch to the mystery of metamorphosis.

The Butterfly Lives on Nectar: The successful chrysalis gradually hardens and alters its colors, usually turning grayish, dark green, or tan. Within its shell the elements that made up the caterpillar are taking on the shape of a butterfly. Then one day, after some weeks of waiting, you will see the upper end break open and a crumpled mass of damp "velvet" come forth. This clings to a support while its wings unfold, dry, and harden. In about half an hour the newcomer is ready for flight. As an adult, it lives entirely on nectar (how fitting!) and acts as an efficient messenger carrying pollen from one blossom to another.

The Migrating Monarch Butterfly: A common species that children can easily learn to recognize is the monarch or milkweed butterfly. With its brilliant copper-red color and vivid black markings it is quite conspicuous. You can distinguish a similarly colored though somewhat smaller species, known as the viceroy, by a black band across the middle of the hind wing.

Monarchs are noted for their migrations. They often gather in large flocks in late summer and then move southward. You may some day discover one of these beautiful butterflies with an identification tag and number in its wing. Many persons in the United States and Canada have for several years been marking and releasing monarchs in an effort to increase the store of scientific knowledge about them. The tag tells where to send the information on your find, and you may thus help scientists learn the full story of this remarkable traveler.

The Hibernating Mourning Cloak: The habits of the mourning cloak—a brownish and yellow butterfly, ornamented with blue spots—are in marked contrast to those of the monarch. The mourning cloak sleeps in hollow trees or crannies during cold weather and is one of the few insects that hibernate in the adult stage.

Flying Fighters: For all their ethereal appearance, you may discover by watching butterflies that they are not at all averse to some very down-to-earth fighting. The males of many species will try to drive away any others that encroach on territory they consider their own. As a result, duels take place, with the contenders darting and dashing at each other, sometimes buffeting their wings to shreds. The red admiral and the buckeye are particularly noted as scrappers.

MOTHS—HOW THEY DIFFER FROM BUTTERFLIES

Children are much more likely to become acquainted with the caterpillars of moths than with the moths themselves, as these winged insects (with few exceptions) sleep by day and fly only at dusk or after dark. This nighttime schedule of activity helps us to distinguish moths from butterflies, as butterflies are abroad during the day.

There are several other features which, as a rule, guide us in telling a moth from a butterfly. When at rest, butterflies hold their wings vertically above their bodies while moths extend theirs—horizontally, or tentlike over their bodies. A moth's body is thicker and more wedge-shaped, and its antennae are feathery or finely tapered. A butterfly's antennae, though smooth, end in knobs or thickenings.

Silk Manufacturers: A moth's life pattern is much like that of a butterfly, except that the caterpillars of certain moths weave about themselves a covering of silk which we call a "cocoon." Most species of moth caterpillars, however, dispense with the cocoon. When the "tomato worm" and the caterpillar of the sphinx moth, for example, are fully grown, they burrow in the earth and there become pupae. If you are digging around the base of a tree in the late fall, you may discover such caterpillars.

By way of contrast, there are moth caterpillars that may be termed "American silkworms": They produce strong lustrous silk rivaling the product of the Chinese silkworms. The American silk never became a commercial success because these creatures proved too difficult to breed in large numbers; in addition, the labor involved in processing their silk was very costly.

The native silkworms are the caterpillars of cecropia, promethea, polyphemus, and luna moths. Even sharp-eyed explorers are not likely to find these insects that have a knack of blending perfectly with the leaves on which they rest and feed.

The Woolly Bear Caterpillar—Weather Prophet: Sooner or later nearly every child in country surroundings encounters the woolly bear caterpillar, which is conspicuous because of its thick coat of hair.

There are many kinds of woolly bears. One species is black at the ends with a middle band of brown. According to popular belief, you can forecast the weather by the size of this band. With the arrival of the fall, if the band is wide—that is, if it measures half the body length or more—on many woolly bears, a mild winter is predicted. By the same token, if most woolly bears have narrow bands, we are told that the coming season will be severe. Scientists have not yet said the last word on the reliability of this belief.

You may often discover woolly bears along the roadside in the bright fall sunshine. If you pick one up, it has the defensive resource of rolling itself into a ball—a trick that it also uses to make itself less attractive to a hungry bird.

Woolly Bears As Pets: If your child brings home a woolly bear for a pet, it must be kept out-of-doors in a sheltering wooden box at ordinary temperatures. Keeping the creature in a warm room is likely to prove fatal to it. During late summer it feeds on grass, clover, and other leaves; with the onset of fall it has reached its full growth and requires little in the way of food.

After sleeping the winter away, the woolly bear rouses in the spring, eats a little grass, and then starts to spin its cocoon, weaving into it the hairs from its "fur coat." The finished cocoon gives the appearance of being made of felt. About the end of May an Isabella tiger moth appears. As the moth flies only at night, you are less likely to become familiar with it than with the woolly bear. It is a dull gray and tawny moth with a few black dots on its wings.

Caterpillars As A Hobby

Where To Look For Caterpillars: The woolly bear is not the only caterpillar that makes an interesting captive. Other larvae of moths that you are likely to find are the leaf-colored polyphemus (often on oak and birch trees), and the colorful cecropia caterpillar, green with bluish tint and marked with yellow, blue, and red.

Collecting butterfly caterpillars is simple if you know the right hunting grounds. Tiger swallowtail caterpillars are most commonly found on wild cherry trees; cabbage butterfly caterpillars on cabbage; monarchs on milkweed plants; and viceroys on poplar and willow trees. In hunting caterpillars it is not only helpful to know the plants on which they feed; it is also advisable to take some of the leaves to feed your captives their favorite food.

Providing Living Quarters: You can make a home for caterpillars from a shoe box or a small wooden box or any other kind of box of convenient size. If any of your captives are the kind that change into a chrysalis in the earth rather than on foliage, it would be wise to put a pot of dirt in the box.

You can keep leafy twigs fresh by placing them in water in the box, but you need a cloth or some other covering over the top of the water container—otherwise the caterpillars might crawl into it and be drowned. The box-cage should be covered securely with mosquito netting or fine wire screening, and kept where the caterpillars will have some sunlight.

The Pleasures of Cocoon Collecting

In the country you may find the cocoons of some of the large silk moths, such as the polyphemus, cecropia, and luna. (The beautiful luna moth usually spins its cocoon between leaves on the ground.) After the leaves have fallen in autumn, it is quite easy to see the brownish wrappings which hold a pupa as it hangs from twigs of bushes and trees.

Children enjoy seeing the cecropia's hammock-shaped product because of its popular name, "cradle cocoon." It has two walls of silk. The inner wall is thin and firm; the outer wall—the one you look for when you go cocoon hunting—is thick and paper-like. Between the two walls there is a mat of loose silk.

Cocoons in the Home: When you collect a hanging cocoon, cut a piece of the twig to which it is attached. Later on, this twig will make the best possible perch for the moth as it emerges and waits for its wings to harden.

If you keep cocoons in your house, they must be left in a place that is not well heated. (An attic or cellar is fine for a cocoon.) If the place is warm, the cocoons will hatch out before spring. They should be sprinkled lightly with water about once a week to keep them from getting dried out by indoor air.

From the first of April or thereabouts, and for the following two months, you can have an exciting time watching for the beautiful winged insects to emerge. Sometimes you are given advance notice of the event when the end of a cocoon grows damp —the effect of an acid fluid the insect discharges to dissolve the silk. Thereafter the moth has no trouble pushing its way through the end of the cocoon.

How to Collect Butterflies and Moths

Collecting insects is a wonderful hobby for children. The boy or girl who is absorbed in this pastime derives ever-increasing pleasure from collecting. Often this interest continues into adulthood, to be keenly enjoyed for a whole lifetime. An outstanding example of how the passion for collecting may develop, is seen in the case of a Pennsylvania youngster who began modestly with the common monarchs, swallowtails, and cabbage butterflies that frequented his back yard. As the years passed, his collection expanded to such proportions that eventually a museum bought it for $20,000!

THE POLYPHEMUS, GIANT OF THE MOTH WORLD

The yellowish or brownish polyphemus moth is one of our largest moths, having a wingspread of six inches. Its name (remember one-eyed Polyphemus—the Cyclops —and how Ulysses escaped from him?) is probably due to the peculiar eye-like spot it has on each wing. At rest, it holds its wings over its back.

How to Handle the Butterfly Net: Butterfly collecting is an ideal hobby to enjoy with your children, sharing the excitement of stalking prey that is elusive without being dangerous. If your child starts collecting at an early age, though, he is likely to be too impetuous for success. Teach him the value of patience and care at the start. A slow and cautious approach to a butterfly is the right one—despite the popular misconception that pictures collectors leaping with abandon and spasmodically lashing out with their nets.

Certain precautions are indispensable to capturing your butterfly, such as avoiding having the sun at your back—otherwise you cast a shadow, alarming the butterfly. You must coach your youngster in acquiring the knack of giving a quick sidewise swoop with the net; then, with the butterfly trapped inside, he must twist his wrist sharply so that the bag folds over the hoop.

Usually this is a good method of attack, but some species have reactions that call for special strategy. For example: A monarch trying to escape, flies straight up in the air, whereas a royal fritillary drops down directly into the grass and weeds. To snare either of these creatures, you must swing your net to cut off escape.

The Best Hunting Grounds: Clear, bright, windless days are most favorable for butterfly hunting. The best hunting grounds are meadows dotted with milkweed, thistles and orange butterfly weed, clover fields, or weed-covered fields near a wooded tract. The best time to trap a butterfly is when it is feeding. Occasionally you will find one so absorbed in sucking nectar from a flower that you can catch your prey between your thumb and forefinger.

Baiting the Trap for Moths: Night-flying moths can often be secured as they cluster about electric lights. However, a more adventurous way to collect them is by "sugaring" tree trunks. For this you prepare bait in the form of mashed, fermented peaches mixed with sugar. (Any similar preparation will also do the trick.)

At dusk your Expedition for Moths takes a generous supply of bait and paints long streaks of it with a stiff brush on the trunks of several trees, making sure to choose the sides sheltered from the wind. A little after dark you again visit the trees—this time armed with flashlight and net. Often you will discover many different species enjoying the bait.

Painless Killing: On any collecting expedition you must have a "killing jar" to quiet your captives quickly, painlessly, and without injuring their delicate wings. You can fashion a homemade container by placing cotton batting soaked with carbona in the bottom of a wide-mouthed pint jar. Over the cotton, place a piece of wire screening to prevent the moisture of the carbona from touching the insect. Keep the jar tightly covered.

When you remove the specimens, it is best to use tweezers rather than your fingers; but if tweezers are not available, pick up the insects by their legs or antennae and not by their wings. Then you may place them temporarily in triangular-shaped holders made of rather stiff paper.

How to Mount Butterflies and Moths: Mounting butterflies and moths for permanent exhibit is not too difficult for children if they have the patience and are guided by expert advice. If the specimens have been kept for a while and have stiffened, you must soften them. You can accomplish this by placing them in a metal box with a tight-fitting cover and a layer of wet sand on the bottom. (Add a few drops of carbolic acid to the water which wets the sand to prevent any mold from forming.)

After twenty-four hours in the sealed box, the specimens are ready for the setting board. This is simply two pieces of soft wood set side by side with a narrow channel between them. At the bottom of the channel there is a piece of cork or balsa wood.

Carefully take the softened butterfly—handling it with tweezers is best; stick a long, fine pin through its thorax and set the body in the channel with the pin pushed down into the cork or balsa wood. Spread the four wings outward on the wooden sides until the wings are in a good position. Do not put pins in the wings, but keep them from moving by pinning narrow strips of cloth across them, placing the pins outside the wings.

The Storage Box: Several days on the setting board are needed before the wings are thoroughly dried out. Now they are ready to be stored in real exhibition fashion. Storage boxes should be shallow and may be made of any of several materials—but some are decidedly wrong for the purpose. In a red cedar box, resin may ooze out and make your exhibits greasy. Cardboard boxes absorb moisture from the air and this will cause the specimens to get moldy. White pine is one of the best woods.

When your box is ready the bottom should be lined with cork, into which you can stick your mounting pins. Two sheets of corrugated cardboard, one placed on top of the other with the corrugations of one running at right angles to those of the other, may be substituted for cork. A few flakes of the chemical dichlor-benzol sprinkled under the cork will prevent tiny beetles from turning the specimens into a fine brown dust.

You can then pin butterflies and moths in rows and columns. The ambitious collector can add a further refinement by organizing the specimens, putting insects of the same family in the same box and placing a male and female of a species side by side.

Many museums gladly furnish more detailed instructions to amateurs, and research in most libraries will yield excellent information about arranging and mounting specimens. The Naturalists' Directory published by the Cassino Press of Salem, Mass., includes the names of places where equipment needed for insect collecting and preserving may be purchased.

BEETLES—23,000 SPECIES IN NORTH AMERICA

Beetles Get Around: Probably the easiest of all insects to collect or to become acquainted with in the flesh are the beetles. Not only can they be found in innumerable places out-of-doors—they appear, unbidden and unwelcome, in city apartments.

Carpet beetles sometimes appear as if by magic in the wool of rugs and upholstery and in stored cheese and cereals. Equally tiny beetles turn up in dried fruits and cereal products. We have already seen that if your family has been collecting butterflies and you begin to notice fine brown dust falling from your specimens, you can be sure that beetles are working on them.

Differences and Resemblances Among Beetles: Once you start looking at beetles with some care, you will appreciate the amazing degree of variation among them; the result is an enormous number of species. Beetles vary in size from minute specimens to some, found in the tropics, that are larger than a mouse. There are at least twenty-three thousand species on the North American continent alone. Varied as the members of this insect tribe are in appearance, nearly all the adults are easy to identify by the hard, veinless forewings that meet in a straight line over the abdomen.

In flight these forewings serve much the same purpose as the wings of an airplane, providing elevation, while the beetle is actually propelled by the hind wings. The forewings also serve as protective coverings for the hind wings, which are folded beneath them. If you could see some of the tropical giants, you would be quick to notice their huge mandibles, or upper jaws; but most of the smaller species also have well-developed mouth parts, as all beetles bite rather than suck.

The Firefly—Childhood Delight: The firefly is a member of the beetle family. Children are always intrigued by the way the insect "lights up" as it flits through the night, and they are forever catching and imprisoning "lightning bugs" in the hope of discovering their secret. In brief, this is the explanation: The firefly produces a substance called luciferin, which glows when it comes in contact with air. Underneath the light-producing area of the body there is a reflecting surface which serves to strengthen the glow.

In some species the females and the larvae have no wings and are therefore limited to ground travel. Both groups are also light-producers—our common glowworms.

Eating Too Much or Too Little: Fireflies are valuable to man because their larvae feed on slugs and snails, which sometimes do damage to cultivated plants. Mysteriously enough, most of the adults, as far as we can observe, do not eat at all! We still have a great deal to learn about the habits of this fascinating beetle.

The Ladybug—Pest Exterminator: Another beetle dear to the hearts of little children is the ladybug or ladybird beetle—which they admonish to fly away home to its burning house. These small, hemispherically shaped insects are also dear to the hearts of fruit-growers—but not for any sentimental reasons. The ladybug preys on great numbers of such destructive fruit pests as aphids and soft scale citrus mealy bugs.

If you happen to be exploring the countryside in the fall you may come on a great assemblage of lady beetles; they congregate in large numbers before going into hibernation under rocks and forest litter and inside hollow trees.

The Ground Beetle—Nighttime Hunter: If you turn over a stone, log, or board lying on the ground—especially damp ground—you are likely to discover a beetle hideout. The "ground beetle" family has many different members, and most of them remain under cover during the day. Usually a ground beetle is plain black or brown and its long, flattened body is carried rapidly over the ground on its slender legs—as you will observe if you disturb one; it runs away as rapidly as possible when it is discovered.

Ground beetles feed mostly by night, looking for food under rocks and refuse or in the soil. Several species are famous for their caterpillar-hunting; the larvae as well as the adults climb up tree trunks searching for caterpillar prey.

Beetles with Gas Bombs: The "bombardier" beetles are among the strangest members of the family. At the first sign of danger these creatures eject a drop of liquid that quickly changes to a tiny cloud of evil-smelling vapor. The source of the liquid is a gland at the tip of the abdomen, and four or five discharges can be made before the liquid "bomb" supply is exhausted.

This unpleasant counterattack will often discourage a bird or other aggressor—at least long enough for the beetle to scurry to safety. Many members of the ground beetle family have this power, but one species makes its discharge with a distinct "pop." This is the true bombardier. It has a yellowish head and a bluish body.

Beetles Near Water: You may find the tiger beetle along the shores of streams, lakes, or the ocean, and also on woodland trails. About half an inch long and often brilliantly colored with metallic greens and purples, this handsome beetle is a prize for any young collector; but, being a swift runner and quick to take flight, it is not easily trapped by a novice.

Sometimes, as you look down at fresh-water ponds or streams, you may see black, oval whirligig beetles cruising around tire-

"TIGER" ANIMALS HAVE STRIKING COLORS

Animals named after the tiger, such as the tiger salamander, tiger swallowtail butterfly, and tiger beetle, are noted for their brilliant coloring. The tiger beetle at the left is purple, the one at the right belongs to the six-spotted species. It is active in the daytime, and found most frequently on woodland paths.

lessly in circles—or dark, shiny diving beetles that stay suspended, head downward, in the water.

How to Collect Beetles: If your child is serious about beetle collecting, he can go about it in a number of ways. Flat rocks and boards on moist earth have been mentioned as good hunting grounds. When he finds beetles on a small tree or bush, he can hold an opened umbrella upside down under it and then hit the branches above, The insects fall into the outspread trap.

An excellent method of snapping up beetles is to use a small, circular pill box in which the cover fits over the bottom portion. If you wish, you can attach the two halves of the box with adhesive tape to the thumb and the index or middle finger. It is possible to find some beetles on sandy shores by pulling up bunches of grass and examining the roots; or moss from stream banks may be shaken over a piece of paper for possible insect finds.

There are several ways of setting traps; one method is to set a tin can or narrow jar into the ground, the open top flush with the surface, and with a bit of meat or fish at the bottom. Also, after spring floods you are likely to find numerous specimens along streams and creeks where they have been drowned and their bodies left stranded.

Carbona or ethyl acetate is the recommended poison to use in a killing jar for beetles. Like butterflies and moths they can be mounted for attractive exhibition in boxes. The mounting pins should go through the right wing-cover.

ANTS—COLONISTS, WORKERS, AND WARRIORS

Ants, like beetles, are almost easier to find than to elude. You see ants on lawns, roadways, and city pavements; in gardens, forests, and pastures. These extraordinary insects vary in size and color from the big carpenter ant to the little brown species that is the most common of all in North America. There are many localities where you may find this brown ant; but because it has been studied chiefly in cornfields, it is widely known as the "cornfield ant."

Ant Colonies: The cornfield ant, like all members of the ant family, lives in colonies. Each colony is made up of three principal types of ants: the queen (or fertile female); the short-lived males that die soon after the mating flight; and the infertile females. These last, the great majority, are the ordinary hard-working citizens of the ant world. They are divided into workers, soldiers, or other specialized castes. The workers have larger heads and part of their front legs is slightly thicker than in other adults of this species.

If you come upon a mound of earth about which ants are hustling, your youngster may exclaim, "There's an anthill!" And if he is of an adventurous turn of mind, he may want to dig into it to see just what an ant colony is like. But in order to examine a nest successfully, you have to dig down with great skill—else you may merely ruin it.

Inside the Ant Colony: Observe the nests of cornfield ants closely and you will realize that these nests vary greatly in size. The mound of a long-established colony covers a much larger area than that of a new one. As a rule, the underground rooms are only a few inches below the surface. But after a long dry spell, or if the nest is located in sandy soil, the rooms are deeper in the earth; for soil that is very dry becomes too crumbly for excavation.

In the winter you would find the apartments occupied only by inactive adults and larvae. In midsummer the rooms bulge with eggs, larvae, pupae, workers, males and females. (The eggs are tiny specks.) The larvae are white maggot-like creatures, and the pupae are enclosed in whitish cocoons about an eighth of an inch long. Often mistakenly called "ant eggs," the pupae are collected in large numbers and sold as fish and bird food.

How Ant Life is Organized: If you were to discover an ant nest on a fine afternoon in August or early September, you might find the occupants swarming excitedly about the entrance; you might also notice that many of them have wings. Every few minutes a winged form takes to the air. Some of these are males, some females. (Apparently their mating takes place in the air.)

When the female returns to the ground she breaks off her wings, then burrows a few inches into the earth or finds an opening beneath a log or stone. Here she forms a small cell. She may then immediately start to lay her eggs—or she may wait until the following spring. As time goes on she eats some of the eggs—they are the only food she has—and continues to lay more. About two months after she begins to raise her young she may have one or two workers.

During the first year, if she does well, her colony increases to about twenty-five adult workers. Their duty is to search far and wide for her food. They feed her and the larvae as well, also helping the larvae to spin their cocoons and in time assisting the new adults as they escape from these cocoons. Their mandibles and forelegs make excellent tools. With these, too, they dig out new tunnels and rooms; and as they dig and bring soil up to the surface of the ground, the "anthill" grows larger. When the soil becomes cold, they close the entrance to the nest and rest quietly in the rooms until the next spring.

Savage Ant Warriors: Not all ants are as settled in their ways as the cornfield ant. There are some that do not bother to build homes at all: They are almost constantly on the move, wandering from place to place in search of food. Among these nomads are the "driver" ants of Africa and tropical America. They march in close formation, in columns an inch or two wide and sometimes a mile long! Even animals as large as a deer will flee in terror from such an army.

Many species of ants are savage fighters. Sometimes battles are fought by two colonies of the same species but more often there is a struggle of one species against another. The fighting may occur between two large groups or even between individuals.

If you stop to watch a lively group of ants on the ground or sidewalk, you may find it is divided into two factions struggling over a bit of food—or you may not even discover the cause of the conflict. I have heard of a sidewalk ant battle that raged for more than five hours, until each colony was reduced to a few battered members.

You may wonder how the ants in such a struggle know friend from foe. Members of different colonies look exactly alike, yet you see individuals meet and at once pass on to another warrior or start fighting. Apparently an ant's antennae help it distinguish its own team mates from the opposition—for as two fighters meet, the antennae of each touch the head of the other. There is also a theory that ants have a characteristic odor that varies with each colony and may thus be an aid to solving the "friend-or-foe" puzzle.

Ant Hangers-on: As you observe some ant colonies you may be puzzled by the presence of other insects that act as though they belong there. If you were able to study ant nests all over the world, you would find there are actually several thousand different kinds of insects that make their home with ants. Some of these—certain kinds of beetles, for example—the ants use to obtain savory secretions. Others are hangers-on, scavengers, thieves, or enemies. Some of them to all outward appearances *are* ants.

Among the best known are aphids—tiny insects that feed on the juices of plants and give off from their bodies droplets of honeydew. Some aphids are popularly known as "ant cows." The ants protect them and even carry them from one food plant to another, "milking" them by stroking their back with their antennae. The milk is the sweet, colorless fluid that we call "honeydew."

Observing Ants Indoors

A child can get a great deal of pleasure by watching ants, and he can learn a great deal about their habits, if you keep some in your home—provided the ants are there through your choice and not their own, and you supply suitable living quarters for them. One type of house that is easy to make might be described as a glass sandwich.

Use two pieces of window glass about ten or twelve inches square. One will serve as the base, the other as the top. Around the edges of the base, glue quarter-inch strips of wood that fit snugly at the corners. Leave two openings in one strip that you will use later—one for food, the other for water. Inside the water opening you keep a sponge that can be kept moist with a medicine dropper. When you are not feeding the tenants, you can keep these two openings plugged with cotton.

How to Collect Ants: You are now ready to collect your ants. Dig around a nest carefully with a small shovel or trowel, lift the dirt with the insects into a carton and close it tightly to carry home. Transfer both dirt and insects to the glass that you have rimmed with strips. At this point you need to work quickly to glue the other square of glass to this base and finally seal all edges with adhesive tape.

Place a piece of cardboard of equal size on top—ants need darkness most of the time. You can use two strips of adhesive as hinges to attach this cover to one side, lifting the cardboard whenever you wish to watch your insects at work.

You may see them constructing a central hall, excavating a system of tunnels, cleaning themselves with tongue and front legs—they do this repeatedly—and sometimes lying down to sleep, their legs pulled close to the body. It is important to have a queen in your colony—otherwise the activities of the captives will show a far from complete story of life in an anthill.

How to Take Care of Captive Ants: The care of ants is rather simple. The soil should be kept moist by inserting water through the opening at least once a week; the insects' home should not be left in bright sunlight or near a radiator. A drawer or closet is a good place to keep them when you are not watching them. A drop of honey should be supplied every few days, as well as a little solid food, such as tiny morsels of mashed walnuts, apples, bananas, and bits of dead insects.

GRASSHOPPERS AND THEIR MUSIC

Katydids—Fiddlers, Not Singers: Katydids have become so closely identified with this name because of their insistent refrain *Katy did, no she didn't,* that people sometimes forget these insects are also grasshoppers. The grasshoppers are divided into two groups: the short- and long-horned families. The "horns" (really the antennae) are considered long if they are nearly as long as, or longer than, the insect's body. Katydids belong to the long-horned group.

A child hearing them on a summer night may refer to their "singing," but "fiddling" is a better word for their kind of music. A male katydid—the females only listen—rubs its left wing over the right wing. The left wing has a file-like row of ridges, while the right wing has a hard little scraper just behind the shoulder where the wings overlap; the rubbing of the wings produces the fiddling sound.

Fiddlers All: It is the broad-winged or leaf-winged katydid that plays its name with insistent repetition. The large oblong-winged tree katydid has a refrain of *Zzzzzz-Ipswich;* the fork-tailed bush katydid plays a slow *zeep-zeep-zeep* now and then; and the common meadow katydid fiddles several soft *zees* in a row, each faster than the one before, and then hits and holds a high *zeee.*

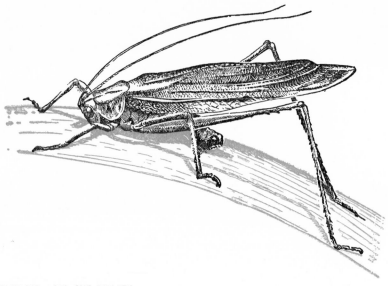

"KATY DID — NO SHE DIDN'T"

Yhe katydids are long-horned grasshoppers noted for their fondness for fiddling. The sound is produced by rubbing the left wing over the right wing. The males do all the playing, while the females are apparently content to listen. The katydid has hearing organs on its front legs.

A short-horned grasshopper has a different fiddling technique. Its long hind leg forms the bow, and a coarse outer wing the fiddle. It may play one leg and wing at a time or both sides together—a "one-man duet." However, little actual music is created by these efforts; you can hear the resulting rasps for only a few feet.

Both males and females have large hearing organs. You can see what looks like an oval window on each side of the first abdominal segment under the wings. What you see is the outer part of the grasshopper's "ears."

Grasshoppers blend so successfully with their surroundings that it is not easy to spot them during the day except when they take wing. Some of the smaller katydids are easily startled into flight from tall weeds and grasses where they spend much of their time. In the country you can have a lively evening tracking down the little insect fiddlers; take a flashlight along and let yourself be guided by their sounds.

Crickets Join the Insect Serenade: The chirpy, cheerful cricket produces music with its wings in the same way as the katydid, but usually with its right wing over the left—whereas the katydid, as we have seen, rubs its left wing over the right. To a listening youngster it may seem that the katydids dominate the insect serenade; but crickets contribute their share of the melodious performance. The tune of the common snowy tree cricket begins as a musical *waa-waa-waa*, played by individuals, each "on his own." But soon they join forces and play as if they were following a conductor's baton.

Crickets As Weather Forecasters: The performance of the snowy tree cricket is directly related to the temperature. By counting the number of notes it produces each minute, you can roughly gauge what your thermometer registers. Thus, a hundred chirps to the minute indicate a temperature of 63 degrees. Increasing its tempo as the temperature rises, this cricket slows down when it gets cooler.

The common black crickets, with their clear chirp, are the first musicians you will hear in summer. You may often discover them, by late August, if you turn over an old board or stone. They run fast but despite their muscular-looking legs they do not imitate the grasshopper's high-jumping tactics.

Cricket on the Hearth: The cricket that may serenade you from indoors after cool weather begins is not necessarily the same kind about which Dickens wrote so appealingly in England; but the American field cricket is also a cheery visitor to have on the hearth. The European cricket is now quite well established in the eastern United States and is a persistent fiddler. Unfortunately, once these musicians are indoors they do not limit their activities to music but may get into food and eat holes in everything made of cloth.

How To Keep Cricket Pets: In the natural state, not many crickets survive the coming of frost. However, if they are adopted as pets, they will often live through the winter with every appearance of enjoying themselves. You can make a cage for a cricket very simply with a flowerpot full of earth and a kerosene lamp chimney.

Sink the chimney into the earth to a depth of two inches and cover the top with a piece of mosquito netting held in place by a rubber band. You can make a similar cage with a large jar, or an aquarium also covered with mosquito netting, and with soil and plants set on the bottom.

Once you have obtained a few crickets, place them inside the cage with a cabbage leaf or other greens and fasten the mosquito netting top. Aside from providing their leafy food, it is a good idea to occasionally drop a little corn meal saturated with water into the glass cage—it will furnish moisture as well as food. Periodically, too, the inside quarters should be sprinkled with water to keep the atmosphere moist.

You may conclude from sad experience that it is not practicable to keep more than one cricket in the cage; they frequently start fighting with fatal results.

BEES—HONEY-MAKERS, POLLINIZERS, AND STINGERS

What probably impresses children above all about bees is their stinging ability. "Is it true that a bee dies after it stings you? Can only females sting? Don't bees sting when they are swarming?" I have heard youngsters put these queries incessantly before the topic of honey-making ever came up.

The Bee's Sting: Tormenting humans is far from the primary use of stingers. When the first queen hatches in a hive, she immediately rips open other queen cells—unless she is restrained by the workers—and stings the inmates to death, thereby removing all possible rivals. Queens have the ability to sting over and over again—but they use their sting only on other queens.

It is a worker bee that will sting you, and it commits suicide by doing so. Stinging brings twenty-two muscles into play; when the stinger is torn out of the worker's body, death results.

The order of insects to which bees—and wasps and ants—belong is the only one in which genuine stingers are found. The stinger is the modified ovipositor (or egg-laying organ) of the female worker, so obviously the males or "drones" possess no stings. In early summer, when a mass of bees leave their hive with a queen to found a new home, they seem especially tolerant of bystanders and almost never sting during this swarming.

Very Few Kinds of Bees Store Honey: Many children and even some grownups have a mistaken idea that all bees store honey. Actually this is true of only a few of the thousands of kinds of bees known to exist. Most of them eat nectar as they take it from the flowers, instead of using it for honey.

The true honeybees, so valuable in fertilizing such plants as clover and fruit trees, are native to Europe; they were introduced to North America by colonists in the seventeenth century. If you find any of these in hollow trees in the woods, they are swarms that have escaped from man-made hives—or descendants of such bees.

The Underground Bumblebee: The large, hairy bumblebee, with its black coat marked with yellow, orange, or red, is probably more quickly recognized by children than most species. This honey manufacturer is native to America. Bumblebees live in large colonies underground, where they construct many-celled combs. In the cells they lay eggs, store pollen and nectar, and make honey.

Playing Bee Detective: Country youngsters have long delighted in tracking down honeybees that have "gone native," and finding their store of honey. The bee detective's equipment is a small box with either honey or sugar water and an opening large enough to enable the bees to get to it. The same purpose is achieved by using one of those frames in which honey is bought in the comb. Putting some flour or cornstarch in the receptacle will give the bees a touch of white as they take the bait. Thus they will be more conspicuous at a distance, making it possible to follow the direction of their flight.

Your bee detective places the box on a stump or post in a neighborhood where bees are working. By moving the box at intervals in the direction of their flight, the youthful hunter gradually narrows down the distance to the bees' storehouse.

The first customers will usually bring other workers with them. Individual bees can be identified after a while, and the lessening time required to complete the round trip will indicate how much the distance to the hive is decreasing. Although the youngster will be overjoyed when he finally locates the store of honey, it is a wise precaution to have him call on adult help in removing the honey from the hollow-tree storehouse.

How Bees Use "Glue": When you see a bee purposefully visiting tree after tree, it may be gathering water from the buds. The other object of its quest may be a brown resinous material—called "propolis" or "bee glue"—that these insects use for smoothing rough places in the hive. This assignment is given to young bees on their first flights.

Pollination by Messenger Service: Later on, the bees set about collecting pollen and finally nectar. They knead the pollen into a little ball and tuck it into a cavity on the hind leg; they obtain nectar by extending their tongue into a flower and sucking the fluid. There are some species of clovers and other plants with long-tubed corollas that depend completely on bumblebees and other long-tongued species of bees for pollination.

Western fruitgrowers keep colonies of bees in the great orchards for fertilizing the fruit-tree blooms. (Some owners rent the bees for this purpose.) Honeybees are more valuable to man in this way than they are as producers of honey and beeswax.

What Goes On In A Beehive: Many children are familiar with the beehives provided by people to keep bee colonies and to take advantage of the bees' honey production. This kind of hive usually has one lower story, in which the frames are used both for the brood and for storing honey which the bees use in winter. There are one or more upper stories with additional frames for storing honey.

As they would do in a natural hive, the bees house their brood in the lower section, then work hard filling the top part with honey. Beekeepers remove the upper frames as they are filled. Small sections of each frame, containing about a pound of honey, are taken out in the form you buy them in at the store. The honey is removed from the larger frames and sold in liquid form.

How Bees Make Honeycombs: To store honey, honeybees manufacture cells from wax produced by certain glands in their bodies. (Bumblebees do this also. Many species make their cells of wood, leaves, or earth.)

The making of a honeybee comb is an amazing example of co-operative effort. A group of bees begin by forming a living curtain of their bodies, each one holding on with its forefeet to the hind feet of the bee above. After they have remained in that position for some time, little plates of wax appear on each insect's abdomen. They then chew the wax and form it into a comb.

The Bee's "Honey Stomach": The nectar that the bees take from flowers becomes honey in the insects' "honey stomach." This organ is not involved in ordinary digestion; the nectar is mixed in the honey stomach with secretions from glands that cause chemical changes. The cane sugar of nectar, for example, turns into the fruit sugar of honey—a form that we can digest more readily.

Money From Honey: Keeping honeybees is a hobby that may be made to pay dividends. Some people are successful at housing them in relatively small back yards, so long as there are nearby meadows to which the insects can fly. Bees need comparatively little care, but before you purchase a swarm or hive, you will do well to seek advice either directly from an expert or from literature on the subject.

Some Unpopular Insects

Wasps—Clever Papermakers

Proud indeed is the young nature collector who can add a hornet's nest to his home exhibits. It is a real showpiece—an impressive example of the skill of the insects often claimed to be the cleverest of the entire six-footed tribe.

The bald-faced hornet is one of several wasps that manufacture paper by chewing bits of wood to a pulp and use it to construct nests sometimes massive in size. Some wasps—like the hornet—suspend the nest from a branch of a tree or bush, while others attach their homes to eaves or barn roofs—or locate them in cavities in the ground or in tree trunks.

How the Wasp Builds Its Paper Nest: If you observe these wasps when they are busy with their home construction, you will see them flying off in search of weathered wood or cut wood fibers in a post, an unpainted old building, or a piece of a dead tree trunk. From something of this sort, a wasp builder bites and tears the fiber with its mandibles, taking enough to form a pellet about an eighth of an inch across the middle. It tucks the pellet under its chin and chews until the wood is sufficiently turned into a mass of doughy pulp.

STYLES IN WASP ARCHITECTURE

When wasps are mentioned, most of us immediately think of their stinging habits. Actually, their abilities as builders are far more remarkable. The "paper" wasp (upper left) chews wood into paper pulp for its nest. The mud-dauber wasps (right) mix mud and saliva to mortar their nests.

The insect now returns to the nest and, alighting astride an unfinished layer of paper, presses down the new ball of pulp, biting it to fasten it in place. Then the wasp walks slowly backward, unraveling the ball and fastening it to the layer of paper below. When the new pulp is all laid out, the wasp runs forward, then once more backs up, biting the pulp all along the way to flatten it. While the moisture is drying out, the wasp is off collect₊ ing more fiber. As these fibers are collected from a variety of sources, the color of the paper may vary in different parts of the nest!

It is usually safe to watch bald-faced hornets or yellow jackets —which are also papermakers—at work as long as you do not disturb them. But if you poke into their nest or meddle with their activities, you will quickly discover the origin of the phrase, "mad as a hornet."

Wasp Homes of Mud: Paper nests are not the only kind built by wasps. Your observant youngster may come across cartridge-shaped cells made of mud and attached to the walls of garages, barns, or other buildings—as well as many out-of-the-way "unlikely" places. Such cells are constructed by mud-dauber wasps.

At first there is only one cell, about an inch long; but soon another is added next to it, and before the builder is finished there may be half a dozen more. On a hot summer day you may catch sight of these wasps collecting little balls of mud at the side of a puddle of water. You can even set up an observation post by forming a mud puddle there.

THE WOOD-EATING TERMITES

Most children know about these notorious insects, and the damage they do to wooden structures; but few people get to see these creatures. Termites live in the dark seclusion of tunnels, and the first intimation of their presence may come when a fence falls down or a wooden step gives way. (They have also been known to eat through table tops and window frames!)

The one time you are likely to see them in the light of day is on the occasion of the marriage flight of a colony. Then swarms of these insects—the male and female winged forms—may emerge from walls, porch supports, or anywhere near the wood foundations of a house.

Though termites are often called "white ants," they belong to an entirely different order of insects. It is easy to recognize them by their shape; termites are broad where the thorax and abdomen join. They do not have the indentation or "waist" that all ants have. The worker and soldier termites are almost colorless and blind. The winged females and males, the future queens and kings of new colonies, are dark-colored and have eyes. Actually termites are more closely related to roaches than to ants.

How Termites Digest Wood: Nearly any child can tell you that termites "eat wood," but few of us are aware of the strange alliance that makes it possible for them to live on this "food." Each termite harbors numerous tiny one-celled animals that break down the cellulose content of wood into digestible substances. If you were to place a termite in a temperature high enough to kill its minute parasites, it might continue to eat wood but would derive no nourishment; before long it would die of starvation!

FLIES—CARRIERS OF DISEASE

We all dislike and mistrust flies. They are generally targets for destruction rather than objects of study. But despite all our efforts to wipe them out, they are so extraordinarily successful in surviving that they become objects of interest for that very reason. There are many species of flies, but probably the most familiar—perhaps the most familiar of all insects—is the common housefly.

A Generation A Month: The difficulty of keeping houseflies in check is easy to understand once we are aware of the rate at which they produce their young. The female lays a mass of from twenty-five to about a hundred eggs at a time. In less than a day these hatch into tiny white maggots about as large as the point of a pin. The maggots—actually larvae—mature in four or five days, then enter the pupa stage which lasts another five days or so. The full-grown fly now appears.

Shortly after, the mother of this brood may lay another mass of eggs; and the new generation begins producing young of its own within a few days after becoming adults. As long as warm weather lasts, generations follow each other from within two weeks to a month.

The arrival of cold weather destroys the adult flies, eggs, and larvae. The pupae in their protective shells survive, remaining inactive during the winter. With the onset of warm weather they quickly complete their development, and the same process begins all over again. The average life of an adult is from two to three weeks; some live considerably longer.

The Fly's Cleaning Routine: If you have ever watched a fly cleaning itself, you must have wondered at its reputation for filthiness. Its grooming is remarkably thorough. First it rubs its front feet together briskly so that the hairs on one leg act as a brush for the other leg; then the fly nibbles at the front feet with the rasping disk it has in lieu of teeth.

Next the creature gives its whole head an energetic scrubbing with its clean front feet. It pulls forward its middle pair of legs, one at a time, and brushes and nibbles them. Finally its hind feet are used to clean each other and to brush its wings and most of its body.

All this careful grooming is deceptive, however, as far as protecting our health is concerned. Flies breed in manure and the odors of fermented or decayed plants and animals have a special attraction for them. Harmful germs cling to their feet and are deposited in food on which they may alight. Typhoid fever and amebic dysentery are among the many diseases they are known to spread. It is true that many kinds of flies render important service as scavengers and exterminators of other objectionable insects; but credit is given them grudgingly,if it is given at all, because their relatives are so unpopular.

The Fly's Wing Structure: Flies differ from most other adult insects in having a single pair of wings instead of two pairs. (Dragonflies, mayflies and others with four wings are not really flies.) Nevertheless they seem able to keep flying indefinitely, as you will notice when you chase one with a swatter. Hind wings are replaced by short stalks, or knobs, which are important in balancing them as they fly.

How Flies Walk Upside Down: You can observe, too, how a fly crawls up walls, windows, and across a ceiling as easily as it walks across the floor. Two tiny claws on the last segment of each foot aid it in walking on rough surfaces. It also has on each foot two small flat pads covered on the lower side with tiny hairs. These hairs give out a sticky fluid which effectively holds the insect on slippery surfaces and upside-down positions. It is these hairs that retain the great number of germs carried by flies.

BLOODTHIRSTY MOSQUITOES

As in the case of the bee's sting, the feature of the mosquito that chiefly interests children is this insect's bite. But while many bees are highly useful to man, little but trouble can be expected from mosquitoes. In the humid tropics they are the dreaded carriers of such diseases as malaria and yellow fever. The relatively harmless and very abundant salt-marsh mosquitoes of the Atlantic and Gulf coasts inflict painful bites but do not transmit disease.

The female mosquitoes, like the female bees, are the trouble-makers; the female of most species has piercing-sucking mouth parts and its thirst for blood makes it a great pest for man and beast. Some males have an elongated "beak," but it is not suited for piercing skin. They live on the juices of fruits and plants. It is the females, too, that "sing" by vibrating thin hard projections that lie across their breathing pores.

How Mosquito Eggs Develop: Mosquito eggs can hatch only in water. Even small puddles are good breeding grounds. Where eggs have been laid on dry land, a hard rain may provide sufficient moisture for them to develop. The water must remain standing long enough—from two to three weeks—for egg, larva, and pupa stages to be completed if an adult is to emerge. If a puddle dries up in less time, the insects die.

A female mosquito lays a mass of from fifty to several hundred eggs. The larvae that develop from these eggs are aptly known as "wrigglers." The pupae, or "tumblers," are also lively in the water and move about lashing their tail-like abdomens. Though they require no food, they must have air, and frequently come to the surface of the water to inhale through their short breathing tubes.

Crane Flies: Often a child believes that he has discovered a giant mosquito when he sees a long-legged, gangling creature awkwardly drifting through the air. The chances are it is a crane fly—an absolutely harmless insect. In spring and autumn you may see large swarms of crane flies dancing a few feet above the ground or water.

The Dragonfly—Beautiful, and Useful Too

"DEVIL'S DARNING NEEDLE" AND OTHER NICKNAMES

Though the dragonfly is one of the most beautiful of all insects, and harmless as well, it may terrify a small child who has heard some of its nicknames and the old fables in which they originated. "Devil's darning needle" recalls the old superstition that this insect can sew up children's ears; "mule-killer" reminds us that the dragonfly was once believed to kill livestock. The name "snake-doctor" was inspired by the weird notion that it brought dead water snakes to life.

An Underlip With Claws: However, "mosquito hawk" *is* a well-deserved title, for dragonflies in their nymphal stage (spent in water) eat quantities of mosquito larvae. As an adult, a dragonfly catches all sorts of insects on the wing—flies, honeybees, butter-flies, and sometimes other dragonflies smaller than itself. The nymph has a long underlip that folds back between its front legs. When it approaches a victim this lower lip shoots out rapidly and grasps the prey with two claws that form a pair of pincers at its end. Though it is a serious threat to mosquitoes and other insects, the dragonfly neither stings nor bites people.

The Metamorphosis of the Dragonfly: If yours is a family of early risers, you may some day thrill to the memorable sight of a dragonfly emerging from its nymph. You would have to go exploring along the edge of a pond about six o'clock of a summer morning and watch carefully for one of the grotesque nymphs crawling out of the water, up a tree trunk, water plant, or other support.

Sure of its support, it now strains at its armor-like covering until the skin of its back splits along its length; then very carefully it begins to pull its soft body from the shell. When this has been accomplished, the two pairs of transparent, glistening wings expand and harden. Sometimes these wings are beautifully tinted in•blue and brown. The insect has an elongated body, and its great, compound eyes cover almost the entire surface of its head.

The Damsel Fly: It is quite a puzzle to distinguish the dragonfly from its close relative the damsel fly. They are alike in many ways, but the dragonflies have larger bodies and are stronger fliers. Also, the dragonfly always holds its wings outstretched when resting, whereas a damsel fly holds its wings together over its back.

Insects that Live in the Water

THE WHIRLIGIG—"LUCKY BUG"

Summer outings are a lot more fun for your children if they can make the acquaintance of some of the odd little creatures found in ponds and streams. One of the most easily observed is the whirligig, a dark, small beetle. You may see the whirligig spinning or skating in circles on the surface of the water. It is known by such charming nicknames as "lucky bug," "submarine chaser," and "write-my-name."

Usually you find whirligigs in groups, sometimes made up of hundreds of individuals. If they are alarmed, they make a sudden dive to the bottom. They prefer shade to bright sunshine and may sometimes be found out of water, resting on sticks or rocks.

The whirligig's eyes are worth special notice; each is divided so that the upper half looks into the air while the lower part looks down into the water! Its legs are also specialized, the middle and hind ones being broad and oarlike, while the front pair are long and slender. Another strange feature of the whirligig is that if you hold one in your hand for a time, you will find it gives off a white milky fluid with a smell recalling that of ripe apples.

This accounts for such local names as "apple bug" and "vanilla bug."

THE SPEEDY WATER STRIDER

Water striders, usually found in fresh or brackish water, have very long slender middle and hind legs. It is difficult to capture them, as they skate away with great speed. The middle pair of legs propel this bug over the water while the hind pair steer. Its color is a dull dark brown above, with a silvery-white underside.

THE UPSIDE-DOWN BUG

Another water insect, the back swimmer, is named for its habit of swimming on its back, which is shaped like the bottom of a canoe. You may first notice it as it hangs head downward in the water; but when it is alarmed, it propels itself swiftly away —bottom side up!—pushing with its hind legs.

The more common species are about half an inch long, and have enormous compound eyes. The back, which you do not see when they are swimming, is pearly-colored; the underside, which you do see, is darker. The back swimmer is easily confused with the water boatman, which is quite similar in appearance; but the boatman is smaller and never swims on its back. All these bugs, with the exception of some wingless water striders, fly at night and are strongly attracted to lights.

THE CADDIS FLY AND ITS PROTECTIVE COVERING

Among the fascinating population of ponds and streams there are some creatures which, like the dragonfly, spend their early life in the water and then, as adults, proceed to live on land and in the air. Look in shallow pools for one of the most interesting of these. At first you may see what appears to be a stick, one or two inches long and half an inch around. If it starts to move itself along the bottom or up the stem of a plant, you know it is "animal" rather than "vegetable."

This is the larva of a small mothlike insect called the caddis fly. Many caddis fly larvae make cases of pebbles, sticks, or other materials, as a protective covering for their caterpillar-like bodies. Those that use sticks are said to construct "log cabins." More commonly they use sand or bits of vegetable matter which adhere to their bodies with silk produced by certain glands.

THE CADDIS FLY — NATURE'S MASTER BUILDER

In the larval stage this small mothlike insect, living at the bottom of a pond or stream, builds a case about itself from bits of plants or pebbles. (Both types are pictured underwater.) The cases, held together with gluelike silk provided by the creature's secretions, are remarkable for their skillful construction.

Still another interesting product of some caddis worms is a silken net. The insect anchors this so that the cup-shaped interior faces upstream. Thus the net serves both as protection against the current and as a food trap for the caddis worm that fashioned it.

The caddis fly emerges from its pupal form in a manner different from that of most water insects. The usual way is for them to leave the water before they attain adult form; but the caddis fly emerges at the bottom of the stream and swims to the surface.

There it usually grasps some object, climbs on it and waits for its wings to dry.

The Fisherman's Friend: A knowledge of these interesting insects is of practical value to the child or grown-up who wishes to do "fly-fishing" in ponds and streams. As part of this fascinating sport the fisherman uses nymphs, "wet flies," and "dry flies" to duplicate the caddis fly in all its stages. He may make these with such materials as bits of feather and hair; but even if he buys them commercially, he ought to have a knowledge of the fly and its habits in order to make the best use of his bait.

How to Keep Water Insects at Home

Housing the Captives

One of the most enjoyable ways for a child to observe the activities and development of water insects is to have an insect aquarium. You can keep a few specimens in jars or buckets; but a rectangular glass aquarium, which is available at a pet store, makes a much better home because you can reproduce the creatures' natural surroundings in miniature.

Cover the bottom with a layer of sand about an inch and a half thick, first taking the precaution of baking it to kill any bacteria. Next, fill the aquarium about two-thirds full with water; then plant water cress, eel grass, chara, or other green plants, anchoring them securely in the sand. If you expect to house nymphs, you will want to have sticks fastened at the bottom of the aquarium and extending a few inches over the surface of the water; when the nymphs are ready to be transformed into winged adults, they can crawl on the sticks.

Capturing Water Insects: To collect specimens, use a large kitchen strainer or a net smaller than the type employed for collecting insects in the air. At a shallow edge of a pond, where the reeds are plentiful, sweep the net a few inches above the muddy bottom. Examine your catch and drop interesting-looking specimens into various jars, adding some of the pond water. Try to keep different kinds separate as a precaution against any flesh-eating species devouring their fellow captives on the way home.

How to Feed Water Insects: When you collect your specimens, it is wise to take extra insects to serve as food. You can also obtain food by sweeping an insect net through weeds and tall grass. Often the flesh-eating nymphs will eat tiny bits of meat. This should be tied to a string and pulled out again if it has not been eaten by the next day. If you wish to keep both flesh-eating and plant-eating species, you will need more than one aquarium.

An insect aquarium should be located in a bright spot, but not directly in the sunlight. Keep the inner sides of the glass cleaned with a piece of flannel wrapped about a stick. This will give you good "observation windows" through which to see a caddis worm building, a dragonfly nymph snatching at prey with its long, hinged lip, or the tiny larva of a whirligig creeping stealthily over the bottom as it looks for other larvae to eat. And if you successfully keep them to maturity, you will have the added thrill of observing them transformed from underwater "personalities" to winged creatures of the air.

Insect Oddities

THE GALLS—WEIRD HOMEMAKERS

Insects provide many of nature's most remarkable oddities. You have discovered one of them when you observe a curious "bump" or ball on a plant stem or flower, reminding you of a large nut growing on a tree branch or leaf. It may be greenish, brown, pink, or red. If you were to cut open one of these bumps, you would discover an insect larva at its center. This identifies it as a "gall," the home of a growing creature that will develop into a small wasp, fly, or moth.

The young nature observer is likely to be puzzled by the imprisoned larva. "How does it get in there? I don't see any opening from the outside."

How a Gall Insect Develops: Actually, the larva doesn't "get in"; its home grows about it! Let us follow the life cycle of one of the common gall insects—a very small wasp responsible for the "oak apple." In early spring we see it deposit its eggs on the leaf of a scarlet oak. When one of these eggs develops into a legless and almost colorless larva, we note an immediate change in the leaf. Vegetable fibers start to grow, radiating out from the little grub. As this process goes on, a thin smooth crust forms around the outer edges.

Now the "oak apple" is formed, and the insect larva is completely surrounded by food and protected by its globular house. Here it eats, completes its growth, changes to a pupa, and at last emerges as a wasp, no more than a quarter-inch in length.

Remarkable Types of Galls: The "apple oak" is but one of the many kinds of galls. Thus, you may frequently see two different types on goldenrod stems. One of them, made by a grub that becomes a fly, is spherical in shape; the other, which is spindle-shaped, develops into a tiny moth.

Then there are the willow cone galls, produced by a little gnat. It lays its eggs on the tip of the bud of a twig. This stops the further growth of the twig, stunting the leaves into small scales which overlap in rows around the larva. The very pretty galls which you may find on wild rosebushes somewhat resemble small chestnut burs but are pink and green when young. Later they turn brown.

Collecting Galls: In wintertime, collecting galls makes a fine outdoor activity. Many of them are dead and deserted by then, to be sure; but in some the grubs are still resting and waiting for the onset of warm weather. The collector will find it rewarding to compare styles. A gall may be large or small, globular or spindle-shaped; its covering may be smooth, shingled, or spiny. You can succeed in identifying the insect builder once you become familiar with these variations and the kinds of plants that each insect characteristically chooses.

THE INTERESTINGLY NAMED ANT LIONS

The larva of the ant lion, one of nature's most remarkable oddities, catches its prey in a trap. It is fairly easy to find the traps it builds, for ant lions live on sandy stretches over most of the United States and southern Canada. As in the case of the gall insects, the adult forms are undistinguished; it is the larvae, often called doodlebugs, that attract our attention.

The Doodlebug's Ambush Technique: The doodlebug, plump-bodied and hairy, is less than an inch long. Its head is small in proportion to its body—but its jaws are enormous in relation to the size of its head! It digs a pit in sandy or powdery soil by shoveling the earth on its head and then with a sharp jerk, throwing it a considerable distance. As it digs, it walks around and around, always *backwards,* in ever-widening circles.

Finally a tiny crater is formed, an inch and a half across or smaller, with the doodlebug buried at the bottom. With only its head and powerful jaws exposed, it waits for an ant or some other insect to slip over the edge and slide down. Then it seizes the victim, makes it helpless by injecting a paralyzing secretion into it, sucks the juice from its body, and flips the lifeless remains out of the pit by an upward jerk of its long jaws.

How to Find Doodlebugs: You may be interested in observing this extraordinary example of how a "lowly" creature can capture its prey by an ingenious trapping technique. You can catch a doodlebug by finding its crater and scooping your hand under to bring the insect-excavator to the surface. Place it in a box of sandy soil and you will quickly see it set to work. If you wish to see the final act of the drama, you must place ants or other insects in the box so the doodlebug will not vainly lie in wait.

The Strange Praying Mantids

I know of one little girl to whom the praying mantis will always seem curious if only because of the way she first became acquainted with this insect. On an August evening a mantis alighted on a window sill of her New York apartment! It would be hard to imagine a more unlikely intruder in such a place than this queer green creature with its pointed, elfin face and big round eyes.

The little girl managed to get it into a box and took it to the American Museum of Natural History in New York in the belief that she had something on the order of a visitor from Mars. There she learned the true nature of her captive, and also that it was quite possible to keep a mantis as a pet.

The Preying Habits of the Praying Mantis: In natural surroundings mantids are great hunters, capturing by stealth such lively insects as butterflies, mosquitoes, grasshoppers, beetles, and flies. The mantis lies in wait with its front legs upraised in a prayerful pose, and when its prey comes near, it snatches at the victim with lightning speed. The prey has slight chance of escaping the rows of sharp spines on the second and third joints of the mantis' forelegs.

"MULE-KILLERS" AND "DEVIL'S HORSES"

These are some of the epithets that have been applied to the praying mantis. Though its forelegs seem to be raised in a devout attitude, the mantis is actually poised to pounce on its prey. Then, holding its victim in a grip of steel, it devours it at its leisure. Green or brown in color, this insect is about two inches long.

How to Feed a Praying Mantis: In captivity a mantis will usually accept bits of hamburger and other meat as substitutes for living prey. Mantids vary quite a bit in their eating habits; some are known to drink milk while others refuse it. They should be watered every day, and you can do this by sprinkling water on leaves in their cage. In time they may become tame enough to drink the water off a spoon.

During the winter, mantids' brownish egg cases, about the size of walnuts, may be collected from weeds and bushes. In the spring at least a couple of hundred babies will emerge from one of them.

The Mantis as a Pest Exterminator: The mantids of our southern states are native to this country, but one species found commonly in the more northerly regions originally came from China and Japan, while another is an import from Europe. Both were introduced here by accident; later more were imported for their supposed value in destroying insect pests. In China they are sometimes tied by a silk thread near a bedroom window where they trap flies and mosquitoes.

WALKING STICKS—MASTERS OF CAMOUFLAGE

A youngster must be really sharp-eyed to discover one of these remarkably camouflaged insects. Aside from the fact that its coloring blends with the tree bark on which it so often rests, the walking stick has much the same shape as a slender twig. Unless it moves, you can scarcely tell it is an animal! In North America you will never see one flying, as all our species are wingless; but some of the tropical kinds have wings.

When a walking stick is detected and picked up, it is quite capable of playing dead—sometimes for several hours at a stretch. Though the largest American species is about six inches long, including the antennae, some found in India are known to reach a length of fifteen inches. Some walking sticks are able to grow a new leg, at least partially, to replace one lost through a mishap.

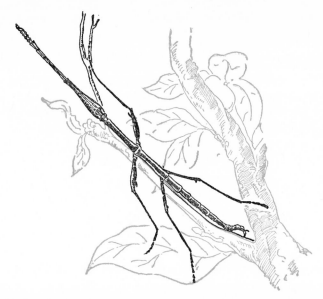

WHICH IS THE WALKING STICK, WHICH IS THE TWIG?
This aptly named insect is one of nature's most amazing examples of camouflage. Its color follows the seasons: green in springtime, brown in autumn to blend with the changing hues of the leaves. The walking stick can also play dead for several hours, if need be. It feeds on leaves, and is active mostly at night.

The Misunderstood Spiders

Most of us think of the classic struggle between the spider and the fly as a war between two kinds of insects. But the spider is not an insect at all! Your youngster can discover this for himself if he watches one closely and counts its legs. The spider has eight legs—two more than an adult insect. Another distinction is that a spider has only two major body divisions—the head and thorax merged into one unit, and the abdomen—whereas an insect has three. Still another difference is that a spider, unlike an insect, has no antennae.

THE SPIDER'S POISONOUS BITE

Spiders are widely misunderstood, much as snakes are. Many people believe that all spiders should be avoided or killed, that a spider bite is often fatal. In the United States we must beware of just two kinds: the tarantula and the black widow. Even in the case of these two species, the deadliness of the bite has been greatly exaggerated. If victims are properly treated, they recover promptly.

It used to be thought that black widows were found only in the South, but they are constantly being discovered—and always with great surprise—in New York, Connecticut, and other northern states. The large, hairy tarantula (the banana spider) also occasionally appears up north, after traveling as a stowaway in a bunch of bananas. In the tropics tarantulas are constantly on the prowl among this fruit for roaches and other insect food; so, chances are strong that a certain number will be moved aboard ship.

The bite of ordinary spiders is poisonous—that is the way they kill for food. Some bites cause swelling and irritation, possibly to the extent produced by a wasp's sting. However, the poison is usually administered in minute quantities; and few spiders are strong enough to be able to bite through a human skin even if they tried.

STYLES IN SPIDER TRAPS

Spiders are past masters at keeping out of sight, but we have little trouble finding the silken traps they weave. Thus we rarely see the little house spider that prefers life indoors; still, we know it has been about when we discover cobwebs in dark and undisturbed corners. The funnel-shaped webs you may see spread over the fields if you go for an early-morning walk are the work of grass spiders.

A close relative of this species frequents cellars, so it is not surprising to find the same kind of funnel-shaped webs in your cellar. The most exquisite of all webs are those constructed by the orb builders, which often do their weaving in gardens or on porches.

Remote-control Traps: Sometimes you may find an orb weaver stationed at the center of its web, waiting for its prey; some species make a habit of this. Others, however, keep themselves hidden nearby. A spider that remains away from its web rests one of its claws on a trap line stretched from the hub of the web. When an insect enters the trap, the resulting vibration is carried to the spider, which rushes onto the web and envelops its victim in a band of silk. It bites the insect either before or after wrapping it, but usually does not eat it at once unless it is hungry.

How the Spider Ingeniously Avoids its Own Trap: A child may wonder, even if he has the opportunity to watch this drama being enacted, why the spider does not become entangled in its own web. He will understand why, if he knows that a web is made of two kinds of silk. One kind is inelastic and does not stick to objects that touch it; the other is very elastic and sticky.

The spokes of the web, the framework, and the guy-lines that fasten it to surrounding objects, are all of the inelastic silk. However, the continuous spiral lines connecting the spokes are very elastic and adhere to anything that touches them. The spider cleverly runs along the spokes and thereby avoids being tangled in its own web.

How the Spider Spins an Orb Web: If the spider is unlucky its web may be destroyed many times during a season. At times the little weaver may have to construct one every twenty-four hours. It begins its work on a well-elevated position by spinning a thread of silk which is soon caught in a passing breeze; the free end is carried along until it reaches an object to which it adheres. The spider then draws in the slack, making the line taut. It fastens the second end and walks across it, doubling its strength with another line of silk.

The spokes are constructed next, extending outward from a central point on this bridge line. Now the spider makes a spiral line a short distance out from the hub of these spokes and attached to each of them, holding them firm. The spider pulls this line tight, then continues weaving spiral lines until it reaches what will be the outer edge of the orb.

Up to this point all the silk has been smooth, tough, and not sticky. Now elastic, adhesive silk is manufactured as the spider makes a second series of spirals, this time working from the outer edge of the web down to the hub. During this process the spider cuts the first spirals with its jaws so that these lines fall away from the web. They have served their purpose as a mere scaffold! If you look very closely at a web, you may possibly see bits of the temporary spiral clinging to the spokes.

Built-in Silk Spinner: What the spider succeeds in spinning is so extraordinary that the result is quite certain to cause an observant child to wonder just how the silk is produced. This is the explanation: A spider has special spinning organs located near the top of its abdomen (in contrast to a caterpillar, which has its near the lower lip). There are two or three of these finger-like spinnerets, tipped with many small tubes. The silk is spun from them as a fluid but it hardens immediately upon coming in contact with the air.

Spiders in Ambush: Not all spiders construct webs; some kinds merely lie in wait for their prey. You may find white crab spiders doing this, though it is not easy to detect one of them. They are great artists at camouflage, taking on the color of the various flowers they hide in. Another spider that dispenses with a web is the trap-door spider, which makes a silk-lined home in the earth from which to stalk victims.

How to Watch Spiders at Work: You may occasionally succeed in moving an orb web with its weaver to your home, if it happens to be attached to a branch that you can break off conveniently. If you set it on a porch or some other likely place, you can then observe it at your convenience. However, it is more adventurous to watch spider traps being prepared in their natural setting.

You may have a chance to do this while you take an evening walk with your child; late in the day is the spider's usual time for spinning. You can even plot to have a web built as you look on. If you find one during the day with its builder lying in wait nearby, break it quietly and gently so as not to frighten the spider into running away. Then return to the scene during "building hours" and you should see a new web under construction.

Spiders have still another use for their silk. Eggs laid in the autumn to hatch in the spring need protection from weather as well as from hungry creatures. Many spiders solve this problem by spinning elaborate silken sacs for their eggs. Those that make cobwebs often suspend the sac from the web—or they may place the sac in a more sheltered spot. Others make nests for their eggs in folded leaves, or in the crevices of rocks and boards. Another custom is to nest on stones and cover the nest and eggs with a smooth, waterproof silken coat.

You may frequently see these little silvery disks as you walk through the fields in autumn. The large running spiders that you are most likely to find under stones not only make egg sacs—the mother attaches the sac to her spinnerets and carries it everywhere. When the young hatch, they climb on her back and stay with her for some time.

Cannibal Spiders: Even a mother's care cannot prevent her off-spring from devouring each other. One of the common orb weavers, the orange garden spider, makes a very fine sac, about as large as a hickory nut, in which she may lay five hundred eggs or more. These hatch early in the winter but the young remain within the protective walls of the sac. By spring, when the sac breaks open, only a dozen or so young may emerge. They are the strong ones that have survived by consuming the rest of the once-large family.

Possibly you have had the disconcerting experience of having a very tiny spider "fly" in your face on occasion. Particularly in the spring and autumn great numbers of these eight-legged creatures sail through the air and, especially to a youngster, it may seem they are actually flying.

However, if you look closely, you will see that the spiderling is attached to a long thread—still one more use for silk! Aided by the thread, it makes use of rising air currents to float from its hatching place to new territory, well apart from its numerous and hungry brothers and sisters.

The Spider's Homemade Parachute: To start its journey, the young spider climbs up a tall blade of grass or a larger plant. There it spins a silken thread and sends it out on the air. When it is long enough, the friction of air currents on it buoys it upward, and the spider, letting go its hold, is off on its journey to an unknown destination. Usually the flight is ended by the spider's bumping against an elevated object, but sometimes it helps decide its own fate by pulling in the streamer till all buoyancy is lost. "Flying" spiders have been discovered in mid-ocean!

Flying or ballooning is not the habit of just a few kinds of spiders. Most species use this means of getting from one area to another.

Daddy Longlegs

If you observe the habits of this creature which, like the spider, is almost "all legs," you will find that it does not have the spider's ways. It does not spin silk, and it lays its eggs under stones or in crevices but gives them no other protection. Though it has eight legs and in many other ways resembles spiders, it is in an animal division of its own. We recognize it quite easily by its hairlike and remarkably long legs. If our legs were as long in proportion to our bodies as "daddy's" are to his, we would stand something like forty feet off the ground!

"Tell Me Where the Cows Are": Some children still learn the strange old custom of grasping a "daddy" and saying, "Tell me where the cows are, or I'll kill you." Its waving legs, as the little creature struggles to get away, are directed to all points of the compass, so that if there are some cows about, they are sure to be indicated. To a very young naturalist, this seems a satisfying experiment! But later he can learn facts about daddy longlegs that are much more interesting than this fanciful idea.

How "Daddy" Uses His Long Legs: This creature has the power of regrowing legs if they are broken off. The several pairs are of varying lengths: The first pair is usually the shortest, the second pair the longest and the fourth pair next in length. When you watch "daddy" running you can see that the second pair of legs are spread wide apart and keep in rapid motion. Their sensitive tips serve as feelers and relay information about the nature of the animal's surroundings. If they pause over something that suggests food, "daddy" stops running to investigate further with the little feelers (palpi) under its head.

Observing Daddy Longlegs: A daddy longlegs makes a most rewarding little captive. You can keep one for a while by simply putting a large glass tumbler over it. Place a few drops of sweetened water within convenient reach of the legs. It is amusing to watch this odd creature pull one leg at a time slowly through its jaws, nibbling it clean. A child can also see a little black dot on top of its body, located between the second pair of legs, which is apparently an eye! However, by examining it under a magnifying lens, he will discover that this is a raised knob, with a tiny shining black eye on either side of it!

"Thousand-Leggers"

Children often call these creatures "bugs"—but they are neither bugs nor insects of any kind. They are in the same major grouping of the animal kingdom as insects, but each is recognized as a separate class in this division. This is quickly indicated by the fact that centipedes and millipedes have many pairs of legs— in contrast to the insects, which have three pairs of legs.

More About "Thousand-Leggers": Centipedes and millipedes have two main parts to their body structure: head and body. The millipede has two pairs of walking legs to each body segment, whereas the centipede has one pair to a segment. Their size and number of legs vary according to species, but all species of millipedes have so many legs that we frequently hear them called "thousand-leggers."

We usually find millipedes in damp places, though they may appear almost anywhere in a garden. They feed on vegetable matter and they do not bite. If they are disturbed, they roll up into a spiral.

The centipedes are not so harmless. They have a pair of poison fangs on the first segment of the flattened body. In northern regions centipedes are small and generally use their poison for killing insect prey. In tropical regions there are larger species of centipedes; their bite may have serious consequences for human victims.

The Lowly Worms

Many a child who digs earthworms for fishing bait thinks he is collecting "insects." This idea is indeed very far from the truth. Worms are not closely related to any other creature; in the animal kingdom they occupy their own major niche, just as distinct as the division of "vertebrates" to which man belongs.

Scientists have classified the many kinds of worms in three main groups, and each of these forms one of the eleven major divisions of the animal kingdom. Some of our most troublesome parasites, such as tapeworms and hookworms, belong to two of these divisions—"roundworms" and "flatworms."

How Earthworms Enrich the Soil

In the third group ("segmented worms") we find our friend the earthworm. "Friend" it is indeed, for earthworms are of immense value to man in growing food. As they move through the ground they do not push the earth around their bodies as a mole does; they actually swallow it! Before they expel the earth again, it is ground fine in the gizzard and lime is added to it in the stomach.

Earthworms usually plow a foot or more beneath the surface of the earth, and are constantly bringing subsoil upward. They also carry down with them from the surface bits of dead leaves, flowers, and twigs, which enrich the soil as they decay. Charles Darwin estimated that an acre of garden land in England held more than fifty thousand earthworms, and that eighteen tons of vegetable mold passed through each earthworm's body every year!

Tug-of-War: If a child watches a bird tugging at an earthworm, he may wonder what enables the worm to "hold on." The holding is done with strong muscles aided by tiny stiff bristles that cling to the earth. There are four pairs of bristles on each segment (or ring) of the worm's body, except for the first three segments and the last one. The bristles are aids in crawling as well as holding.

The Earthworm's Eggs: In the giant earthworms of the tropics which may grow to a length of six feet, it is easy to see how the body is composed of segments—one behind the other. On the common earthworm an extra, saclike ring is formed about the body toward its tail-end. The worm lays its eggs in this ring, and then works it forward and over its head. Cast off, the ring becomes a football-shaped capsule of yellowish brown, no larger than a grain of wheat. You may sometimes come across such a capsule in the fields, under stones or sticks, in May or June, before baby earthworms have hatched from the egg.

Earthworms Are Profitable: With the value of the earthworm fully recognized, raising worms has become a successful business enterprise. The earthworms are sold as fish bait to sportsmen throughout the United States and Canada—and, more important, they are supplied commercially to farmers who appreciate their ability to increase the fertility of the soil.

The Insect World—Tiny or Immense

We have come to the end of our exploration of the enchanting world of insects, spiders, and other small creatures. It is a world tiny in scale but brimming over with fantastic, "wonder-full" things to observe: How insects see with their curious compound eyes, how they walk upside-down, walk backward, swim on their back, whirl in circles, make music, and change into gorgeous creatures through the magic of metamorphosis; how they make paper, produce honey, and weave silk; how they kill by piercing, sucking, trapping, entangling, or injecting nerve-killing fluid; how they build nests, combs, webs—or house themselves by fashioning a case over their bodies; how they live in huge colonies and fight in vast armies commanded by queens and served by slaves.

Once you turn from man-made structures of wood, concrete, and steel, and allow your eyes to dwell on nature and its creatures, you can never know a boring, empty moment. There is so much to see, so much to be inquired into and understood. Exploring nature, I have said earlier, is a natural and rewarding outlet for our children's energy and our own. It opens windows on the world, through which the tensions produced in all of us by modern living may escape. That is what George Orwell, the noted British novelist and critic, meant when he declared: "I think that by retaining one's childhood love of such things as trees, fishes, butterflies and . . . toads, one makes a peaceful and decent future a little more probable."

CHAPTER **10** The Fascination
of Flowers

HILDREN LOVE things that grow. That is
probably why few toys can ever hold their
attention as long as a garden will. Everything about a garden appeals to them. Planting a seed is a privilege they are ready to fight
for, and day after day they will come back to see if it has begun
to sprout. Watching a bud unfold is another experience that fills
them with wonderment. It is no exaggeration to say that the youngster who does not have his own garden or flower box, or just a
single flowerpot, is being deprived of one of childhood's most
treasured possessions.

A child's interest in the plant world is by no means limited to
flowers. Vegetables and flowerless plants, or even grass, will absorb
his attention, too, and he will give them devoted care. What
attracts him to plants is that they are living things, growing, expanding, changing.

Once your youngster becomes fully aware that plants have
life just as animals do, a number of questions are bound to arise
in his mind if he takes nature exploring seriously. Not so easy
to answer as it is to ask is this one: "What's the difference between
plants and animals?"

Plants Move Too: The younger child may be satisfied with the
popular answer—quite oversimplified—that animals are capable of
motion, moving from place to place by their own efforts—whereas

plants cannot move. Often this answer will not do for an older child. As he thinks it over, he may realize that plants *do* move in certain ways.

For example: They move upward and outward as part of the growing process. Some develop runners that creep over the ground. Violets—and others—shoot their seeds; the dandelion is one of many plants that parachute seeds to new growing grounds, while portions of the stems of Florida moss break off and are blown about by the wind until they alight and start to grow. The water lily, like numerous other species, closes its petals each night and opens them again in the morning. (What probably impresses children even more is that the water lily floats.)

So we see there is plenty of motion on the part of plants. The older child will conclude that many characteristics observed in animals are also present in plants. Both plants and animals move; both are made up of living cells, are born, breathe, feed, grow, and reproduce themselves.

How Plants Feed Themselves: There is one vital difference between plants and animals, however, and that is in the way they feed themselves. A plant is in effect a factory which produces its own food *by turning nonliving matter into living matter.* This process, one of nature's wonders, is made possible by the green substance known as chlorophyll.

We often call chlorophyll "leaf-green," as it is found chiefly in leaves. When this leaf-green is worked on by the action of light from the sun, chemical changes occur which transform lifeless (inorganic) matter into life-giving and life-sustaining matter. (Animals do not have chlorophyll, but we now find it used in all kinds of products, from toothpaste to dog food, mainly for the purpose of killing odors.)

The Leaf—Nature's Great Chemical Laboratory

If you examine leaves, you will notice that as a rule they are a darker green on the upper side than on the underside. The chlorophyll-bearing cells on the top surface are packed more closely to catch as much sunlight as possible. (As we have seen, sunlight is one of the "raw materials" needed for making living matter.)

The "manufacturing" cells are protected on top and bottom surfaces by a skin, or epidermis, which is perforated with innumerable tiny holes. Each hole is surrounded by two guard-cells—the only surface cells that contain chlorophyll. Through the little holes the leaf constantly takes in and gives off oxygen, carbon dioxide, and other gases as well as water vapor.

How Chlorophyll Makes Food for Plants

Before the leaf "factory" can operate, it requires one more item. This is a watery solution, containing many substances, that originates in the soil, enters the plant roots, works its way up the stem and at last into the leaf.

Within each leaf, carbon dioxide—much of it comes from the air we exhale—is separated into carbon and oxygen. In the same way, water is broken down into oxygen and hydrogen. The leaf cells combine the carbon with the hydrogen and oxygen into a form of sugar that will nourish the plant. It is the chlorophyll that accomplishes this remarkable feat—but it can be done only when sunlight, or artificial light equal to sunlight, is shining on the plant.

In the daytime plants are our benefactors by releasing oxygen, which purifies the air we breathe. At night, though, they give off carbon dioxide, a gas which is poisonous when it is present in considerable quantity. (This explains why a room with many large house plants should be well aired at night.)

A scientist has estimated that during the course of a summer a single leaf, suitably exposed to sunlight, manufactures enough sugar to cover itself with a solid layer about one twenty-fifth of an inch thick—and this is aside from protein and other food elements!

Plants Turn Toward the Sun: Your house plants will give you a fine opportunity to observe how leaves are affected by the need for sunlight, in order to continue feeding the plants. Even a small child can observe how the location of the leaves at or near the ends of branches helps expose their surfaces to a maximum of light.

The youngster can also notice the way the plants sometimes change their position according to the direction of the source of light—and how, when a new length of stem grows, its young leaf bends and turns its stalk to escape, as much as possible, the shade of surrounding leaves. The leaves of nasturtiums, begonias, and others, are noticeably adept at keeping in a favorable light.

Out-of-doors there are some plants, such as one of the wild lettuces, which fix their leaves so consistently in a north-south plane that they are known as "compass plants."

Some "Dew" Doesn't Fall: Going out-of-doors in the early morning, a child always notices the dew, with some such exclamation as, "Look how much dew has fallen!" But like as not the drops of moisture he calls dew, did not "fall"; they are probably water that passed out of the grass and leaves as water vapor and condensed into drops as it emerged. If the night was humid and cool, the vapor could not become part of the air as rapidly as it came out of the leaves.

What Flowers Are For

There is much that a child can learn from house plants, but the real fun of studying flowers is mostly found outdoors. There he can watch insects traveling from one bloom to another in quest of nectar. As he observes flowers in numbers, he will see countless interesting variations in the shapes and colors of petals and in the forms of complete flowers. But there is a purpose in flowers beyond mere looks, beautiful though they are.

A child may be old enough to understand that what flowers are really for is to continue the life of the plants that bear them; yet, looking at a blooming garden and with real curiosity in his voice, he will ask, *"How do they?"*

How Flowers Develop Seeds

A brief answer is that flowers produce seeds. But before a flower can produce seeds, it must receive grains of pollen that will fertilize it. What is involved in the fertilization of a flower? To answer this question, we must be familiar with the different parts that make up a flower.

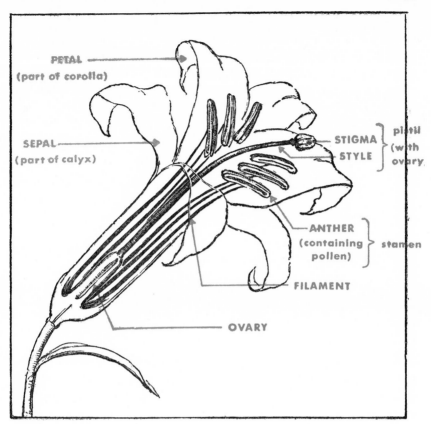

PETAL
(part of corolla)

SEPAL
(part of calyx)

STIGMA
STYLE
pistil
(with
ovary)

ANTHER
(containing
pollen)

stamen

FILAMENT

OVARY

A SEED-PRODUCING FACTORY
All seeds are produced by flowers, but there is considerable variation in the forms of flowers. Not all types have both male parts (stamens) and female (pistil) within one blossom. Those that do are termed "perfect" flowers. This diagram of a lily (shown with transparent petals and sepals) illustrates one of them.

Here a difficulty arises: Not all flowers conform to the same pattern. Suppose, then, we consider the simplest types. One of these is the "perfect" flower—such as the lily—which has a pollen-bearing stamen and an ovary in which seeds develop.

The other simple type is a plant which bears two different types of flowers—the pussy willow is an example; one flower bears only the pollen-laden stamens while the other flower bears the ovary. In this case, we might call the flower with the stamens the "male" flower, while the flower with the ovary is the "female" flower.

The Parts of a Flower and What They Do: It is a great help, in understanding how a flower functions, for a child to look at a diagram in which flower parts are pointed out. If he has a diagram illustrating a perfect flower (as shown here), he will find:

The *ovary*—a well-protected structure in the center of the flower. In it are

The *ovules*—which contain egg cells, destined to become seeds. (Some ovaries contain a single ovule; others have many ovules.) The ovary has a rather slender stalk, extending upward, and known as

The *style*. At its top, the style expands into a broadened tip with a sticky surface—a perfect trap for pollen. This expanded tip we call

PETALS ARE A FLOWER'S CROWNING GLORY

The corolla (meaning "crown") of a flower may vary in countless ways. It is made up of petals, and these have numerous colors and shapes. Sometimes, too, each petal is separate (as in the lily, left); sometimes they are joined and show only as separate points (as in the squash flower, center); and sometimes (as in the petunia, right) there is no separation whatever.

The *stigma*. The combined stigma, style, and ovary form a complete *pistil*.

Also within the flower are

The *stamens*. A stamen consists of

The *filament*. This is a slender stalk, on the top of which rests

The *anther,* which encloses a powder (nearly always yellow) that we know as

The *pollen*. The pollen grains are formed by the division of cells within the anther. In our typical flower the pistil and the stamens are surrounded by

The *corolla,* composed of petals. This word, meaning "crown," is well chosen, for the corolla is the most beautiful part of the flower. In many flowers it is made up of separate petals; in other flowers—the squash flower, for one—the petals are joined together and show only as separate points. Then there are still other flowers—the petunia and morning-glory are among them—which have a corolla all in one piece, without any separation of the petals. In any event, the petals are encircled by

The *sepals*. All together, the sepals make up

The *calyx,* which serves to protect the flower, especially in its budding stage. The sepals, which are really specialized leaves, vary in size, shape, and number in different kinds of flowers. Often the sepals are green, as on the rose; but sometimes—as in the case of the tulip—you find them the same color as the petals. On some kinds of plants sepals fall off as soon as the flower opens; on many others—roses and apple blossoms, for example—these leaves remain even after the seeds have ripened.

How the Seed Starts

The first step in the development of a seed is for pollen to reach the flower's stigma. The pollen may be blown into the stigma from the anther of some flower. What happens more commonly is that an insect, going from one flower to another in search of nectar, gets pollen on its body and the grains later rub off on a stigma.

Once a pollen grain has become attached to the sticky surface of the stigma, it quickly forms a tiny tube much like a root hair.

This tube forces its way down the style to reach an egg cell in the ovule. As soon as the tube makes its connection with the egg cell, the life-germ in the pollen slips through the tube to combine with the life-germ in the egg cell. Thus the seed starts, developing on food furnished by the plant and on warmth given by the sun.

How the Seed Is Nourished and Protected

A fully developed seed is the embryo of a new plant, with food stored around it in a form that can be used whenever new growth begins. One of the amazing things about seeds is that the stored food remains usable even though new growth does not start for weeks, months, or even years! (This dormant period varies, of course, with different kinds of seeds.) The embryo and the food supply are protected by one or more layers of the ovule.

Nuts and Tomatoes Are "Fruit": In some seeds, such as peas and beans, the food supply is stored within certain parts of the embryo itself. In other plants, corn and wheat for example, the food is stored around, rather than in, the embryo. And still other plants develop elaborate structures about their seeds. These structures are called "fruit"—apples and pears are familiar examples. When a scientist speaks of a "fruit," he may be referring to the ripened ovary of any kind of plant, be it the pod of a pea, a hard nut, or a juicy tomato.

There are many opportunities for examining seeds—for example, when you are preparing dinner. To a hungry diner, peas, beans, and corn are food; to a nature explorer, they are seeds! A child is thrilled to see the first sprouting of the plant embryo after he plants a few seeds in a glass with moist soil. If the seeds are placed just inside the glass, they can be seen sprouting.

How Flowers Attract Insects

When a child learns that pollen is transferred from one plant to another by messenger insects, he may wonder what attracts an insect to flowers—is it their sweet scent or the color of their petals? This is the kind of problem that scientists still ponder and sometimes debate about. For many years it was a generally accepted "fact" that the chief value of color in flowers was to attract insects.

Scent Is the Attraction: Along came a scientist who had made a study of the insects' pollinizing role. He pointed out that bees and other flower-visiting insects have poor vision but a well-developed sense of smell. He also demonstrated that in addition to the colors that we can see, some flowers emit ultraviolet rays. Though these rays are not visible to our eyes, insects can see the rays as well as, or even better than, the colors which our eyes perceive. His over-all conclusion was that color is, at most, only incidentally responsible for bringing insects to flowers.

Since that time, countless observations and experiments have shown that insects are attracted by the scent of flowers. In the course of one of his famous experiments, for example, Luther Burbank worked patiently to develop a petunia that would have fragrance. He knew that he had succeeded at last when he saw several bees hovering over one of the plants in a large bed of his experimental petunias. He quickly verified the fact that this particular plant's flowers *were* perfumed.

How Pollen Is Carried from Plant to Plant

It is vital for insects to visit flowers for, as we have seen, they carry pollen from plant to plant and thus help bring about the fertilization of flowers. Corn and all other plants known as "grasses," and most cone-bearing plants—such as pine trees—depend on the wind to convey their pollen.

Breeding Flowers: But sometimes man takes a hand in pollinating plants, especially when he wishes to create a hybrid, for a variety of reasons, by "crossing" the pollen of two different species in the same family. This may be done to increase the hardiness of a beautiful but fragile plant, or to make the colors of flowers more vivid.

Crossing different kinds of plants calls to mind the name of Luther Burbank. He will undoubtedly be remembered for all time as the great genius among plant breeders; it was he who made the science of "training plants to work for man" really practical.

He made countless improvements in vegetables as well as in flowers; bigger and better potatoes, sweet corn that matures early in the season, luscious blackberries on thornless bushes, and freestone plums of excellent flavor and texture, are just a few of them. There is no secret about the methods he used to bring about his "miracles" with plants. These methods have often been described, and a book by Mr. Burbank *(Partner of Nature)* telling about his work is exciting reading.

How Seeds Are Scattered

One of the most intriguing aspects of the flower story involves the ways in which seeds are scattered. Many children get their first notion of seed dispersal when they blow at a dandelion "gone to seed." Each seed, attached to a filmy parachute, flies away.

Other times, say after a country hike, a youngster may find his clothes (or his dog's fur coat) covered with sticktights or cockleburs seeking transportation with their sharp little hooks. If he realizes these "burs" are seeds, unconsciously trying to use him or the dog as a means of reaching new growing grounds, he may find the job of prying them loose less tedious.

Other Ways That Seeds Travel: Although the seeds that are dispersed by the wind are the most conspicuous ones, we can observe other ways they travel. Some plants, including violets, pansies, and touch-me-nots, shoot their seeds. Water lilies and several other water plants bear seeds that manage to float to some desirable growing spot without becoming water-soaked.

180,000 Seeds from a Plant: Countless seeds are unsuccessful, as a youngster may realize when he throws the burs into a scrapbasket; but this is of little importance as the number of seeds borne by each plant is incredibly large. Charles Darwin reported counting the seeds of an orchid; he found more than six thousand in a pod. As there were thirty pods on the plant, the total number of prospective seedlings from this parent would be something like 180,000!

A Garden of His Own

The modest blooms children raise themselves will easily thrill them as much as, if not more than, the most spectacular plants to be seen at a flower show. Window boxes and other indoor planting can give city youngsters some of the joy of raising plants; but families with land at their disposal have endless opportunity for engaging in one of the most solidly satisfying of all occupations—working in a garden.

An important point for you to bear in mind is that a youngster may be only casually interested in a family project—whereas if he is given a small plot of his own, the chances are that he will tend it with conscientious zeal. He enjoys having the power to decide what is to grow in that special piece of earth, he finds new delight in poring over seed packets and catalogues, and he is stimulated by the challenge of trying to bring his plans to a successful conclusion. He is not likely to ask for advice or help but he will probably welcome a little of each if it is offered tactfully.

ANNUALS, BIENNIALS, AND PERENNIALS

In planning his garden, a youngster will find annuals, biennials, and perennials from which to choose. Most plants that flower the same season they are sown are usually included with the annuals in flower books. However, the true annual is a plant that not only flowers the first season, but, if left to itself, dies in the fall.

Biennial plants may flower during their first season, but more often do so the next year. Unless they are given special treatment by the gardener during their first season, biennials die after their second season.

Perennials—with the exception of woody types—die down to the ground in the fall. But the roots continue to live, and new branches and flower stems are thrown up for years.

TREES, SHRUBS, AND HERBS

Another interesting point for the young gardener is that most flowering plants belong to one of three general forms: trees, which have large, erect stems; shrubs, with stems that are smaller and bushy; and herbs, with stems that are more or less soft, and with little woody tissue. We most commonly use the term "herb" to describe plants valuable for medicinal purposes or for their flavor or sweet scent. Nevertheless, the majority of flowers (domesticated as well as wild), grasses, and weeds are herbs.

Favorite Flowers

FLOWERS FOR A BEGINNER

If you are a beginner, there are several points you will want to bear in mind. It is important to have plants that will thrive with the amount of sun that reaches the plot you are using. It is fun to have at least a few showy flowers—such as hollyhocks or salvia—as well as flowers good for cutting. Phlox, dianthus (pinks), zinnias, and asters are a few of the many that provide generous floral decoration for your home. Plants should be arranged so that those which grow tall will be at the back of the garden; the lowest ones should be in front, or else grown to form a border.

Plan Your Color Scheme: Your child can begin to enjoy his garden well ahead of the planting season if he works out a "theme" for his plot. It may be an all-yellow color scheme (marigolds, California poppies, nasturtiums, calliopsis); or purple and white (petunias, asters, baby's breath, hollyhocks); or red (salvia), white (petunia), and blue (ageratum). These flowers are a few of the many annuals from which a child should choose to obtain an abundance of blooms.

Protect the Seeds: If seeds are put in the earth too early they may freeze or rot. It is therefore advisable to start some annuals—pansies, for example—indoors or in a protected seed bed, and then move the young plants to the garden when the weather is suitable. Many flower enthusiasts eliminate this step by purchasing plants from commercial growers. Pansy plants produced from seeds planted outdoors do not bloom until the end of summer.

PANSIES—PERFECT FOR CHILDREN

Youthful gardeners can ask for no more delightful flower than the pansy. Its coloring is beautiful and its markings often give it an appealing face. The dark spots at the bases of the side petals and the lines radiating from them suggest eyes and eyelashes, the opening of the nectar tube makes a nose, and the spot near the base of the lower petal will pass for a mouth.

Many varieties of pansies may be easily raised from seed sown in the spring or early summer, and seedlings may be set out in the garden in early spring. They do better in shady areas than in full sunshine.

Pansies Are Ideal for Picking: Children love to pick flowers. This makes the pansy an ideal plant for a child, as the flowers should be picked as soon as they open, or shortly afterward. If the pansy's seeds are allowed to ripen, the plant will bloom for only a short time, its life purpose having been accomplished. Persistent picking of the blooms, on the other hand, constantly produces new buds.

How Bees Help Fertilize the Pansy: The nectar sought by bees in the pansy is contained in the spur formed by the lower petal extending behind the flower. As the insect probes the nectar well with its tongue, pollen from a flower previously visited brushes off against the stigma. At the same time the bee receives a fresh coating of pollen dust. Shortly after a pansy has been fertilized, you can notice the ribbed seed pod becoming prominent. Finally this opens in three valves, and the seeds are scattered as the edges of each valve curl inward.

TULIPS—THE NATIONAL PASSION OF HOLLAND

This famous flower was introduced into Europe from the East in the sixteenth century, and about a hundred years later became the national passion of Holland. The Dutch growers speculated in outstandingly beautiful varieties of the tulip as some people speculate in stocks! Anyone who is familiar with these lovely flowers will understand the hold they took on Dutch tulip-fanciers.

Tulips Are Planted in the Fall: Tulips are excellent material for youngsters who enjoy gardening in every season of the year. They may be put in the earth during September or October. Each bulb is formed of several layers of leaves, all of which may open above ground if the planting is done properly—with the tip of the bulb pointed upward. The leaf layers are fleshy, for they contain the food that was stored up during the previous season. This food nourishes the flower bud in the heart of each bulb and the other growing parts. The roots, forming a thick white tassel below the bud, bring minerals and water up from the soil.

The Tulip's Spring Buds: In the spring, the anxious gardener first sees his tulip buds appear, protected by three sepals. As the bud stretches upward and becomes larger, the green of the sepals changes to the color of the petals. When the flower finally opens there is no very noticeable difference between petal and sepal. The sepals are below the petals and stand out around them, giving the flower a triangular shape. When the sun is not bright, the sepals partially close about the flower.

BACHELOR'S-BUTTONS—COMPOSITE FLOWERS

Most children love this hardy and beautiful plant, often called the cornflower. It may have special interest for them, too, if they realize it is one of the "composite" plants—a group in which different kinds of flowers are attached to one head. Those at the center of this compound flower head work for the production of seeds, while the flowers surrounding the center serve merely to attract insects.

The bachelor's-button usually has from seven to fourteen marginal flowers and they may be white, pink, blue, or purple. Each of the center flowers has a white corolla tube, enlarged toward the upper end to a purple bulb, and a purplish anther tube which is bent far over so that its tip opens toward the middle of the flower head.

On no other flower will you see a more obvious nectar well; that of the geranium extends almost the whole length of the flower stalk. The long narrow nectar tube explains why you often see butterflies on geraniums; this shape is especially suitable for the long-tongued insects.

Some of these plants are called "horseshoe" geraniums because of the horseshoe pattern on many of the leaves. Botanically they are not true geraniums, being the descendants of the pelargonium —a plant that was brought to England from South Africa more than two hundred years ago. These African plants were the ancestors of many of our popular garden geraniums. Other varieties have been bred; Luther Burbank, for example, created the now popular crinkled-leaf species from a single wild geranium plant that did not have the customary smooth-edged leaves.

Seeds Spread by Explosion: Some geraniums have depended for so long on man for planting that they have almost lost the power of producing seed. However, in the single blossoms you may sometimes discover the ovary changed into a long beaklike seed pod—a feature that reveals its relationship to the wild geranium. The seeds are dispersed by an explosive action of the pod.

How Geraniums Open: It is interesting to watch geranium flowers opening. Several buds are grouped together in a nest of specialized leaves known as "bracts." Besides having this protection, each bud is individually guarded by its own sepals. As the flower stalk grows longer and droops from the weight of the buds, the bracts often fall off. In each mass of drooping buds, the ones in the center open first. It sometimes happens that by the time those on the outside are in bloom the center flowers have begun to wither.

NASTURTIUMS AND THEIR REMARKABLE METHOD
OF POLLINATION

The most remarkable aspect of the nasturtium is its special method of pollination. The five beautiful petals are set around the mouth of the long tube leading to the nectar well. The two upper petals are erect, suggesting colorful display signs. They are marked with lines that point toward the opening of the nectar tubes. The lower petals stand out to form a landing platform for visiting insects.

Despite this, the flower is not actually designed for hospitality; it can accommodate only big insects such as sizable bees or butterflies for its pollination work, and it is able to thwart smaller, useless creatures that might creep into its treasure house of nectar. Each of the lower "landing" petals narrows to a fine strip at its inner end, making it in effect a footbridge to the nectar tube. These bridges are covered with projecting fringes and numerous little spikes that prove an effective barrier to any small creeping visitors.

Mechanized Pollination: When a nasturtium first opens, its several stamens are all bent downward. But when the pollen-containing anthers—located at the end of each slender stalk of a stamen —are ready to function, the stalk lifts up so that it is directly in the path of the nectar store. When a bee or butterfly, or occasionally a hummingbird, touches the stamens, it is sometimes bombarded with pollen. Equally remarkable is the action of the anther: No sooner has it discharged its pollen than it shrivels, making way for a new anther.

While all this is going on, the flower's three-lobed stigma lies quietly below and behind the anthers. (The stigma is located on the prolongation of the ovary known as the style.) But, once all the pollen has been shed, the stigma rises up and opens. Now the stigma operates like a three-pronged fork, and as more insects come in quest of nectar, it rakes pollen from them. Thus the ovary is fertilized and the seeds are ready to develop.

PETUNIAS AND THEIR INTERNATIONAL BACKGROUND

Profusely blooming petunias are so much a part of our American garden scene that it comes as a surprise to us to learn that they have an international background. They are the result of a cross between two species of plants from different parts of South America. The first of these, with long-tubed white flowers, was brought to Europe a little more than a hundred years ago.

Shortly afterward seeds of the second species, having small, broad-tubed, red-purple flowers, were sent to the Glasgow Botanical Gardens where the two species were brought together. Today we find petunias of many colors, but red-purple and white still predominate.

Pollen for Petunias: The petunia's wonderful arrangement for pollination is one of the marvels of nature. Near the bottom of the long tube lies the stigma, with two well-developed anthers in front of it and two more—not quite so advanced—behind it. The stalks that support the front anthers are longer than those of the second pair. There is still another anther—a fifth—on a stalk shorter than all the others. This is apparently a little pollen supply held in reserve by the flower.

For about half its length, each stamen is attached to the base of the flower's tube. The rest of the stamen curves abruptly inward. This makes it snuggle up to the pistil, the base of which is set in the nectar well at the bottom of the flower. When an insect pays a visit, its tongue reaches along the flower tube toward the nectar and it presses against the stamens at the point where they curve. This causes the anthers to move about, and as they move their pollen is shaken off on the insect!

In an older petunia the stigma, standing above the empty anthers, opens into two lobes and is ready to receive pollen from other flowers.

The Petunia and the Hummingbird Moth: The most notable insect partners of petunias are the sphinx or hummingbird moths, which can often be seen hovering over these flowers in the early evening. Petunias are members of the "nightshade" family, which also includes the tomato, the potato, and tobacco. Hummingbird moths are distinctly partial to all these plants.

POPPIES—THEY FASCINATE BEES

The poppy is distinctly a bee's flower. The insects apparently delight in wallowing in the pollen that lies along the ridges of the flower's pistil.

This pistil resembles a tiny vase with a circular cover. After a poppy has been fertilized, the circular cover develops a scalloped edge. Sharp ridges run from the center of each scallop down the length of the vaselike pistil. These ridges are the outer edges of partitions. Countless seeds develop inside these partitions and, when ripe, they fall into the hollow capsule which forms the center of the pistil.

The Poppy's Seed-Shaker: An observant child is charmed to see how poppy seeds make their way in the world. As each segment of the capsule loosens at the top and curls back from the circular cover, openings are formed. The upshot is that the "vase" has been made into a perfect seed-shaker. When the wind blows on it, or when it is brushed by any passing creature, the contents—the seeds—are sprinkled a little at a time in all directions.

There are a great many varieties of poppies, but only four species are commonly cultivated: the corn poppy and the opium (both of them annuals); the arctic and the oriental (both perennials).

The California poppy in its native setting blooms abundantly from February to April in the desert and the foothills. In gardens in the East you can see the shining orange flowers from midsummer until frost arrives.

Irises—Large and Showy

The large, showy iris, also called "blue flag," is another plant favored by bees. It has an interesting shape because of its unique style, which is divided into three branches so large and broad that they appear to be petals. These branches combined with the sepals form a tunnel through which bees pass. Between the sepals and the style are the true petals, marked with decorative purple lines.

How the Bee Maneuvers on the Iris: The bee uses the lip of a sepal for its landing platform, then pushes forward through the tunnel to the nectar well. As the insect moves, pollen that it has collected from another flower is rubbed off against the stigma, which hangs like a tent flap above the nectar well. The stigma is so fashioned that it gathers pollen from an incoming insect but turns a blank side to the departing visitor.

The small solitary bees are persistent callers; so are bumblebees and honeybees, though they seem to prefer different varieties of the iris.

ROSES—THE WORLD'S MOST POPULAR FLOWERS

It has been said that children see so many roses that they take them for granted. I doubt that this is really their attitude, as so many of them choose roses when asked to write about their favorite nature subject. Certainly the rose appears to be the world's most popular flower. It is grown wherever gardening is practiced, in all temperate climates and in some tropical regions as well. It is also believed to be the oldest of cultivated flowers.

Though no flower is more readily identified, many people are perplexed by the question, "What *is* a rose?" Looking for an answer, we may be inclined to find more sense than nonsense in Gertrude Stein's famous statement, "A rose is a rose is a rose"; for the rose has endless varieties and it is neither an ordinary seed plant nor a tree. There are single blooms, having only one row of showy petals, and double blooms with their rows of petals arranged in regular sequence or in loose informal patterns.

Five Thousand Varieties of Roses: The roses' bright colors cover a wide range from white, through delicate pink, yellow to rich tones of red. As to size, they vary from dime-small miniatures to exhibition blooms seven inches and more across. Believe it or not, in the United States alone there are more than five thousand varieties, each differing in some detail. The plant is a woody shrub which may stand erect or climb on supports. It has an extensive root system that sometimes goes as deep as twenty feet into the ground.

Roses and Strawberries Are Relatives: Aside from the innumerable kinds of roses produced in gardens, there is the simple but very beautiful wild rose with its broad blossoms that display five pink petals. On a wild rose or a full-blown garden rose you can easily see the great number of stamens, about twenty, as a rule, a characteristic feature of the whole family. Usually there are a great many pistils also.

Many of our common fruits belong to the rose family; the plants include the creeping strawberry as well as the sturdy blackberry bush and apple tree. Though these plants differ considerably in size and general appearance, their blossoms have a great similarity to the rose.

Chrysanthemums—Japanese Favorite

The chrysanthemum has a double flower head, numerous petals, and lovely coloring (generally red, yellow, and white). It gets wide publicity every fall as the star attraction of countless flower shows. But it is not only the spectacular prize-winning varieties that merit popularity. There are many kinds that will flourish without highly skilled care, bringing fresh beauty to our gardens in the fall when most flowers are dying.

Until fairly recently "mums" could be grown in northern climates only inside a greenhouse; but now we have hardy types that bloom out-of-doors through light frost. These perennials usually survive the winter, and each spring you can separate the new growths and replant them. Thus your chrysanthemum display can expand considerably from a very few plants.

Two Thousand Years of Chrysanthemums: Two thousand years ago, a chrysanthemum much like a colored daisy was a popular garden flower in Japan. (A figure of a sixteen-petaled chrysanthemum is used as the crest of the Japanese imperial family.) Early in the eighteenth century some of these flowers were brought to England, and China and India contributed other species. English gardeners and plant breeders went to work with them and in less than a hundred years produced new varieties bearing flowers three times as large as any of the originals.

Dahlias—They Grow Even on Ash Heaps

The dahlia, a reddish flower that originated in Mexico and Central America, is a popular show flower. Because of their size and beauty, you might suspect that dahlias are difficult to raise. The fact is, though, that dahlias are adaptable to almost any kind of soil, if it has been properly prepared.

Clayey soil may be lightened with coal ashes or sand, plus vegetable matter and manure. A light sandy loam will produce healthy plants and exquisite blooms; gravelly fields have been known to support fine dahlia beds; and a plant may even be found growing in an ash heap where a tuber (the underground stem) has been discarded.

How to Protect Dahlia Seeds: You can raise dahlias from stem cuttings as well as from tubers. For a real gardening adventure, your youngster may enjoy trying to develop new dahlias from seeds. The project begins at the height of the blooming season, when he must be on the lookout for any particularly large, rich-colored flower. This should be tagged "For Seed," so that it will not be picked.

The chosen flower must now remain in the garden until insects have carried pollen to it and it "goes to seed." When the flower shrivels and turns brown, you tie a small paper bag over it so that you can save the seeds if the seed pod bursts.

How to Plant Dahlia Seeds: Late fall is the time for you to gather the seeds, drying them and storing them in an airtight bottle. Early in May you plant them in a box with one part soil to two parts sand mixture. When seedlings appear about two weeks later, transplant them to a sunny spot in the garden.

Until the buds finally open, the young gardener will go through the suspense of wondering whether they will be double or single flowers and what their color will be. It all depends on what pollen was carried to his flowers during the previous season.

Indoor Gardening

If you live in an apartment and cannot have a garden outdoors, you and your child can share the rich pleasures of starting a garden indoors. Bulbs are especially suitable. (Bulbs are buds made up of a stem surrounded by leaves.) You can buy them inexpensively at many department stores, hardware stores, or florist shops.

Narcissus Bulbs Are Easy to Grow: The narcissus, a popular favorite with yellow or white varieties, need only be supported in a shallow dish with pebbles or bits of broken shell, and given just enough water to show through the pebbles.

Unaided, a youngster can easily prepare a dish for a narcissus bulb, and will be thrilled at having something his very own. To enhance his enjoyment, a narcissus grows rapidly and thus rewards daily watching. Care should be taken when watering that water does not leak in where old leaves have broken off, as this causes a bulb to rot.

When it is first planted, the bulb should be kept in a dark cool place until its roots have formed. Outdoors this would take from eight to twelve weeks, but indoors only a few weeks are required. The plant should then be brought into sunlight gradually, being kept away from drafts. Two or three weeks will elapse before a flower appears.

Hyacinth, Tulip, and Crocus Bulbs: Such bulbs as hyacinths and tulips do better in soil. As bulbs have a built-in food supply, the soil need not be rich. Sandy garden soil well mixed with peat moss is excellent. A hyacinth bulb should be placed so that its top projects over the top of the pot; a tulip bulb should have its top level with the top of the soil. As for crocus and other small bulbs, they should be covered with an inch of soil.

If you keep the bulbs in a cool dark place for several weeks, the roots will be well developed before the leaf stalks begin to grow. When the roots press against the sides of the pot or show at the bottom opening, you know that the plants are ready for a sunny window.

OTHER EASY INDOOR GARDENING TECHNIQUES

You need not limit your indoor gardening to bulbs. You have the choice of plants growing directly from roots, such as the sweet potato; from stem cuttings—begonia, geranium, or cactus, among others; and from certain fleshy leaves, such as those of the African violet. Also, many seeds thrive when they are planted indoors.

A wooden cigar box will do to give stem cuttings or leaves their start. Bore holes in the bottom and spread pebbles or chips from broken flowerpots. Then fill the box with clean sand to within half an inch of the top. Moisten the sand and press it down firmly. Make a hole in this soil for each stem cutting you wish to plant. (A pencil is a very good tool for this purpose.)

Now place a freshly cut stem in each hole, making sure that in every case you have buried at least two "nodes" — juncture points for leaves that have been removed. Keep the little garden moist, in a cool place, and before long, roots should form at each node.

How to Propagate Plants

AFRICAN VIOLETS

You can work out an excellent arrangement for propagating African violets from leaves by using two flowerpots—one an eight-inch size and shallow, the other a three-inch pot. Cover the hole of the larger pot with a piece of crockery and partly fill the pot with sand. Close the hole of the smaller pot with a cork, and place this pot inside the larger one, filling the space between the two pots with more sand. If you keep the small flowerpot filled with water, the sand will be moist at all times. Set the base of the violet leaves in the moistened sand.

BEGONIAS AND SNAKE PLANTS

Begonia leaves may simply be pegged down with toothpicks on moist sand and slit across the main veins. Small plants will develop at the wounds. The ever-popular snake plant, or Sansevieria, may be propagated by cutting leaves into sections an inch or more in length and pegging them into moist earth. The leaves of this white or yellowish plant take root easily but grow slowly.

Any plant you are raising from leaves or stems should be covered by a glass jar or globe until it has become well rooted. The covering keeps the air immediately surrounding the plants moist; an excessively dry atmosphere would soon kill them.

GROWING FLOWERS INDOORS

If flowers interest you more, you will find that marigolds, petunias, and other plants will flourish in your window boxes. Smaller seeds should be planted about a quarter of an inch deep, and larger ones slightly deeper; allow at least an inch between seeds. When your seedlings are large enough to handle, transplant them to window boxes or flowerpots. An excellent mixture in which to plant them at this time combines two parts garden soil, one part sand, and one part leaf mold.

Vegetables—for Decoration and Food

SWEET POTATOES

Of all the plants that can be raised from roots, the sweet potato is probably the most satisfying. It needs nothing but water. A sweet potato should be placed in a glass or bowl so that about one-third of it is in water. If necessary, you can push three toothpicks into the plant to support it on the rim of the bowl or glass. Although this will not yield a vegetable harvest, the leaves produced are extremely decorative.

WORKING WITH SEEDS

If you wish to work with seeds, you will need a shallow tray with holes in the bottom (for drainage) to start your gardening. Place small stones or pieces of broken flowerpots over the holes; then sift soil into the box and press down firmly until the soil is within an inch of the top. If you want to try a miniature vegetable garden, you can plant such seeds as peas, beans, and radishes.

GROWING DANDELION GREENS

A child who shows real enthusiasm for gardening may derive great pleasure from growing a few indoor "crops" during the winter which may be used on family menus. However, a warm cellar is usually essential for such activity. There are several plants that will flourish in a box of earth set beside a furnace. Dandelion greens, which are a tasty substitute for lettuce, are among the easiest to obtain and raise.

Dig up the plants, including roots, before the ground freezes, and cut off a good two inches of the leafy top. Then set the roots in a box of good garden soil, and keep them in a constantly warm location—if possible, near a furnace. They require some watering but need no light.

Growing Rhubarb

Rhubarb will thrive under cooler conditions. A temperature of about 50 degrees is best; but the atmosphere should be moist and the plants should not be in a draft. To provide an occasional winter pie or breakfast fruit, dig up clumps of rhubarb root in November; you can allow them to freeze under natural conditions or in a freezer. Then store them in a cool place and plant portions from time to time in a box of earth or sand. Tender young shoots will grow from the nourishment stored up in the roots.

Young Dirt Farmers

There is something about working with earth that is deeply satisfying to boys and girls—and out-of-door vegetable gardening provides a splendid combination of physical exercise plus the challenge of producing food from the soil.

When space is limited, we sometimes feel it is best to "bother" only with flowers. However, a small corner devoted to vegetables can give youngsters a wonderful sense of accomplishment. I know of two ten-year-old boys who raised radishes, lettuce, corn, string beans, tomatoes, beets, and carrots in one plot just six by ten feet. They were able to make substantial contributions to the table, and the only help their parents gave was in the spading.

Radishes—A Fast Crop

Radishes are a special boon to young gardeners—particularly those with limited planting space. Some radish seeds may be mixed in with seeds of other vegetables, perhaps beets and carrots, for they pop up above ground in a few days. Thus the planted rows are almost immediately marked, and weeds cropping up between them can be dealt with promptly. Another good point about radishes is that they mature in a month or so and can then be pulled out and eaten—while the slower-growing vegetables continue to develop and occupy space vacated by the radishes.

CORN—A SOMEWHAT PUZZLING PLANT

Even children who do not aspire to raise their own vegetables are likely to be interested in growing corn. Corn is a universal food favorite. Not only that—it is something of a symbol of our American heritage—of lessons learned from the Indians and the bountiful harvest that inspired our traditional Thanksgiving.

Corn is in a class by itself and something of a puzzle. What is the silk tassel comparable to on other plants? Are those green husks that encase each ear regular leaves? How do the green husks differ from the long narrow leaves that hang loosely from the stalk? Is each kernel of corn a seed, or is the whole cob a seed? And why do we sometimes find tiny, undeveloped kernels among others that are fully ripe?

Early Development of the Corn Plant: If a child could observe the progress of a corn plant, he would see that when it first appears above the ground, its leaves are wrapped in a colorless sheath in a pointed roll. These leaves soon spread apart. Growth is slow; but presently the main stalk becomes visible—and once above the ground, it stretches up rapidly.

The main stalk develops more leaves and also ears which are located at the leaf joints, or nodes, where the stalk is hollowed out in order to hold the ear more snugly. The ear is actually on a branch stalk, and the leaves of this stalk are those that are wrapped around the portion we call the "cob." It is on the cob that the seeds, or kernels, will develop.

Flowers—the kind bearing pistils—now appear in pairs along the sides of the cob, and the corn "silk" develops. Each strand of silk is really a pistil, with the stigma at the upper end of a very long style (the prolongation of the ovary). In order to secure pollen, this silk, or pistil, must extend from each flower to the tip of the cob, and beyond the leaf wrapping.

How the Corn Plant Is Fertilized: Meanwhile brown tassels have appeared at the top of the main stalk. These are the plant's flowers which bear stamens and produce pollen. The tassel is made up of many florets, each having two anthers hanging from it; half of each anther is a little bag of pollen grains. When the pollen is ripe, this bag opens and the grains fall on the silk below. The ends of the silk are now branched and covered with fine hairs, to catch the pollen.

After "landing," a pollen grain goes on a remarkable journey—through the entire length of the corn silk until it reaches the ovule. Now that the ovule is fertilized, it will develop into a kernel or seed. If a strand of silk from one of the flowers does not receive a pollen grain, no kernel will develop. An ear with some of these undeveloped kernels is called "imperfect." If pollen from another variety of corn reaches the stigmas of the silk, the ear shows a mixture of the two kinds of kernels.

Self-Preservation in the Corn Plant: Corn stalks are so tall and slender that heavy winds can damage them seriously. Yet the structure of the plant provides some defense against wind. The cylinder-like stalk with its pithy center is sturdier towards the base, as the hard nodes, or joints, occur closer together there. Towards the top the nodes are farther apart, allowing the stalk to bend with the wind and recover.

The leaf structure also affords protection against the wind. The true roots go deep into the soil, but even so they are inadequate for holding a tall heavy plant upright in a windstorm. However, aside from these roots the corn has other roots about the base of the plant—they suggest a tentlike frame—which hold the stalk erect.

PUMPKINS—SOURCE OF DELICIOUS PIES

Every year harvest pictures remind us that corn and pumpkin are constant garden companions. A child may guess that these two vegetables are planted together because one grows high while the other barely rises above the ground. The real reason, however, is found in the nature of the respective roots: The pumpkin is a shallow-rooted plant, whereas the true roots of corn go deep into the earth. The consequence is that the two plants do not fight each other for minerals and water.

The Classic Beauty of the Pumpkin: The fruit of the pumpkin plant, being the source of jack-o'-lanterns and delicious pies, rather overshadows its flower and foliage. The rugged, broad-based leaves, with their three to five lobes, form a decorative design of classic beauty. The delicately curved tendril on the pumpkin vine is worth observing. Possibly the tendrils are a holdover from a remote past when pumpkin vines lifted themselves off the ground, as certain gourd vines do today. Occasionally you may notice a pumpkin vine reaching out as it climbs on the edge of a field, over mounds of earth or fences as if it were actually a climbing plant.

Pumpkin Seeds: At first a young pumpkin is held up by a stiff stem, but as it grows heavier it rests on the ground. If you cut across a green pumpkin, you will notice that instead of a cavity inside, there are a number of partitions within which seeds are borne. (A cucumber has much the same arrangement.) As the pumpkin ripens, the partitions around the seeds become stringy— a very different texture from the "meat" that forms a thick solid layer between the skin and the inner chamber.

The pumpkin is a plant that requires no aid from man aside from planting. Another favorable trait is that it helps to check obnoxious weeds.

Weeds Are the Farmer's Enemy

The child who has a chance to work in a garden develops a new respect for nature—the greatest farmer of them all. As he comes to realize what labor and skill go into producing plants, he looks appreciatively at natural "crops" that no man has aided. He concludes that although these plants which cover the countryside may be attractive and have certain uses, they are nothing but weeds if they spring up where they are not wanted.

WEEDS—PESTS THAT MAY BE BEAUTIFUL

Children are sometimes perplexed about weeds. We usually speak of them with disdain or annoyance, yet the flowers that some produce are as lovely as those we carefully tend in a garden. It is not the looks of the weeds that disturb us; their ability to produce fantastic numbers of seeds makes them a nuisance in little gardens, and a serious problem to farmers.

Members of the composite family, which includes daisies and goldenrod, are among the chief offenders; bindweed (a morning-glory), devil's paintbrush, and others swell the ranks. Because of their attractive flowers, many types of weeds were intentionally brought to America from Europe, where they had been kept in check by the nature of their surroundings—farms, forests, and cities. In the great open spaces of America they ran wild, and today they are more of a pest than a pleasure.

Wildflowers to Look for in Springtime

People in the tropics are fortunate in having flowering plants throughout the year, but few northerners would exchange the joy of hunting the first spring flowers for all the luxury of endless blossoms.

As you search for the elusive hepatica, trillium, and other flowers that appear soon after the last snows have melted, you may wonder how it is that these flowers are on hand in so short a time after the end of cold weather. After all, daisies, irises, and many others will not bloom until summer, and still others—such as asters and chrysanthemums—wait almost until fall.

Is it only the warm weather that brings forth flowers? If so, why do plants have such varying timetables? Here is the answer: Tests have shown that plants react differently to the amount of daylight they receive. Some are stimulated to bloom by short days and long nights.

At first it sounds contradictory to say that hepaticas and other early spring flowers are "short-day" blossoms—they make their appearance as days are growing longer! However, they have actually been formed *the previous year*. Formation takes place underground; when the temperature becomes favorable, these flowers rise up into the light and air.

On a quest for early spring flowers, you are likely to observe that many of them are white. Later in the season you will find more color. There is a definite reason for this. Flowers formed underground are white to start with because no pigment has been developed. When they are exposed to light, many of these flowers take on various hues, among them blue, red, or yellow.

HEPATICAS CLOSE FOR THE NIGHT

One of the earliest flowers of spring, the hepatica must be hunted among the decaying foliage of the previous fall. As its blossoms grow they rise about three inches above the brownish leaves of the year before, and the new leaves may appear very soon after. The petal-like sepals are white, pink, or bluish-lavender. Young blossoms close during the night and on dark days; older ones remain open all the time.

You are most likely to find the wood anemone, a member of the same family as the hepatica, along the borders of woodlands. The anemone is an inch or more taller than the hepatica; its flowers are white or delicate purple.

ADDER'S TONGUES ARE LILIES

Yellow adder's tongue favors moist woods and brook sides, though it sometimes grows in open fields in the East. White adder's tongue is common in the West and South. The small bell-shaped flowers appear in early spring, but the leaves, pale green mottled with brownish purple, are found carpeting large irregular areas long after the blossoms have gone. The yellow adder's tongue, though a member of the lily family, is often called "dog-tooth violet."

VIOLETS—NOT ALWAYS SHY

In the true violet family there is a "dog" violet found especially in the sandy soils of the Northwest. This is a low, creeping species with light purple flowers. Fairly widespread also is the downy yellow violet which blooms almost anywhere in low ground. It is tall in comparison to most violets—sometimes as high as seventeen inches.

As for the common violet, you may find it almost anywhere in low ground. As a rule, the deep green heart-shaped leaves usually grow a little taller than the flowers. In marshes, however, the flower stalks are longer than the leaf stalks and the flowers are exceptionally large. The flowers of the common violet range from rich purple to light violet. There is also a rare variety which is white with purple veins.

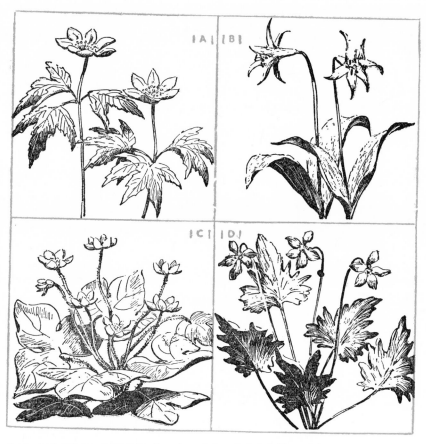

[A] THE WOOD ANEMONE.—Sometimes it is called "windflower" because of the way it sways in spring breezes.

[B] THE YELLOW ADDER'S TONGUE.—It is known by several names; "trout lily" properly identifies it, for it is a member of the lily family.

[C] THE HEPATICA —Each flower is covered with a soft, hairy coat.

[D] THE COMMON BLUE VIOLET —Besides the lovely spring flowers, in summer it bears small greenish flowers beneath its leaves.

TRILLIUM FOR THREEFOLD

The season for trillium begins in April with the poetically named wake-robin, a species that produces purple, red, and sometimes purplish flowers. There are other species, but it will be June before you find the white large-flowering trillium. It is this handsome kind that flower-fanciers often cultivate.

The trilliums grow mostly in damp, rich wood soils. You can help children in identifying these flowers if you explain the meaning of "trillium," which comes from the word *triplum,* meaning "threefold." These flowers always have three petals and the plants have three leaves and three sepals.

JACK-IN-THE-PULPIT—MINIATURE PREACHER

No plant is easier to remember and recognize than jack-in-the-pulpit, for to an imaginative child the club-shaped flower head does represent a miniature preacher, while the spathe (a bract or modified leaf) forms his pulpit.

Moist woods are the best place for locating this plant. When it first pushes through the earth it looks like a pointed peg. Inside the pointed and mottled sheath are the leaves, rolled lengthwise and forming the point. The club-shaped spathe is at the center.

As the leaves grow and open, flowers develop at the base of the spathe. There are two different kinds; greenish, round pistillate flowers, packed like berries on the stalk; and tiny, almost white flowers, which bear the pollen. The two kinds grow on separate plants. You may sometimes find both types on the same plant, with the pollen-bearing kind set above the others. In such a case only the pollen-bearers function.

By the time summer comes around, the "pulpit" falls away from Jack, revealing shining green berries formed from the pistillate flowers. In August, when the leaves may have also disappeared, you will find that the berries have turned a brilliant scarlet.

[A] JACK-IN-THE-PULPIT —Its flowers are well hidden in the depths of the "pulpit." This plant is related to the skunk cabbage.

[B] THE WHITE TRILLIUM —Though this charming member of the lily family belongs to woodlands, it is also a successful garden flower.

[C] THE DANDELION —At the left of the drawing is a flower head at its height of blooming. At the right is a flower head gone to seed.

CACTUS—NOT JUST A DESERT PLANT

We usually associate cactus plants with the desert. Some cacti, though, thrive in such contrasting localities as the high South American Andes and the Pine Barrens of New Jersey.

Many varieties of this hardy, spiny plant have been adapted for indoor gardens, so you don't have to be anywhere near a desert to enjoy the flowers of a cactus. (This ought to interest television-minded children, accustomed to viewing hard-riding cowboys among desert scenes!) Cacti may bloom in your home any time during the year—not just in the spring as the desert plants do.

It is in the springtime that we see desert plants at their best. Outstanding are the pink, yellow, and rose blooms of the prickly pear, the white flowers of the giant sahuaro, and the yellow blossoms that form a ring about each round column of the barrel cactus.

Storehouses of Water: Most children are fascinated by the curious forms that cacti take. They can see some of these plants in the hothouses of botanical gardens, and they are very likely to wonder about their lack of leaves. Actually the cacti do very well without leaves.

"Leaf-green" in their thick fleshy stems takes care of manufacturing their food, and the absence of leaves prevents the water inside the plants from evaporating. They store water in the stems to such an extent that they can survive periods of drought for an amazingly long time. Many people lost in the desert owe their lives to these natural water tanks.

Plant Survival in the Desert: In humid regions plant species are largely assured of survival by their great numbers. In deserts, where plants are comparatively sparse, they have evolved a number of defenses to keep humans and animals from preying on them. Notable are the spines, thorns, and toughness of the cactus. Other plants depend on bitterness or unpleasant odors, a few on poison.

Aside from cacti, the desert offers many other colorful floral displays. Visitors from near and far are attracted every year to desert areas—the vicinity of Bakersfield in California, for example —to see lilies, poppies, violets, primroses, and verbenas blooming in a riotous profusion of brilliant colors.

The Charm of Summer Blossoms

DANDELIONS—PERSISTENT WEEDS

This golden-headed flower, one of the most persistent of all weeds, is occasionally a source of income to youngsters, who earn money by helping rid lawns of dandelions. In early summer dandelions can provide a lot of fun for children. The youngsters can whistle through the hollow stems, or make dandelion curls of them; they may even pretend to tell time by the number of puffs required to blow away all the seeds on a ripened stem.

The Adaptable Dandelion: Children have done such things to dandelions for ages, man has tried his best to exterminate them, animals have grazed on them, other plants have attempted to crowd them out—all in vain. The dandelion has had extraordinary success in surviving. One of the many reasons for its survival is its adaptability to circumstances. For example: In a meadow of tall grasses the plant sometimes reaches a height of two feet—and more; but on a lawn the flower stem may be less than two inches tall, saving the flower head from the blades of the lawn mower!

The Dandelion is a Composite Flower: The dandelion belongs to the great family group that we call "composites"—a word that comes from the Latin and means "made up of parts." Aside from the dandelions, the composites include asters, thistles, and a great many other kinds of flowers. All have compound flower heads (the term "head" is commonly used for a cluster of flowers) .

Petals and Buds in the Composites: Some of the composites have a disk in the middle of the flower head. This disk is made up of tiny tubular florets, and around it are brightly colored ray flowers, or petals.

The dandelion belongs to another type of composite which has a petal-like part on each flower. In a just-opened dandelion you can see the buds at the middle all curving slightly toward the center. They are also shorter and a darker yellow than the outer florets, for they are younger. The flower head is well protected by long bracts; shorter bracts near the stem curl back, forming a frill.

How the Dandelion Opens and Closes: Dandelions close on dark days and at night. It is often eight o'clock before they begin to wake up, and it may take a full hour for the golden head to be

completely opened. When all the florets on a head have blos-
somed, the dandelion closes for good until its seeds are formed.
Each seed is equipped with a fluffy, parachute-like head. When
this head is dry it can "parachute" the seed to new growing
ground.

How the Dandelion Got Its Name: You need a good imagination
to see that the notched edges of dandelion leaves resemble lions'
teeth; but that is what they looked like to someone in France who
named the plant *dent-de-lion,* whence we get our name for it.

From "Day's Eye" to Daisy

This flower, which has much in common with the dandelion, is a great favorite with children. Like the dandelion, it is
an amazingly persistent weed; and it is also a composite. At its
center we find numerous short, yellow, tubular disk flowers.

These are surrounded by twenty or more ray flowers—"petals"
to children, who love to pull them off one by one with "he loves
me, he loves me not." If you look closely at these ray flowers you
will see that each has a pistil which shows a two-part stigma at
its base. The flowers ripen many seeds but they lack the traveling
equipment of the dandelion.

In the yellow daisy, commonly called "black-eyed Susan," the
purple-brown disk flowers form a conical, button-like center for
the orange ray flowers. Still more color is added to the flower
when brilliant orange pollen appears.

Like the dandelion, the daisy opens in the morning. It owes its
name to this trait—people in Old England called it "day's eye,"
which finally became our "daisy."

Buttercups—Sometimes Three Feet High

Growing as they do in the same fields, buttercups and
daisies are commonly associated in children's minds. There is an
essential difference, however; whereas the daisy is a composite,
the buttercup is a single flower. The five (and sometimes more)
wedge-shaped petals are slightly curved, giving the flower its cup-
like form.

"Do You Like Butter?": The bright yellow color of the buttercup gives it a shiny finish which in bright sunlight quite easily reflects on another surface. That is why the answer is nearly always positive when a child follows the old custom of holding a buttercup under a playmate's chin to see if he "likes butter." (If yellow is reflected on the chin, the answer is "yes.") Outside the reflecting petals are five sepals, about half the length of the petals and pale yellow with brownish tips.

There are many different kinds of buttercups; the common one of fields and meadows is properly called the tall buttercup. It may grow as tall as three feet! Though you are likely to find buttercups as early as May, they bloom through August and sometimes until frost appears.

Lucky Clover

Among our most popular superstitions is the one that promises good luck to the finder of a four-leaf clover. It is a fact, however, that the clover plant is good fortune for all of us.

25,000 to the Inch: In addition to being a valuable food crop for horses and cattle, clover has an almost magical way of bringing fertility to the soil. The secret of this power lies in the little swellings—sometimes called root tubercles or nodules—that you will find on the rootlets. Each swelling is occupied by bacteria, so many that 25,000 of them, lined up, would cover only an inch of space.

These bacteria extract nitrogen, a valuable chemical fertilizer, from the soil and change its form so that clover can absorb it. When a crop of clover is harvested, the roots remain in the ground with their precious supply of fertilizer. This is one reason why farmers, in rotating their crops, plant clover every few years.

Collecting Clovers is Fun: It is fun for a child to make a collection of clovers, for there are many attractive species, including crimson, red, white, rabbit-foot, buffalo, and yellow. Both leaves and blossoms can be kept for several years when pressed between pieces of wax paper or cellophane. It is even possible to become an expert at finding the rare four-leaf clover to add to one's collec-

[A] **THE WHITE DAISY**—One of the best-known wild flowers of America, this plant originally was an immigrant, coming from Europe with early colonists.

[B]   **THE BUTTERCUP**—It is sometimes called "crow's-foot" because the shape of its leaf suggests a bird's claws.

[C]   **RED CLOVER**—It has an unusually long period of blooming. Flowers may be found from April until November.

[D]   **COMMON MILKWEED**—Its small, purplish-brown clustered flowers, rich in nectar, are especially attractive to insects.

tion. These leaves turn up here and there in the midst of stalks with three leaflets.

The three-leaved grouping is the customary one and has given the plant its scientific name, *trifolium* ("three-leaved"). To find the out-of-the-ordinary stalk with four leaflets, you need to practice looking for a *square* pattern in a carpet of *triangles*. Stand erect and scan the clover design; where one four-leaf specimen is found there are apt to be more.

Milkweed and its Strange Secretion

This plant has two products that fascinate children: its milky juice of rubber-like composition and its skeins of shining silk. To see the "milk," all they need do is break the stem of the plant or cut across a leaf.

The "milk" is a special secretion—not the sap of the plant. If you cut across the stem and then blot the end so that you can see the details clearly, you will find that the liquid oozes from a dark green ring around the hollow stem. On a plant that is only partially broken or gashed, the "milk" soon heals the wound.

Murder by Milkweed: The extremely complex flowers growing at the junction of the milkweed's leaf stem and plant stem are fertilized mostly by bees. Every once in a while one of these insects loses its life on the flowers! It is actually trapped by the anther, and this is how: Instead of being free, the pollen is held in paired sacs that are joined in a V-shape. The bee, busy collecting nectar, may stand in the V, and the little sacs of pollen-producing anthers may close on its legs. If the grip is too tight, the insect cannot free itself.

Milkweed for Life Jackets and Aviators: Once the milkweed flower has been fertilized, the seed pod begins to grow. The fully developed pod bursts apart at the seam, and you can see the brown, overlapping seeds inside with exquisite silk attached to one end of each seed. When the silk is dry, each fluffy mass of threads parachutes off in the breeze carrying a seed with it—in some cases for a very long distance.

Milkweed floss has been used commercially to stuff life jackets—it is more buoyant than cork—and to line aviators' uniforms, as it is six times lighter than wool, and just as warm.

This plant is very beautiful, as its name suggests, but it is also a very troublesome weed. You are likely to find it in waste places and fields almost anywhere. It is also called the wild carrot, and it is really closely related to the garden carrot. On a fully grown plant, the yellowish root is six inches long or more; but it isn't good to eat.

The Flower Cluster: Each large flat flower cluster, with its radiating pattern as fine as lace, is made up of many small flower clusters, each in turn with a stalk of proper length to fit into just the right place in the medallion pattern. These small flower clusters each have twenty or thirty tiny white blossoms in a rosette design.

If you look down at one of the large flower clusters, you will notice that the outside blossoms have small bracts—the special leaves which, in this case, resemble the petals. These are larger than the petals and create a pleasing border effect for the complete cluster. Often you will find a single wine-colored floret in the center on its own stalk.

When Queen Anne's lace begins to wither, each of the small clusters curves inward until the whole unit suggest a tiny bird's nest. Thousands of seeds develop on each plant, and many live to germinate.

From early summer to late fall you can see these bright yellow flowers on dry, sandy roadsides, along moist riverbanks and seashores, at the edges of woods, in sunny meadows, in mountainous regions, and on flat barren plains. In all these localities there are many kinds of goldenrod—more than fifty all told.

The goldenrod is another interesting example of a composite flower. Each flower head is very small, but the plant makes a bright showing because the florets are set close together. On each delicate branch there is a procession of ray flowers with short but brilliant banners, and a few tubular disk flowers that open out like bells. Look at the disk flowers closely and you will see in them the pollen tubes or yellow two-part stigmas.

Insects of many shapes and sizes carry the goldenrod's pollen far and wide for it.

Asters—Attractive to Bees

Like goldenrod, asters are to be found in all sorts of places, and there are numerous species. They too are composites, but the flower heads are different in form from the goldenrod. At the center of their circular flower heads there are yellow disk flowers that turn a dull purplish color as they age.

These disk flowers yield an abundance of nectar, and you frequently see bees, small butterflies, and beelike flies visiting them. One of the most beautiful and best known is the New England aster; it is widespread throughout the eastern United States and is frequently cultivated. Its numerous flowers, blooming from August to October, vary in hue from pale violet to deep purple.

Some Sunflowers are Twelve Feet High

Because of its size, this giant plant serves best of all to show us the make-up of a composite flower. One wild species— the "tall sunflower"—is common to swamps and the borders of wet meadows. It grows as high as twelve feet and has a flower head about two inches across. On the common garden sunflower the flower head may have a width of ten inches.

First to unfold are the wide, flaring ray flowers that are largely responsible for the sunflower's spectacular appearance. There may be two or three rows of these. When they are a few days old, you can see inside them a circle of florets from which ripened pollen and stigmas have already disappeared. Below the florets fertilized seeds are now developing.

Inside this circle is another composed of florets where coiled-back stigma lobes protrude from the anther tubes. Next, moving toward the center of the flower head, you may see several rows of florets in which pollen is just being pushed out; and within this ring may be florets with the anther tubes still closed. At the center

[A]   QUEEN ANNE'S LACE—These flowers, grouped in lacy, geometric designs, seem especially suited for decorations in "modern" settings.

[B]   GOLDENROD—The different kinds of goldenrod vary somewhat in form, but all are easily recognized by their masses of small golden flowers.

[C]   WILD ASTERS—This beautiful fall flower is sometimes called "Michaelmas daisy" because it blooms near Michaelmas Day.

[D]   SWAMP SUNFLOWER—Because its leaves were once used for making snuff, this plant is known also as "sneezeweed."

are buds with the inmost few still covered with the green spear points of their bracts, or specialized leaves.

Sunflower Myths: Children who have not had a chance to observe sunflowers may be interested to know if it is true that these blossoms twist on their stems in order to face the sun all day. This widely circulated story is charming but not particularly accurate. Some of these giant flowers have been observed turning with the sun to a certain extent when they first unfold—but not after they grow heavy with seeds.

Another published observation is that many turn for their last few weeks of bloom to the east and remain that way. Watching those that grow in my neighbor's garden—they are planted, by the way, to raise seeds for her winter bird-feeding station—I have not seen any evidence of the flower heads following the sun. The direction they usually face is south.

Wildflower Bouquets and Gardens

Part of the joy of flowers comes from picking them and arranging them in enchanting bouquets. Unfortunately, we are limited for the most part to garden plants. Many wild species have become so rare that they are protected by law; others, such as wild roses and asters, though plentiful, wilt quickly after they are plucked.

WHAT FLOWERS TO CHOOSE

Despite these limitations, we still have some excellent material for wildflower bouquets. The common blue violet is one of the very few spring flowers not on the "protected" list of most states, and in summer, buttercups, daisies, black-eyed Susans, goldenrod, and Queen Anne's lace lend themselves to charming floral decorations.

When you have a chance to pick wildflowers, it is best to cut them with scissors or regular garden clippers. Later, the stems should be cut on a slant with a sharp knife. Then, if they are left in a pail of water for a few hours or overnight, they may regain much of their freshness.

GROWING A WILDFLOWER GARDEN

Few hobbies are more delightful than a wildflower garden. With very little trouble you can transplant daisies, black-eyed Susans, and certain other hardy species, making them thrive close to your home. You can usually move even the rarer plants, such as red trillium, violet, and wild geranium, if you take along a generous amount of earth. As a matter of fact, many commercial growers specialize in quite rare plants; you can obtain the wild-flowers in this way when it is not feasible to take them from their native growing places.

How to Press and Mount Plants

Pressing wildflowers is still another way in which children can get pleasure from them. They can also have a world of fun arranging the flowers in attractive groupings and framing them as wall pictures. You will again want to stress to youngsters, before they do any picking, that only plants that are plentiful should be taken. It is well for children to make a habit of asking their parents about protected wildflowers before doing any picking. The parents can then check conservation laws with local authorities.

Techniques for Pressing Flowers: When you collect plants for pressing, keep them damp until you are ready to place them under pressure. You can manage this by taking a few damp newspapers on a collecting trip and carrying the plants between the pages. For ease of handling, you can roll up the papers—not too tightly, however, or the leaves may crack.

When you are ready for pressing, place a piece of newspaper about twelve by eighteen inches on the floor, and lay plants or flowers on top of it. As you may want to frame them later on, take care to arrange petals, and leaves in natural positions. A violet, for example, usually looks more natural if pressed in profile. A few buds with the full-bloom flower and some leaves make a complete story and an interesting composition. Make sure that no plants overlap during the pressing.

How to Dry Out Plant Moisture: Now that you have laid out the plants on newspaper, cover this arrangement with a layer of newspaper equal in thickness to the thickest part of the plant or plants below. Add layers of plants and paper until your entire collection is taken care of. Over this pile, place a board or other flat object equal in size to the newspaper, and on top of this put weights such as books, rocks, or other heavy things. If the weight is not heavy enough, the plants will wrinkle.

Change the paper or move the plants to a dry location every day for at least four days—then less often, for about ten days. The more rapidly the plant loses its moisture, the better its delicate colors will be preserved.

How to Mount Plants: To mount a plant you need a piece of glass as large as the specimen you are preparing. Cover the glass with a thin coating of glue diluted a bit with a drop or two of vinegar. Place the dried plant on the glue (to get the glue on one side), then quickly transfer the plant to a piece of mounting paper. Now you are ready for framing. If a plant is too delicate for this treatment—it may curl when it is picked up from the glue—you can mount it by placing thin strips of gummed paper at intervals across the stem.

Some Plants Have No Green Parts

Knowing as we do how vital "leaf-green" is to the growth of plants, the mushroom and other fungi that develop without a trace of green seem rather mysterious to us. No wonder that generations ago, when not too much was known about plant life, people stood in superstitious awe of the magic "toadstools," which seemed to spring out of nowhere and were sometimes good food and sometimes poisonous. When you are on a woodlands hike with your youngster, especially in late summer or early fall, you can get a lot more out of your trip if you watch for members of this fungus family growing wild.

What Fungi Feed On

Lacking leaf-green, mushrooms are unable to manufacture starch, sugar, and other elements, and must absorb them from dead wood, withered leaves, or soils enriched by remains of plants. They are the kind of fungi we know as "saprophytes" (living on dead or decaying matter), and they are valuable plants because they prevent forests from becoming choked with dead wood. As mushrooms and other fungi absorb tissue from stumps and old logs, the wood softens and falls apart.

Fungi That Prey on Living Things

The other kinds of fungi, the "parasites," take their food from the cells of living things. These fungi are often dangerous enemies to the plants and animals on which they grow. It is a parasitic fungus that causes "potato blight"; another is responsible for the costly disease known as "wheat rust." The simplest forms of parasitic fungi that take their nourishment from animals are the bacteria that cause diphtheria, typhoid fever and other serious diseases.

Mushroom Spores Instead of Seeds

As mushrooms have no flowers, a child may wonder what they do about seeds. Flowerless plants have their own special kind of "seed." Microscopic in size, it is called a "spore." After landing in a favorable growing place, the spore of a mushroom develops rapidly into a threadlike form. From this a whole mass of threads grow out for weeks or even months, until there is enough tissue to produce a fruiting body—then, with startling suddenness, the mushroom appears!

Precautions Against Poisonous Mushrooms

Mushrooms are usually abundant in damp, wooded spots, as they do not need sunshine. If we happen to be in one of these localities, we may be tempted to find some mushrooms suitable for eating. *It is a temptation best denied.* Unfortunately some people rely on tests that are supposed to indicate when a species is poisonous—they believe such mushrooms turn a silver spoon black or change color when bruised. None of these tests are of the slightest value. A number of characteristics do help to distinguish the poisonous from the nonpoisonous species, but only an expert should attempt to draw the distinction for eating purposes.

Mosses Favor Moist Places

There is a shrub known as the "flowering moss," but you can be sure it is not really moss—no moss bears flowers. The so-called flowering moss merely suggests moss in a superficial way because of its appearance.

Mosses, like mushrooms, produce spores. The moss spore grows a branched green thread on which leafy buds soon appear. They develop further into leafy stems which in turn produce rootlike projections—not true roots. Some of the plants bear eggs at their leaf tips while others produce sperms. Wind, or films of water supplied by rain or dew, may bring sperm and egg together. After fertilization they develop delicate upright stalks on which spore cases full of green-colored spores will form.

The Moss as a Compass

In June you can generally see mosses in all stages of development. Usually you find moss only in rather moist places, on woodland floors and on rocks and tree trunks where strong sunlight does not penetrate. The American Indians commonly used this bit of nature lore to determine their direction—moss usually grows on the northern side of tree trunks where there is least exposure to sunlight.

The Best-known Moss

What is probably the best-known moss has several names: common hair-cap, bird wheat, or pigeon wheat moss. It grows not only in woods but in open fields and meadows as well as in all parts of North America; it is found also in Europe and Asia. It is rather a large moss with stems a foot long, and in fall or winter you will see it as a greenish-brown mass of bristling stems.

By the arrival of summer the new growth tips these with vivid green. During dry spells the small leaves shut lengthwise into mere threads and huddle against the stem to prevent their moisture from evaporating. After a rain they open up again. In Europe this moss is used for making small brooms and for mattresses.

Ferns, Fronds, and "Fiddle Heads"

Most children love ferns as much as they do flowers. Ferns lack colored petals, but by way of compensation they have gracefully shaped fronds, or leaves, that are a delight to the eye from the time they come through the ground and uncoil like a watch spring until the divided leaves are fully developed. While the leaves are still partly coiled they are called "fiddle heads," as their shape resembles the top of a violin.

FERNS FOR DECORATION

Ferns are frequently cultivated and used for decoration; consequently a fernery makes a very rewarding project. To begin with, the ground for a fern garden should be dug up and treated with well-rotted leaves and humus. When you transplant specimens from the woods, take a large ball of earth with each plant, and water the ferns well for several days after each planting. Give the ferns the same conditions of shade and sunshine, as far as possible, as they had in the natural state.

Among the most attractive species are the Christmas fern of the East and its close relative, the sword fern of the West. They are very similar in appearance—except that the sword fern grows much larger.

FERNS AND THEIR SPORES

Ferns, like the mosses and mushrooms, produce spores. Some ferns also have a creeping underground stem, called a "rootstock," which pushes forward and sends up new fronds each year. One species is known as the "walking fern" because new growth is started where the tips of the fronds come in contact with ground or rocks. Look closely at a Christmas fern in early spring and you will notice on the underside of some of the leaflets a double row of circular, raised fruit dots, looking like pale blisters.

Later on these "dots" turn brown, and by the middle of June masses of pinpoint-size globules push out from under them. Each globule is a case packed with spores so tiny that even under a magnifying glass they look like yellowish powder. By July the brown covers have shriveled into irregular scrolls but still cling to the ferns.

Fronds and Frondlike Foliage: Not all fronds are fertile. The infertile ones—those without the fruit dots—are much prettier. Coming back to the fertile fronds, the brown spots are not always recognized as being covers of spore cases; many people take them for fungus growths. Another cause for confusion is that Queen Anne's lace and other plants with frondlike foliage look enough like ferns to be mistaken for them. A good test in case of doubt is to examine the center of the plant to see if the leaves are rolled into a coil. If they are, you are almost certainly looking at a fern.

How to Make Fern Prints

You can press fern fronds by using the methods described for flowering plants (page 332). A child will also enjoy making blue prints of fronds, and here is how it is done:

You can buy sheets of blueprint paper in any store which sells artists' supplies. Keep the paper in the dark at all times; the safest course is to keep it rolled and wrapped up in other paper. You will also need a picture frame with a glass and tight-fitting cardboard back. Then you can cut the blueprint paper into sheets the size of the picture frame—always being careful to avoid exposing the blueprint paper to light.

Finally, take two shallow pans, each somewhat larger than your sheets of blueprint paper, fill them half full with cool water, and add a teaspoon of hydrogen peroxide to one of the pans of water. Now your equipment is complete.

Printing the Fronds

A bright sunny day is best—but not essential—for your blueprinting operations. Working in a dimly lighted room, place the picture frame, glass down, on a table and remove the cardboard back. Place the ferns on the glass, and lay over them a sheet of blueprint paper with its greenish-blue side down, against the ferns. (Fronds that have been pressed for a day or two may give better prints than those freshly picked.)

Now replace the cardboard and fasten it firmly. The frame is ready to be exposed to sunlight at a window or outdoors—from two to five minutes depending on the intensity of the sunlight. After exposure, remove the blueprint paper from the frame and let it soak in the pan of clear water. In a few minutes, after the background of the fern has turned white, transfer the paper to the other pan of water to which the peroxide has been added. In this second bath—which fixes the print—the background will turn a deep blue and the outline of the frond will appear in white.

You can now remove the paper, wash it again in the clear water, and dry it. Dry the print between blotting paper or paper towels and leave it for several hours pressed between books or other heavy objects until it is completely flat and dry. This project can be managed even by a fairly young child, and the process can be used not only for ferns but for a collection of all kinds of leaves as well.

NATURE'S FERN PRINTS

Countless ages ago nature made fern prints of a somewhat different sort. Today workers in coal mines frequently find these "prints"—for they are a part of the great coal deposits in Ohio, Pennsylvania, and other regions. When our earth was several hundred million years younger, ferns and their relatives were the principal land plants. The massive but weak fern trees crashed down and gradually filled swamps and marshes.

Later the pressure of overlying sand and mud that drifted and oozed over these regions turned the fern masses into peat and finally into coal. As this was happening the outline of an occasional fern frond was imprinted in the slate or rock which formed from the muddy deposits as it pressed against the vegetation which was changing into coal. These ancient prints reveal that the appearance of ferns has not changed much in all these millions of years.

CHAPTER 11 Trees and How to Know Them

Ost adults seem to take trees for granted, but in the child's world they loom large. They are natural play equipment, to be climbed for fruit or for fun. City children are doubly grateful for them in summertime, when the hot sun blisters the pavements and the only comfortable place to play is under widespread, sheltering leaves.

There are other reasons for appreciating trees—because they give homes to the birds and squirrels, and yield to man the wood that he uses in so many ways. Even a young child cannot remain unmoved by the beauty of the trees: the majesty of their boughs and rugged bark, the changing colors of their leaves, the splendid bounty of their fruit, blossoms, and cones. No wonder that most children love the trees and delight in telling the seasons by these living calendars.

Tree Rings and What They Tell Us: You can find the record of a tree's growth in the trunk or a branch that has been cut across. There, in the wood, are the rings that mark each year of its life. In adding to its girth the tree depends on a layer of cells called "cambium," which lies just inside the protective bark. Each year the cambium builds a layer of bark on its outer side and a layer of wood on the inner side.

During spring and early summer, when conditions for growth are most favorable, wood cells develop. During late summer and early fall, new though somewhat smaller wood cells are still produced. During the winter, growth stops entirely. When it resumes once more with "spring wood" next to "fall wood," the contrast between the two kinds of wood produces a line around the trunk. This line we know as the "annual ring."

How Trees Record Their Autobiographies: In a sense the annual rings are the biography of the tree—wide spaces between rings indicate good growing years, whereas narrow spaces tell of seasons of drought or other climatic conditions unfavorable to growth. A series of rings with little space between them at the center of the trunk, changing to wider-spaced rings toward the bark, might also be a clue to improved growing conditions. The thinning out of surrounding trees, for example, would provide more sunlight and the roots would have less competition for the water and minerals of the soil.

Annual growth rings are common to most of the trees that grow in North America. But in some regions, such as the rainy tropics, there is no distinct growing season. There tree growth is constant, and the wood has a more uniform structure instead of annual rings. When these trees are sawed into boards they do not show the intricate grain that our trees do; what we call the "grain" is simply the annual growth rings sawed lengthwise.

Watching a Tree Develop

In attaining its height, a tree does not merely stretch upward. If you observe one from the time it is a sapling until it is a mature tree, you will see that the height of the lowest limb always stays at exactly the same distance from the ground. It gains height as a result of "leaders" at the top of the tree.

Buds—New Life for the Tree: If you open a bud from the tip end of a branch in wintertime, you will find tiny but perfectly formed stems, leaves, and perhaps clusters of flowers. Many of our familiar trees produce all these in the same bud; others, like the American elm, have twigs and leaves in one type of bud, flowers in another. The buds, folded neatly and tightly, are protected by scales that overlap like shingles on a roof.

In the spring you can see the buds open when the scales are cast off and the new twigs lengthen and form new side branches. On most trees the new twigs are only a few inches long, but on some the growth is more noticeable.

How to Grow Tree Buds Indoors: Children can observe this unfolding at close range by putting a few twigs of different kinds of trees into vases partly filled with water. Collect the twigs in the fall after the leaves have been shed, and cut them carefully with a sharp knife. Through the winter, change the water each week and rinse the twigs in cool water to keep the bud scales fresh and clean—a task performed out-of-doors by winter rains and snow.

If you keep the twigs in a warm, fairly dark place, the buds will enlarge ahead of those on the trees outdoors. When the buds seem almost ready to burst, they should be moved to a sunny window.

Trees Have Their Own Birthday Candles: Trunks are not the only parts of trees that have growth marks. Branches and twigs have them too, and you don't have to cut down a tree to see them. Every year a bud leaves a little circle of scars as it casts off its scales. Consequently the distance between every two circles of scars on the branch shows the growth achieved in a year's time. An imaginative child will enjoy likening the bud scars to birthday candles—by counting them he finds the age of any twig.

Bursting at the Seams: The child who makes a habit of observing some of the details of tree structure will soon notice that while young trees have smooth bark, that of older trees is furrowed and frequently sheds untidily. This also is caused by growth; as the girth of the trunk increases, the constant pressure causes the bark to split. A special layer of cells in the bark forms new corky layers that patch the damaged parts but do not smooth the "wrinkles" that have formed. Trees, like people, often look their age.

How Trees Are Nourished

Though we cannot see a tree obtain its food the way we can watch an animal feed, we can observe to some extent how the leaf "factories" secure the materials with which they work. Put a leafy twig into ink and you will see how the color is carried up through the wood into the leaves. The minerals and water taken from the earth by the rootlets are carried in much the same way up the larger roots, on up into the sapwood of the trunk, and out through the branches and twigs to the leaves.

When you look carefully at the leaves you can see many veins that serve as channels for spreading water and minerals. From these raw materials, and with the help of sunlight, the leaves produce a sugary liquid that travels back to the trunk and through the fibers of the innermost layer of bark to all parts of the tree to nourish it.

The work of making food and distributing it, goes on throughout the spring and early summer. By midsummer the tree has achieved most of its growth for the year and it can begin to store extra food in its trunk, branches, twigs, and roots. During the winter the tree rests; the following spring the reserve food is available to help buds open and new leaves can begin to grow.

The Most Famous Tree Food of All: At this point maple sugar and maple syrup come into our story. Everyone knows they are processed from the sap of the maple tree—but what makes that sap so deliciously sweet? As it surges through the maple trees in springtime, the sap dissolves the sugar they have stored up. Thus sugar and sap flow out together into containers the canny Vermonters have mounted under holes they make in the trunks. Boiling does the rest.

Why Leaves Change Color and What Makes Them Fall

As children first notice the reds and yellows about the time of the first cold snap, they often conclude that frost causes the leaves to change from green to bright fall coloring. As it happens, frost is not the cause, though lower temperatures do have some bearing on the change. With the coming of colder weather the earth starts to harden and the trees are no longer able to draw much water from it.

Lacking water, the green pigment of the leaves begins to fade and is gradually replaced by yellow and orange pigments that have been present all along but in smaller quantities than the green. Red coloring has a different origin: It is formed in the cell sap by the same sort of "dye" that colors red cabbage and beets. You can look for lovely red displays on sugar maples, white oaks, and sumac.

Poplar, hickory, and linden are some of the trees that have golden-yellow fall coloring. The green pigment of evergreens is so hardy that—as we might guess from the name of this tree—it is not affected by winter conditions.

How Leaves Die and Drop Off: While the leaves are changing color, a thin corklike layer of cells develops between the leaf stems and the twigs to which they are fastened. This layer of weak tissue reduces or shuts off completely the flow of sap to the leaf. This not only contributes to the death of the leaf—it also weakens its attachment so that it falls at a slight breeze or even from its own weight.

How Knots and Knotholes Are Formed

Trees Prune Their Own Branches: Children often have the opportunity to watch trees being pruned in city parks or on suburban lawns. But they are surprised to learn that trees growing under natural conditions are also pruned. The trees do this pruning themselves! One process, called natural pruning, works like this: Lower branches become undernourished because excessive shade prevents their leaves from manufacturing food, with the result that these branches die and drop off.

In willows, poplars, and other trees, layers of weak tissue, similar to those that cause leaves to fall, form somewhere along certain branches—sometimes at the base. After a while the branches break off, even though many fresh leaves may still be attached to them. This process is known as self-pruning.

Knotholes and Peepholes: When a branch is lost to a tree by pruning, the remaining short stump of branch eventually becomes overgrown by the trunk. If the tree is felled and cut for lumber, the end of the branch shows up as a knot. In cases where the branch was quite dead when it dropped from the tree, the knot is a dead one and falls out readily, leaving a knothole—a boon to many a child who wishes to peep through a board fence.

The Underground Life of Trees

Trees vary in many respects, but all kinds are alike in being made up of two main parts. Every tree has a trunk and a crown— or head—which is made up of branches and spray (the term used for its great mass of twigs). We can easily see this part of the tree, but there is another big section which is concealed.

Below the Surface: The root system of a tree is often so extensive that its size would equal that of the crown if this upper part were somewhat compressed. The roots of some species grow almost straight down; other species have roots extending outward close to the surface of the ground. Certain oak trees have been found with roots two or three times as widespread as their branches!

Sometimes roots that have pushed partly above the surface help a child to picture the extent of a root system—or he may come upon an uprooted stump to which roots are still attached. City youngsters occasionally see work being done on pavements or watch the installation of pipes under sidewalks which uncovers or cuts into the roots of shade trees. They may well be impressed by the amount of abuse the trees will take, yet there are limits to the damage that a tree can stand.

Repairing Injured Roots: Often the injured roots require treatment. Sometimes it is enough to trim away the ragged edges; in other cases the broken sections should be removed completely. If any considerable amount of root material is taken away when a tree is transplanted, the crown should also be trimmed. This reduces the needs of the foliage for food and water at a time when the root system can no longer do its full part in providing them.

Keeping a Tree Biography

Once a child has a general understanding of tree growth, he will very likely enjoy keeping a record of one particular specimen. Choose a tree fairly near home so that he can observe it often: about once a week in spring and fall and every two weeks in summer and winter. If he looks at it closely for just a few minutes at a time, he will see whatever developments there are: buds noticeably larger, buds opening, flowers blossoming, fruits forming, and so on through changing leaf colors to bare branches.

Insects found on the tree, birds nesting in it, or squirrels using it for their home—these are all part of the story. Such a record kept in a notebook may be illustrated with a few sketches of the tree's changing silhouette, its leaves, flowers, or fruit. At the end of the year the youngster is quite sure to have felt something of the fascination of first-hand observation, and to have an increased interest in all trees.

How to Recognize the Trees

Certain trees have something so special about them that children have no trouble remembering them. The drooping form of the weeping willow, the bark of the slender white birch—these are quite unforgettable. However, you will find dozens of trees in your own neighborhood that look more or less like many others. It would be rash to conclude that it is quite impossible to recognize them all; there are numerous ways in which each reveals its name to us.

Oaks—Grandeur, Strength, Endurance

If there are oak trees in your neighborhood, you might begin with this group. So impressive are the grandeur, strength, and endurance of the oak that it is frequently used as a symbol of these qualities in literature and art. The oak group has many different members. It is not always easy to identify each of its species; there are numerous kinds that vary in size, type of leaf, and other features.

Usually, though, an oak is ponderous, with scaly or furrowed bark. The leaves are marked by prominent branching veins and the winter buds are clustered at the ends of the twigs. These buds are covered with chestnut-brown scales which leave a ringlike mark on the twig when they fall. All oaks are alike in producing those delightfully sculptured seed containers, the acorns.

The White Oaks: All oaks are divided into two classes: white oaks and black oaks. In identifying a member of the white group—

"GREAT OAKS FROM LITTLE ACORNS GROW"

The mighty white oak, with branches that may extend fifty feet or more, develops from a seed that may be only three-quarters of an inch long. Its wood is a great favorite where durability is needed; it is used in shipbuilding, for railroad ties and cars, flooring, agricultural implements.

which includes the white oak proper, the bur, post, and California white oak—it helps to examine the leaves. They have characteristically rounded lobes (segments), though the chestnut oak is a well-known exception with its long narrow leaves. Usually they are light-colored on the underside.

Another characteristic of these trees is the grayish or light-brown bark which you may often notice breaking off in loose, flaky scales. (This, again, is not true of the chestnut oak.) Acorns of the white oaks mature in one year; you will never see acorns of old and new crops on a tree at the same time.

The Black Oaks: The black oak group, by contrast, has leaves with angular lobes, ending in sharp points. Members of this group, including the black, pin, red, scarlet, Spanish, and willow oaks, require two years to mature their acorns; so you may observe fully grown acorns started the previous year and the new crop clinging to the branches at the same time.

As for differentiating oak species, you will find such distinc-tions as the pin oak's horizontal, slender branches that arch out gracefully and on the lower part of the tree droop and spread out into fine branchlets most unusual for an oak. The willow oak is distinctive in that its slender leaves have no lobes. The black oak has rough, dark bark growing in ridges; the bark of the scarlet oak is even rougher. The red oak's acorns are large and set in broad, shallow cups especially adaptable for the toy cups and saucers that children enjoy fashioning from them.

Many oaks do not begin to produce acorns until they are about twenty years old. Oaks are comparatively slow-growing and long-lived; you may find some that have apparently been growing for several centuries.

Oak Buds: There are noticeable differences in the shapes of oak buds. On most of the white oaks they are blunt; on black oaks they are large and sharp-pointed. They also differ in color. All oaks do have a family resemblance, however, in the way several buds, all fairly equal in size, cluster at the tip of a branch or twig. (Other trees may have only one bud at, or near, the tip of the branch. Still others may also have several placed like the buds of the oaks; but in such cases the buds are very unequal in size.)

The Sturdy Oak: The sturdy wood of the oak has played a great role in our history. Pioneers built blockhouses, log cabins, bridges, and barns of oak. Gun deck, keel, and other parts of the frigate *Constitution* were made of white oak, and all-oak ships were built for years. Today oak is still a wood of great importance. It is used especially for flooring and furniture and serves the United States Navy in mine sweepers and patrol boats.

MAPLES

Sugar Maples: The form of the sugar maple is determined by the conditions under which it grows. When there is plenty of room the tree has a short trunk and an oval head; in a forest its granite-gray trunk in search of sunlight may reach a height of a hundred feet while its leaves and branches blend with the surrounding foliage to form the forest's green canopy. The glossy leaves, dark green above and pale beneath, have five main lobes between the edges marked with a few large teeth.

When the leaves fall, you see a silhouette with many branches—these divide into fine spray—set close at sharp angles to the trunk. You can notice, too, a fine graduation in color as the dark gray of the trunk shades to lighter tones on the branches. The spray is purplish—the color of the long sharp-pointed winter buds. In late winter the bud scales become downy and turn almost golden. Soon afterward you see them pushed off by the yellowish, downy leaves. Greenish-yellow flowers appear at the same time, grouped in tassel-like clusters.

The sugar (or rock) maple's hard, close-grained wood is used in much of our high-quality furniture.

Red Maples: Other species of maple native to America can also be distinguished quite readily. The red maple gets its name from usually having something red about it. It has red buds in winter and early spring; in late spring the flowers are most frequently

THE VERSATILE SUGAR MAPLE

In early spring this maple yields delicious sweet sap. During the summer its leaves provide glorious shady shelter. With the coming of autumn the crimson, orange, and yellow coloring of the leaves makes the tree a work of art. In winter, with the leaves gone, we can appreciate the fine tracery of the sugar maple's branches and twigs. This hardy tree may live as long as three hundred years.

red (though sometimes yellow); the leaf stalks in summer are noticeably red; and in fall the leaves are a lovely crimson or wine-red.

Silver Maples: These maples turn a pale yellow in the fall. In summer you can appreciate their interestingly two-toned leaves: bright pale green above and silvery white below. Whenever the wind ruffles this foliage, a silver maple may seem to change before your eyes from an ordinary green hue to silver. This tree is the fastest growing of all our maples and attains a good size.

Bigleaf Maples: The bigleaf maples, found along the Pacific coast from Alaska to southern California, have the largest leaves of any native maple. They may be as long as twelve inches, and their width is slightly greater!

Norway Maples: The Norway maple is one of several species introduced to America for ornamental planting. Its leaves are very much like those of the sugar maple, but they are broader than they are long. If you break one of the leaf stalks, a milky juice will ooze forth. The bark of the Norway maple is dark gray and fairly smooth; its twigs are about twice as thick as those of a sugar maple.

Seeds with Wings: What acorns are to the oaks, the paired, winged seeds are to the maples. Any time after the first of June you may look for maple seeds on the sidewalks, roads, and woods. In the case of the sugar maple, though, the seeds do not fly until the fall. Sometimes maple seeds have two wings attached, other times a wing is broken off. Though they have the appearance of two separate seeds joined together, usually only one seed of the pair is developed.

The twin green wings do a good job of carrying seeds to new growing grounds. Children are quick to appreciate their efficiency and similarity to man-made gliders.

SYCAMORES—MASSIVE SHADE TREES

You will easily recognize this massive tree in winter as well as summer by its mottled whitish bark, its thick trunk, and its broad oval crown. However, the bark takes on a variety of forms and colors according to the sycamore's age and the conditions under which it is growing. Until it is moderately old, large thin plates of bark peel off, exposing areas of whitish, yellowish, or greenish inner bark—probably the result of the outer bark's inability to expand.

THE UNPREDICTABLE SYCAMORE

Young sycamores are generally flat at the bottom and round at the top, but as they age their forms show interesting individuality. The branches spread and twist at every angle, and their leaves, broader than long, provide heavy foliage. Some sycamores grow tall straight trunks, others have trunks dividing close to the ground.

In older trees, the bark is two or three inches thick and broken by numerous shallow fissures. This results in a scaly appearance, and the light-colored mottled look is replaced by dark gray or reddish brown.

"The Button-Ball Tree": The inconspicuous flowers of the sycamore blossom when the leaves unfold early in May. By October, the fruit that develops from them provides an excellent "trade-

mark." It is a dense ball about an inch thick which is green at first but later turns brown.

Because of this button-like fruit, the sycamore is sometimes called the button-ball tree or buttonwood. A "button" dangles from a long slender stem throughout the winter. When spring arrives, the button breaks up into many hairy nutlets.

Sycamores are chiefly useful as shade trees, but their wood is of some value for musical instruments.

American Elms—Graceful and Tough

In summertime this tree, when it is growing in the open, is likely to remind you of a huge vase filled with foliage. From its rounded wide-spreading top it tapers downward in the manner of many graceful flower-holders. After it sheds its first foliage, you will notice how the trunk divides gradually at ten to twenty feet above the ground into two or more stout branches. The gray bark is furrowed in perpendicular flat-topped ridges.

The Elm's Purplish Haze: In early spring you may wonder whether your eyes are deceiving you, or if there really is a purple glow over that elm tree a short distance ahead of you. Your eyes are not playing tricks: The purple haze is produced by clusters of light-green blossoms with red stamens, all over the tree. Seeds develop from them even before the leaves are fully open in May or June; they are flat and surrounded by a broad papery wing. When the seeds are planted, some may germinate within a few days; many, however, remain dormant until the next spring.

Lopsided Leaves: The leaves of this elm have the peculiarity of being lopsided; one side of each leaf is larger than the other. Their parallel veins are evenly spaced and go directly from the midrib to the sawtooth edges. The upper surface is somewhat rough and the undersurface softly hairy.

What Elm Wood Is Used For: The wood of this tree is so hard as to make it impractical for many uses; yet the very hardness of elm wood makes it ideal for such purposes as the hubs of heavy

THE AMERICAN ELM — GRACEFUL SHADE TREE

Many trees derive their graceful charm from their foliage, but the American elm is lovely for its shape as well. Its lower branches sweep upward and bend at the ends; the higher branches form a rounded top with a multitude of slender twigs. This arrangement gives the elm an attractive vaselike outline.

wagons, floors that must take considerable punishment, and chopping boards and bowls. The more this wood is scrubbed, the more it shines.

Some Other Elms: The American elm, sometimes also called the white elm, grows naturally on low, fertile hills and river bottom lands. Of the other species of elm native to America, the slippery elm is next in importance. It rather resembles its larger relative but lacks its graceful symmetry. The whitish inner bark of the slippery elm is very gummy (though quite tasteless) , and chewing it is fun for children.

POPLARS—INCLUDING THE QUAKING ASPEN

Of the eleven different members of the poplar group that we find in North America, the quaking aspen (or aspen poplar) carries to the furthest extreme the family characteristic of having foliage that trembles with the breeze. The small broad leaves of this poplar quiver almost incessantly even when the air is calm.

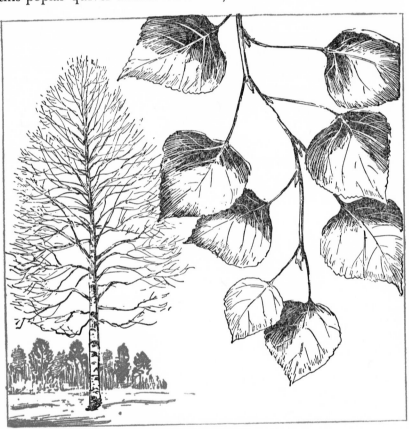

THE RESTLESS FOLIAGE OF THE QUAKING ASPEN

The slightest breeze sets in motion the foliage of this poplar. Its dark green leaves, which turn clear gold in autumn, are attached by long ribbon-like stems. Its twigs and bark of blotched white keep many a rabbit alive in winter, and its bitter inner bark is a favorite food of beavers. It is also known as the trembling aspen.

The Quaking Aspen: The quaking aspen's leaves are shiny green above and pale dull green below; in the fall they turn golden yellow some time before they are shed. In spring the quaking aspen flowers appear in the form of drooping catkins—a compact spike of flowers from an inch and a half to two and a half inches long.

Young trees have yellowish-green or nearly white powdery bark which is marked with horizontal creases and scars. On old trees the bark near the base is almost black, and roughened by bands of wartlike growths. For years the wood was considered quite worthless. Today it has a very real value as a source of paper, especially magazine stock.

The Popular Cottonwood: Another widespread and well-known poplar is the cottonwood. You are likely to encounter it on dry western plains where other trees cannot gain a foothold—or in a large city where its shiny, leathery leaves successfully shed smoke and dirt. However, many cities prohibit the planting of the cotton-wood because its extensive shallow root system often breaks up sidewalks and its tiny rootlets, in their quest for water, fill drain-pipes.

Cottonwoods Grow Fast: Children who are impatient for things to grow up can enjoy watching cottonwoods develop. These trees have been observed adding four or five feet to their height in a year; some have grown a hundred feet in fifteen years. This is rather more than average height for a cottonwood, yet you may find one growing as tall as 150 feet, given favorable conditions. It develops a massive trunk that divides near the ground.

WILLOWS—GENERALLY FOUND NEAR WATER

Children are quickly attracted to some of the willows. One introduction is all they are likely to need to the huge but extremely graceful willow, with its long, narrow, pointed leaves, some of which droop to the ground. A boy with his first jackknife loves the willow because the bark is easily removed in whole sections from branches or twigs and can be used to fashion a variety of whistles.

The wood of the willows has a few practical uses but most members of this group, especially the weeping willow (an import from Asia), are mostly valued for their grace and beauty.

The Pussy Willow—Children's Favorite: The pussy willow, a great joy to children, is related to the weeping willow though they differ considerably in size. The pussy willow rarely reaches a height of twenty feet. Its prominent soft pussies are welcomed as one of the first promises of spring and enjoyed for their silky "fur" as much in florists' shops as in their natural setting.

Willow Seeds and Pollen: There are quite a few other species of varying sizes and characteristics, but they all have the distinctive elongated catkins (scaly spikes), and our American willows bear long narrow leaves that turn yellow in the fall. In each species the seed-bearing flowers and the pollen-bearing flowers are produced on separate trees.

The showy pussies are pollen-bearing flowers. In winter they are covered by a shiny brown tentlike bract. When these open you can see two stamens and anthers (the pollen bearers) underneath each fur-bordered scale. But you will find no pistils.

On another tree, however, you may discover greenish-gray catkins, similar to the ones just described, but not so soft and furry. In these, each fringed scale has a pistil at its base, and projecting from it is a Y-shaped stigma that is fertilized by the pollen and produces the seed. You can observe the process closely by keeping a few in water until the catkins open.

At the base of both kinds of flowers are small glands of nectar. Bees make their way to these, and as they do they carry pollen to the pistils. Wind also plays a role in the pollination project. When the willow seeds ripen in June, you find the catkins made up of tiny pods. When the seeds pop open, they are equipped with fuzz and fly away, balloon-fashion. A frequent comment is, "The willows are shedding cotton."

WHY WILLOWS ARE FOUND AT WATERSIDES

We are so accustomed to seeing willows at the edges of streams, that these trees have come to seem most "at home" there. As a matter of fact, the planting of willows near stream banks has practical value; their roots, powerful and extensive, have a restraining effect on the soil and help hold it in place in case of a flood.

Willows and Their Roots: Willows are most likely to be found near water, and they are valuable in controlling watercourses in floodtime because of their extensive roots. By placing willow twigs in water you can demonstrate how easily they form rootlets. A twig lying on moist soil will develop them in the same way along its entire underside as shoots appear from the buds on the upper side.

BEECHES—HANDSOME AND PRACTICAL

If there are beech trees in your neighborhood, your children are likely to be familiar with the nuts even though they pay scant attention to the rest of the tree. By early fall they are ripe and edible—two or three small triangular, highly polished nuts enclosed in a small prickly bur. Another distinctive characteristic of the beech is its smooth, blue-gray, skinlike bark which hugs trunk and branches, even on old trees.

THE HARDY AND LONG-LIVED AMERICAN BEECH

The American beech, a relative of the oaks, has striking beauty of form, foliage and bark. This hardy and long-lived tree is easy to recognize by its smooth gray bark. The family name of the beech, *Fagus*, comes from a Greek word meaning to "eat"—perhaps a reference to the tasty beech nut, which makes good eating.

From Beech to Book: This bark offers youngsters a tempting opportunity to carve their initials on its smooth surface. The idea of using it as a slate is far from new! It is said that centuries ago in Europe some of the first writing was done on beech-bark strips, and there is an interesting connection between the words *beech* and *book*. Beech comes from the Anglo-Saxon *beeche,* to which our word *book* is closely related.

What Beech Wood is Used For: Though unsuitable for important building, beech has a number of practical uses, serving for such humble articles as boxes, crates, barrels, and clothespins. Seeing one of these handsome trees with its many long, wide-spreading branches, you are hardly likely to associate it with such lowly though essential products.

The glossy, dark blue-green leaves of the beech are between three and five inches long, and each vein ends in a small sharp tooth. The leaves sometimes cling stubbornly to the branches throughout the winter.

Ash Trees—Pliant But Tough

Of the eighteen different species of ash growing in the United States, the white ash is the largest and handsomest. You may discover it on a variety of soils—most often on well-drained fertile sites along streams and on north or east slopes. Its compact, oval head is a rich green that derives from the dark tone of the lancelike leaflets. These are the compounded type of leaf; from five to nine short-stalked blades are attached to each leaf stem.

Possibly the ash got its name from its dark ashy gray bark. In any event the color of the bark serves as a reminder of the tree's name. The bark is cut by deep diamond-shaped fissures with broad flattened ridges between them. The seeds are equipped for flight, each being enclosed in a single wing.

Ash for Baseball Bats: There are not many purposes for which the white ash is esteemed, but some of the special uses to which it is put provide a lot of fun for boys and girls. White ash is the only wood used for making good baseball bats, and it is excellent for

BATS, PADDLES, SKIS, HOCKEY STICKS
The wood of the white ash is ideal for many kinds of sports equipment, including baseball bats, canoe paddles (this goes back to Indian times), frames for tennis racquets, skis, polo and hockey sticks. Incidentally, the tree of the universe in Norse mythology (Igdrasil) was a white ash.

tennis racquet frames, hockey sticks, skis, and other sports equipment. What makes it peculiarly suitable for these purposes is that it is pliant yet tough. It can be bent into the required shapes, but it is durable enough to stand up under strenuous use.

Black ash wood also serves specialized purposes: It splits easily into very thin, yet tough pieces, and as a result makes ideal barrel hoops and woven chair bottoms.

BIRCHES—FROM CANOES TO FURNITURE

The Paper Birch: It is a pity that the bark of this graceful tree
appeals so much to children; the temptation to peel strips from
the trunk is usually irresistible, with the result that countless trees
are disfigured or fatally injured. Some children may have the good
fortune to fashion some article or other from a birch that must be
felled; but as a rule parents need to admonish them against mis-
treating standing trees. We have to hoard our natural resources

BIRCH BARK FOR CANOES

Long before the arrival of the white man in America, the Indians were using the
bark of the paper birch for their canoes. Though the paper birch varies in form
all the way from a bushy and rather dwarfish tree to one that reaches a straight,
sturdy sixty feet, it can always be recognized by its white bark, which peels into
thin, papery layers. This may be worked into fancy objects, such as baskets.

nowadays, unlike the Indians and early American settlers, who used birch bark freely to make canoes and a variety of receptacles.

In the young birches the bark is smooth and peels easily. As the tree ages, the outer bark rolls back in irregular, frayed sheets, and the black lower trunk develops deep fissures. Aside from the characteristic bark, the paper birch is distinguished by its slender trunk and an open crown with small branches and a quantity of flexible twigs.

In April or May you may find it interesting to watch for brown, slender tassel ends on the twigs. (These are the male flowers.) A short distance back from them are the short, greenish female cones. By fall these have become loose, conelike fruit. You will usually find the paper birch growing among white or red pine, spruce, and aspen.

The Gray and Yellow Birches: Gray birch is much like paper birch, as it also has chalky white bark; but it does not peel off readily, and it has short thick horizontal lines. You can easily recognize the yellow birch by the lustrous silvery yellow bark on young trunks and on the limbs. Bark on older trees peels into thin papery strips. Yellow birch is usually associated with maple, beech, ash, and red and white pine.

The Cherry Birch: The cherry birch (also called black birch) provides furniture manufacturers with an excellent wood just as hard as mahogany. Before the days of synthetics, an oil was extracted from it that was widely used to flavor candy and medicines. Though this oil is rarely used nowadays, children still love to chew the bark of tender young branches and twigs. Another product of the cherry birch in bygone days was birch beer, made from the tree's sap.

HORSE-CHESTNUTS—IMPORTED FROM ABROAD

It is almost impossible to find an American chestnut tree, for it has been practically wiped out by the chestnut blight—a parasitic fungus that lives on its bark. Throughout our country this tree has virtually been replaced by a popular ornamental species imported from Europe and Asia, known as the horse-chestnut. Because of the similarity in names, many people connect this tree with the vanishing chestnut. However, the two are not related. The nuts of the horse-chestnut, far from being deliciously sweet, are so bitter that even squirrels shun them.

It is claimed that the seeds of the horse-chestnut were used long ago as medicine for horses—hence the tree's name. When the green prickly balls encasing the fruit open in the fall, the highly

THE LUXURIANT FOLIAGE OF THE HORSE-CHESTNUT

This favorite shade tree carries a suggestion of tropical growth in the size and profusion of its leaves and its showy flower clusters. Now a favorite American tree, it was originally found in Balkan countries and introduced into England before reaching our shores. Though inedible and despised even by squirrels, this tree's shiny rich brown nuts are prized by children.

polished reddish-brown nuts become the prized treasures of children. Designs can be carved on these nuts, and if they are hollowed out they can be turned into pipes, baskets, and other toys. Even when they are put to no use whatever, they have a tremendous appeal and are hoarded by boys and girls as if they were precious, hard-earned legal tender.

In June and July you find the horse-chestnut tree at its loveliest; showy white flower clusters from six to twelve inches high appear then and the leaves are fully developed. Its leaves suggest tropical foliage in their size and luxuriance, for leaflets from five to seven inches long are grouped together like a palm with six or seven fingers. Its bark is dark brown, with deep furrows and scaly ridges.

Another imported tree furnishes many of the chestnuts that we now buy at the market. It is the Japanese chestnut, a rather dwarfed and compact tree that stays free of blight and is excellent for orchard growth.

Ginkgos—Admirable for City Streets

City streets are the place to find ginkgos, or maidenhair, trees. This species, imported from Japan and China as a shade tree, is excellent for city use because it thrives on poor soil and is not harmed by heat reflected from pavements.

The name "maidenhair" was suggested by the fanlike leaves which are shaped like the leaflets of the maidenhair fern. They are deep green and turn a brilliant yellow. The tree is naturally cone-shaped, but as it responds so well to pruning you may see it rounded or otherwise trimmed to a form suitable to narrow city streets. The bark of the short trunk is grayish brown with shallow furrows.

The Cone-Bearing Evergreens

Firs for Christmas

The firs are so closely associated with the delights of Christmas that children are likely to be particularly interested in these trees. We cannot help admiring the symmetrical form and rich green of the persistently clinging needles which make the balsam fir the ideal evergreen for Christmas decorating.

This tree retains its beauty even when it is quite dried out after many days indoors. Not so all evergreens—the spruce, for example, begins to shed its needles fairly soon after being cut, as each needle is attached to the twig by a small joint. Boys and girls love the evergreens for the happiness they bring at Christmas; and while grown-ups feel the same way, they may also appreciate them as our major source of paper and lumber.

The Fir's Fragrant Aroma: People living close to balsam firs become so accustomed to their fragrant aroma that they are no longer aware of it. But city children and their parents delight in the lovely "Christmasy" smell and sometimes enjoy it the whole year round by using cushions stuffed with the fir needles.

Canada Balsam: These firs yield another useful product: Canada balsam, used in making turpentine. The balsam comes from resin blisters under the thick, rich brown bark which are a great fire hazard for the trees. In case of fire, the resin quickly turns the whole tree into a torch.

SPRUCES—ONCE USED FOR CHEWING GUM

Our native black spruce has a wide natural range in North America—from coast to coast, as far south as West Virginia and as far north as Labrador and Alaska. Young spruces are often used as Christmas trees, despite the fact that they shed their needles early in a warm house; but you do not often see them adorning landscapes. As cultivated trees they are relatively short-lived and their dead branches give them an uneven appearance.

Children are usually intrigued to know that spruce resin was once an important source of chewing gum—now replaced by *chicle* from the tropics. The Indians used spruce gum to waterproof their canoes.

How to Recognize a Black Spruce: Among the distinctive features of the black spruce are its bluish-green, blunt-tipped needles

(Left) THE BALSAM FIR MEANS CHRISTMAS

To children the beautiful and fragrant balsam tree means Christmas. Outdoors, the fir, with its straight trunk and graceful, symmetrical branches, adorns many a landscape of Canada and the northern United States. The balsam fir is particularly attractive in wintry surroundings, when it is effectively outlined against a snowy background. It is not a long-lived tree; it seldom survives ninety years.

(Right) THE SPRUCE AND ITS VARIED FORMS

There are many kinds of spruce trees. The black spruce, pictured above, varies its shape according to the natural forces with which it has to contend. On lowlands the spruce grows narrow and tall, on mountains you may see dwarfed firs no more than five feet tall. The cones of this spruce may remain on the tree for decades.

averaging half an inch in length and growing in spirals along the twigs. New twigs are yellowish brown and covered with short reddish-brown hairs. Tiny flowers appear near the top of the branches in May or June. Small, clustered grayish-brown cones mature in August, but they may remain on the trees as long as twenty or thirty years!

You will find the oldest cones at the base of the branches, nearest the trunk. The straight mastlike trunks of spruces are covered with bark of grayish brown or reddish brown tinged with gray. The bark is scaly rather than furrowed.

The Norway Spruce: While we have other important native spruces, it is the one imported from Norway that you are most likely to enjoy. The Norway spruce has been planted for forests, as an ornamental tree, and for farm windbreaks in both the northern and western states. The dark shiny needles, each with tiny white lines, point upward and forward, but their bases entirely surround the twig. They remain on the twig for six or seven years.

HEMLOCKS—USEFUL AND ORNAMENTAL

While we enjoy this magnificent tree for its appearance, it is more than merely ornamental as far as many animals are concerned. Its dense foliage furnishes valuable shelter for birds in winter, and branches of young hemlocks drooping to the ground form cozy hideouts for mice, rabbits, and other small creatures during severe weather. And sometimes you may catch sight of squirrels feasting on the seeds that develop in the cones.

Though hemlocks grow to massive proportions, the cones of the eastern hemlocks are among the smallest of all tree cones. The largest are about three-quarters of an inch long. They mature in one year and normally fall in the spring. The cones of the western hemlocks are nearly twice the size of the eastern species.

Three Centuries to Mature: When you look up at the foliage of a hemlock, it appears whitish because the needles are light underneath. On top they are a rich dark green. Hemlock branches are seldom broken by snow—they droop to let it slide away. These slow-growing trees require nearly three hundred years to reach maturity, and often live more than twice that long. Countless seeds are formed each year and sail away on tiny transparent wings, but they reproduce poorly. Those that find moist, shady conditions have the best chance of survival.

Useful Hemlock Bark: The thin brownish-red to purplish rough bark of the eastern hemlock is rich in tannin. Long ago the Indians used this as a curative for sores and burns. For many years it was the basis of our tanning industry and in some places tannin is still used for this purpose. It not only preserves the leather but gives it an attractive reddish tone. Hemlock wood is used chiefly in making pulp for wrapping paper and newsprint. Hemlock poison, notorious in ancient times, is not derived from this tree but from herbs.

PINES—MAJESTIC TREES

Some pine trees reach a height of two hundred feet—and even more. An age of two hundred years is not unusual, and the sturdiness of pine wood makes it particularly suitable for the masts of ships. And pines are handsome too. Branches of the white pine make especially graceful decorations. If you look at them closely you will see that this graceful quality derives from their length and also from the way that the needles are attached to the branches in bundles.

Needles—The Key to Identification: The pines can generally be distinguished from other evergreens by their longer needles. The grouping of the needles provides a key to the various species because the number varies from one type of pine to another. For example, on all true white pines there are five needles to a bundle; the pitch, red, and ponderosa pines generally have three; and the piñon and lodgepole pines have needles grouped in pairs. White pine needles are long, soft and pliable; those of the pitch pine are stiff and coarse.

The shape of pine needles is such that the wind blowing through them makes the soft sighing sound that we like to fancy as whispering. The "whispering pines" and other cone-bearing evergreens were growing on earth long before the more modern type of tree—the deciduous or "leaf-dropping" kind, which sheds

(Left) THE STUBBORN HEMLOCK

The needles of the eastern (or Canadian) hemlock, pictured here, are flat, but the needles of some hemlocks are angular. This tree likes mountains and the shady north sides of hills. The great rocks that may abound in such locations are no handicap; the hemlock's roots straddle them when necessary, and in time crack them apart! This pyramid-shaped tree may grow to a height of one hundred feet.

(Right) THE MAJESTIC WHITE PINE

This magnificent tree sometimes reaches a height of two hundred feet and may live two hundred years or more. It is very easy to identify by its needles, which are bluish green, from three to five inches long, and grow in groups of five. The cones are from four to eight inches long and droop gracefully.

its foliage each year—and they have clung to their ancient custom of retaining their needle-like leaves all year round.

Pine Cones: Boys and girls enjoy gathering the cones of evergreens. Some of these cones are splendid collector's pieces. Small ones may be painted or used in natural color for Christmas trimmings; larger cones, such as those of the western sugar pine, which weigh a pound or more, are spectacular items for nature collections.

Pine cones, which develop from small pistillate flowers, require two years to mature. In May and June you can see the bright pink flowers of white pine growing near the tips of new twigs. On the new shoots of lower branches, yellow staminate conelike blossoms appear and produce quantities of pollen. Soon after this pollen has been carried off by the wind, these blossoms wither and fall; but meanwhile the pistillate flowers, which have been pollinated, are turning into cones.

By the end of a season's growth the cones are about an inch long, green and upright. By the second season they are longer and turn downward. By August they have turned brown and are from five to eleven inches in length. If you look at them carefully at this time, you will find two little winged seeds beneath each scale. In September the cone scales open out and the wind carries the seeds away—perhaps as far as a quarter of a mile.

Massive Sequoias—Thousands of Years Old

The likeliest place to find these huge trees is in the national parks of California, though giant sequoias have been successfully planted in other parts of California and occasionally in parts of the eastern United States and Europe.

The sequoia is the most massive, as well as the oldest, of all living things. Some of the very trees that stand majestically today on the high slopes of the Sierras were growing in the time of Christ—roughly two thousand years ago. Some sequoias are more than three hundred feet high! These magnificent trees were named in honor of Sequoyah, a gifted Indian chief who invented an alphabet over a hundred years ago for his people of the Cherokee tribe.

The Sequoia's Foliage and Bark: The rich evergreen foliage is in the form of scalelike sharp-pointed needles that overlap closely on the branches. You can see the tiny flowers in February or

March. From the seed-producing flowers there develop yellowish-brown, egg-shaped cones between two and three inches long. These mature in two years and the seeds are blown away, but the empty cones often remain on the tree. Sequoias are better able to resist fire than other trees because their spongy red-brown bark is at least twelve inches thick—sometimes as much as twenty-four—on mature trees.

The Towering Redwood: The giant sequoia has a cousin, the towering redwood, which grows to an even greater height—though its girth is less than that of the sequoia. The redwood gets its name from the straight-grained red wood which varies in tone from light cherry to dark mahogany. It is a popular wood for building. As in the case of the sequoia, the thick, fibrous bark is exceptionally fire-resistant. It is reddish gray with fissures running up and down the trunk, giving it a fluted appearance.

The Redwood Grows Readily: Sometimes one finds old stumps or roots of redwood from which vigorous sprouts are growing into sizable new trees. In this respect they differ from the giant sequoias, which grow only from seeds. The redwood cones also produce many seeds that may germinate and become young trees. The tree's readiness to sprout is emphasized by redwood burls, the large knots that grow on the trunks. If you place a burl in water, it quickly produces sprouts to form an attractive "redwood plant."

How to Mount Evergreen Specimens

Youngsters can make attractive exhibits of evergreens with little or no aid. You start by finding a shallow cardboard box and cutting a square out of the lid, leaving a half-inch margin around the edge. Fill the box with cotton, right up to the top. Place the evergreen spray on this, removing just enough of the cotton under the stem so that the spray will lie flat.

Now place a piece of glass over the square opening in the lid and fasten it neatly with a tape binding. Put the lid on the box and fasten it by inserting pins on all four sides. You can of course decorate or paint the box in advance, and the tape may be colored to provide an even more handsome setting.

Some Spring Beauties

When we look forward to flowers that bloom in the spring, we usually have in mind the small, shy blossoms of woodlands and meadows. However, certain trees make a gorgeous if brief display with their flowers. If any of these are within reasonable traveling distance of your home, you will be well rewarded if you keep track of the best time to see them. There is a great delight in viewing the massed array of their colors.

FLOWERING DOGWOODS

The flowering dogwood with its beautiful mass of showy white flowers is among the loveliest of all trees. It blooms from late April to early June, depending on the locality. The spectacular part of its display is not actually the flower, but four white or pink bracts—specialized leaves that look like large petals.

Your first chance to see these bracts comes in wintertime when, as purplish-brown scales, they are wrapped snugly about the flower buds. In early spring these scales grow rapidly and spread out. The artistic notch on the tip of each bract is telltale evidence of its winter form. The true flowers, which are yellow green and inconspicuous, cluster at the base of the four bracts. Such a cluster consists of about twenty bracts.

MAGNOLIAS

The display put on by tulip trees (members of the magnolia family) is another sight to reward a journey to the country, though you may also find them on lawns or along city streets. The large greenish-yellow and orange tulip-like flowers that give the tree its name show themselves among the glossy leaves of late spring and early summer.

We find the magnolia tree beautifying many a park and lawn with its striking pink and white flowers. Scattered over forest areas are seven other species of magnolia, all of tree size. One of these is the hardy cucumber tree, which produces bell-shaped pale yellow or green flowers from April to June. You must look closely to see them—their coloring is so much like that of the spring foliage of the tree.

APPLE BLOSSOMS

The blossoms of apple and other fruit trees make a lovely floral display. Children can appreciate the individual beauty of an apple tree in bloom, if they examine the cluster of blossoms that grows at the tip of each twig. With soft green leaves surrounding each cluster, the effect is that of a conventional bouquet. By contrast, peach and cherry blossoms grow along the sides of the branches.

Though we find five, six, or even more blossoms in a cluster of apple blossoms, only one or two of each tend to develop into fruit. It is interesting to examine an apple and a blossom together, observing the parts of the flower that may still be seen in the fruit. The five scales at the bottom of the apple are the remains of the calyx lobes that originally enclosed the blossom; and within them are the dried and shrunken stamens and styles.

You will find many buds on an apple tree branch that produce only leaves; whereas at the side and below the spur (where the apple develops), there is a bud that will continue the growth of the branch. The following year the blossom buds will appear on this new growth.

Shrubs—Mostly Decorative, Occasionally Harmful

HOW TO TELL A SHRUB FROM A TREE

It is not easy to be exact enough to satisfy a boy or girl who wants to know the difference between a shrub and a tree. Both shrubs and trees are woody, perennial plants. Trees are generally much larger—but you may find some shrubs, such as the witch hazel, almost rivaling a small dogwood tree in size. There is a definite line of cleavage, however, in that trees have a single trunk, whereas shrubs are divided into many primary stems at the ground, or near it.

Witch Hazel and its Popgun Seed

You can look for witch hazel blossoms long after those of other plants have disappeared. Sometimes the witch hazel blossoms open in late September, but more often it is October or November before the yellow, starlike flowers open. As most flowers have fallen by that time, the long-petaled flowers are particularly effective in enhancing the landscape. If you keep watching a bush, you will see that once the flower petals fall, the calyx forms a little urn in which a nut will develop.

At first the small nut is green, but later it turns brown. It requires a year to mature. Then, if you take it indoors, the heat will soon cause the edges of the seed cup to curl inward, shooting the seeds out as it does so. When this shooting device functions out-of-doors, the seeds are propelled many feet from the parent bush to new growing grounds.

Lovely Mountain Laurel

By fall the flowers of mountain laurel have long since died away, but you still find this lovely shrub a beautiful part of the landscape. The lustrous leaves do not die with the onset of cold weather but remain green throughout the winter. With the coming of spring, leaves grow on the new wood, arranged below the clusters of flowers in formal bouquet design. You can easily recognize the new wood: It is greenish and rough while the older wood is brownish red. Mountain laurel is a woodland shrub, with a special adaptation for rocky mountain sides and sandy soil.

Staghorn Sumac—Brilliant Scarlet

In open fields and on hillsides you are likely to come upon staghorn sumac. This is how you can recognize it: In early fall the leaves are usually the most brilliant scarlet of any on the landscape. These leaves are of the kind that has a number of separate blades attached to both sides of the long leaf stalks, though they are not always set exactly opposite each other. The number of these blades varies from eleven to thirty-one.

After the leaves have fallen, you can realize why this sumac is named "staghorn" when you see the upper branches widely spread in the form of a stag's antlers. In the spring the new growths of wood and leaf stems are covered with fine hairs, giving them a velvety feel—again suggestive of a stag's antlers "in velvet."

By the time summer has arrived, the sumacs resemble giant ferns with their long narrow leaf blades drooping somewhat from the mid-rib. In June a shrub shows two different kinds of blossoms: one, a whitish form that bears the pollen; the other, a reddish pistillate flower that later develops into the dark red seed on the upright fruit cluster.

Poison Sumac

One of the hazards of nature exploring is the "poison sumac," which, when handled, sometimes causes painful itching and swelling. You may recognize this species partly by its location (swamps rather than sunny fields); by its smooth-edged leaves (staghorn sumac has sharp-toothed leaves); and by its fruit (a drooping arrangement of white berries). Any sumac with a *red* fruit cluster is harmless.

Poison Ivy and Poison Oak

Other offenders that may give us discomfort in the course of outdoor exploring are poison ivy and poison oak, which belong to the same family as the sumacs. As in the case of the poison sumac, their foliage contains an oil that poisons the skin of many people who come in contact with it. You will find poison ivy climbing up trees and over walls and fences. It does so by means of rootlets—not by tendrils such as vines use. The poison oak, on the other hand, is shrubby in form.

Harmless vines—this is especially true of the Virginia creeper— are often mistaken for poison ivy although there are several ways to distinguish the nonpoisonous from the poisonous plants. Poison ivy is best identified by its leaflets which are shiny and arranged in groups of *three*. The Virginia creeper leaves are grouped in fives and are dull rather than shiny. When berries develop, those of poison ivy are white while the Virginia creeper's are dark blue.

Relief for Poison Ivy: A thorough washing with heavy suds (preferably yellow soap) is an old precaution if you suspect that you have been exposed to these plants. Several preparations are available in drugstores to treat cases of poison ivy, in which redness and burning of the skin is followed by the appearance of small white blisters. When commercial preparations were not at hand, I have used a mixture of half a cup of vinegar and a teaspoon of salt with success. Dabbed on frequently, this relieves the itch and tends to dry up the blisters.

Making Leaf Collections

Children, as we know, are avid collectors; and collecting leaves often provides a completely satisfying outlet for this instinct. They can obtain foliage of many kinds of trees in late summer and early fall by simply picking the leaves off the ground. To preserve them, place each leaf between sheets of newspaper, with several sheets above and more below, and with a heavy weight on top of the pile. In a few days the leaf will be dried out and flattened so that it can be fastened in a scrapbook with narrow strips of cellophane tape.

How to Make Spatter Prints

Older boys and girls may enjoy the more elaborate process of making leaf prints. There are several methods. One of them is the "blueprint" made like the fern prints described on page 337. Possibly the simplest method is the spatter print, which requires the use of ink, a toothbrush, a small piece of wire screening (or a thin stick), sheets of paper, and fresh—not dried—leaves.

First place the leaf on a sheet of paper and pin it down absolutely flat. Then dip the toothbrush into the ink, remove it and allow the surplus to drain back into the bottle. Now, working from side to side and from top to bottom of the paper, hold the brush a few inches above it and rub the bristles against the wire screening (or stick) to spatter the ink. Scrape the bristles *toward* you as this throws the ink in the opposite direction. (It may be a good idea to have the youngster practice this stroke several times before trying it with ink.)

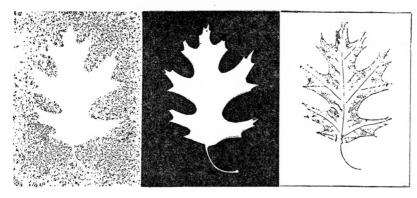

INK SPATTERING   BLUEPRINT   PRINTER'S INK PRINT

When the whole surface of the paper is covered, you can finally remove the leaf—and what remains is a perfect outline of the leaf, surrounded by hundreds of little spatters of ink. You can get interesting effects by varying the combination of ink and paper colors.

How to Make Prints with Printer's Ink

Leaf prints made with printer's ink have the advantage over spatter prints that they show not only the outline of the leaf but also many of its veins. The materials you need for this third process are: a tube of printer's ink (any color), a sheet of window glass slightly larger than the leaves, a rubber roller, and several sheets of paper.

Roll out a thin film of ink on the surface of the glass. Next place the leaf, with its underside down, on this inked surface. Put a piece of paper over the leaf and work the roller over it several times. Now you can discard the paper and lift the leaf from the ink.

To make your print, place the leaf, with the inked side down, on a sheet of clean paper. Place another sheet of paper over it and work the roller back and forth directly over the paper-covered leaf. Now remove the top paper and leaf and allow the finished print to dry.

When the youngster has made a series of leaf prints or mounted the actual leaves, his collection will mean a great deal more to him if he labels each leaf with the name and a few short notes about the characteristics of the tree on which it grew.

Growing Trees At Home

Aside from the pleasure of observing trees in their natural environment and in decorative landscapes, it is also fun to watch them start growing from seed. It is far more difficult to get tree seeds to grow than flower seeds; even under natural conditions only one out of thousands may develop into a tree. But if you keep certain facts in mind, you should have a rewarding measure of success.

Among the better seeds to try your green thumb with are acorns, horse-chestnuts, sycamore, and beech seeds. They germinate quickly and, if successful, they put forth their first leaves the spring after they are planted. You can prepare ground in flowerpots or flat, lightweight wooden boxes such as the ones used for packing certain kinds of cheese. If you use the box, make several drainage holes in the bottom and cover them with broken bits of pottery, rounded sides up, so that the holes will not become clogged.

Now put a layer of pebbles over the bottom of the box or pot, followed by garden soil or sand, mixed half and half, until the box is filled to within half an inch from the top—and press down firmly. Plant the seeds, place a light covering of soil over them, and press the soil down again. (Such seeds as acorns and chestnuts should be soaked in water for two days before planting.)

Keep your "tree garden" very close to a window which admits plenty of sunshine. The soil, which should be kept moist but never wet, is best watered with a bulb spray or sprinkler. Until the seeds sprout, it is helpful to cover the top with a pane of glass, thus preventing the surface from drying out.

You can keep small trees in pots for years. They remain dwarfed and do not flower, but otherwise they are as interesting as forest trees. If you have land with space for more trees, it is naturally a thrilling experience for a child to transplant one of the seedlings in its second year to the out-of-doors, where it may soon out-distance him in growth!

Seeds of fruit trees are almost always available. Those of the orange, lemon, and grapefruit may be planted thickly in shallow flowerpots. They need little attention and will grow slowly all winter, producing attractive green decorations. Apple, peach, cherry, and plum seeds should be mixed with dampened peat moss, placed in a jar and put in the refrigerator for some seven or eight weeks. Once a week thereafter, look at the seeds and turn them a little in their mossy bed. As soon as they start to sprout, take them out and plant them as you would other tree seeds.

12 Our Earth and Its
Fellow Planets

E HAVE NOTHING ON EARTH so sublime as the star-filled night sky. We gaze in wonderment at this vast and mysteriously ordered universe where a million miles is a short distance and where each of the countless stars moves in its own sphere without disturbing other heavenly bodies. Who, looking heavenward, can fail to feel trivial by comparison?

A small child may not share all our adult feelings about this miracle of the skies. Yet even to him the night sky has an irresistible fascination. When a child recites "Twinkle, twinkle, little star, how I wonder what you are," he is unwittingly giving expression to mankind's old curiosity about what a star is, and why it behaves as it does. But the child can ask more questions about stars than does the poem. Why do stars disappear in the daytime? What makes stars twinkle? Why can't we fly to them in an airplane? Don't they ever bump into each other? These are questions that many a child has asked me.

Some of them are quite easy to answer. We cannot see stars in the daytime because the brilliant light of the sun blots them out. A youngster can understand this more easily when he looks at the night sky from a brightly lit city and finds how dim the stars seem—and then sees their brightness from dark country fields.

When the sun is overhead, every bit of air and dust catches its light and scatters it. Thus in the daytime the air is brighter than the starlight and prevents it from shining through to us.

Stars *appear* to twinkle because we see their light through an unsteady atmosphere. The fact that there are no collisions of heavenly bodies is explained by the force of gravitation, which makes the stars, planets, and moons move around each other in fixed paths, or "orbits." They pull and tug at their neighbors, but the net effect is to hold all in place rather than pull them off course.

We cannot fly to the stars—though we sometimes feel we can reach up and almost touch them—because they are really millions of miles away. Up to now no one has penetrated beyond the mere six miles of air that surround our earth.

THINGS ARE NOT WHAT THEY SEEM

The youngster who observes the heavens appears to be easily learning a number of facts. He watches the sun rise in the east and move across the sky until it sinks in the west. He sees the moon gradually disappear each month, then gradually return to view. When he can see it, he knows it rises and sets, as the sun does. He may notice that the stars, too, seem to travel from east to west across the sky.

But these are *apparent* happenings. Our children have the benefit of centuries of study by people who questioned what their eyes perceived; and before a child is ten, he usually begins to learn at school some of the facts discovered by the astronomers. He is taught that much of what appears to be the behavior of the heavenly bodies is actually the result of our earth turning on its axis and revolving around the sun; and that the moon is a sphere that reflects the light of the sun and revolves around the earth in a period of about twenty-nine days.

Yet, even while they are learning, today's children are being exposed to a new type of fantasy that is likely to become confusing even to parents. Science fiction and television depict people racing in rocketships from one planet to another; they describe distant planets inhabited by humans, and present "new" planets to explore.

The imaginative child who accepts and thrills to this fantasy is reassured to learn that at least some of it may become reality. For, since scientists have learned how to use the energy inside the atom, they seriously predict that atomic-energy-propelled rocket-ships may in due course be sent to the moon. So, what only a few years ago would have been regarded as completely fantastic is today given serious consideration.

Yet these fanciful facts are so intermingled with out-and-out fantasy in young minds that we are actually bringing our children down to earth—in more than one sense!—when we tell them the truth, as we know it today, about planets and stars.

LOOKING AT THE SKY

Though the people of long ago watched the skies closely and made keen observations, they could not understand many things because they assumed that the earth stood still while the planets and stars moved around it. Only about 350 years ago the great Polish astronomer. Copernicus announced his startling hypothesis: The movements of the planets became understandable if the earth was a planet and if all the planets revolved about the sun. Copernicus added that the earth also turns on its axis once a day. Thus, while we are apparently watching heavenly bodies move from east to west, we are instead seeing the effects of the earth whirling eastward on its axis.

Galaxies and More Galaxies: We call the earth and its eight fellow planets that travel around the sun, the "solar system." Beyond our solar system—a seemingly endless distance beyond it—there are billions of stars! All these heavenly bodies are a part of our universe, or galaxy. At one time, universe (meaning "everything there is, combined into one") seemed a suitable word to use for our galaxy; but, as exploration of the heavens continued, astronomers found that our universe was not "everything." Many other galaxies of stars are scattered throughout the endless space that surrounds our own galaxy!

What Telescopes Tell Us: Powerful modern telescopes reach out across hundreds of millions of light-years to penetrate some of these distant galaxies. (A light-year represents the distance that can be covered by light in a year's time: 6,000,000,000,000 miles!) But even the comparatively "close" stars of our own universe are so far away that they appear as mere points of light. Our most powerful telescopes make these stars appear brighter, but with no more defined form than when we observed them with the naked eye.

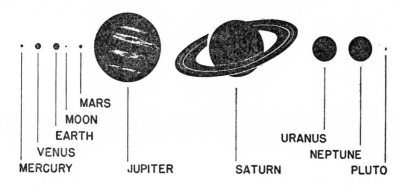

MARS
MOON
EARTH
VENUS
MERCURY

JUPITER

URANUS
NEPTUNE
SATURN   PLUTO

(*Courtesy A.M.N.H.*)

OUR PLANET NEIGHBORS VARY GREATLY IN SIZE
The earth is neither the largest nor the smallest of the planets. From Jupiter, the largest, with a diameter of eighty-seven thousand miles, to Mercury with a diameter of only three thousand miles, there are remarkable differences among the members of the sun's family. However, all move around the sun in the same direction. A year on any planet is the time it takes that planet to make a complete revolution around the sun. The planets are dwarfs, compared to the sun, with its 864,000-mile diameter. The sun, a ball of flaming gas, is not a planet but a star.

On the other hand, when we look at any of the planets (except Pluto, the most distant one) through a large telescope, they appear as round disks, similar to our moon. Jupiter, largest of the planets, which is hundreds of millions of miles distant from the earth, needs to be magnified only fifty times to appear as large as the moon.

Telescopes for Everyday Use

If your family becomes seriously interested in stargazing, you may consider a telescope of your own a worth-while investment. Either of the two types that are used by the great observatories devoted to astronomy, can be obtained in vastly reduced size.

REFRACTOR TELESCOPES

The kind that looks as you might expect it to—that is, resembling a long spyglass—is known as a refractor, or lens, telescope. It is called a "refractor" because starlight, as it passes through the lens, is bent or *refracted* by the curved surface of the glass, then brought together at the focus.

REFLECTOR TELESCOPES

The other type is a "reflector" or mirror telescope. It brings the light from the stars to a focus by reflection from a mirror, which is not flat like an ordinary mirror but slopes gradually towards its center. The world-famous telescope on Mt. Palomar in California is a reflector.

Each type, refractor and reflector, has its advantages for the professional astronomer, but on the whole the refractor seems best for a child. It is less subject to damage from inexperienced handling and as a rule the stars are seen more sharply through it.

Choosing a Telescope: If you are buying a telescope, it is wise to choose a small one with a good lens and a tripod (mounting), rather than a large one without these assets. A mounting that is not firm will show you "dancing stars" as you look through it. Equipment of this kind may require an investment of more than a hundred dollars; however, you may find satisfactory an extension type of telescope that is held to the eye. The cost of such an instrument is less than half that of a mounted telescope.

In many towns and cities groups of young people interested in the stars have astronomy clubs. Belonging to such an organization often gives a child the opportunity to use a telescope regularly, thus saving his family the expense of investing in one. The club

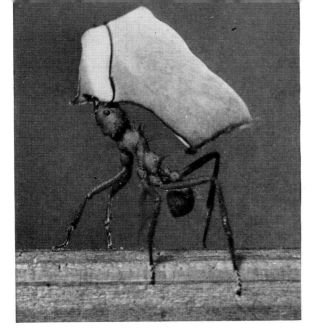

PARASOL ANT— SCIENTIFIC GARDENER

This ant bearing a piece of leaf, parasol-fashion, is not shading itself from the sun but is carrying out an important part of its farm program. Parasol ant workers cut leaves underground and on them plant fungus spores which produce food for the colony. In dense tropical forests a procession of these large ants may extend a good part of a mile.

New York Zoological Society

THE BEAUTIFUL, USEFUL, AND ALARMING DRAGONFLY

Many people regard this handsome insect (note its exquisite transparent wings) with almost superstitious fear. But not only is it harmless to man—it helps to keep mosquito pests in check. Dragonfly eggs are often laid right in the water.

Harold K. Whitford

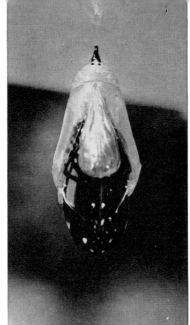

American Museum of Natural Hi.

A MONARCH BUTTERFLY IS BORN

Behind the creation of every butterfly is a fanciful story. The ugly caterpillar turns into a chrysalis of rare beauty. The monarch chrysalis, shown first at the upper left, is a jewel of gold and green, hanging from a leaf or fence. It gets darker; after twelve days the butterfly emerges.

A MONARCH ON ITS FAVORITE PERCH

When the butterfly emerges from the chrysalis, its wings are damp and limp, but soon they harden and the insect becomes a sturdy flier. The monarch can sail in strong breezes or light rainstorms, and is notable for its long-distance migrations. The females, as they travel north in the spring, lay eggs on milkweed plants like this.

American Museum of Natural History

has the additional excellent feature of giving youngsters an opportunity to compare notes with other stargazers of their own age level.

The Planets

"Is there much difference between stars and planets?" your sky-minded youngster may ask.

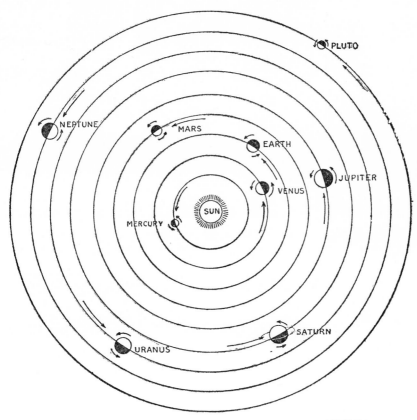

(Courtesy A.M.N.H.)

THE PLANETS TRAVEL ABOUT THE SUN — OUR DAYTIME STAR

Two planets are closer to the sun than is our earth; six others are farther away. The drawing shows the planets in the order of their distance from this great blazing mass. It may be that beyond our solar system, there are other planets revolving about stars which furnish them light and warmth as our sun does for us.

There is, indeed. Stars are blazing masses of glowing gas, like our sun. We are told that something like two or three billion years ago a great piece of our sun was drawn away from the main body and separated into nine parts. The generally held theory is that the gravitational attraction of a passing star pulled away a portion of the sun's mass, which later broke up into separate drops. Some of these went much further away from the sun than others, but all cooled into solid balls, and all—controlled by the sun's pull or force of gravitation—proceeded to revolve about the sun. These are the planets.

From planet Earth we can see five of the others—Mercury, Mars, Venus, Saturn, and Jupiter—without using a telescope. The remaining three—Uranus, Neptune, and Pluto—are too faint to be seen with the naked eye.

How Planets Differ from Stars

It will help you to distinguish planets from stars if you keep several points in mind. Planets shine steadily—they do not twinkle as stars always appear to do. This difference comes about because the beam of light that radiates from a planet is wider than that from a more distant star, and is therefore less influenced by our atmosphere. Also, the way the planets move about the sky is different from the movement of the innumerable stars that surround them.

Like stars, the planets appear first in the east and seem to travel westward; but you will notice that the position of the stars with relation to one another remains constant. The position of the planets among the stars, however, is variable.

If you start to keep track of a planet, you will see it change its heavenly neighbors week after week. More than two thousand years ago, the Greeks noticed these "stars" that behaved differently from the rest, and named them *planets*—in Greek this means "wanderers."

How to Locate the Planets

The night sky may well bewilder parent and child as they first try to distinguish planets from stars, and one star group from another. Charts which indicate the positions of these heavenly bodies will help you to recognize them and also indicate where to look for them as their positions change. You can find sky charts in many newspapers and in publications devoted to astronomy.

When your child has looked carefully at timely charts, he will be thrilled as he traces with you the paths of the planets. Over a period of time he will have the exciting experience of seeing them travel along with the stars, then seemingly move backward—then soon turn again and go forward in their original direction.

WHY THE EARTH IS "DIFFERENT"

It is quite natural for a child to suppose that since our earth is one of a group of planets, the others are worlds just like our own. When he learns that this is not so, he will surely be intensely curious about the difference between the earth and the other planets.

Is it because the other planets are too far away from the sun— or too near it—that he could not live on them? Some planets are larger than the earth (which has a diameter of nearly eight thousand miles) and others are smaller. Is the size of a planet important in regulating the possibility of life on it?

Why Life is Possible on our Earth: Most scientists agree that a combination of favorable factors makes our form of life possible on earth.

Among these are the size and weight of the materials of which the earth is made. They are just right to produce the gravity that is needed—not too great to crush us by our own weight, and yet great enough for the earth to hold sufficient atmosphere to sustain life.

Another condition is that we are neither too close to, nor too far away from, the sun; and the length of our seasons is apparently stimulating to organic life. Not only are these particular conditions missing on other planets, but they have other conditions definitely unfavorable to our form of life.

As we look at the other planets, it appears that if there is life in these other worlds, it must be of a kind that is beyond our experience and understanding.

Mars—Science-Fiction Favorite

Of all the planets, Mars is the one most often used by science-fiction writers as the home of a race of people similar to ourselves. They choose Mars because they have more information on which to base their stories than they have about the other planets. It is one of our closest planetary neighbors, and while many of the other planets are hidden behind dense clouds, the atmosphere of Mars is so thin that we can see through it clearly.

Mars Through the Telescope: If you look at Mars through a telescope it appears mostly orange in color; but patches of other colors show, too. At the top, or at the bottom, of the disk (and sometimes at both locations at once), there is a great patch of white. These patches are apparently fields of snow and ice which we call polar caps. When the northern half of the planet's axis begins to tilt toward the sun, the northern polar cap begins to grow smaller, while the southern polar cap shows a gradual increase in size.

The diameter of Mars is about 4,200 miles—only about half of our earth's.

THE "CANALS" ON MARS

The discovery of "canals" on Mars about seventy-five years ago quickly gave rise to the exciting idea that people like ourselves live on that planet. But actually the canal theory started from a misunderstanding! When an Italian astronomer, Giovanni Schiaparelli, was observing Mars through his small telescope, he saw on its surface what looked like a network of fine lines. He noted them as *canali*, an Italian word meaning "channels." English translations immediately turned this into "canals"—a word we use for artificial waterways made by human beings.

Ever since that time the canals have been a subject for debate; the astronomers have not been able to agree on their description of the "canals," and some even refuse to recognize anything that even resembles channels. Some scientists believe they are volcanic cracks; others say they are watercourses; still others hold they are formed by vegetation.

Life on Mars: Today the idea that there is human life on Mars is generally discredited but we are fairly sure that plant life, at least, does exist there. An analysis of the planet's atmosphere reveals similarities to our own—including free oxygen. This indicates that plant life is possible, and looking through a telescope we see greenish markings (probably caused by vegetation) that appear to move across the face of Mars.

The motion that we see is due to the fact that Mars is turning on its axis—just as the earth does. And because the axis of Mars is tilted just about as much as ours, we conclude that Mars must have seasons like our own. But it takes Mars nearly two years to complete a journey around the sun; its seasons are therefore much longer than ours, and its "year" is nearly twice as long as one of our years.

Mars Without a Telescope

When you look at the sky unaided by a telescope, Mars appears reddish—in contrast to the blue of other planets and stars. It was this reddish tinge that led the ancients to associate the planet with their god of war. Sometimes Mars is brilliant, at other times dim. The variation is caused by its changing distance from the earth and by its distance from the sun; Mars shines by reflected sunlight.

Sometimes Mars is 250 million miles away from the earth, and sometimes as close as thirty-six million miles. When the earth is between Mars and the sun, Mars is at its brightest as viewed from the earth. When Mars is on the opposite side of the sun from us, Mars is very dim.

Martian Invasion

Many years ago H. G. Wells wrote a work called *The War of the Worlds,* in which he described with great imaginative skill a Martian invasion of our planet. When a dramatized version of this story was broadcast on a Sunday evening in 1938, the narration was so "realistic" that great numbers of people were caught in the unreasoning grip of hysteria. The popular reaction to this broadcast is the most convincing proof that scientific knowledge of the planets is not very widespread. Their distance is so great, of course, that no object could proceed from them toward our planet without its movements being noticed long in advance of its arrival.

Mercury—Submerged by the Sun's Brilliance

Though Mars is probably our most frequently discussed planet neighbor, Venus and Mercury are also reasonably close—close, that is, in comparison to the other five remaining planets. Together with Earth and Mars, they are sometimes called the "terrestrial planets." All are made up of solid, fairly heavy material. All are roughly comparable in size, and all rotate on their axis at moderate or slow speed.

LIFE IS IMPOSSIBLE ON MERCURY

The smallest member of the sun's "family," Mercury is also closest to the sun. Because of its small size and slight mass (it is only three thousand miles in diameter and the earth has twenty-five times as much mass), the attraction of gravity on its surface is not enough to retain an atmosphere. And because of its nearness to the sun, Mercury's surface is hot. The heat and lack of atmosphere make life impossible.

WHEN MERCURY IS VISIBLE

Submerged by the sun's brilliance, Mercury is generally invisible to us. During the year there are only six periods of two weeks' duration when we can see it clearly, shining with a white light. These are the times when it is farthest, east or west, from the sun as seen from the earth. When it is far to the east of the sun, Mercury sets soon after the sun. We then see it in the west, and know it as the "evening star." About two months later, when Mercury is farthest to the west of the sun, it rises in the east a while before the sun, and we know it as the "morning star." Mercury requires eighty-eight days to complete its trip around the sun.

Venus—Most Brilliant of the Planets

This planet, named by the ancients for their goddess of beauty, is also close to the sun, but it shines with remarkable brilliance. In fact, aside from the moon, Venus is the brightest object in the night sky. It is invisible for certain periods, like Mercury; but these periods of invisibility are far less frequent than Mercury's. We can hope to see Venus about sunset or dawn, and occasionally we can see it, with the naked eye, in broad daylight.

THE ATMOSPHERE OF VENUS

Venus has an atmosphere, and in fact it is completely covered by dense white clouds—one reason for its brilliance, as the clouds reflect light. Unfortunately the clouds hide all fixed points on the planet, so we do not know what its surface is like. Astronomers have not detected oxygen and water vapor in the upper atmosphere of Venus—a fact which leads us to conclude that life does not exist there. However, we do not know what conditions exist below the heavy surrounding curtain of clouds.

With a small telescope you can watch Venus go through phases similar to those of the moon. When it is nearest to the earth it appears as a crescent; when the planet is farthest from the earth it is "full."

Earth—Just Another Planet

With solid ground under his feet, and firmly rooted trees, solidly constructed buildings, and many other stationary objects all about him, a child finds it difficult to think of our earth as a heavenly body moving freely through space, just like the other planets. Probably the most convincing evidence you can offer the youngster to show that we do live on a moving planet is to cite our change of seasons and alternating periods of light and darkness.

That the sun stands still (aside from rotating on its axis) has been known since the time of the astronomer Copernicus. Consequently the earth must be moving, or we would have no change from winter to summer or from day to night. The earth and all the other planets travel around the sun and, at the same time, turn, or spin, on an axis (the imaginary line that connects the North Pole with the South Pole, in the case of the earth).

NIGHT AND DAY

A good way to give a child a clear picture of some of the causes and effects of the earth's motions is to have a lamp represent the sun. An inexpensive globe may be bought at many five-and-ten-cent stores, and as you rotate the globe and make it revolve around the lamp, the youngster can see how light from the sun varies at different parts of the earth.

As the Earth Whirls Through Space: If we could stand out in space to watch our earth, as we can observe the lamp and globe in our room, we would see that the earth makes one complete turn on its axis every twenty-four hours. This may seem very slow, but at its widest part—around the equator—it is whirling at a rate of

DAY CHANGES TO NIGHT AS THE EARTH TURNS ON ITS AXIS

As the earth rotates, some of it always faces the sun and has daylight. As rotation continues, this portion is gradually turned away from the sun and night descends there. All the planets rotate in this manner, and the length of a day on each depends on the time it takes to make one complete turn on its axis. A day on Mars is thirty-seven minutes longer than our twenty-four-hour day. Jupiter's day is less than ten hours, while one day on Mercury equals eighty-eight of our days!

more than a thousand miles an hour! At places north and south of the equator the rate is not quite so fast. The rotating speed at San Francisco, Chicago, and New York is 750 miles an hour.

Sunrise, Noon, and Night: Just as our lamp illumines only half the globe at a time, so the light of the sun shines on only half the earth at a time. This is what gives us our alternation of night and day. As the earth turns so that we can see the sun from our particular spot on earth, we say that "the sun is rising."

The earth continues to turn eastward and the sun appears to rise higher and higher in the sky. When the sun is as high as it "can go," we have "noon." After that the sun seems to sink lower and lower until the earth has turned so far that we can no longer see the sun from our particular spot on earth. We say that "the sun has set." It is now night on *our* side of the earth—but on the other side of the earth, day is beginning.

Why the Amount of Daylight Varies: The path that the sun *appears* to follow in the sky varies according to our location on the earth. If we were at the equator, we would find night and day of equal length throughout the year. But the farther north we are from the equator, the farther around to north does the sun rise and set in summer (making for long days and short nights).

Thus if we travel far to the north in summertime, we find the days still longer than they are in the United States. When we get as far north as the capital of Sweden, for example, a summer day is nearly nineteen hours long. Still farther north, beyond the Arctic Circle, there is a time in midsummer when we would find the sun shining continuously for forty-eight hours!

In wintertime, however, the farther north we are from the equator, the farther to the south does the sun rise and set. This produces short days and long nights.

What causes these changing lengths of night and days? The earth's axis is tilted and always pointed in the same direction—with the North Pole toward the north pole of the sky. There is a certain stage in the journey of the earth around the sun when our North Pole is tipped farthest *toward* the sun. One result is that sunshine goes far beyond the Pole, making long days (summer) on the northern half of the earth. When the earth reaches a different stage in its journey around the sun so that the North Pole—always pointing in the same direction—begins to tip further and further *away* from the sun, daytime on the northern half of the earth grows shorter: Winter is approaching.

If the earth's axis were not tilted—if the axis were straight up and down in relation to its path around the sun, the sun would always appear directly over our equator, and throughout the earth the days and nights would be of equal length.

Why We Have Changing Seasons

The slant of the sun's rays affects the earth's seasons. In the United States the rays are most nearly vertical—coming almost

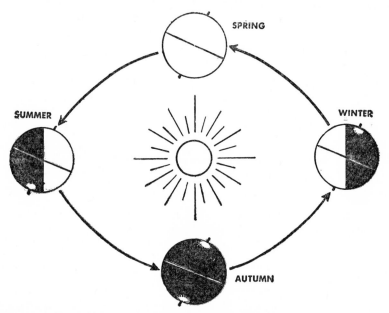

SEASONS CHANGE AS THE EARTH TRAVELS AROUND THE SUN

The variation in the way the sun's rays reach us causes the seasons of spring, summer, autumn and winter; and the variation results because the earth's axis is not exactly perpendicular to its path around the sun, but is tipped toward the north. The axis always points in the same direction, but the fact that it is tipped causes the North Pole to point away from the sun during our winter and toward the sun in summer. We receive only one two-billionth of the sun's energy.

straight down—on June 21 (beginning of summer). On December 21 (beginning of winter) they come to us on more of a slant than at any other time.

We notice, however, that we have our hottest weather in July and August, and our coldest in January and February. This lag is explained by the fact that the earth takes time to grow warm again after the cold of winter, and to become fully cooled off after the accumulation of summer heat.

Winter in June: On the day that *summer* begins in the Northern Hemisphere, *winter* begins in the Southern Hemisphere; at the stage of the earth's journey around the sun where the North Pole is tipped farthest toward the sun, the South Pole is tipped farthest away from the sun. Thus we see that the seasons in the Southern Hemisphere are the reverse of those in the Northern Hemisphere at the very same time. This shows that winter and summer are not caused by the earth being farther away from, or nearer to, the sun. It is the tilting of the axis that produces the changes of the seasons.

Jupiter—Largest of the Planets

This planet is often one of the brightest objects in our night sky, and this may give us the impression that it is at least as close to the earth as Mars. The fact is that Jupiter is hundreds of millions of miles further away from us than Mars is; however, the tremendous size of Jupiter enables us to see it clearly. It is the largest of all the planets (perhaps that is why the ancients named it for the king of their gods) , with a diameter about eleven times that of the earth.

An Atmosphere Thousands of Miles Deep

With only a small telescope you can get a closer view of Jupiter, making out soft shades of red, yellow, tan, and brown that form bands across the distant white planet, parallel to its equator. These bands are actually clouds, composed in the main of two poisonous gases—ammonia and methane. Their presence rules out any possibility of life as we know it on earth. Scientists believe that the atmosphere of Jupiter is thousands of miles deep and that the solid core of the planet is comparatively small.

JUPITER HAS MOONS

What is possibly the most interesting feature of Jupiter, the procession of moons that circle about the planet, cannot be seen with the naked eye. There are twelve of these moons—four of them visible through powerful field glasses. Looking at these four through a small telescope, you may see them circling around Jupiter, first in front of, then vanishing behind, the giant planet.

It was about 350 years ago that the great Galileo discovered these four moons, which are about the size of our own moon. They were the first moons ever seen that belonged to any other planet than the earth. The development of more powerful telescopes led to the discovery of eight smaller moons around Jupiter, the most recent one coming in 1951.

Saturn and Its Strange, Gigantic Rings

This planet, too, has moons, but it has an even more fascinating feature. Saturn is encircled by three strange, gigantic rings that whirl around it continually. These rings are one of the unsolved mysteries of astronomy. Why should Saturn—but no other planet—have rings?

The rings of Saturn are not solid—they are apparently made up of innumerable tiny particles, perhaps no larger than grains of dust. These great rings are probably not more than ten miles thick—which is paper-thin in relation to its enormous diameter.

LOOKING AT SATURN'S RINGS

If we view Saturn through a small telescope, we see the rings as a single flattened object. However, a more powerful instrument reveals all three of them, one inside the other. The innermost ring is very faint; the middle one is the brightest. They are inclined at an angle that is unchanging, but, as the planet moves around the sun we see them at varying angles according to Saturn's position with respect to the earth.

Saturn takes twenty-nine and a half of our years to revolve about the sun. Twice during that period the rings are so tilted that only a narrow edge faces the earth. At that stage we cannot see the rings at all through a small telescope; we succeed with a powerful instrument only because of sunlight shining through the rings. When they appear upward or downward, the three rings are distinct.

It is fascinating to observe the changing aspects of the rings as the shadow of Saturn is thrown on them, and again as the shadow of the rings appears on the planet as a dark, sharply outlined band. They move around the planet at varying speeds—the ring nearest Saturn is the fastest; the outer ring, the slowest.

Saturn is the last of the planets that we can see with the naked eye. It is another of the "giants," second only to Jupiter in size. As in the case of Jupiter, clouds of poisonous gases form bands across the surface of Saturn, but they are much fainter than Jupiter's bands. Despite its great size, Saturn does not appear nearly so brilliant to the naked eye as Jupiter does. Saturn is millions of miles farther away from us.

Uranus and Neptune—Distant Planets

These planets are so far away from us that only a person with exceptional eyesight can possibly see Uranus without the aid of a telescope, while Neptune is always invisible to the naked eye. Both of these planets resemble Jupiter and Saturn in having clouds of ammonia and methane in their atmosphere. And though they are smaller than Jupiter and Saturn, they are nevertheless classed as giants.

Uranus is about thirty-two thousand miles in diameter and takes eighty-four of our years to complete its revolution around the sun. Even through a telescope there is little to look for on Uranus. It appears as a small greenish disk with vague belts across the surface. It has four satellites.

Neptune, as we have seen, is completely invisible except with the aid of a fairly powerful telescope. Still, it has a diameter of about thirty-three thousand miles, and its period of revolving about the sun requires almost 165 of our years. It has one satellite and, like Uranus, is greenish in color.

How Uranus and Neptune Were Discovered

It is interesting to realize that Uranus was discovered purely by accident in 1781—thousands of years after people first began to watch the heavens and firmly concluded there were no planets beyond Saturn. The discoverer of Uranus was Sir William Herschel, a great British astonomer, whose name is sometimes given to it.

Neptune was found independently in 1846 by two different astronomers—each unknown to the other! They noticed that Uranus did not always follow its expected course, and they speculated that this might be due to the influence of another, hitherto unknown, planet. After several years of study and calculations, each man in his own way located the "new" planet, which was named Neptune. Science had rung up another curtain, revealed another secret of the mysterious universe that is our home.

Pluto—Most Distant of Them All

The most recently discovered planet (it was first seen in 1930), Pluto is completely beyond the range of a small telescope. Small wonder—Pluto is almost four billion miles away from us! It is the planet most distant from the sun, and requires nearly 250 of our years to complete one trip around it.

Pluto does not compare in size to the giant planets, and is probably somewhat smaller than the earth. One interesting theory about the origin of Pluto is that it may have started as an escaped satellite of its nearest planetary neighbor, Neptune. Scientists believe that Pluto has little or no atmosphere, as it reflects light very poorly. Pluto is yellowish in color.

Though this planet was named for the god of the underworld, the first two letters PL are used for its symbol, and these are the initials of a great astronomer, Percival Lowell. It was Dr. Lowell who calculated how a planet in the realm of Pluto must move.

However, Pluto was not discovered until twenty-five years after his death!

The Mysterious Minor Planets

With a telescope you may make the acquaintance of another group of heavenly bodies that are not stars—for they are within our solar system—and yet lack the full status of planets. These are the asteroids (from the Greek word *aster,* meaning "star"). They are found in the great gulf of space between the orbits of Mars and Jupiter.

Even through the telescope the asteroids show up only as points of light (like the stars), though they have the solid mass of planets. This is explained by the far smaller size of the asteroids as compared to the full planets; the largest asteroid is less than five hundred miles across and the smallest, only five or ten miles.

SOLVING THE PUZZLE OF THE MINOR PLANETS

The answer to the puzzle of why several thousand of these minor planets (or asteroids) exist in an area where one single planet might be expected, may lie in the theory that once a single planet did move along this path. This unknown planet may have broken into the thousands of fragments that now continue to move in the same path. Meteorites that strike our earth are also believed to be the remains of this vanished planet.

The Moon—Our Neighbor in Space

To young children, the moon is probably the most interesting object in the sky. It is by far the brightest of the night sky; and though the sun is overwhelmingly brighter, it does not have the moon's rather mysterious appeal. The moon's gradual disappearance and equally gradual return to view each month may seem very odd, to say the least, until a child understands the cause.

A child may take in all seriousness talk about "the man in the moon," and by the time he realizes that this is merely an imaginative phrase, he may have begun to wonder about such terms as the "craters" and the dark plains (often called seas or "maria") of the moon—terms concerned with facts rather than fancy. As he grows older he may have the exciting dream of going to the moon by rocketship; being the nearest of the heavenly bodies, the moon is the first that scientists hope to reach.

What Makes "The Man in the Moon"

A powerful telescope gives spectacular results when it is trained on the moon, but we can still learn many things about its surface by observing it with field glasses or a small telescope. Conspicuous even to an unaided eye are the large dark spots we like to associate with a man's face, a rabbit, and other fancies.

Through a telescope we can see these spots better. They are craters—great circular depressions. Some are fifty miles or more in diameter, with walls thousands of feet high; others are small pits without walls. Many astronomers believe the craters were formed by volcanoes, but others suggest that large meteors falling upon the moon created them.

Phases of the Moon

The dark spots give further emphasis to the fact that the moon (like the planets) *has no light of its own;* the brilliance of the moon is all *reflected* light. And because it borrows its light from the sun, the moon has "phases" that range from crescent to "first quarter" to "full" to "last quarter" to crescent again. With light of its own the moon would not be so changeable.

What Produces the Phases: To understand the phases, we must keep in mind several facts: The sun is ninety-three million miles from our earth. The moon is a mere 240,000 miles from us. The moon revolves around the earth, as the earth revolves around the sun. But whereas the earth takes a year to make its revolution the moon requires only a month for its journey. (The word "month" is derived from "moon.")

We cannot see the moon at all when it comes between us and the sun, for the side of the moon that faces the earth then reflects no light. When we are able to see a thin sliver of light on its edge, which now faces the sun, we call it the crescent or "new" moon.

About a week later, when the moon has moved a quarter of the way around its orbit, we can see half of its bright side (first quarter).

In another week the moon is opposite the sun, and appears full, for we can see all of its bright side. (During this period the moon rises about sunset and remains in the sky all night.) Still another week brings the moon three-quarters of the distance of its orbit and we again see half of the bright side (third quarter). The moon goes through all these phases each month.

It happens that the moon rotates on its axis in just the same time that it revolves about the earth, with the result that the same face is always turned towards us! No one has ever seen the other side—the intriguing "hidden side" of the moon.

What We Will Find on the Moon

If the time comes when we can shoot in a rocketship to the moon, we shall have to take oxygen tanks along; there is no air on this planet-like heavenly body. The territory to be explored will be far less than on the earth, for the moon's diameter is only 2,160 miles—in contrast to the earth's 7,918-mile diameter.

We probably would not regret the small size, for there is a terrible sameness about the moon's landscape. Rocks, rocky plains, and rocky mountains are on all sides of us. No trees, flowers, or even grass break the monotony and no birds or other animals give life to the scene. If we clap our hands to break the eerie quiet, we still hear nothing!—without air there can be no sound waves.

Knowing as we do that the force of gravitation on the moon is low compared with that of our earth, we check our weight. Whereas on earth we weighed 120 pounds, we are now just twenty pounds—only a sixth of our accustomed weight! In this feather-weight condition we find that we can get around with great strides. So we climb easily over the moutains, dome-shaped hills, and mountain-ringed plains. We have no worries about weather for the moon, being without moisture, has no clouds, rain, snow, or wind.

These things we know about the moon, but many others we do not. Its first explorers will doubtless find out much we on earth cannot possibly discover even with our wonderful scientific instruments.

How the Moon Was Formed

Satellites are generally very tiny in relation to the size of the parent bodies around which they revolve. The other planets, for example, have several hundred thousand times the mass of their satellites. But the moon is an exception: Our earth has only eighty-one times the mass of the moon. One explanation of this is found in the theory that our moon separated from the earth at a comparatively late stage of the earth's development, when it had cooled to a liquid form.

At this point, so runs the theory, gravitational forces from the sun acted to form a bulge on our earth. In time this bulge separated as a giant teardrop and moved out into space to occupy its present orbit encircling the earth. Held in its orbit by the continual pulling force of the sun as well as by that of the earth, the moon exerts its own pull on the earth. (This pull of the moon is reflected in our tides. The highest tides each month come with the full moon and the new moon.)

To support this interesting theory the astronomers have brought geology to their aid by suggesting that the moon's tearing away from the earth left a visible scar on our planet. The fact that the entire Pacific Ocean basin has a different surface rock structure— basalt rather than the granite common to other areas—has led some scientists to accept this area as the region where the moon carried away a large portion of our forming earth.

Why We Have Eclipses of the Moon

Every once in a while the moon stages a show that fascinates children as well as adults. This happens at the times when the moon goes into the shadow of the earth, and we say there has been an eclipse of the moon.

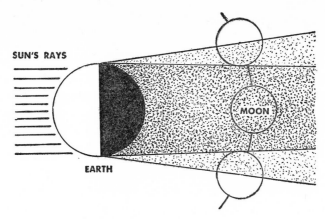

SUN'S RAYS

MOON

EARTH

THE MOON IS ECLIPSED WHEN COVERED BY THE EARTH'S SHADOW

An eclipse of the moon does not occur each time the moon makes its circle around the earth; usually the sun passes above or below the earth's tapering shadow, which is nearly a million miles long! But when sun, earth, and moon are in line, the earth blots out the sun's rays. However, some of these rays are bent in passing through the earth's atmosphere—enough to make the moon faintly visible, with a coppery tint. Astronomers predict these eclipses with extraordinary precision.

In its journey around the earth, the moon usually passes once a month either below or above the shadow cast from the darkened side of the earth. But sometimes the moon passes through this earth shadow and then becomes nearly invisible—eclipsed. A whole year may go by without a lunar eclipse; in another year there may be as many as three eclipses.

On some of these occasions the moon passes through the edge of the shadow and only part of it is darkened; at other times it is completely in the shadow. But even during a total eclipse the moon does not entirely disappear from view—it only dims and changes color. The point is that it does not completely lose all sunlight. Some of that light is refracted (bent) by the earth's atmosphere; and because red, orange, and yellow pass most easily through the atmosphere, the moon appears a deep copper color when it is eclipsed.

Astronomers can predict eclipses. Newspapers and almanacs tell when they will occur, and from what places they may be seen.

Seeing the Skies "Indoors"

If it is at all possible, you will not want to miss the experience of visiting one of the great planetariums. It is the best way for a child to get a good basic understanding of our solar system and the stars that surround it. There are six planetariums in the United States—in Los Angeles, Chicago, Pittsburgh, Philadelphia, New York, and Chapel Hill, North Carolina.

When you enter a planetarium, your child will be curious about the weird-looking instrument that stands on a platform in the center of the domed room. This is the projector—rather like a motion-picture projector but far more complicated. The "show" begins, the room is plunged into darkness, and the projector throws on the rounded ceiling images of the stars and planets. As these bodies move about in "the heavens," the speaker explains their movements; inside an hour you may watch them go through motions that would normally take days, months, or years.

The sky may be pictured as it was at the birth of Christ or when Columbus arrived in America; or it may be shown as it should appear hundreds of years from now. As he looks on, the child can feel a thrilling closeness to the distant past when intrepid explorers guided their ships by the stars and peaceful shepherds used the stars to tell time. He can feel, too, a comforting confidence in the future as it becomes evident that though stars, moon, and planets disappear from view, each in its own proper time will be back again.

————————————————————————————————

THE SUN is of course the most familiar of all the stars—and yet not everyone realizes that it is a star! It appears large and red, instead of small and cool like other stars, because it is closer to us. The sun is more important to us than any other body in the heavens. Without it, the scientists tell us, life could not have begun on our planet; and if the sun were to vanish, life would be hard put to survive.

We can see all about us the results of the energy that the sun gives to the earth. We owe almost all our heat and light as well as energy, to the influence of this great ball of fiery gas. Plants cannot grow without its beneficent rays, and the animals in turn draw life-sustaining energy from the plants. It is not surprising that ancient peoples worshiped the sun as their supreme god, and that to us the word "sunshine" means "happiness."

The sun is blazing hot—hot beyond belief. It helps us to get some idea of the sun's temperature when we consider how hot it is in midsummer despite the fact that the nearest we ever come to the sun is well over ninety million miles! The surface temperature of the sun is about 5,800° centigrade. Inside its burning body the temperature may be millions of degrees higher.

The sun gives the illusion of varying in brightness and also in size. Late in the day, as the sun sinks toward the western horizon, its glare is reduced so that you can watch it briefly without ill effect. At this time it appears to grow larger; but if you roll a sheet of paper into a tube and look through it, the sun will resume its usual size. The "change" of size is one of nature's interesting illusions.

Spots on the Sun

If you look at the sun through a telescope equipped with a specially darkened filter, you may observe some dark spots on its bright yellow surface, possibly grouped in pairs or clusters. You would see them apparently moving across the disk a short distance each day as the sun turns on its axis.

These "sunspots" would appear very tiny in your telescope, but in reality each one of them might be as large as our earth—or larger. The earth is a mere speck compared to the sun, which requires twenty-five of our days to complete a turn on its axis and has a mass 332,000 times greater than that of the earth!

What Sunspots Are: A sunspot is believed to begin in a column of gas that rises from far below the surface of the sun. This column is pushed upward to the surface by energy supplied by its own heat. This expended energy results in a shallow layer of gas at the top of the column. The top layer is cooler than its surroundings and therefore appears darker.

The number and frequency of sunspots vary, but they have a way of increasing and gathering in larger groups for several years, then becoming less and less frequent until the sun is quite clear of them. On the average, about eleven years elapse between one period of great spottedness to the next.

Tracing the Influence of Sunspots: There has naturally been a great deal of speculation about the possible effects of sunspots on our earth. Occasionally scientists have thought they could trace a connection between "storms" on the sun and stormy weather on the earth. However, observers in the United States Weather Bureau have not yet succeeded in tracing any direct influence of sunspots on our storms.

However, these observers feel more certain about a connection between sunspots and the northern lights (aurora borealis) often seen from Alaska, Canada, and northern Europe, and also between sunspots and the so-called magnetic storms that sometimes interfere with radio reception. These storms and the northern lights have never been traced to any particular sunspots, but they have been most numerous during years when the sun was heavily "spotted."

"Granules" Hundreds of Miles Across: You would need to use a large telescope to discover that the sun's surface is not smooth, but apparently made up of countless grains (usually called "granules") that are believed to be rising streams of hot gases. Though they look small to us, they have been estimated as anywhere from about four hundred to a thousand miles across! The sun probably contains the same chemical elements as its daughter, the earth, but these remain in the form of gas because of the intense heat.

Eclipses of the Sun

When the moon is in a direct line between the earth and the sun, we have a total eclipse of the sun. This kind of eclipse does not happen often; hundreds of years may pass between total eclipses in any one part of the earth. Sunlight is so taken for granted that even the prospect of an eclipse is of wide interest and appeals not only to scientists, but to all people, young and old.

We can see an eclipse of the sun from only a small area—for a total eclipse the area is about sixty miles wide—while an eclipse

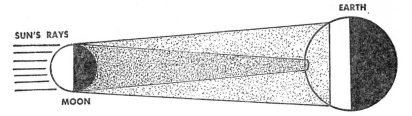

THE MOON, BETWEEN SUN AND EARTH, MAKES A SOLAR ECLIPSE

When the moon passes between the earth and sun, the sun is eclipsed. However, we see a *total* eclipse of the sun from no more than a small portion of the earth—that area on which the tapering shadow of the moon falls. From a much wider area the sun is only partly hidden and here observers see a partial eclipse.

of the moon can be seen anywhere on the side of the earth where it is night. This is explained by the fact that the earth's shadow is large enough to cover the whole moon (during a lunar eclipse), whereas the moon's shadow is small and covers only a small part of the earth.

How the Sun is "Blotted Out": "How can the moon ever 'blot out' the entire sun, if the sun is so much bigger?" a child may wonder.

If he holds a dime at arm's length he will find that the small coin seems to more than cover the moon. This same principle operates when we see the nearby moon between us and the distant sun. While the sun's diameter is four hundred times larger than that of the moon, the sun is also four hundred times farther away, and the two disks *seem* of equal size.

ATOMIC ENERGY AND THE SUN

Children take a lively interest in the information that the sun's energy is atomic, and that this giant heavenly body was producing atomic energy before the earth began. Long ago people believed that the sun was merely a great burning mass; but if this had been true, it would have burned itself out in less than two thousand years. When scientists realized that this idea must be wrong, they were puzzled about the secret of the sun's energy— until they discovered, quite recently, that an atom could be split, releasing an enormous amount of energy. This solved the puzzle of the sun's energy!

The term "atom" (taken from a Greek word meaning "indivisible") had been chosen for what was believed to be the tiniest possible unit of matter. We now know that these units are made of still smaller particles that are in motion—and are constantly changing into new forms. The change may be sudden and violent, as in an atomic bomb, or slow and gradual.

In the case of the sun, hydrogen atoms are changing into helium atoms. To be specific, four hydrogen atoms are changed into one helium atom, and one per cent of their weight is converted into atomic energy. This means that the sun, with its countless active atoms, is constantly growing smaller, or losing weight; but it is *so* enormous that it can continue to shrink at its present rate for billions of years without affecting the earth!

SAFETY MEASURES FOR SUN OBSERVATION

If you are interested in sun-watching, you must always keep in mind how dangerous it is to look directly at it, even for a moment. To impress this on your child, you can hold a reading glass in the sunlight so that it will focus the rays on a piece of paper. Before long a hole will burn in the paper—a dramatic illustration of the power of the sun.

As for using an instrument, anyone looking at the sun through a telescope not equipped with a darkened lens, would be blinded. Observing the sun is safe only with a proper telescope, or heavily smoked glass, or several thicknesses of photographic film.

For interesting and easily managed sun observations, you can note and record the time of sunset and sunrise over a period of several months and also the points on the horizon at which the sun rises and sets during the same period. In this way you have first-hand information about its gradual shift northward (as seen from northern latitudes) from December 21 to June 21; you can then chart its reverse trip southward from June 21 to December 21.

Stars Beyond the Sun

The sun is four hundred times farther away from us than is the moon. Yet the sun, in comparison to the other stars, is a *nearby* star!—that is why it appears large and red. This fact will give a youngster some notion of the incredibly vast distances between us and the other stars.

The average size of a star is about equal to the size of the sun. Many stars that we can see with unaided eye are much larger than the sun; on the other hand, countless stars that can be seen only through telescopes are smaller than the average size.

HUNDREDS OF THOUSANDS OF LIGHT-YEARS AWAY

The real stars (as distinguished from the wandering planets) we know as "fixed" stars. Scientists have reckoned that light, moving at a rate of 186,000 miles a second, takes four years to travel from the nearest fixed star—other than the sun—to our earth. This impressive figure is a useful one to remember, for it involves the "light-year" previously mentioned, which is used as a unit of measurement in astronomy. (A light-year is the distance light travels in one year.)

Looking at the night sky, we have the illusion that all the stars are the same distance from us, with some larger than others. However, their apparent size is partly dependent on their location. Some of these stars are hundreds of thousands of light-years away!

How Stars Seem to Move

When we talk about "fixed" stars, it is a good idea to remind a child that the earth rotates on its axis. It is this *real* motion of the earth that explains the *apparent* motion of the stars. The youngster should also bear in mind that the axis of the earth, if it could be extended, would pierce the northern sky a short distance from the North Star, or polestar, known also as Polaris.

Polaris, the North Star: Polaris is the *only* star in the sky that never seems to move. While it remains nearly stationary, the other constellations seem to move around it. If we look for Polaris from a position just north of the equator, we will locate it barely above the horizon. As we travel northward, it seems to be higher and higher in the sky. If we went as far as the North Pole, we would find Polaris directly overhead.

The North Star has guided sailors for centuries in determining their position at sea. In the southern sky, where the earth's axis would touch if extended, there is no star bright enough to serve as a comparable guide to seamen.

The heavens look different depending on what part of the earth you view them from. Thus, from the United States and Canada we cannot see the stars that circle the South Pole; and the people who live in Australia, southern Africa, or South America, cannot see the stars around the North Pole. It is only from locations along the equator that all the stars can be seen.

Constellations in the Night Sky

With their vivid imagination and quick flair for fanciful patterns, children seize eagerly on the constellations, those pictorial star-groups that hark back to the childhood of civilization. At the time of Christ, more than forty of these sky pictures had become generally accepted; over the succeeding centuries more were worked out, and today astronomers officially recognize eighty-eight constellations. (The word "constellation" is taken from two Latin words meaning "stars together.")

The stars in a constellation may differ in brightness, distance from us, and in size; their only relationship is created as our eyes move from one to another and we draw our imaginary picture bringing a group into focus. Some constellations, such as Sagitta (the Arrow), have few bright stars and the area they cover is small. Ursa Major (the Great Bear), Hydra (the Water Monster) and Hercules are among the very large constellations.

The constellations near the North Star go around the pole (in terms of apparent motion) every twenty-four hours and are visible throughout the year. How many constellations you can see constantly, depends on your location between the pole and the equator. From the greater part of the United States we can observe six that never set: the Great Bear, the Little Bear, the Dragon, Cepheus (se fus), Cassiopeia (kas io-pe yah), and Camelopardalis (kah-mel o-par-dah-lis). From Canada and the northernmost United States about ten others can be seen, wholly or in part, through all seasons.

THE GREAT BEAR AND THE BIG DIPPER

The Great Bear is usually the first constellation with which children become familiar. "Great Bear" is the translation of the Latin name Ursa Major; in the United States a part of the constellation is famous as the Big Dipper. This is the most easily recognized of constellations, and of further importance as the guidepost to the North Star.

If you imagine a line joining the two stars that form the side of the Dipper's bowl farthest from the handle, and then extend

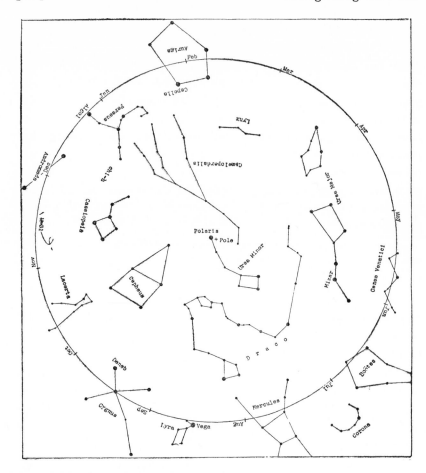

USE THIS STAR MAP TO FIND THE CONSTELLATIONS
IN THE NORTHERN SKY, AT ANY TIME OF YEAR

Inside the circle, you see the star groups around Polaris. You can always find them on any clear night in the year, for they never go below the horizon. If you'd like to locate some of these northern star groups tonight, here is what you do:

Find the name of the present month on the circle, and turn the book so that this name comes at the top. Then look on the map for the Big Dipper (Ursa Major).

If the month on top of the circle is February, you will find the bowl of the Dipper at the *right* of the polestar. If May is on top, the bowl will be high *above* the pole. If it is August, the bowl will be at the *left;* and in November the Dipper will be directly *below* the polestar. The sky turns a quarter way round every three months; one-twelfth of the circle each month.

This map shows the positions of the Dipper (and the other star groups) at about eight o'clock in the evening. If you look for them two hours later, you will find them advanced (in a counterclockwise direction) another twelfth of the way round the circle. Each twelfth is two hours; each twenty-fourth is one hour.

this line through the top of the Dipper for five times that length, it will end at the North Star. For this reason, the two stars at the Dipper's bowl are often called the "pointers."

All four stars that form the bowl of the Dipper and the three that make the handle are of about the same degree of brightness, making the form of a dipper especially clear. If you keep track of the Dipper for three or four hours, you will see that it is moving like a giant clock hand—"counterclockwise," however—around Polaris. Unless you look carefully you may not see the stars contained within the bowl of the Dipper; but with close observation on a clear night, you should be able to distinguish ten or twelve faint stars.

THE LITTLE BEAR AND THE LITTLE DIPPER

You will not find the Little Bear so easily as the Big Bear, for many of its stars are dim and may be overlooked in moonlight or haze. Seven of its stars form the Little Dipper, with the bright North Star forming the free end of the handle. The two stars that correspond to the pointers in the Big Dipper (farthest from the handle) are also bright. These two stars are known as "the guardians of the pole" because they circle closer to it and to Polaris than do any other bright stars.

THE WINDING DRAGON

Winding about the Dippers is Draco, the Dragon. To locate it, you must look for a stream of stars that starts near the pointers in the Big Dipper. From there the dragon makes a semicircle around the guardians of the pole, then turns sharply back for some distance; the dragon's head lies between a very bright star, Vega, and the guardians.

CASSIOPEIA AND CEPHEUS

Cassiopeia is nearly directly opposite the Big Dipper, on the other side of the pole. Hence, when one of these constellations is not in a good position for observation, the other is. Five of the brighter stars of Cassiopeia form a giant irregular W (or M, depending on your location). One less bright star is sometimes included in the group, and when it is, the constellation may be fancied as a broken-backed chair, sometimes called Cassiopeia's chair.

In Greek mythology Cassiopeia was a queen, and Cepheus was her king. In the heavens, Cepheus is located next to Cassiopeia. Cepheus contains no very bright stars, but you can locate it by looking along an imaginary line from the pointers of the Big Dipper through the North Star, and then continuing on for about the same distance again. Some of its stars form a crude square and others make a triangle resting on the square. The Milky Way runs through Cepheus.

CAMELOPARDALIS

When you go sky-exploring in quest of Camelopardalis you will want to choose a clear moonless night; this constellation is made up of nothing but faint stars. Though its name suggests a camel, the constellation is actually supposed to represent a giraffe. It lies quite close to the North Star. Astronomers worked out Camelopardalis to fill in a large area of the sky that the ancient constellations did not include.

STARS OF THE SUMMER NIGHT

Just as we can learn to tell time by the position of the Big Dipper constellation, we can follow the seasons by tracing certain stars. In the summertime, if you look to the east and slightly north, you will see three exceptionally bright stars, located so as to form a gigantic triangle. The Milky Way, passing through it, may help you to discover this triangle. The stars that form it are Vega, Altair, and Deneb.

Vega, a brilliant bluish-white, is the brightest star in the summer sky. Arcturus, orange in tone, is second brightest. You may notice these two stars as darkness falls (Arcturus to the southwest), for they are the first to appear. The three "summer triangle" stars are not a constellation; in fact each belongs to a different star group. Vega is in a constellation known as the Lyre. Altair is part of Aquila the Eagle, and Deneb belongs to Cygnus the Swan.

Another brilliant star you will find in the southern sky of summer is Antares, of rosy hue in contrast to Vega's bluish-white. It is a part of the constellation Scorpio. These and many other stars and constellations will become sky friends to look for, year after year, once you have made their acquaintance.

Winter Stars are Exceptionally Brilliant

On winter evenings the stars are exceptionally brilliant— brighter than any "sky pictures of summertime." In guessing at the explanation, a youngster may give all the credit to the clear, cold atmosphere. True, this clarity is a help, but it is a fact that many of the most brilliant and striking star groups come into view only in winter.

Some Wintertime Favorites: It is in the winter that we see the supergiant star, Betelgeuse (**bet** el gooz). Early in the winter two bright stars, Castor and Pollux, may be located by extending the line of the Big Dipper's handle through its bowl. Then, through the season we have an animal parade of star groups with the Little Dog (Canis Minor) and Big Dog (Canis Major), and Leo, the Lion. Many of the stars that form these "animal" outlines are of exceptional brilliance, including the Dog Star (Sirius) situated in the Big Dog, and Regulus, which marks Leo's heart.

You may be interested to know that Sirius is twenty-five times as bright as our sun—though most of the effect is lost on us as Sirius is fifty trillion miles away from our earth!

If the clearness of the winter atmosphere does not account for the variations in the brilliance of stars, what then is the explanation? The distance of a star from the earth is part of the story; but if all stars were equally distant from us they would still not be equally bright. Some stars are larger than others, some have a higher temperature than others. All these factors affect the degree of brilliance associated with a given star.

The Zodiac

Millions of children undoubtedly met this ancient word for the first time through a sinister television villain known as

Doctor Zodiac. Their parents generally had a vague notion that the zodiac was concerned with the heavenly bodies, though many were unable to say just what it was.

The zodiac is an imaginary wide zone in the sky, within which the sun, moon, and planets move. In addition, twelve constellations are considered part of the zodiac, although their boundaries may extend beyond it, and other constellations have at least a few of their stars within it.

The Signs of the Zodiac: The twelve zodiacal constellations are divided into six northern signs and six southern signs. Here they are, with their Latin names and English translations:

Northern signs for spring: Aries (the ram), Taurus (the bull), Gemini (the twins); northern signs for summer: Cancer (the crab), Leo (the lion), Virgo (the virgin); southern signs for fall: Libra (the balance), Scorpio (the scorpion), Sagittarius (the archer); southern signs for winter: Capricornus (the goat), Aquarius (the water-bearer), and Pisces (the fishes).

The astronomers of ancient times divided the zodiac into twelve equal parts, and we know these sections as "the signs of the zodiac," with the same names as the twelve constellations of the zodiac.

Discovering the Constellations

Although our modern observatories have to be equipped with all the latest refinements in the way of observing, recording, and calculating, you can have the fun of looking for the constellations without resorting to a telescope.

At the start it is helpful to obtain sky maps or charts giving the positions of the stars for the season in which you are interested. You can avoid discouragement if you are aware that even the ever-present constellations are not always in a good position for study. (When they are near the horizon, some of their stars are too faint for you to see.)

A youngster will get the best results, and hence the most fun, seeking constellations that are high in the sky. Help him recognize

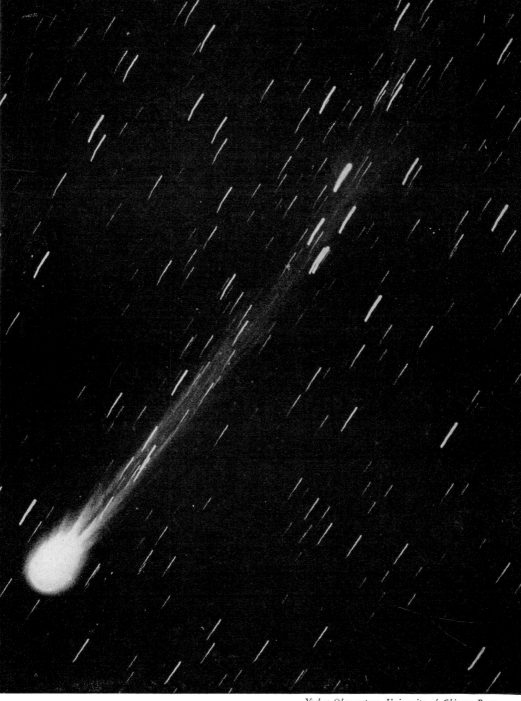

Yerkes Observatory—University of Chicago Press

THE HEAD OF A COMET MAY BE LARGER THAN THE EARTH

is a rare and unforgettable sight, with its bright, starlike head and long,
. The head probably consists of countless small meteorites, and the tail
fied gas. In its travels around the sun the same comet may become visible
earth a number of times, but centuries may elapse between these appear-
some cases. The photograph above is of Daniel's Comet, sighted in 1907.

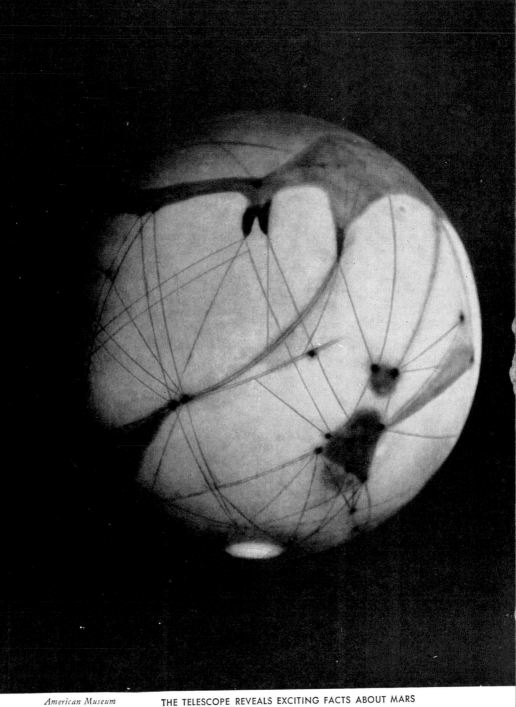

THE TELESCOPE REVEALS EXCITING FACTS ABOUT MARS

Mars is one of our closest planetary neighbors, and astronomers can see clearl
through its thin atmosphere. On the model shown above are lines indicating th
long-disputed "canals" of this planet. Also prominent is a "polar-cap," apparent!
a field of snow which varies in size with the seasons. Although it is believed tha
people do not inhabit Mars, many scientists claim that plant life flourishes there

the Big Dipper first; after that it is not too difficult, with the aid of a sky map, to find other nearby groups. The best sky-exploring is done away from the bright lights of a big city, and an excellent position from which to do it is flat on your back. It is important not to rush matters by trying to discover or recognize too many constellations or stars in a short time. Become really acquainted with one or two before going on to others.

How Astronomers Study the Stars

As you explain facts about the stars to a child, he may very well be puzzled. Some of these facts are so fantastic of themselves, some go counter to "common sense," some contradict what a child may have taken for granted. How can he be sure that the informa- tion given him is accurate—especially as he learns that early studies of the stars led to many incorrect conclusions?

TELESCOPE AND CAMERA

It was the telescope that gave tremendous impetus to man's exploration of the stars. But his observations were still limited until the camera came along and considerably enhanced the value of the telescope. A camera can be fastened to the viewing end of a telescope, doing the observer's work more efficiently in some respects.

The combination of telescope and camera is particularly effective when a driving clock is attached causing the instrument to turn about an axis parallel to the axis around which the earth turns. The instrument moves at the same speed but in the opposite direction. Thus a photographic plate may be exposed for several hours, and stars too faint to be seen through the telescope, will register dots on the plate.

THE VERSATILE SPECTROSCOPE

Even before the camera was being used by astronomers, the spectroscope had been invented. To understand how this instrument works requires a knowledge of physics, but even the layman can appreciate the immense usefulness of this instrument.

The spectroscope analyzes the light of the stars and reveals what chemical elements go into their make-up. On the basis of this analysis the spectroscope estimates the rate at which the stars are moving, and the direction of their motion toward the earth or away from it.

The spectroscope does more—it reveals the age of the stars through their size, color, and composition. The younger ones are giant size and are composed of thin gases that shine with a rosy hue. An older star is more condensed and shines yellow. In the next age cycle it would shine white and blue; after that it is really an old star and begins to cool.

Through all its stages a star condenses and contracts. After its old age, a star shines white, then yellow, then red—at last becoming cold and dead. Although a new star and a very old one both shine red, their age can be distinguished by their size: A giant red star is young, a small red star is old.

The Interferometer and Other Aids

Another invention that has proved of great value to astronomers is the interferometer, a remarkable instrument that can be attached to a telescope to measure the size of certain stars. There are still other instruments that help us to know the stars. Scientists use these instruments to measure the intensity of light and heat on these far-distant heavenly bodies. Whatever instrument is used, mathematical techniques are the key to success. Geometry, trigonometry, and the calculations they involve, originated with the measurement of land on the surface of the earth, but they ended up by leading us to the stars.

Spectacular Sights in the Skies

The Milky Way—Forty Billion Stars

On a clear night, in open country, even a child will be able to find the Milky Way without having it pointed out to him—the band it forms in the sky actually does have a milky-white appearance. This cloudy band of light is made up of an enormous number of stars—an estimated forty billion!—one of which is our sun. Many of these stars are too dim to stand out separately, but their light adds to the glow of the star-band. A number of important constellations, such as Sagittarius and Cassiopeia, are included in it.

If you were to take a trip around the world you would find that the Milky Way (also called the Galaxy) forms a nearly continuous belt about the heavens. At home you can, at best, see half of this starry band crossing the sky from horizon to horizon. When it lies near the horizon, it can be observed only with some difficulty, and on cloudy nights, not at all.

The Southern Cross

South of the equator, the Milky Way includes the famous constellation that we call the Southern Cross (Crux). To the people who live in the far south it is what the Great Bear is to those in the north, for it lies closer to the South Pole than does any other outstanding constellation. While the Southern Cross is sometimes seen from the farthest southerly parts of the United States, most of us know it from reading or from pictures.

However, a picture of the Southern Cross may be disappointing to a child; the bright, reddish star (Gamma) at the top of the cross does not photograph well on ordinary plates because of its color. The outline of the Southern Cross is formed by four stars of almost equal brightness. In the northern skies we have a group of stars, also lying within the Milky Way, which form a cross and are often called the Northern Cross—though the official name for the group is Cygnus, meaning "swan."

Comets—Millions of Miles Long

Children are naturally interested in learning more about this amazing spectacle of the skies. Whenever a comet is bright enough to be seen with the unaided eye, newspapers make a big story out of its appearance, and give the position in which the comet will be found. Though astronomers watching the sky with telescopes can see possibly six or more comets every year, on the average not more than two or three a century will be large enough to attract wide attention.

What Comets are Made of: A comet has a bright starlike head and a long filmy tail. We know that it is made partly of solid matter (as it reflects sunlight) and partly of gas; but the solid matter does not form one great solid body like the earth. It is made of many solid pieces of greatly varying sizes with gases between them.

Millions of Miles, Thousands of Years: The tremendous distance that separates us from the comets makes them appear small. Actually the head of a comet may be as big as the earth, if not much larger, and the tail is millions of miles long! The apparent motion of comets through space is affected, too, by this distance. They seem to move slowly because they are millions of miles away, but they are really speeding through space. In the course of their travels—which take them around the sun in elongated ellipses— they may return a number of times within sight from the earth, but hundreds or thousands of years may pass between the successive appearances of any one comet.

While the actions of most comets are unpredictable, the famous "Halley's comet"—a bright one that can easily be seen without a telescope—has been observed at intervals of about seventy-seven years. It was last seen in 1910 and is predicted to return about 1987.

A comet may be seen with the naked eye or with a telescope for a number of nights, perhaps running into weeks. Each night its position is somewhat changed as it progresses through the heavens.

"Shooting Stars" are not Stars

The term "shooting star" is a very natural one for a bright spot streaking across the sky. Astronomers avoid the term, however, as the objects that look like shooting stars are not stars at all. The proper name for them is meteors.

Meteors and "Fireballs": Meteors are made up of solid material that suggests stone or iron. We do not know whether meteors are fragments left over from the forming of our planets or matter that entered our solar system from the outside; but we do know that comets sometimes break up into meteors.

As it shoots through the sky, a meteor may give off sparks or appear to have a bright train; and it may travel in a straight or wavy line. You are most likely to see one that appears white or yellow; but there are also very bright ones, red or green, and these are called "fireballs."

The light given off by meteors is produced by the terrific speed at which they race through the atmosphere, and the resulting friction. Their average speed is anywhere from seven to nearly fifty miles a second!

"Meteor Showers": At certain times of the year meteors appear in such numbers that we talk of "meteor showers." You can look for a shower about the tenth of December in the eastern sky; another, about the sixteenth of November. There are others in August and October, but as they do not occur until after midnight, it is not practical to keep young children up to watch for them.

Two Thousand Meteors a Day: Some meteors are no larger than a small pea; others may weigh thirty tons or more. The small ones burn themselves out by the friction they create, but many of the larger ones land on earth. About two thousand meteors hit the earth every day! After landing they are called meteorites. About fifteen hundred of them have been found (the biggest weighs fifty tons), and a number of them are on exhibition in museums throughout the country.

When a big meteor strikes the earth it may smash a gaping hole, or crater, in it. The largest meteor-made crater in the United States, known as El Diablo (the Devil), is in Arizona. It is more than four thousand feet across, and 575 feet deep. For years prospectors have hunted in vain for the meteorite that created El Diablo. Despite all the evidence of huge meteorites and the discovery of some big ones, it does not seem that anyone has ever been injured by a meteor.

"FLYING SAUCERS"—OPTICAL GHOSTS

The baffling challenge of unsolved mystery confronts us in the provocative reports of these strange objects which are supposed to have been seen from time to time in the sky. The first accounts in 1947 of disks hurtling through space aroused more amusement than serious attention. It was recalled that fifty years earlier, glimpses of unaccountable "objects" in the skies were exciting people, first in California and later as far east as Chicago. The verdict on the flying saucers was that they were not material objects, but lights and reflections.

"As Real as Rainbows": Then came a new series of flying saucer episodes. The first reports spoke of round objects—hence the name "saucer"—but later saucers were described as cone-shaped and even rocket-like in form. Several observers, including an authority on meteors, reported globes of green fire rushing through the night sky which did not seem to be ordinary fireballs.

These accounts—and others like them—started some astronomers and the United States Air Force on exhaustive investigations. Dr. Donald Menzel, an astronomer and expert on radar, summed up his researches with the statement: "Flying saucers are as real as rainbows."

What Causes Optical Illusions: Behind this apparently simple remark are many complicated facts concerned with warm and cool air currents, and lights from cars, airplanes, and other sources, that make us see things when there are none. Even children may be familiar with some simple optical illusions. A common one is to "see" water shining on a road that is actually dry. The effect is caused by a thin layer of warm air above sun-heated pavements. The layer of hot air and another, colder and more dense, above it, together refract (bend) upward the light that comes to them from the sky; and it is this that gives the illusion of a wet pavement.

Other, less common, types of mirages may explain the majority of flying saucers. In the Southwest, where most of them are re-ported, atmospheric conditions are especially favorable for mir-ages, or "optical ghosts." In some instances, weather balloons or other objects have been mistaken for flying saucers.

Seeing is not always believing. Our eyes and nature itself often conspire to deceive us. Someday genuine flying saucers, intelligently directed, may scoot across our skies. I expect then that we shall be able to find, without much difficulty, unmistakable, verifiable, and abundant proof that they are real. Until evidence of a reputable kind is forthcoming, we must consider the saucers a popular fantasy, like the Loch Ness monster, but still not close our minds to unexpected possibilities.

CHAPTER 14 Understanding
the Weather

PEOPLE ARE ALWAYS talking about the weather, and with good reason. The weather has a vital bearing on our plans, our work, our leisure, and even on our dispositions. Weather is important in great and small things—all the way from planning a picnic to growing successful crops and keeping our nation and the world well fed.

Children are even more dependent than grown-ups on the state of the weather. Clear, sunshiny days mean happy play out-of-doors; rain often means the opposite, to many a mother's despair; an abundance of snow promises endless hours of merriment on a strange and wondrously transformed landscape. So, be it fair or foul, weather is always a meaningful and absorbing topic to explore with children. They are keenly interested in it even before they can talk, and words like "rain" and "sun" are often among the first they learn.

Later on, as the children grow older, flashes of lightning, claps of thunder, blizzards, wind, rain and ice storms give rise to a never-ending series of *whys* and *hows*. They discover a fascinating fellow called the weatherman; the younger ones may be under the impression that he "makes" the weather, but the older ones sagely pooh-pooh this juvenile belief and ask to know something of the secrets of weather forecasting.

In our grandparents' time people relied on various signs for hints of coming weather. Some of these signs we still believe in—on the whole, with good reason, as they often have scientific backing. Others are wholly unreliable and have no such backing; where they "work," the effect is wholly coincidental and cannot serve as a basis for further prediction.

RING AROUND THE MOON

Perhaps you have heard that "a ring around the moon means rain." This old belief is accurate enough—rain often follows the appearance of a moon halo. The big question—and it is sure to come—is *why*. The ring indicates that the moonlight is refracted (bent) by ice particles in clouds that are miles overhead. Those ice particles warn us of a change of temperature, and thus of a probable change in weather.

THE RAINBOW HAS PRACTICAL VALUE

"Rainbow at night, sailors' delight; rainbow in the morning, sailors take warning," is another fairly accurate saying. Rainbows are formed when raindrops in the air break up the sunlight into distinct colors. This takes place in the part of the sky opposite the sun. When you see a rainbow in the late afternoon sky, you know that the moisture causing it is to the east. Why? Because the rainbow must be opposite the sun, which is now in the west.

Now add to this the pertinent bit of information that our storms usually move from west to east; you can see that the moisture (a potential storm), being already in the east, has passed us. But, by the same reasoning, a morning rainbow (in the west while the sun is in the east) means that there is a large amount of moisture in the west. As this comes toward us, it is likely to arrive as a storm.

NIGHT RAINS

"Rain before seven, shine before eleven," is likely to prove a dependable forecast if the rain is light or moderate. Rain usually lasts only a few hours; and when it starts in the cooler hours of

the night, the morning sun often evaporates the clouds and stops
the rain. However, the proverb does not apply to heavy storms
that are often connected with northeast or southerly winds.

When the Sun "Draws Water"

Still another weather prediction we can depend on to a
certain extent is that rain is on the way if we see "the sun drawing
water." This expression, which is used to describe light rays
streaming toward the setting sun, is inaccurate.

Actually the rays are formed by sunlight streaming through
openings in the clouds and shining on vapor. However, as the
rays appear when there is an exceptional amount of moisture in
the air and when the sun is hidden behind a cloud, it often happens that they precede rainy weather. But often, of course, they
do not.

Unreliable Predictions

Among the many false notions is the one that we can tell
how many days will pass before it rains by counting the number
of bright stars within a ring that may be around the moon. Another entirely incorrect idea is that whenever the moon goes into
a new phase, the weather changes.

If all these old tales were true, the weatherman could close up
shop. As it is, he has to stay on the job twenty-four hours a day,
using the most modern equipment devised by scientists; and at
that he cannot be as certain as he would like to be! But more of
this later.

The Wind and Its Ways

We can blame most of our severe storms on the wind. Rain is
not unpleasant unless it is lashed by strong winds. Snow usually
seems very beautiful—unless wind turns it into a blizzard. Wind-
storms, unaccompanied by rain or snow, often do fearful damage,
especially in the form of tornadoes and hurricanes.

The air that is all about us is made up of a number of gases—
chiefly oxygen and nitrogen. Although we cannot see these gases,

they have mass, and gravitation pulls them downward, giving them weight. As a rule you do not think of the pressure of air against your body; but when you drive from mountain heights to a lower level the change to "heavier air" is very noticeable—especially on your eardrums.

How Winds are Formed

For a number of reasons we have high-pressure areas, in which the air is cooler and therefore more compact, and low-pressure areas, in which the air is warm and expanded. (One reason for this is that different portions of the surface of the earth heat up or cool off at unequal rates.) Wind is air moving from high-pressure areas to areas of low pressure—nature's effort to equalize pressure differences in the atmosphere.

A high or low-pressure area may range from a few hundred to a thousand miles in diameter. In a "high," the pressure increases steadily toward its center, and in a "low" it gradually decreases. The speed of a wind depends on the degree of pressure difference between a low-pressure area and the high-pressure area next to it. When we have stormy weather these variations show up sharply on the weather map in your daily newspaper; this is an especially good time to study the weather map with your child.

Why It Rains

"Look at the *size* of those raindrops!" is an exclamation that may start a child wondering about why we have raindrops at all, and why they are of varying sizes.

The "makings" of rain are around us all the time—tiny droplets of water that we know as vapor and bits of water-attracting dust. These dust particles—two important kinds are salt from the sea, and smoke—become the center of the droplets when the vapor in the air takes the form of moisture. Air can hold only a certain amount of vapor (warm air can hold more than cold air), and when there is too much vapor, the droplets of water join together and form raindrops.

How Air Currents Affect Rain: When the raindrops are formed in gently rising air, the condensation takes place very slowly and quite small drops may fall in a drizzle. But when the drops are formed in powerful upward currents, the drops may be held aloft until they are very large (to a fifth of an inch in diameter). This kind may fall with great splashes—the kind you often see just before a thunderstorm downpour. At times the larger raindrops flatten out and split up as they fall.

Sun Showers: Occasionally we have the odd effect of rain falling from a clear sky overhead. This may be due to the drops being delayed in their fall by rising air currents or by friction with the air. Thus before the drops reach us the clouds from which they started have blown away or evaporated.

Another curious sight is rain falling on one side of a street while the other remains dry. This is simply caused by small clouds meeting with a cold air current that turns their vapor into raindrops which fall only over the area the clouds had covered.

A child may think of rain as blowing to his neighborhood from great distances—possible from over the ocean. This is never the case: Rain falls where it forms. The moisture may have been absorbed into the air many miles away, but it is never blown to us as "ready-made" rain.

Billions of Snowflakes, No Two Alike

Probably no other event in nature is so thrilling to children in our latitudes as the first snowfall of the season. It is as if snow were a substance designed to turn the humdrum world into a dazzling fairyland. Observation only strengthens the fairyland illusion, for if a youngster studies a flake through a magnifying lens, he notes that each snow crystal has a lovely, delicate design, as if woven on a fairy loom.

Though billions of snowflakes may fall, no two are exactly alike in design, except that *each one* is six-sided. Some flakes, as you can see with a magnifying glass, are more solid than others. They are formed in clouds very high above the earth. The most beautiful flakes, of lacelike design, usually form in warmer air currents, close to the earth.

Snow and Sleet

"Aren't snowflakes frozen water?" your alert child may wonder. "What makes them soft and white? Why aren't they little pieces of ice—like sleet?"

Good questions, these. Snowflakes *are* frozen moisture, like ice, but they are formed when the moisture in the air condenses (changes from vapor to liquid form) at a point below freezing. If, on the other hand, the moisture condenses into rain first and *then* freezes, sleet results. The time when the freezing takes place accounts for the difference.

Snow is Mostly Air

As the crystal particles of the snowflake take shape, many tiny reflecting surfaces are formed with air spaces between them. It is these air spaces that make snow soft and dazzling white as it reflects the light of sun and moon. Also, it is odd but true that the fluffy, new-fallen snow forms an effective blanket, protecting whatever it covers from freezing. (Air is one of the best insulators against heat and cold.) Newly fallen snow usually contains only one part of ice to ten or twelve parts of air; and even an old snow is at least half air.

The popular theory that the temperature may be "too cold for snow" is definitely wrong. The extreme dryness of very cold air does make heavy snow unlikely, but even then a warm wind may move into the upper atmosphere bringing moisture with it and thus resulting in snowfall.

Frost on the Windowpane

The appearance of frost on windowpanes is nature's artistic announcement of the arrival of winter. In many modern homes, where storm windows are used, this lovely effect is not so common; but sooner or later most children have an opportunity to see these exquisite icy window decorations. It is pleasant to credit them to the magical hand of Jack Frost, but they are of course the result of low temperatures outside, cold enough to chill the indoor air which touches the windowpane. (Storm windows protect the pane and prevent frost from forming on windows.)

If the chill is sufficient to cause the moisture to condense on the inner surface, frost begins to form. Usually crystals first appear around some tiny irregularity in the glass surface or around a bit of dirt. Often these first crystals continue to grow, and as some of the smaller ones evaporate, their moisture condenses again on the larger crystals. Thus spectacular designs, numerous and interestingly varied, are created.

How to Make Frost Prints

As window frost rarely lingers more than a brief time, children may get a great deal of pleasure from making prints of some of its lovely designs. This may be done with blueprint paper. Sheets of this paper, about twelve inches square, should be kept in a dark place until ready for use. Some morning when the sun is shining brightly though frost prints have not yet melted from the window, take a piece of blueprint paper and quickly attach it with scotch tape to the pane. Press the sensitive side directly against the frost design for two or more minutes.

The sunlight turns parts of the paper light blue but leaves the pattern of the frost in white. Remove the sheet of paper and immediately immerse it in a pan of clear water for a few minutes. Then transfer it to another pan of water to which a tablespoon of peroxide has been added. When the blue part has turned an attractive shade, rinse the paper in clear water, then spread it flat to dry. It will make an attractive decoration for any child's room.

Hail—"Hot-Weather Ice"

To some people, hail is "hot-weather ice," as it is usually seen during violent summer thunderstorms; it is quite rare in wintertime. Hailstones are formed when raindrops are caught in swiftly uprushing air and are carried high into the cloud tops where they may meet snow crystals. Mixing with the crystals, the raindrops become globules of cloudy ice. These globules may fall, on descending air currents, into warmer rain levels of air and take on a layer of ice from contact with rising drops. Again the growing ice pellets may be tossed far up, and again a layer of snowy ice will be added to them.

This up-and-down movement may continue until the ice pellets have a dozen or more layers. Records show that hailstones having twenty-five layers, and as big as baseballs, once fell at Annapolis, Maryland!

Thunder and Lightning

Many children are frightened by thunder and lightning. Their timidity usually fades in the course of time if they see that grownups are undisturbed by storms, and if they can understand just what takes place during a storm. This last, unfortunately, is easier said than done.

It is easy for a child to believe that there is such a thing as air all about him, for he can often feel it blow. It is more difficult for him to understand that electricity is always there as well. Nevertheless, every bit of dust and droplet of moisture has its charge—a fact closely connected with lightning flashes. It may be enough to explain to a young child that lightning is electricity— the same force that furnishes our modern lighting—but on a grand scale. Older children may be eager for more details.

What Causes Lightning

About the time a thunderstorm breaks, you may notice a wind spring up as though from nowhere and blow toward the storm. Scientists believe such currents of air may be part of a chain of events somewhat on this order: As the wind blasts its way upward, it cools and the vapor in it is changed to liquid form. The speed of the rising current tears apart the drops of water that form. The fine drops are carried to the top of the storm cloud while the larger drops fall to lower levels.

Now, it seems that the fine drops have a negative charge, while the large drops are positively charged. When the electrical pressure between these two parts of the cloud becomes powerful enough to break through the air so they can join each other, a tremendous spark—lightning—is created.

"Lightning" In a Storage Battery

If you are interested in things electrical, and have some simple equipment, you probably know how to give your child a dramatic illustration of how lightning is formed—and thunder too. All you need do is connect the positive and negative poles of a storage battery with a piece of wire. As the youngster looks on, he will see how quickly a spark is created there, caused by the negative particles (electrons) leaping toward the positive pole. He will hear, too, a crackling sound accompanying the spark.

In just the same way the giant sparks that flash across the sky produce a crackling sound of tremendous volume. We call it thunder.

Forked Lightning and Other Kinds

Lightning comes in different forms. The most common type is forked lightning with a brilliant zigzag flash, as the electrical discharge takes the path of least resistance—an irregular one—through the air. A second kind, "sheet" lightning, is caused by a flash hidden in the clouds which brightly but briefly lights up a whole cloud or a sheet of rain.

Finally, there is "heat" lightning—a description we often give to a sudden lighting of the atmosphere that appears near the horizon though no thunderclouds are in sight. Heat lightning is usually explained as the reflection of lightning flashes below the horizon by the hazy air within our range of vision. It is appropriately named "heat lightning," as we encounter it during hot, muggy weather.

When Lightning is Dangerous

Though we want to reassure a child on the subject of lightning, we must not fail to let him know the circumstances under which it can be a real danger. Most flashes are from one cloud to another; very few come down to earth, and only when the negative charges in a cloud are attracted to positive charges on the ground.

Probably the safest place to be is indoors when there is a storm in your neighborhood. If you happen to be outdoors and without available shelter, be sure to avoid high ground, trees standing alone, the edges of woods, and wire fences. In case the lightning is unusually severe and directly overhead, your safest course is to lie or sit in a ditch.

How Many Miles Between You and Lightning?

Most children enjoy being able to reckon how far lightning is from them; and knowing how to do this is especially comforting to the nervous child who imagines that every flash is directly over his head. The calculation is based on the lapse of time between a flash and the moment the resulting thunder is heard. So quickly does light travel that the lightning is seen almost the instant it flashes. Therefore, if you count the number of seconds that elapse between the flash and the thunder, you know, roughly, the distance between you and the storm center.

You can train yourself to count seconds without a timepiece by repeating some such phrase as "storm in the sky," which takes a second to say. A lapse of fifty seconds means the lightning is about ten miles away (a mile distant for each five seconds). You cannot hear thunder from a greater distance than ten miles, except under unusually favorable circumstances.

Thunderstorms

You have probably noticed that there are different kinds of thunderstorms and that they have different effects on the atmosphere. Moreover—contrary to popular belief—they may even occur in winter. The two kinds that most often visit us in summer are the local or "heat" thunderstorm and the "cold front" type.

Heat Thunderstorms: The heat thunderstorm is generally a small-scale affair leaving the atmosphere as oppressive as before it broke. This kind is most common in the late afternoon or early evening following an extremely hot day. The overheating of the surface air when the atmosphere is fairly quiet brings about an unstable condition, and the storm is the outcome.

"Cold Front" Thunderstorms: The "cold front" thunderstorm is frequently more severe. It may form a nearly continuous line hundreds of miles long where cool air from the west or north meets hot, moist currents. As a result, the vapor in the air turns rapidly into water, and with the heavy downpour of rain great electrical disturbances take place. Such a storm is often accompanied by wind squalls and hail. Though it may break at any time of day or night, the most likely time is in the afternoon.

Winter Thunderstorms: Winter thunderstorms, which usually come at night, almost always announce the arrival of a sharp change in the weather. Toward the close of a cold spell, when a warm wind blows over a region, thunderstorms may occur whenever there is a great contrast between the cold and warm air masses. Or again, where warm air currents are being displaced by cold air, thunderstorms may give warning of the coming cold wave.

Storms of Violence

TORNADOES—SEVERAL HUNDRED MILES AN HOUR

The thunderstorm is a relative of the dreaded tornado and often accompanies it. The tornado has a distinctive feature: It always includes a funnel-shaped whirling cloud. This terrifying spiral, green gray to yellowish black, moves at a rate of thirty to fifty miles an hour, and within the tornado itself the wind moves at more than a hundred miles an hour!

In fact, the speed of a tornado has been estimated up to several hundred miles an hour; but since recording instruments are destroyed in such a storm, no exact records are available. Fortunately, tornadoes do not occur everywhere, and even in regions where they are apt to strike they are infrequent.

CYCLONES—A CONFUSING TERM

Many people use the term "cyclone" for these violent storms. In fact, the "cyclone cellar" is the common description of an underground retreat used for escaping tornadoes. The word is rather confusing, for to weathermen a cyclone is a low-pressure area which is not violent and may extend over thousands of square miles. These cyclones pass over us every few days and generally cause no more of a change than increased cloudiness.

However, it became customary to apply the term "cyclone" to a certain type of storm that developed about low-pressure centers in the Indian Ocean. From this the usage of the term broadened until it became identified with tornadoes.

Hurricanes—Several Hundred Miles Wide: A hurricane is not accompanied by a funnel-shaped cloud; but its speed may reach 150 miles an hour and the width of its path is far greater than that of a tornado. This width is generally several hundred miles. Hurricanes always start on the ocean.

Forecasting the Weather from the Clouds

CLOUDS AND FOG

The best way for a youngster to "get the feel" of a cloud is simply to walk through fog—for fog is nothing more than a cloud in contact with the ground or a body of water. Once a child knows that cloud and fog are the same, his logical question then is, "What keeps some clouds up in the sky?" and, "Why don't they fall down to earth like this one?"

FEATHERY AND BILLOWY CLOUDS

These questions are fairly easy to answer if we can forget that constantly repeated phrase, *"floating* clouds." Clouds really do not float; they tend to fall earthward. However, certain forces act to prevent their falling. For example, the great billowy white mounds that we call cumulus clouds are supported by the strength of ascending air currents. In the more feathery ("cirrus") type of cloud formation we may see some of its moisture fall as snow or rain; yet the cloud stays aloft if conditions favor condensation, and if the particles it has lost are replaced.

Most clouds are formed by rising, warm, moist air that becomes visible as billowy masses of moisture when it comes in contact with the cold upper atmosphere; and generally this same process which produces clouds counteracts their natural tendency to fall earthward.

We get fog when warm, humid air meets a cool surface such as that of a lake or sea, or ground which has rapidly lost the heat it absorbed during the day. As in the case of clouds, the vapor in the warm air then condenses and becomes visible.

How to Read the Clouds

Anyone, young or old, enjoys playing the role of weather prophet. While many factors enter into the predictions made by the weatherman, you can nevertheless have the fun of making reasonably accurate forecasts just from clouds. And because you are concerned only with your immediate vicinity, your prediction may be more successful than that of the professional forecaster!

As far as a youngster is concerned, the simplest indications for clear weather are high, white clouds, while dark, heavy, low clouds point to bad weather. Long before people knew much about clouds, this much was about all that anyone looked for in them. Today, however, we have the benefit of years of study of the clouds, and we know that scientists have divided them into three general classes. Each class has its own story to tell about conditions high above the earth.

Spectacular Cumulus Clouds

The spectacular cumulus is the kind of cloud that children are likely to notice first. Its name, taken from the Latin word for "heap," is a good description; these clouds are heaps upon heaps of billowy mounds that may reach a height of several miles! The name becomes easy to remember when you associate it with "accumulated."

When cumulus clouds are glistening white they are an indication of good weather; but on a summer afternoon they may gradually darken and become an unmistakable threat of a storm—often accompanied by thunder and lightning.

Artists are fond of ornamenting their landscapes with cumulus clouds, but the cloud "portraits" they produce are often decidedly incorrect. They show the clouds as rounded masses at both top and bottom—whereas the base of a cumulus cloud is always flattened. The base forms at the level where rising warm air cools enough to cause its water vapor to condense. Then, if the current of rising air is strong, the cloud grows upward with its rounded head marking the top of the rising air column.

Cirrus Clouds—"Mares' Tails"

The white feathery wisps that you are likely to see on a fine summer day belong to a second cloud group. These are cirrus clouds (from the Latin word meaning "curl"). "Cirrus" sounds a little like "icy," and this helps us remember that cirrus clouds are made up of tiny particles of ice—not merely moisture. They are the highest of all clouds, and may range from two to seven miles aloft. As cirrus clouds suggest long wisps of hair, they are often called "mares' tails."

If cirrus clouds are moving from the southwest, the temperature is apt to fall. If they are coming from the north, it is probably going to be fair and warm.

Stratus Clouds

Thin flat clouds make up the third group, well named "stratus," for this is the Latin word for "spreading out." Stratus clouds do spread out across the sky, sometimes as far as we can see. To remember this name, think of the similarity of "stratus" and "straight." Most often the stratus clouds appear as low, gray sheets. They may merge with rain clouds and precede a storm, or they may clear away like lifting fog.

OTHER CLOUD FORMS

"Nimbus" is one of the descriptive words that are frequently combined with the three cloud forms when dark, heavy portions build up in them. For example, a cumulus that grows black and threatening is a cumulus-nimbus, and a nimbo-stratus is a rain sheet.

"Alto" ("high") is also combined with cloud names, and "fracto" ("broken") is another element of cloud descriptions. Add these terms to combinations of main cloud forms like cirro-cumulus and cirro-stratus and you have a descriptive name for all the many cloud formations that decorate the sky. Cirro-cumulus clouds are small and fleecy, arranged in even rows high overhead and producing what we often call a "mackerel sky"—a sign of coming rain.

How the Weatherman Operates

Young children sometimes look upon "the weatherman" as a very definite person—either a hero or a villain, depending on how well the weather fits in with their plans. Of course it does not take long before they realize that this somewhat mysterious figure has nothing to do with producing rain, snow, or sunshine—he only predicts them. In the next stage they begin to wonder why, when predictions prove wrong for several days, we show any further interest in them.

FORECASTING THE WEATHER

We can understand why some predictions fail to materialize when we have a clear picture of the complex factors that enter into weather forecasting. Our United States Weather Bureau has more than five hundred observers stationed throughout the entire country. Every morning each observer reports by teletype to headquarters in Washington, D. C. all the weather facts in his region as recorded on sensitive instruments. These facts are all immediately recorded on a map by symbols.

The Chief Forecaster studies this map, compares it with the weather map of the previous day, and prepares his predictions for

Washington. Similar forecasts are made for other sections of the country and a radio station in the Weather Bureau broadcasts them, while teletype sends them to airports, newspapers, and commercial organizations. A daily weather map is also printed and widely distributed.

Yet, despite all the skill and care of the experts in reading signs, it is not always possible to be certain about the coming weather. An unexpected shift of winds may blow storm clouds from an area that was prepared for rain, and drench another where sunshine was expected!

The Weatherman's Tools: The observers who report to the Weather Bureau depend on a variety of instruments. The weather vane, which indicates wind direction, is the one with which most children are familiar. More complicated are the barograph which writes down the pressure of the air, the anemometer which measures the speed of wind, thermometers (of course!), a very precise barometer, an instrument to measure moisture, and another to record sunshine. These tools, and many others, help the observers to prepare their account of weather conditions close to earth.

Studying the Upper Atmosphere: Besides assembling this information, weathermen have become increasingly interested in ascertaining the condition of the upper atmosphere. To obtain this data the Weather Bureau sends aloft equipment attached to a large balloon. A radio device called a radiosonde is attached to a parachute carried in the balloon. This instrument is a small radio station in effect, telling, as it rises, about the temperature, winds, and other conditions.

The information supplied by the radiosonde is recorded on a complicated receiver at the Weather Bureau. The parachute carries a small balloon which both prevents the larger one from going up too fast and also helps to steady it. When they reach fifteen hundred feet, the smaller balloon bursts, causing the remaining balloon to rise faster—which it does for about thirteen miles. Then the larger balloon bursts—the parachute opens—and the radiosonde descends safely.

Weather Study as a Hobby

Weather forecasting provides many hobbies for older children. They can construct instruments for a weather station of their own, keep records of their observations, and study the weather maps in the daily newspaper.

ESTIMATING WIND VELOCITY

Besides learning to know the clouds, boys and girls of even first and second grade can have fun with weather in other ways. While they may not be able to construct a wind vane, they can learn to describe the direction of the wind by observing where the narrow, weighted part of the vane points.

They can also learn to judge the speed of wind fairly accurately without an instrument. For example: If smoke is seen rising straight up, the wind is moving less than a mile an hour. If the smoke drifts in the wind—though wind vanes are not turning—its rate is from one to three miles an hour.

When wind keeps leaves and small twigs in motion, it is described as "gentle" and is traveling from eight to twelve miles an hour. When it raises dust and papers and keeps small branches moving, it is "moderate"—from thirteen to eighteen miles an hour.

If you have trouble walking against the wind and it is bending trees, it is "strong"—more than thirty miles an hour. Wind that does such damage as the uprooting of trees is a gale, and may move up to seventy-five miles an hour. A wind in excess of this is a hurricane.

How to Make a Rain Gauge

A small child who enjoys making things can construct a measuring instrument for rain and snow—a rain gauge. The weatherman uses a gauge to measure periodic rainfall in an area, or the depth of water that would lie on the ground if the rain had not escaped.

All your child needs in order to make his own gauge is a large watertight can—eight inches across is close to the size used by the United States Weather Bureau. You can also make a measuring glass by pouring water to the depth of one inch in the can; then pour it into a tall thin jar (such as an olive jar) about a third as big around as the can. Mark the level to which it comes, using permanent paint, and divide the space between this level and the bottom of the jar into ten equal parts.

Place the can with its top removed on a stand so that the top is level and about two and a half feet from the ground. After a rain, pour the water that has accumulated in the can into your measuring jar. In this way you can easily measure even as little rainfall as a tenth of an inch. By keeping a chart for recording the results of each storm, a youngster has the added fun of weather recording.

Studying the Weather Is More Than Fun

There is a real need among weather scientists for greater knowledge of local weather variations. Your child might even succeed in making a useful contribution to this field; and, no matter what occupation or profession he follows in later life, his interest in the weather will never leave him. If his activity is connected with aviation or related sciences, weather study may be of great importance to him. Or—at the other end of the scale—he may merely want to know whether he can expect clear weather for taking his family on an outing.

Whatever your child grows up to be, his first experiences as a weather recorder or prophet will be prized memories. Indeed, all his happy associations with the out-of-doors—his enjoyment of animals and his appreciation of trees and flowers—will be greatly enriched if he has pleasant memories of a childhood in which he explored the surprises and delights of nature with his parents.

Index